A. C. S. Joel
1950

NAME THIS FLOWER

*BY THE SAME
AUTHOR*

BRITISH FLORA
Translated and adapted
from the French

BY

ETHEL MELLOR, D.Sc.

NAME THIS FLOWER

A SIMPLE WAY OF FINDING OUT THE
NAMES OF COMMON PLANTS WITHOUT
ANY PREVIOUS KNOWLEDGE OF BOTANY
WITH 372 COLOURED DRAWINGS
REPRESENTING PLANTS TO A UNIFORM SCALE OF
ONE-THIRD THEIR NATURAL SIZE, AND 2797
OTHER FIGURES

BY

GASTON BONNIER

Professor of Botany at the Sorbonne
Member of the Academy of Sciences
Foreign Member of the Linnean Society

LONDON
J. M. DENT & SONS LIMITED
NEW YORK: E. P. DUTTON & CO. INC.

J. M. DENT & SONS LTD.
Aldine House · Bedford St. · London

Made in Great Britain
by
The Temple Press · Letchworth · Herts
First published 1917
Last reprinted 1949

TRANSLATOR'S PREFACE

THIS book was originally written by M. Bonnier in French for use in France. It contains descriptions of nearly 700 species generally distributed throughout the plains of France and Western Europe, about half of this number being represented in the coloured plates. Most of these plants generally distributed in France are equally so in the British Isles; but they include a few that will not be found wild in this country, though they may occur as escapes from gardens. Some common British species have been added in this edition; but the small number of plants peculiar to the mountains or to the sea-shore are not as a rule included. A few of the names have been altered to the form commonly to be found in more advanced English books; but none of these changes have been made without the consent of the author.

Special attention is drawn to M. Bonnier's method of finding out the names of plants without troubling about their classification, which he distinguishes as " The Simple Way "; to the Index of the English Botanical Names of Plants, which indicates their application to agriculture, industrial uses, and herbal medicine; and to the Index of Popular Names.

G. S. BOULGER.

TABLE OF CONTENTS

THE SIMPLE WAY

An example of how to find out the name of a plant

THE object of the Simple Way is to make the finding out the names of plants as straightforward a matter as possible, without any knowledge of the structure of flowers and without any previous notion of Botany. To do this it is only necessary to read the successive alternatives, or questions which are propounded, in the order indicated.

Let us take an example. Suppose we have picked a Poppy in the fields and want to know its popular names, its properties and what it is called in Botany. It is necessary to pick the flowering stem as low down as possible, so that the shape of the leaves may be clearly seen.

Open the book at page 2. (The pages are numbered at the bottom.) At the top of the page are written the numbers of the questions—Nos. 1, 2, 3, 4, and we will begin to find the name of the plant by reading the two questions, each preceded by the sign +, which are grouped under the number 1. They are:

1 { + Plant with flowers, etc.
{ + Plant without flowers at any time, etc.[1]

As our plant has flowers, we choose the first question, " + Plant with flowers," where we are referred to No. 2, which is lower down on the same page.

No. 2, in its turn, offers us the choice of two questions, each preceded by the sign — • :

2 { — • Herbaceous plant, etc.
{ — • Tree, shrub, or undershrub, etc.

After having read these two questions, we see that the stems in our plant have none of the appearance or hardness of wood.

We choose, therefore, the first question : " — • Herbaceous plant," where we are referred to No. 3, which is lower down on the same page.

At No. 3 there are again two questions to choose between, each preceded by the sign △. The first, " Flower composite," is accompanied by an explanation and some figures. As our flower is not made up of a collection of little flowers packed close together, without stalks, as it is not surrounded by a collarette of little leaves or scales, and as it in no way resembles those there figured, we choose

---

[1] It is very important that the questions should be read to the end, and that all the questions put under the same number should be read, before choosing the one which agrees with the plant the name of which we wish to find.

the second question: " △ Flower not composite," where we are referred to No. 4, which is lower down on the same page.

At No. 4 we are given the choice of five questions at once, each with the sign ⋈ before it. These questions refer to the colour of the flower. Our flower is red, so we choose the first question, which sends us on to No. 5, which is on the next page.

At No. 5 we are faced by three questions, each with the sign ○ before it and accompanied by figures. After having read all these questions, seeing that our flower has four red similar parts arranged regularly round the centre of the flower and very nearly equal to one another in size, we choose the first question, which takes us to No. 6, on the next page. (If, as sometimes happens, we find that our flower is not regular, because its petals are unequal in size, and we choose, therefore, the second question " Flower irregular," we shall get to the name of the plant, though by another route.)

At No. 6 we have to choose between four questions, each preceded by the sign — and accompanied by explanations and figures. We may find that our plant has simple leaves, that is to say, the leaves are not cut more than half their width. We choose, therefore, the third question: " Leaves simple." (It may happen that our plant has its leaves deeply cut, in which case we shall choose the second question, which will also bring us to the name of the plant.) Supposing, however, that the plant we have gathered has simple leaves, we are referred to No. 7, which will be found on the next page.

At No. 7 we are faced by five questions, each preceded by the sign ✳ and accompanied by explanations and figures. After reading these questions we shall choose the third, " ✳ Leaves alternate," because the leaves of our plant are attached to the stem one by one and at different levels. This brings us to No. 8, which is on the next page.

Two questions, each with the sign ═ before them, present themselves at No. 8. After having read the explanations, we see that we can detach each red petal of our flower down to its base without tearing the other petals. We choose, therefore, the first question: " ═ Each flower has its petals separate from one another down to the base," which refers us to No. 9, which is on the next page. At No. 9 there are four questions, each with the sign ⊖ before it. As our flower has four red petals, we shall choose the first of these questions, which will bring us to No. 10, lower down on the same page.

Here, under No. 10, we have the choice of two questions with the sign × before them. On examining one of the flower-buds of our plant we see that it is made up of two green pieces mutually overlapping and enclosing the crumpled petals. It is readily observed that these two green pieces fall off as the bud expands into a flower. We therefore choose the first question, which directs us to No. 20.

Let us turn over, and we shall find No. 20 on page 9. Once more we are faced by two questions, each preceded by the sign — . As the leaves of our plant are hairy and do not surround the stem by their base, and as the petals are red with a black stain, we shall choose the first question, which gives us the name of the plant as it is known in Botany: " → Common Poppy." This name is followed by popular names by which it is also known in the country (Corn Poppy or Corn Rose); after which will be found the two words which make up the Latin botanical name of the plant: [*Papaver Rhœas*]. After this come the announcements: " medicinal, harmful to cattle." On looking out the name " Poppy, Common " in the Index of English botanical names which is at the end of the book, we shall find notes on the medical properties of the plant, what parts of it are used, in what proportions it should be infused, etc. It is also there stated in what way the plant is harmful to cattle.

Then turning back to the first description (on p. 9) we find the note " — Shown in colour: 1, Plate 5." This means that on turning to Plate 5, among the coloured photographs of the more common plants at the beginning of the book, we shall see that Fig. 1 on this plate represents our plant in its natural colours. This will show us clearly that we have not been mistaken in the name which we have found out by means of the successive questions propounded to us.

Lastly, we find the word *Papaveraceæ*, which means " plants resembling the genus *Papaver*," or, in other words, " the Natural Family of the Poppies and their allies." In the case of each plant-name we shall find at the end some such name which will be that of the Natural Family to which the plant belongs.

(In those cases in which some parts of the plant have to be measured, the scale of inches and centimetres on p. 290 can be used.)

The sign 🐝 shows that the plant yields honey, that is to say, that it is visited by bees for the sake of the sugary liquid produced by its flowers, or, in some cases, by the leaves.

Other examples of how to find out the name of a plant are given on pages 291-297.

WITH REGARD TO
THE SIMPLE WAY

WHEN we simply wish to find out the names of plants with ease, it is not necessary to trouble about their classification.

People who are really well acquainted with plants know how to name them even at a distance, or by a mere glance at the flowering stalk which they have gathered. These experienced people do not need to take into account the technical characteristics of plants in order to distinguish them; nor to trouble themselves by verifying whether the ovary is superior or inferior; in what way the stamens are joined, or not joined, either to the corolla or to the calyx; if the seed is, or is not, albuminous, etc. They need not know the characteristics either of the families or the genera. In order to give the correct name of the species all that will not trouble them at all.

To find out the names of plants and to find out how to classify them are, in reality, two entirely different problems. This is what Linnæus recognised when he established his classification of the vegetable kingdom with the view, not of constituting natural groups, but of making it easy to determine plants. Linnæus thought that the simplest means of attaining this end was first to count the stamens of flowers and afterwards to count their carpels. But this procedure is not always as easy as might be thought, and admits of great difficulties especially where the carpels are concerned. Nevertheless, the Linnæan System was a great success by reason of the relative facility with which it enabled us to arrive at the names of plants, and this success has been so complete and so lasting that the Floras of Sweden, Norway, and Denmark and some German and Swiss Floras are actually still arranged on the Linnæan System.

When Lamarck invented the dichotomous keys, that is to say, a set of alternative questions put successively to the student, he tried to devise a means even easier than that of Linnæus for finding out the names of plants; but he wished to describe at the same time the plants of the *Flore Française* in their natural order under family, genus, and species. Soon, however, he found himself obliged to reckon with the impossibility of this arrangement. Quite at the outset Lamarck gave up making a key to the families, family characteristics being subject to such numerous exceptions, and he instituted a key to genera directly, or rather to groups of species. The collection of these dichotomous tables, intended for finding out the names of plants, was placed by him outside the Flora properly so-called, the keys referring you to the genus by numbers whose order was not at all the same as that of the plants described in the natural series. What plainly demonstrates that the finding of the names of plants was for Lamarck an end altogether apart from the establishment of a natural classification is that we see, following one on the other, and in the same page of these tables, the names of plants belonging to the most different Families—as, for example, *Epimedium, Euonymus, Fraxinus, Moehringia, Tribulus, Ruta, Pyrola, Peplis, Dianthus.*

In the systematic description of species in the same Flora, these names are widely separated without any relation to the preceding order.

The keys of Lamarck are very convenient to use, owing to his method of successive questions. Nevertheless, the characteristics employed by the illustrious naturalist, more especially those which relate to the first series of questions propounded, are still very difficult of recognition by any one who has not made a study of botany.

I may be allowed to quote here certain extracts borrowed from the philosopher, Ernest Bersot, who, when he was director of the Upper Normal School, published among his Reflections of a Moralist a *Letter on Botany*.[1] These quotations (which I have already used elsewhere) find a fit place here, which is my reason for reproducing them.

" Botany," he says, " is one of the most deceitful sciences. As flowers are so charming one imagines that it also must be charming ; but how soon one is disillusioned ! And why ? Ah, why ? Because the *savants* have thought about themselves and not about us. They have wished for a science complete in itself ; and they have put each thing in its place without troubling themselves to ascertain whether it would be easy for other people to find it there. How many times have I tried to become a botanist, and each time I have been vanquished.

" I had thought that in order to distinguish a flower it would suffice to recognise certain main characteristics, plainly visible, plainly marked, and always united ; but it seems that one must not trust to appearances. . . . Many have gone to the learned men in order to be directed to the more hidden and delicate characteristics, but with the result that they can do nothing without the scalpel and the microscope, and without having at one and the same time the flower and the fruit, without having had to follow pretty nearly the whole history of the plant. It is disheartening at the very least."

Further on the author speaks of illustrations accompanying the descriptions of plants, or as a help to finding out their names, and expresses himself thus :—

" Yes, to the ignorant these books with illustrations are precious. If it is only a drawing 'tis well ; if it is a coloured one 'tis better still. How much trouble it saves us ! Suppose we were obliged to seek through a number of rooms for an unknown person, how difficult, even if aided by the most minute description, it would be to recognise him, and how easy to stumble upon some one else ! If, on the contrary, he himself or his portrait is shown to us, in a glance, without analysing any details, an image of his general appearance is formed in our minds by which we can always recognise him.

" In a word, then, what is the real matter in question ? *Recognition ;* for to be learned is too lofty an ambition for the greater number of us."

The question then puts itself in this way. The botanists who discouraged Bersot—were they right ? Is it impossible to find out the names of plants without knowing any botany ? The people who know plants, did they not arrive at naming them simply by dint of long

[1] Ernest Bersot, *Lettre sur la Botanique* (Un moraliste), p. 277, Paris, 1882.

practice? And these characteristics, of which they make use without thinking of them, is it impossible to translate them into language simple enough to be understood by the general public?

Like all those who have studied systematic botany, I thought for a long time that an answer in the affirmative ought to be given to these various questions; and, nevertheless I had constant evidence that usually it was not by the aid of classificatory characters that I recognised different species but, on the contrary, by direct and, so to say, unconscious determination.

I have also asked myself whether, by combining the method of Lamarck's dichotomous keys with the examination of these " big, plainly visible, well marked-out, and always united characteristics " of which Bersot speaks, and by adding to them, as he desired, numerous illustrations both in black and white, and in colour, the names of plants might not be made easy to find out by those who have not made any preliminary study of botany.

It is the result of such an attempt that I present in this book under the name of *The Simple Way*. It is for my readers to decide if I have succeeded.

GASTON BONNIER.

Note.—In spite of the numerous determinations which have been made by means of *The Simple Way* by very many different people, all ignorant of the slightest botanical knowledge, and in spite of the corrections made in this fresh edition, there will certainly be some errors left to point out, and some improvements to be made in the keys that I have drawn up. I shall be very grateful to the readers who will point out to me any errors they may find, or any improvements which the use of this little book may suggest to them.

PLATE 1.

Plate 1.

RANUNCULACEÆ

1 Bulbous Crow-foot (Buttercup, Golden Cup). — [*Ranunculus bulbosus*]. — poisonous; medicinal.

2 Field Crow-foot (Hedgehog). — [*Ranunculus arvensis*].

3. Water Crow-foot [*Ranunculus aquatilis*].

4. Wood Anemone (Windflower). — [*Anemone nemorosa*].

5, 5 bis. Pasch Anemone (Pasque-flower) — [*Anemone Pulsatilla*]. — poisonous; medicinal; 5, plant in flower; 5 bis, fruit.

6. Wild Clematis (Traveller's Joy, Old Man's Beard). — [*Clematis Vitalba*]. — irritant.

PLATE 2.

Plate 2.

RANUNCULACEÆ
(*Continued*).

1. **Yellow Meadow-rue** (Meadow Rhubarb).—[*Thalictrum flavum*]

2. **Figwort Crowfoot** (Lesser Celandine, Figwort, Pilewort).— [*Ranunculus Ficaria*].—poisonous; medicinal.

3. **Marsh Caltha** (Marsh-marigold, King-cup, Waterblobs).— [*Caltha palustris*].—poisonous.

4. **Annual Pheasants-eye** [*Adonis annua*].

5. **Field Nigella** (Love-in-a-mist) [*Nigella arvensis*].—medicinal.

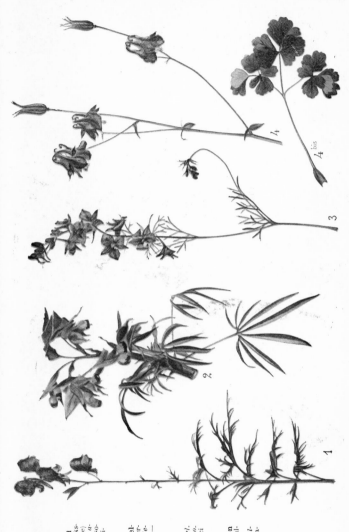

PLATE 3.

Plate 3.

RANUNCULACEÆ.
(*Continued*).

1 Monkshood Aconite (Monkshood, Wolfsbane) — [*Aconitum Napellus*]. — poisonous; — medicinal.

2 Stinking Hellebore (Setterwort). — [*Helleborus fœtidus*]. — medicinal.

3 Consound Larkspur [*l el. phinium Consolida*]. — medicinal.

4, 4 bis. Common Columbine (Culverkeys) — [*Aquilegia vulgaris*]. — ornamental.

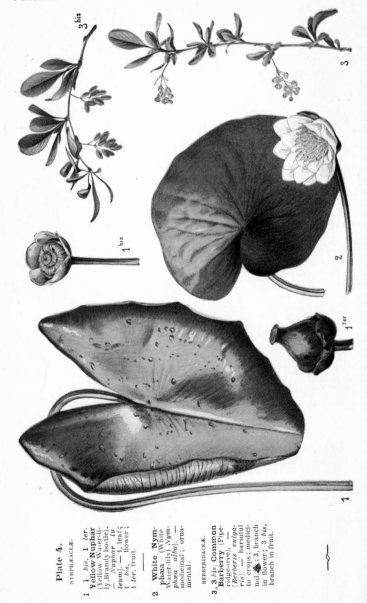

PLATE 4.

Plate 4.

NYMPHÆACEÆ.

1 1 *bis*, 1 *ter*.
Yellow Nuphar
(Yellow Water-li-
ly, Brandy bottle).
— *Nuphar lu
teum*]. — 1, leaf;
1 *bis*, flower;
1 *ter*. fruit.

2 **White Nym-
phæa** (White
Water-lily *Nym-
phæa alba*]; —
medicinal ; orna-
mental.

BERBERIDACEÆ.

3, 3 *bis*, **Common
Barberry** (Pipe-
ridge-tree). —
[*Berberis vulga-
ris*]. — harmful
to crops ; medici-
nal ; 3, branch
in flower ; 3 *bis*,
branch in fruit.

PLATE 5.

Plate 5.

PAPAVERACEÆ.

1. **Common Poppy** (Corn Poppy, Corn Rose) [*Papaver rhœas*]. — medicinal.

2. **Opium Poppy** [*Papaver somniferum*]. — poisonous, medicinal. — used in the arts.

3. **Greater Celandine** (Felonwort). — [*Chelidonium majus*]. — poisonous ; medicinal.

FUMARIACEÆ.

4. **Officinal Fumitory** [*Fumaria officinalis*]. — medicinal.

CRUCIFERÆ.

5. **Field Mustard** (Charlock). — [*Sinapis arvensis*]. ❀.

6. **Cooking Cabbage** [*Brassica oleracea*]. — food plant ❀.

PLATE 6.

Plate 6.

CRUCIFERÆ
(Continued).

1. **Common Wallflower** (Gilliflower). — (Cheirant us Cheiri). —ornamental.

2. **Meadow Cardamine** (Lady'ssmock, Cuckooflower). — (Card amine pratensis).

3. **Official Watercress** [Nasturtium officinale]. — foodplant; medicinal.

4. **Spring Whitlowgrass**[Draba verna].

5. **Common Shepherd's-purse** [Capsella Bursapastoris]. — medicinal.

PLATE 7.

Plate 7.

CISTINEÆ.

1 Common Rock-rose [Helianthemum vulgare]. — medicinal.

VIOLACEÆ.

2 Tricolor Viola (Pansy, Hearts-ease), — [Viola tricolor]. — orna-mental; medici-nal.

3. Sweet Viola (Violet). — [Viola odorata]. — orna-mental; medici-nal.

POLYGALACEÆ.

4. Common Milk-wort [Polygala vulgaris]. — me-dicinal.

RESEDACEÆ.

5. Yellow Reseda (Wild Mignonette). — [Reseda lutea] ✿

6 Yellow-weed Reseda (Weld, Dyer's Rocket). — [Reseda luteola]. — used in the arts ✿

PLATE 8.

Plate 8.

CARYOPHYLLACEÆ.

1. **Official Soap-wort** [*Saponaria officinalis*]. — used in the arts; medicinal.

2. **Carthusians' Pink** [*Dianthus carthusianorum*].

3. **Broad-leaved Silene** (Bladder Campion, White Bottle). — [*Silene latifolia*].

4. **Corncockle Lychnis** (Corn-cockle) [*Lychnis Githago*]. — poisonous.

PLATE 9.

Plate 9.

CARYOPHYLLACEÆ
(Continued).

1 **Cuckoo-flower**
Lychnis (Ragged
Robin). — [Lych-
nis Flos-cuculi].

2 **Evening Lych-**
nis (White Cam-
pion). — [Lychnis
vespertina] Seed-
bearing stalk ; —
2 bis, stalk which
does not yield
seed.

3 **Field Ceras-**
tium (Mouse-ear
chickweed) [Ce-
rastium arvense].

4 **Intermediate**
Starwort (Com-
mon Chickweed).
— [Stellaria me-
dia]. — Food for
small birds.

5 **Bone-set**
Starwort
(Greater Stitch-
wort, Cuckoo's-
meat, Adder's-
meal). — [Stel-
laria Holostea].

—○—

PLATE 10.

Plate 10.

LINACEÆ.

1. Cultivated Flax (Common Flax). — [*Linum usitatissimum*]. — economic; medicinal: a plant in flower; 1 *bis*, a flower, natural size.

2. Slender-leaved Flax [*Linum tenuifolium*].

TILIACEÆ.

3. Small-leaved Linden (Lime-tree). — [*Tilia cordata*]. — medicinal.

MALVACEÆ.

4. Common Mallow [*Malva sylvestris*]. — medicinal.

5. Alcea Mallow [*Malva Alcea*] (Not truly wild).

PLATE 11.

Plate 11.

GERANIACEÆ.

1. Herb-Robert Crane's-bill (Wild Geranium). — [Geranium Robertianum]. — medicinal.

2. Hemlock Stork's-bill [Erodium cicutarium]. — medicinal.

HYPERICACEÆ.

3. Perforate Saint-John's-wort [Hypericum perforatum]. — medicinal.

ACERINEÆ.

4. Sycamore Maple (Greater Maple). — [Acer Pseudo-Platanus]. — ornamental. Branch in flower; 4 bis, fruit.

5. Norway Maple Fruit. — [Acer platanoides].

6. Field Maple (Common Maple). Fruit. — [Acer campestre]. — economic.

PLATE 12.

Plate 12.

HIPPOCASTANEÆ.

1 **Common Horse - Chest - nut** [*Æsculus Hippocastanum*]. — economic; medicinal. Flowering branch. 1 *bis*, fruit, opened.

CELASTRACEÆ.

2. **European Spindle-tree** (waieringe-prickwood) — [*Euonymus europæus*]. — used in the arts : branch in flower; 2 *bis*, Branch in fruit.

ILICINEÆ.

3 **Needle-leaved Holly** [*Ilex Aquifolium*]. — Used in the arts. Branch in flower. 3 *bis*, Branch in fruit.

PLATE 13.

Plate 13.

PAPILIONACEÆ.

1. **European Furze** (Gorse, Whin), — [*Ulex europæus*]. — Fodder

2. **Common Broom** [*Sarothamnus scoparius*]. — used in the arts; poisonous; medicinal.

3. **Dyers' Greenweed** (Woadwaxen), —[*Genista tinctoria*]. — used in the arts.

4. **Laburnum Cytisus**(Laburnum, Golden Chain), — [*Cytisus Laburnum*]. — poisonous; used in the arts.

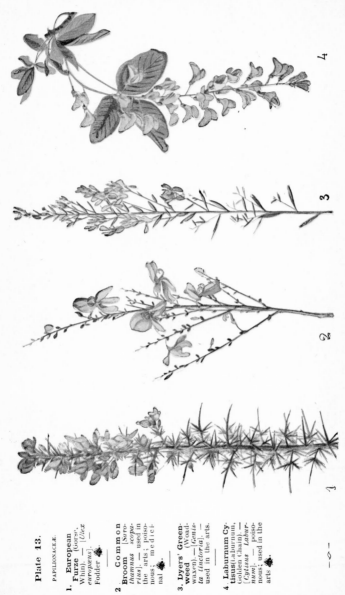

PLATE 14.

Plate 14.

PAPILIONACEÆ.
(Continued).

1. **Birds'foot Lotus** (Butter-and-eggs, shoes-and-stockings). — [*Lotus corniculatus*]. — Fodder. 🌸

2. **Common Haricot** (French Bean, Haricot Bean). — [*Phaseolus vulgaris*]. — Food-plant. 🌸

3. **Creeping Trefoil** (Dutch Clover, White Clover). — [*Trifolium repens*]. — Fodder. 🌸

4. **Meadow Trefoil** (Red Clover) — [*Trifolium pratense*]. — Fodder. 🌸

5. **Crimson Trefoil** (Trifolium). — [*Trifolium incarnatum*]. — Fodder. 🌸

— ○ —

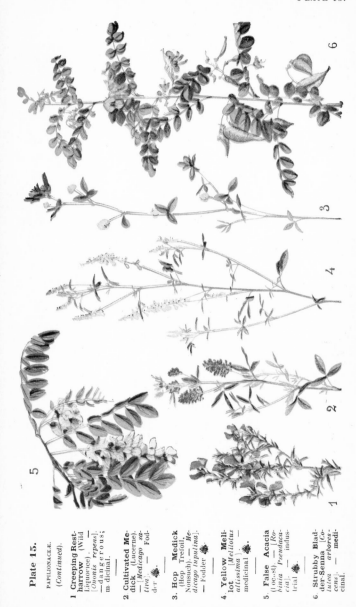

PLATE 15.

Plate 15.

PAPILIONACEÆ.
(Continued).

1 **Creeping Rest-harrow** (Wild Liquorice). [*Ononis repens*]. — dangerous; medicinal.

2 **Cultivated Medick** (Lucerne). — [*Medicago sativa*]. — Fodder.

3. **Hop Medick** (Hop Trefoil, Nonsuch). — *Medicago lupulina*. — Fodder 🐝.

4 **Yellow Melilot** [*Melilotus altissima*]. — medicinal 🐝.

5 **False Acacia** (Locust). — [*Robinia Pseudacacia*]. — industrial 🐝.

6 **Strubby Bladder-Senna** (*Colutea arborescens*). — medicinal.

PLATE 16.

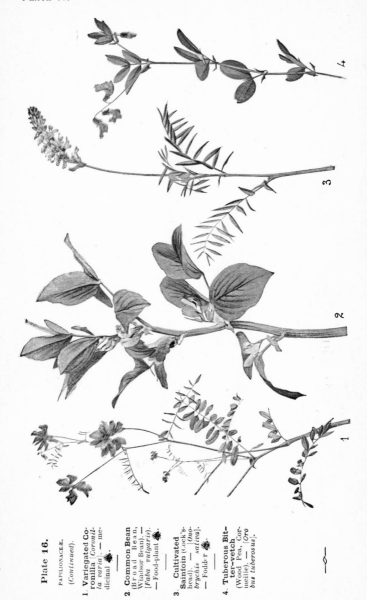

Plate 16.

PAPILIONACEÆ.
(Continued).

1 Variegated Co-
ronilla (Coronil-
la varia). — me-
dicinal ✱.
——

2 Common Bean
(Broad Bean,
Windsor Bean).
— [Faba vulgaris].
— Food-plant ✱.

3 Cultivated
Saintoin (Cock's-
head). — [Ono-
brychis sativa].
— Fodder ✱.

4 Tuberous Bit-
ter-vetch
(Wood Pea, Cor-
neille). — [Oro-
bus tuberosus].

PLATE 17.

Plate 17.

PAPILIONACEÆ.
(Continued).

1. Cultivated Pea (Green Pea). — [*Pisum sativum*]. — Food-plant.

2. Aphaca Vetch-ling [*Lathyrus Aphaca*].

3. Wood Vetch-ling (Narrow-leaved Everlasting Pea). — [*Lathyrus sylvestris*]. — Fodder-plant.

4. Meadow Vetch-ling [*Lathyrus pratensis*]. — Fodder-plant.

5. Cultivated Vetch (Common Vetch). — [*Vicia sativa*]. — Fodder-plant; medicinal.

6. Bush Vetch [*Vicia sepium*].

7. Tufted Vetch [*Vicia Cracca*]. — Fodder-plant.

PLATE 18.

Plate 18.

ROSACEÆ.

1. **Bird's Prunus** (Gean, Black Cherry). — [*Prunus Avium*]. — Food-plant : Industrial.

2. **Spinous Prunus** (Black-thorn, Sloe). — [*Prunus spinosa*]. — Industrial. Branch in flower. 2 *bis*, Branch in fruit.

3. **Edible Strawberry** (Wild Strawberry). — [*Fragaria vesca*]. — medicinal.

4. **Elm-leaved Spiræa** (Meadowsweet). — [*Spiræa Ulmaria*]. — medicinal.

PLATE 19.

Plate 19.

ROSACEÆ
(*Continued*).

1. **Tormentil Po—
tentil** (Tormen-
til). [*Potentilla
Tormentilla*]. —
medicinal.

2. **Creeping Fo—
tentil** (Cinque-
foil). [*Poten-
tilla reptans*]. —
medicinal.

3. **Eupator's Agri-
mony** (Agrimo-
ny). — [*Agrimo-
nia Eupatoria*].
— medicinal.

4. **Dog Rose** [Wild
Briar) — [*Rosa
canina*]. — medi-
cinal. — Flowers.
4 *bis*, Fruits (hips).

5. **Shrubby
Bramble** (Black-
berry). — [*Rubus
fruticosus*]. —
Food-plant. —
medicinal.

6. **Bloody Burnet**
(Salad Burnet)
[*Poterium San-
guisorba*].

PLATE 20.

Plate 20.

ROSACEÆ
(*Continued*).

1. **Sharp-spined
Hawthorn**(Whitethorn. May).
— [*Cratægus Oxyacantha*]. — medicinal. Branch in
flower. *bis*,
Fruits (haws).

2. **Cultivated
Sorb** (Service-tree.). — [*Sorbus
domestica*]. —
Food-plant. 🌑

3. **Common Pyrus**
(Pear-tree).
— [*Pyrus communis*]. — Food-plant;
industrial 🌑.

4. **Common Apple**
(Crab-apple).
— [*Malus communis*]. — Food-plant;
industrial 🌑.

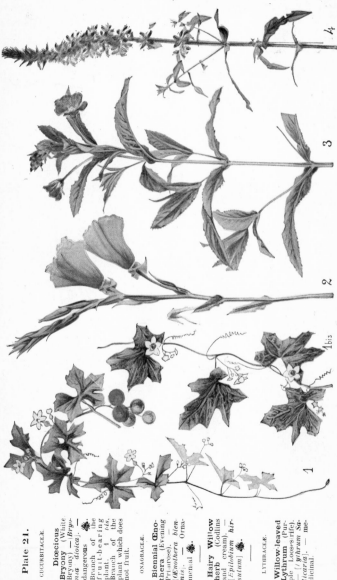

PLATE 21.

Plate 21.

CUCURBITACEÆ.

1. **Diœcious Bryony** (White Bryony) — *Bryonia dioica*]. — **dangerous** 🐝.
Branch of the fruit-bearing plant, 1 *bis*, Branch of the plant which does not fruit.

ONAGRACEÆ.

2. **Biennial Œnothera** (Evening Primrose). (*Œnothera biennis*). — Ornamental 🐝. ——

3. **Hairy Willow herb** (Codlins and cream). — [*Epilobium hirsutum*]. 🐝. ——

LYTHRACEÆ.

4. **Willow-leaved Lythrum** (Purple Loosestrife). (*Lythrum Salicaria*). — medicinal.

Plate 22.

CRASSULACEÆ.

1 **Orpine Stone-crop** (Live-long), [*Sedum Tele-phium*]. — medicinal. ✽.

2 **Reflexed Sto-necrop** [*Sedum reflexum*]. — medicinal.

3 **Biting Stone-crop** (Wall-Pep-per). — [*Sedum acre*]. — Poisonous ; — medicinal. ✽.

4 **White Stone-crop** (Great Sto-necrop). — [*Sedum album*]. — medicinal. ✽.

5 **Roof Semper-vivum** (House-leek) [*Sempervi-vum tectorum*]. — medicinal ✽. — Flowering branch. 5 *bis*, Young shoot.

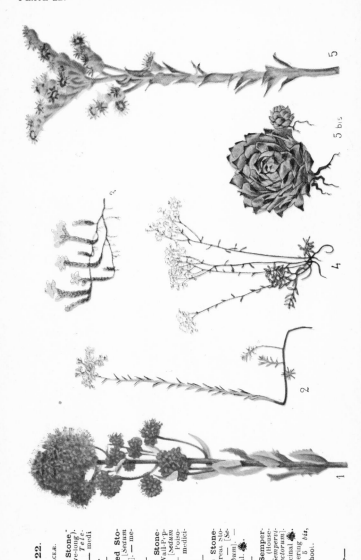

PLATE 23.

Plate 23.

SAXIFRAGACEÆ.

1. **Tuberous Saxifrage** (Pretty Maids). — [*Saxifraga granulata*].

2. **Three-fingered Saxifrage** [*Saxifraga tridactylites*].

RIBESIACEÆ.

3. **Red Currant** [*Ribes rubrum*]. — Food-plant. ✿

UMBELLIFERÆ.

4. **Field Eryngo** (Watling-street Thistle, Hundred-headed Thistle). — [*Eryngium campestre*]. — medicinal. ✿

5. **Wild Carrot** [*Daucus Carota*]. — Food-plant.

PLATE 24.

Plate 24.

UMBELLIFERÆ
(*Continued*).

1. **Official Fennel** [*Fœniculum officinale*]. — medicinal. Flowering top. 1 *bis*, a leaf.

_____

2. **Cultivated Parsnip** [*Pastinaca sativa*]. — Food-plant. ✿

_____

3. **Common Cowparsnip** (Hogweed). — [*Heracleum Spondylium*]. — medicinal. ✿

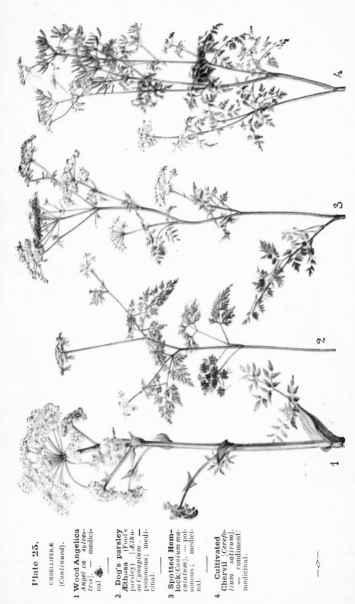

PLATE 25.

Plate 25.

UMBELLIFERÆ
(Continued).

1 **Wood Angelica**
(*Angelica sylvestris*). — medicinal.

2. **Dog's parsley**
Æthusa (Fool's parsley) [*Æthusa Cynapium*]. — poisonous; medicinal.

3. **Spotted Hemlock** (*Conium maculatum*). — poisonous; medicinal.

4. **Cultivated Chervil** (*Cerefolium sativum*). — condiment; medicinal.

PLATE 26.

Plate 26.

ARALIACEÆ.

1. Climbing Ivy
(Common Ivy)
[*Hedera Helix*].
— medicinal 🌿.
Branch in flower.
1 *bi*, Fruits.

CORNACEÆ.

2. Bloody Cornel
(Do wood). —
[*Cornus sanguinea*] 🌿. Branch
in flower. 2 *bis*,
branch bearing
fruits.

LORANTHACEÆ.

3. White Mistletoe [*Viscum album*]. — medicinal 🌿. Branch
in flower. 3 *bis*,
Branch bearing
fruits.

CAPRIFOLIACEÆ.

**4. Common
Honeysuckle**
(Woodbine).
[*Lonicera Periclymenum*]

5. Dwarf Elder
(Daneworth).
[*Sambucus Ebulus*]. — medicinal 🌿

6. Black Elder
[*Sambucus nigra*]. — medicinal.

7. Mealy Guelder-rose (Wayfaring-tree). —
[*Viburnum Lantana*].

PLATE 27.

Plate 27.

RUBIACEÆ.

1. **True Bedstraw** (Lady's Bedstraw, Yellow Bedstraw).—[*Galium verum*].—industrial; medicinal.

2. **Cross-wort Bedstraw.**—[*Galium Cruciata*].

3. **Hedge Bedstraw** [*Galium Mollugo*].—medicinal.

VALERIANACEÆ.

4. **Cooking Valerianella** (Lamb's Lettuce, Cornsalad).—[*Valerianella olitoria*].—Food-plant.

5. **Officinal Valerian** [*Valeriana officinalis*].—medicinal. Flowering branch. 5 *bis*, Leaf.

Plate 28.

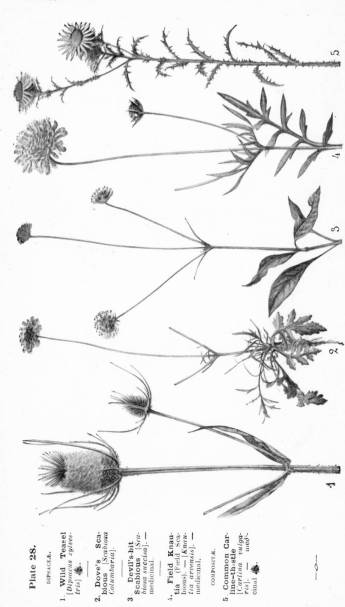

Plate 28.

DIPSACEÆ.

1. **Wild Teasel** [*Dipsacus sylvestris*].

2. **Dove's Scabious** [*Scabiosa Columbaria*].

3. **Devil's-bit Scabious** [*Scabiosa succisa*]. — medicinal.

4. **Field Knautia** (Field Scabious). — [*Knautia arvensis*]. — medicinal.

COMPOSITÆ.

5. **Common Carline-thistle** [*Carlina vulgaris*]. — medicinal.

PLATE 29.

Plate 29.

COMPOSITÆ.

(*Continued*).

1. **Acanthus-Lea-ved Cotton-Thistle** (Scottish Thistle). — [*Ono-pordon Acan-thium*]. ❀

2. **Corn Plume-thistle**. — (Corn Thistle). — [*Cir-sium arvense*]. — Harmful in crops. ❀

3. **Nodding Thistle** (Musk Thistle). – [*Car-duus nutans*]. ❀

4. **Spear Plume-thistle** [*Cirsium lanceolatum*]. ❀

Plate 30.

Plate 30.

COMPOSITÆ.
(Continued).

1 **Blue Knap-weed** (Cornflow-er, Blue-bottle). — [*Centaurea Cyanus*]. — medicinal.

2 **Brown Knap-weed** [*Centaurea Jacea*]. — medicinal.

3 **Great Bur-dock** [*Arctium Lappa*]. — medicinal.

4 **Dyers' Saw-wort** [*Serratula tinctoria*].

5 **Perennial Daisy** (Common Daisy) [*Bellis perennis*]. — ornamental.

6 **White Chrysan-themum** (Moon-daisy, Ox-eye Daisy, Margue-rite). — [*Chrysanthemum Leucanthemum*]. — medicinal.

7 **Chamomile Matricaria** [Wild Chamomile] [*Matricaria Chamomilla*]. — medicinal.

Plate 31.

COMPOSITÆ.
(Continued).

1. **Hemp Eupatorium** (Hemp Agrimony) [*Eupatorium cannabinum*]. — medicinal.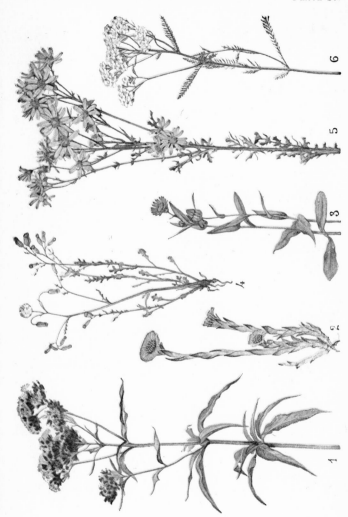

2. **Colt's-foot Tussilago** (Colt's foot) [*Tussilago Farfara*]. — medicinal.

3. **Field Calendula** (Common Marigold) [*Calendula arvensis*]. — medicinal.

4. **Common Senecio** (Groundsel. Birdseed). [*Senecio vulgaris*]. — medicinal.

5. **Ragwort Senecio** (Ragwort) [*Senecio Jacobæa*]. — medicinal.

6. **Milfoil Achillea** (Milfoil. Yarrow) [*Achillea Millefolium*]. — medicinal.

PLATE 31.

Plate 32.

COMPOSITÆ

(Continued).

1 Common Artemisia (Mugwort). —[Artemisia vulgaris]. — medicinal.

2 Common Tansy [Tanacetum vulgare]. — medicinal.

3. Canadian Erigeron [Erigeron canadensis]. — medicinal.

4. Scurfy Elecampane [Plouchman's Spikenard].—[Inula squarrosa].

5. Golden-rod Solidago (Golden-rod) [Solida o Virgaurea] — medicinal

PLATE 33.

Plate 33.

COMPOSITÆ
(Continued).

1. **Common Nip-plewort** [*Lapsana communis*]. — medicinal.

2. **Succory Chicory** (Succory). — [*Cichorium intybus*]. — Food-plant; medicinal 🌼.

3. **Officinal Dandelion** (Common Dandelion) [*Taraxacum officinale*]. — Food-plant; medicinal 🌼.

4. **Meadow Goat's-beard** (Jack go-to-bed-al-noon). — [*Tragopogon pratensis*] 🌼.

5. **Perennial Lettuce** [*Lactuca perennis*].

PLATE 34.

Plate 34.

COMPOSITÆ

(Continued).

1. **Cooking Sow-thistle** [Sonchus oleraceus].

2. **Autumnal Hawk-bit** [Leontodon autumnalis].

3. **Mouse-ear Hawkweed** [Hieracium Pilosella].

4. **Umbellate Hawkweed** [Hieracium umbellatum].

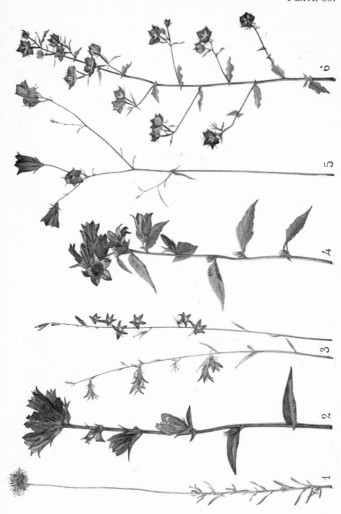

Plate 35.

CAMPANULACEÆ.

1. **Mountain Sheep's-bit** (Sheep's Scabious) —[*Jasione montana*].—

2. **Clustered Bellflower** [*Campanula glomerata*].—

3. **Rampion Bellflower** (Rampion, Ramps). [*Campanula Rapunculus*. Food-plant.]—

4. **Nettle-leaved Bellflower** (Canterbury Bells).—[*Campanula Trachelium*].— medicinal.

5. **Round-leaved Bellflower** (Harebell).— [*Campanula rotundifolia*].—

6. **Looking-glass Speeularia** (Venus' Lookingglass)[*Specularia Speculum*].—

PLATE 36.

Plate 36.

ERICACEÆ.

1. **Hoary Heath**
[*Erica cinerea*].

———

2. **Common Ling**
(Heather) — (*Cal-luna vulgaris*). —
ornamental.

———

PRIMULACEÆ.

3. **Common Pri-mula** (Primrose).
— [*Primula vul-garis*]. — orna-mental.

———

4. **Official Pri-mula** (Cowslip,
Paigle). — [*Pri-mula officinalis*].
— medicinal.

———

5. **Moneywort
Loosestrife**
(Creeping Jenny).
— [*Lysimachia
Nummularia*].

———

6. **Field Pimper-ne** (Scarlet Pim-pernel, Poor
man's weather-glass). — [*Anagal-lis arvensis*]. —
6 bis. **Blue Pim-pernel** [*Anagal-lis cærulea*].

PLATE 37.

Plate 37.

OLEACEÆ.

1. **Lofty Ash** (Common Ash) [*Fraxinus excelsior*]. — Industrial; medicinal.

2. **Common Privet** [*Ligustrum vulgare*]. — Industrial. Branch in flower. *2 bis*, Fruits.

3. **Common Lilac** [*Syringa vulgaris*]. — ornamental.

APOCYNACEÆ.

4. **Lesser Periwinkle** [*Vinca minor*]. — ornamental; medicinal.

ASCLEPIADACEÆ.

5. **Officinal Swallow-wort** (Tame-poison). [*Vincetoxicum officinale*]. — poisonous; medicinal.

PLATE 38.

Plate 38.

GENTIANACEÆ.

1. **Common Cen-**
   taury [*Erythræa*
   Centaurium]. —
   medicinal.

2. **Cross-leaved**
   Gentian [*Gen-*
   tiana Cruciata].
   — medicinal.

CONVOLVULACEÆ.

3. **Field Bind-**
   weed (Small
   Convolvulus). —
   [*Convolvulus ar-*
   vensis]. — medi-
   cinal.

4. **Hedge Bind-**
   weed [*Convol-*
   vulus sepium].

PLATE 39.

Plate 39.

BORAGINACEÆ.

1. **Common Viper's-bugloss** [*Echium vulgare*]

2. **Narrow-leaved Lungwort** [*Pulmonaria angustifolia*]. — medicinal.

3. **Officinal Comfrey** [*Symphytum officinale*]. — medicinal.

4. **Officinal Borage** [*Borago officinalis*]. — medicinal.

5. **Field Bugloss** [*Lycopsis arvensis*].

6. **Scorpioid Myosote** (Forget-me-not). — [*Myosotis scorpioides*].

PLATE 40.

Plate 40.

SOLANACEÆ.

1. **Black Henbane** [*Hyoscyamus niger*].— poisonous; medicinal.

2. **Bittersweet, Nightshade** (Woody Nightshade). — *Solanum Dulcamara*].— poisonous; medicinal. Branch with flowers. 2 *bis*, A flower, natural size.

3. **Chinese Boxthorn** (Duke of Argyll's Tea-tree). — [*Lycium chinense*] Branch with flowers. 3 *bis*, A flower, natural size.

4. **Tuberous Nightshade** (Potato). — [*Solanum tuberosum*]. — Food-plant; medicinal.

SCROPHULARINEÆ.

5. **Great Mullein** (Hag-taper). — [*Verbascum Thapsus*].

PLATE 41.

Plate 41.

SCROPHULARIACEÆ
(Continued).

1. **Greater Snap-dragon** [*Antir-rhinum majus*]. — ornamental; medicinal. ✿

2. **Ivy-leaved Toad-flax** (Mother of Thousands) [*Lina-ria Cymbalaria*]. — ornamental.

3. **Common Toad-flax** [*Linaria vulgaris*] ✿

4. **Nodulo-s Fig-wort** [*Scrophu-laria nodosa*] — medicinal ✿

5. **Purple Fox-glove** [*Digitalis purpurea*]. — ornamental; poisonous; medicinal. ✿

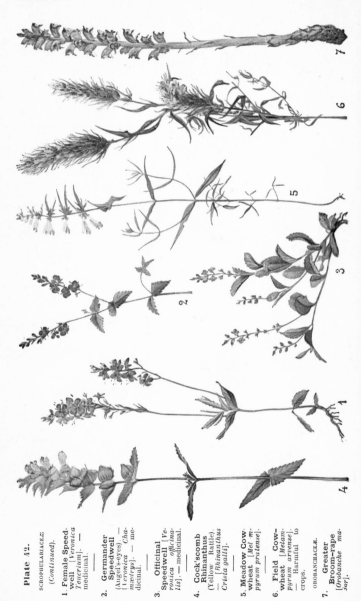

PLATE 42.

Plate 42.

SCROPHULARIACEÆ
(*Continued*).

1 **Female Speed-well** [*Veronica Teucrium*]. — medicinal.

2. **Germander Speedwell** (Angel's-eyes) [*Veronica Chamædrys*]. — medicinal.

3. **Officinal Speedwell** [*Veronica officinalis*]. — medicinal.

4. **Cock'scomb Rhinanthus** (Yellow Rattle). [*Rhinanthus Crista galli*].

5. **Meadow Cow-wheat** [*Melampyrum pratense*].

6. **Field Cow-wheat** [*Melampyrum arvense*]. Harmful to crops.

OROBANCHEÆ.

7. **Greater Broom-rape** [*Orobanche major*].

PLATE 43.

Plate 43.

LABIATÆ.

1. **Official Ca-
   lamint** [Cala-
   mintha officina-
   lis].—medicinal.

2. **Foot-stool
   Calamint** (Wild
   Basil).—[Cala-
   mintha Clinopo-
   dium].

3. **Common Mar-
   joram** [Origa-
   num vulgare].—
   medicinal.

4. **Long-leaved
   Mint** (Horse
   Mint).—[Mentha
   longifolia].

5. **Round-leaved
   Mint** [Mentha
   rotundifolia].—
   medicinal.

6. **Common Self-
   heal** [Prunella
   vulgaris].—me-
   dicinal.

7. **Meadow Sage**
   (Meadow Clary).
   [Salvia praten-
   sis].—medici-
   nal.

PLATE 44.

Plate 44.

LABIATE
(Continued).

1. **Official Woundwort** (Wound Betony). — [Stachys officinalis]. — medicinal.

2. **Scented Hemp-nettle** [Galeopsis Ladanum].

3. **Balm-leaved Melittis** (Bastard Balm). [Melittis Melissophyllum]. — medicinal.

4. **Ivy-like Nepeta** (Ground Ivy, Ale-hoof). — [Nepeta hederacea]. — medicinal.

5. **Amplexicaul Dead-nettle** (Hen-bit Nettle). — [Lamium amplexicaule].

6. **White Dead-Nettle** [Lamium album]. — medicinal.

7. **Black Horehound** [Ballota nigra].

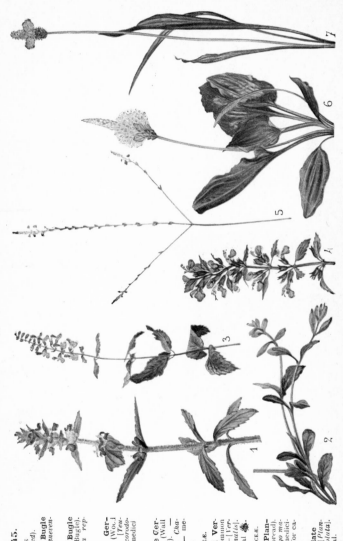

Plate 45.

LABIATÆ
(Continued).

1. **Geneva Bugle**
[*Ajuga genevensis*].

2. **Creeping Bugle**
(Common Bugle).
— [*Ajuga reptans*].

3. **Wood Germander** (Wood Sage). — [*Teucrium Scorodonia*]. — medicinal.

4. **Prostrate Germander** (Wall Germander). — [*Teucrium Chamædrys*]. — medicinal.

VERBENACEÆ.

5. **Official Vervain** (Common Vervain). — [*Verbena officinalis*]. — medicinal.

PLANTAGINACEÆ.

6. **Greater Plantain** (Way-bread). — [*Plantago major*]. — medicinal. Food for cage-birds.

7. **Lanceolate Plantain** [*Plantago lanceolata*]. — medicinal.

PLATE 46.

Plate 46.

CHENOPODIACEÆ.

1. **Good - King - Henry Goosefoot** (Mercury, All Good). — [*Chenopodium Bonus-Henricus*]. — Food-plant.

2. **White Goosefoot** (Fat Hen). — (*Chenopodium album*)

POLYGONACEÆ.

3. **Sorrel Dock** (Common Dock). — [*Rumex Acetosa*]. — Foodplant; medicinal.

4. **Buck-wheat Knotgrass** [*Polygonum Fagopyrum*]. — Foodplant.

5. **Birds' Knotgrass** [*Polygonum aviculare*].

ARISTOLOCHIACEÆ.

6. **Climbing Birthwort** [*Aristolochia Clematitis*]. — medicinal.

PLATE 47.

Plate 47.

EUPHORBIACEÆ.

1 **Evergreen Box**
[*Buxus semper-virens*]. — Industrial; medicinal.

2. **Annual Mercury** [*Mercurialis annua*]. — Harmful; medicinal. Shoot which produces seed. *2 bis*, Shoot which does not produce seed.

3. **Sun Spurge** [*Euphorbia Helioscopia*]. — medicinal.

4. **Cypress Spurge** [*Euphorbia Cyparissias*].

5. **Almond-scented Spurge** (Wood Spurge). [*Euphorbia amygdaloides*].

PLATE 48.

Plate 48.

CANNABINACEÆ.

1. **Rough Hop** [*Humulus Lupulus*]. — Industrial; medicinal. Branch of a plant which does not produce seed. 1 *bis*, Part of a seed-bearing plant.

2. **Cultivated Hemp** (Common Hemp). — [*Cannabis sativa*]. — Industrial; medicinal. Plant producing seed. 2 *bis*, Plant which does not bear seed.

URTICACEÆ.

3. **Officinal Pellitory** (Pellitory of the wall) [*Parietaria officinalis*]. — medicinal.

4. **Diœcious Stinging-Nettle** [*Urtica dioica*]. — medicinal.

— 9 —

PLATE 49.

Plate 49.

CUPULIFERÆ.

1. **Woodland Beech** (Beech) [*Fagus sylvatica*].— Industrial; medicinal. Branch with flowers. 4 *bis*, Branch with fruits.

2. **Strong Oak** (Common Oak). [*Quercus Robur*].— Industrial; medicinal. Branch with flowers. 2 *bis*, Branch with fruits (acorns).

3. **Hazel Nut** [*Corylus Avellana*].— Industrial; food plant; medicinal. Branch with flowers (catkins). 3 *bis*, Branch with fruits.

4. **Cultivated Chestnut** (Spanish Chestnut). [*Castanea sativa*].— Food-plant; industrial; medicinal. Branch with flowers (catkins). 4 *bis*, Fruits.

PLATE 50.

Plate 50.

CUPULIFERÆ
(continued).

1. Birch-like Hornbeam (Common Hornbeam). — [*Carpinus Betulus*]. — Industrial † and 1 *bis.* Branches bearing two different kinds of flowers.

SALICACEÆ.

2. Tremulous Poplar (Aspen). — [*Populus tremula*]. — Industrial.

3. Black Poplar [*Populus nigra*]. — Industrial; medicinal 🌸. Branch with flowers (catkins). 3 *bis.* Leafy branch.

4. 4. *bis* Goat Willow (Great Sallow). — [*Salix caprea*]. — Industrial 🌸

5. Crack Willow (Withy). — [*Salix fragilis*]. — 🌸

6. Osier Willow [*Salix viminalis*]. — Industrial 🌸

PLATE 51.

Plate 51.

PLATANACEÆ.

1. **Oriental Plane**
[*Platanus orientalis*].

BETULACEÆ.

2. **Silver Birch**
(Common Birch).
— [*Betula alba*].
— Industrial;
medicinal ❀

3. **Sticky Alder**
(Common Alder).
— [*Alnus gluti-
nosa*]. — Indus-
trial; medicinal.
Branch with un-
ripe fruiting cat-
kins. 3 *bis*, Branch
with flowers of
two kinds, one in
long hanging cat-
kins, the other in
smaller upright
spikes.

PLATE 52.

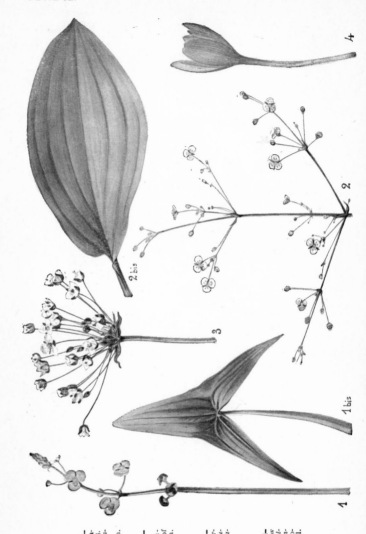

Plate 52.

ALISMACEÆ.

1. Arrowhead-leaved Sagittaria (Arrowhead). —[*Sagittaria sagittifolia*]. Flowering branch. *1 bis*, A leaf.

2. Water-plantain Alisma [*Alisma Plantago*]. — Top of flowering stem. *2 bis*, Leaf.

BUTOMACEÆ.

3. Umbellate Butomus (Flowering Rush).—[*Butomus umbellatus*].

COLCHICACEÆ.

4. Autumn Colchicum (Meadow Saffron). — [*Colchicum autumnale*]. — poisonous; medicinal.

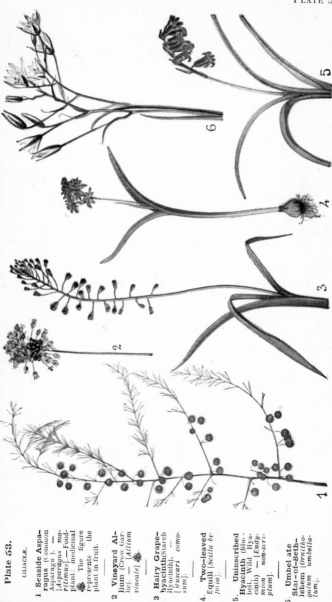

PLATE 53.

Plate 53.

LILIACEÆ.

1. **Seaside Asparagus** (Common Asparagus). — [*Asparagus maritimus*].—Food-plant: medicinal. The figure represents the plant in fruit.

2. **Vineyard Allium** (Crow Garlic). — [*Allium vineale*].

3. **Hairy Grape-hyacinth** (Starch Hyacinth). — [*Muscari comosum*].

4. **Two-leaved Squill** [*Scilla bifolia*].

5. **Uninscribed Hyacinth** (Blue-bell, Wild Hyacinth). — [*Endymion non-scriptum*].

6. **Umbellate Star-of-Bethlehem** (*Ornithogalum umbellatum*).

Plate 54.

LILIACEÆ
(Continued).

1. **Spine-pointed Ruscus** (Butcher's-broom, Knee-holm). — [*Ruscus aculeatus*]. — medicinal.

2. **Official Solomon's-Seal** — [*Polygonatum officinale*].

3. **May Convallaria** (Lily-of-the-Valley). — [*Convallaria majalis*]. — Poisonous; medicinal.

AMARYLLIDACEÆ

4. **False Narcis** (Daffodil, Lent Lily). — [*Narcissus Pseudo-Narcissus*]. — Poisonous; medicinal.

IRIDACEÆ

5. **Acorus-like Iris** (Corn Flag, Yellow Iris). — [*Iris Pseudacorus*]. — medicinal.

PLATE 55.

Plate 55.

ORCHIDACEÆ.

1. **Purple Orchis** (Old Lady Orchis). *Orchis purpurea*.

2. **Mountain Orchis** [*Orchis montana*].

3. **Broad-leaved Orchis** (Marsh Orchis). —*Orchis latifolia*. — medicinal.

4. **Pyramidal Orchis** [*Orchis pyramidalis*]. — medicinal.

5. **Monkey Orchis** [*Orchis simia*.].

6. **Goat Orchis** (Lizard Orchis) [*Orchis hircina*.].

PLATE 56.

Plate 56.

ORCHIDACEÆ

(Continued).

1. **Spider Orchid**
   [*Ophrys sphegodes*].

2. **Drone Orchid**
   (Late Spider Orchid).— [*Ophrys fuciflora*].

3. **Bee Orchid**
   [*Ophrys apifera*].

4. **Fly Orchid**
   [*Ophrys muscifera*].

5. **Egg-shaped Listera** [Twayblade].— *Listera ovata*].

6. **Bird's-nest Neottia.** *Neottia Nidus-avis*,

7. **Broad-leaved Epipactis** [*Epipactis latifolia*] — medicinal.

PLATE 57.

Plate 57.

NAIADACEÆ.

1. **Floating Pond-weed** [*Potamogeton natans*]. —

ARACEÆ.

2. **Spotted Arum** (Lords-and-ladies, Cuckoo-pint). [*Arum maculatum*]. — medicinal. Leaves and flowers. 2 *bis*, Fruits.

TYPHACEÆ.

3. **Broad-leaved Reed-mace** (Bulrush). — [*Typha latifolia*].

JUNCACEÆ.

4. **Spreading Rush** (Rush). — [*Juncus effusus*]. — industrial.

5. **Field Wood-rush** (Chimney-sweeps, Good Friday Grass). — [*Luzula campestris*].

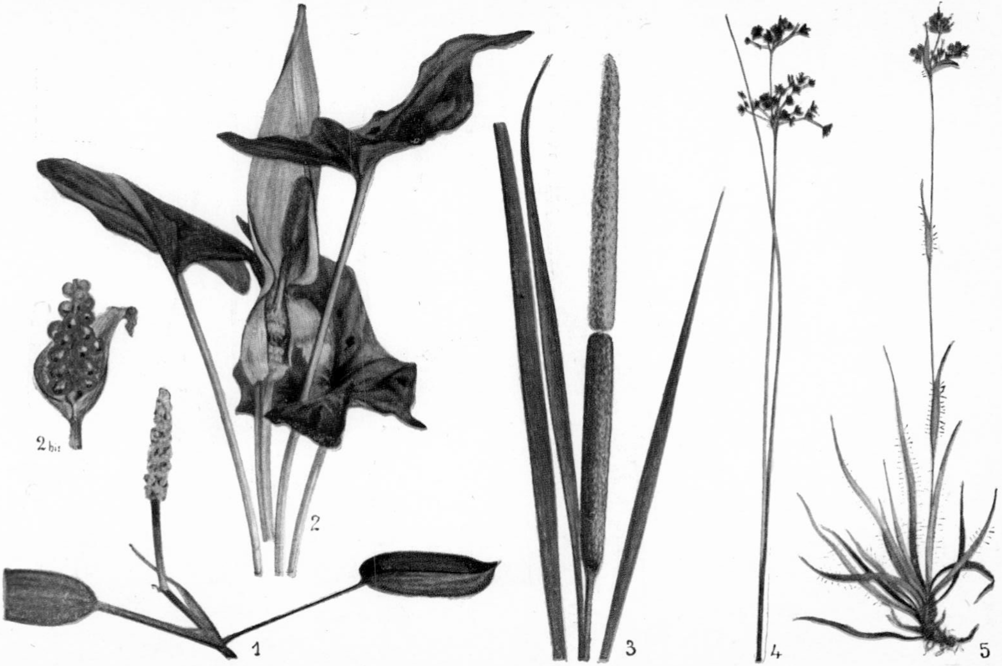

Plate 58.

CYPERACEÆ.

1. **Many-ranked Cotton-grass** [*Eriophorum po-lystachion*].

2. **Lake Scirpus** (Common Club or Pannier Rush).— [*Scirpus lacustris*].—Industrial.

3. **Wood Sedge** [*Carex sylvatica*].

4. **Pond Sedge** [*Carex paludosa*].

GRAMINEÆ.

5. **Maize Zea** (Indian Corn).— [*Zea Mays*]. Food-plant; fodder; medicinal.

PLATE 59.

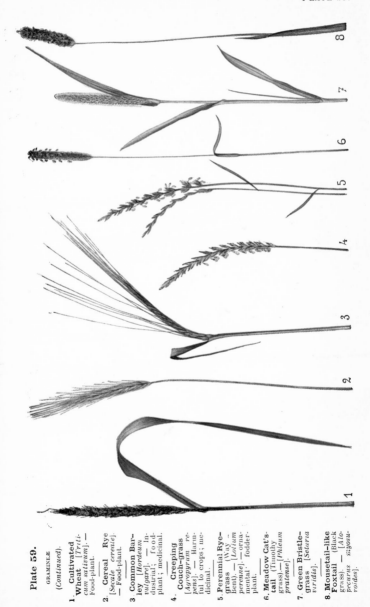

Plate 59.

GRAMINEÆ
(*Continued*).

1. **Cultivated Wheat** [*Triticum sativum*]. — Food-plant.

2. **Cereal Rye** [*Secale cereale*]. — Food-plant.

3. **Common Barley** [*Hordeum vulgare*]. — Industrial; food-plant; medicinal.

4. **Creeping Couch-grass** [*Agropyrum repens*]. — Harmful to crops; medicinal.

5. **Perennial Rye-grass** (Way-Bent). — [*Lolium perenne*]. — ornamental fodder-plant.

6. **Meadow Cat's-tail** (Timothy-grass) — [*Phleum pratense*].

7. **Green Bristle-grass** [*Setaria viridis*].

8. **Mousetail-like Foxtail** (Black grass). — [*Alopecurus agrestis*].

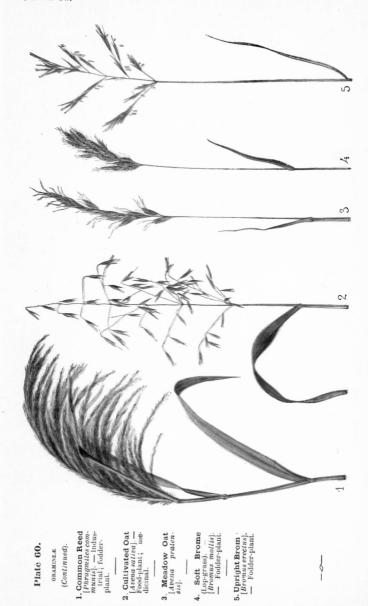

PLATE 60.

Plate 60.

GRAMINEÆ
(Continued).

1. **Common Reed**
[*Phragmites communis*]. — Industrial; fodder-plant.

2. **Cultivated Oat**
[*Avena sativa*].
Food-plant; medicinal.

3. **Meadow Oat**
[*Avena pratensis*].

4. **Soft Brome**
(Lop-grass).
[*Bromus mollis*].
— Fodder-plant.

5. **Upright Brom.**
[*Bromus erectus*].
— Fodder-plant.

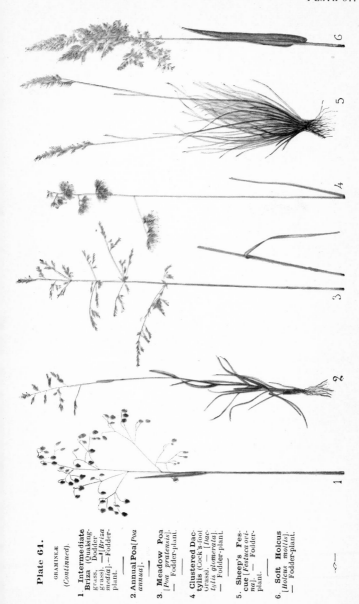

PLATE 61.

Plate 61.

GRAMINEÆ
(*Continued*).

1. **Intermediate Briza** (Quaking-grass, Dodder-grass). —[*Briza media*].—Fodder-plant.

2. **Annual Poa**[*Poa annual*].

3. **Meadow Poa** [*Poa pratensis*]. — Fodder-plant.

4. **Clustered Dactylis** (Cock's-foot grass). — [*Dactylis glomerata*].—Fodder-plant.

5. **Sheep's Fescue** [*Festuca ovina*]. — Fodder-plant.

6. **Soft Holcus** [*Holcus mollis*].—Fodder-plant.

PLATE 62.

Plate 62.

ABIETINÆ.

1. **Forest Pine** (Scots Fir, Northern Pine). — [*Pinus sylvestris*]. — Industrial. ❀ (The figure represents a branch in flower.)

2. **Lofty Spruce** (Common Spruce Fir), [*Picea excelsa*]. — Industrial. ❀ (The figure represents a branch with a seed-bearing cone.)

3. **Comb-like Fir** (Silver Fir),]*Abies pectinata*]. — Industrial; medicinal. ❀ (The figure represents a leafy branch.)

CUPRESSINEÆ.

4. **Common Juniper** [*Juniperus communis*]. — Industrial; medicinal. — (The figure represents a berry-bearing branch.)

PLATE 63.

Plate 63.

FERNS.

1. **Common Poly-
   pody** [*Polypo-
   dium vulgare*].—
   medicinal.

2. **Maidenhair
   Spleenwort**
   [*Asp.nium Tri-
   chomanes*].—me-
   dicinal.

3. **Wall-rue
   Spleenwort**
   [*Asplenium Ru-
   ta-muraria*].

4. **Eagle-marked
   Bracken** (Com-
   monBracken.)—
   [*Pteris aquilina*].
   —medicinal.
   (The figure re-
   presents the up-
   per part of a
   frond.)

PLATE 64.

Plate 64.

FERNS

(Continued).

1. **Male-fern Polystichum** (Male fern). — *Polystichum Filix-mas].* — medicinal.

EQUISETACEÆ.

2. **Field Horsetail** [*Equisetum arvense*]. — medicinal. Branched stem without spore-cases. 2 *bis*, Stem bearing spore-cases at its apex.

3. **Greatest Horsetail** [*Equisetum maximum*]. — (The figure represents the top of a branched stem without spore-cases).

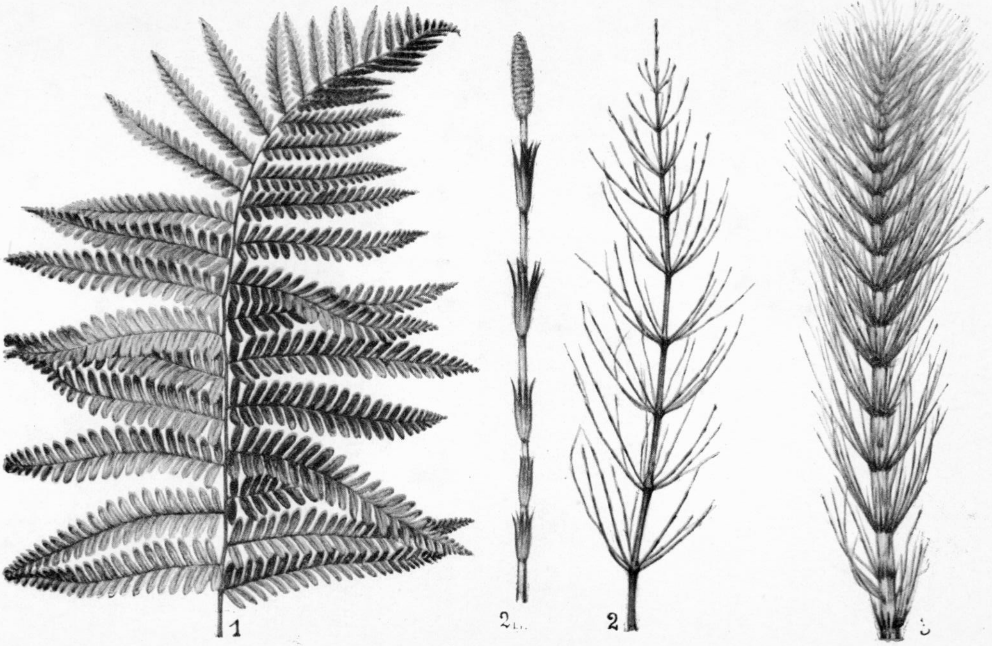

→ *The questions which are to be read to lead us to the names of plants begin at the top of the next page.*

Readers who have become accustomed to the use of this book can shorten the search for the name of a plant by beginning with the ABRIDGED TABLES on Page 286 and the following pages.

The tab fastened to the top of Page 287 enables us to turn at once to these Tables.

A

1 {
  + Plant **with flowers** (the flowers may sometimes be very small, or green, or scarcely visible)................... 2

  + Plant **without flowers** at any time, that is to say, a plant of which there is never anything to be seen but the leaves or the leafy stems, as, for example, the Ferns (see the figures at Nos. 1092 to 1104) 1092
}

2
(following on 1). {
  −• **Herbaceous plant**, that is to say, one with stems or branches without the appearance or hardness of wood 3

  −• **Tree, shrub, or undershrub**, one, that is, with stems or branches with the appearance and hardness of wood, except in the case of the very youngest branches 942
}

△ **Flower composite**, that is to say, that what is ordinarily called the flower is in reality a collection of little flowers packed close together, without stalks, and surrounded by a collarette of little leaves or scales, the whole resembling a single flower 770

Familiar instances of composite flowers : Daisy (Figs. M, MA, MAR) ; *Thistle* (Figs. C, CH) ; *Dandelion* (Figs. D, DE, DT). The little flowers which collectively form the composite flower are marked *flt, fll, fl :* the collarette of little leaves or little scales is marked *co.*

3
(following on 2).

In turning over the pages between No. 771 and No. 929 many figures representing very varied forms of composite flowers will be seen.

△ **Flower not composite**, that is to say, not having the arrangement above mentioned 4

N.B.—If there is a doubt as to whether the flower is *composite* or *not*, either question may be chosen and in either case the name of the plant will be reached.

4
(following on 3). {
✢ Flowers **rose colour, rosy, red, purple, reddish, brown,** brownish, or of a blackish brown.................. 5

✢ Flowers **blue, bluish, lilac, violet,** or violet purple . 228

✢ Flowers **yellow or yellowish** 354

✢ Flowers **white or whitish** 506

✢ Flowers **green or greenish**..................... 705

Note.—If there is a doubt between two colours, either may be selected, and in either case the name of the plant will be reached. —In deciding on the colours of flowers, no notice need be taken of the colour of the little parts terminating the threads which we find in the flower, nor of that of the organs in the centre of the flower.
}

○ Each flower **regular**, that is to say, that the similar parts of the flower which are coloured rose, red, or brown, are arranged regularly round the centre of the flower and are obviously equal to one another in size 6

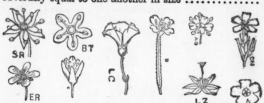

The above figures represent some examples of regular flowers.

○ Each flower **irregular**, that is to say, the flowers have not the characteristics above described 123

Note.—Flowers which have their right half similar to their left need not be considered as regular.

The above figures represent some examples of irregular flowers.

○ Each flower **reduced to little brown or reddish scales (or to little oval bodies)** 146

The above figures represent some examples of groups of flowers reduced to scales.

Note.—If we hesitate as to whether a flower is regular or irregular—as, for example, in the case of the flowers represented by Figs. VT and V, we may take either of the numbers to which we are referred (6 or 123) and we shall get to the name of the plant.

There may also be a doubt between flowers reduced to scales and regular flowers, because some flowers, although regular, are made up of membranous parts and seem to be reduced to scales, as, for example, the flower represented by Fig. ML or the group of flowers represented by Fig. LG. Here again either the No. 6 or the No. 146 may be chosen and either will bring us to the name of the plant.

5 following on 4).

— **Compound** leaves; that is to say, that the entire leaf is formed by the union of secondary leaves called *leaflets*, each of which is often mistaken for a leaf. The entire compound leaf is attached to the stem at its base, or by a stalk which bears all the leaflets. The compound leaf is *not* directly attached in the axil of another leaf: that is to say, it is not in the angle between a leaf and the stem 88

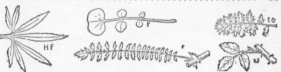

The above figures represent some examples of compound leaves.

— **Deeply divided** leaves (except sometimes those leaves which are quite at the top of the stems), that is to say, each leaf is, as it were, cut to more than half its breadth.. 88

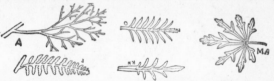

The above figures represent some examples of divided leaves.

— **Simple** leaves; that is to say, either not cut for more than half the breadth of the leaf, or only notched at the edge, or even without any notches at the edge....... 7

The above figures represent some examples of simple leaves.

— **Undeveloped** leaves 8

Note.—If there is a doubt between compound and deeply divided leaves, the matter is of no importance, as in both cases you are referred to the same number (88).

If there is a doubt between deeply divided and simple leaves (as, for example, Fig. A) either question may be taken. In both cases the name of the plant will be reached. It will be equally arrived at if the plant should have both simple and compound, or divided, leaves (with the exception of some simple leaves which may be found quite at the top of flowering branches).

6
(following on 5).

✱ **Opposite leaves** (except sometimes at the top of a stem or its branches) ; that is to say, leaves arranged in couples, at the same height, and facing one another 60

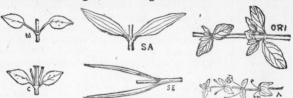

The above figures represent some examples of opposite leaves.

Note.—There will often be found developed in the axil of opposite leaves small leafy branches (as in Fig. ORI above), so that the leaves might be supposed to be grouped in a large number at the same level on the branch, and not in opposite pairs only; but in looking carefully at the base of such groups of leaves, the two opposite ones are easily distinguished.

✱ **Whorled leaves**, at least towards the middle of the stem : that is to say, 3, 4, 5 or even more leaves attached to the branch at the same level, and arranged regularly round it 85

The above figures represent examples of whorled leaves.

✱ **Alternate leaves** ; that is to say, leaves attached one by one to the stem at different levels................... 8

The above figures represent alternate leaves.

✱ **Grouped leaves** ; that is to say, two or more leaves attached to the stem at the same level, but arranged, at this level, on the same side of the stem (as, for example, Fig. BE) 8

✱ **Leaves all at the base** of the plant (for examples, Figs. C, ME) 8

Note.—If a plant has both alternate and opposite leaves (as, for example, Fig. PD) or alternate and whorled leaves at the same time, either one or the other question may be chosen, and in either case the name of the plant will be arrived at

7 (following on 6).

— Each flower having its petals **separated from one another down to the base**; that is to say, it is possible to remove from the base one of the petals (that part of a flower which is coloured pink, red, or brown) without tearing the others. These petals are those parts of a flower which, collectively, form the corolla that surrounds the little threads and other organs situated in the centre of the flower. When the blossom fades each petal or coloured portion falls or withers separately[1] **9**

Figs. E and G represent flowers having separate petals in which one can distinguish the 4 detached petals (Fig. PE) or the 5 detached petals (Fig. PG). The other figures (PY, BO, LA, and FA) represent some examples of flowers with separate petals.

8
(following on 7).

= Each flower having its petals **joined together**, at least at the base. In trying to detach one of the coloured parts, pink, red, or brown, of such a flower, one is obliged to tear the corolla at least at its base. When the flower fades the whole corolla falls, or is withered, at the same time **45**

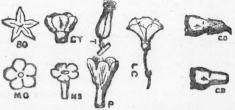

The petals are joined together at different heights in various flowers. Fig. MC represents the corolla of a flower in which the petals are very slightly joined together at the base. In the corolla BO the petals are more united. They are even more so in the corollas CY, MS, and P, where they form a tube at the base. In flower T the petals are only separated at their tips where they form little teeth. In flower LC the petals are joined together almost to the tip.—Fig. CO represents a flower, the detached corolla of which is shown in Fig. CD.

---

[1] In most flowers there will be found, outside the corolla, another covering for the flowers, generally green in colour, which is called the *calyx*, and which encloses the base of the corolla. In other flowers it is difficult to distinguish the calyx from the corolla, they being more or less blended in one floral covering (for example, Figs. LA, FA, T). Finally, there are other flowers which have only a single floral covering, pink, reddish, or brown in colour, like a corolla. Under the names petal and corolla here, then, must be understood the coloured parts, pink, red, reddish, or brown, which immediately surround the tiny threads or other organs placed in the centre of the flower.

<table>
<tr><td>—
9
(following on 8).</td><td>

⊖ **Each flower** having 4 petals, or 4 parts, pink, red, or brown **10**

⊖ Each flower having 5 petals, or 5 parts, pink, reddish, or brown **21**

⊖ Each flower having 3 **or 6** petals, or 3 or 6 coloured parts, pink, red, reddish, reddish green, brown, brownish, or pink and white **33**

⊖ Each flower having more than 7 petals, pink, red, brown **44**

</td></tr>
</table>

10
(following on 9).

× Petals **crumpled in the flower-bud** inside two green parts which drop apart as the flower expands (Fig. PR) .... **PR** 20

× Petals **not** crumpled in the bud and not enclosed in two green parts which fall when the flower opens **11**

11
(following on 10).

☐ Plants **which** exude a white milk when they are cut, or when the stalk is broken.→Spurge [*Euphorbia*].—For the principal kinds of Euphorbia see No. **706**

☐ Plants **without any** white milk **12**

12
(following on 11).

✱ ✱ Each flower **almost stalkless** and with the flowers arranged in long clusters (Fig. LS). The green

part which encloses the petals at their base (the calyx) is shaped like a tube and has **8 or 12 toothed points** arranged in two rows (6 of these toothed points in the outer row are visible in Fig. SI (enlarged)). → Willow-leaved Lythrum (Purple Loosestrife) [*Lythrum Salicaria*]—medicinal.—Shown in colour: 4, Plate 21. (Family *Lythraceæ*.)

✱ ✱ Each flower **supported by a stalk of more or less** length **13**

13
(following on 12).

☉ Flowers having no small leaf, or leaflet at the base of their stalk (see Figs. HM, LB on the next page) **14**

☉ Flowers which have a small leaf, or leaflet at the base of their stalk (for example, Fig. ET). → Willow-herb [*Epilobium*]. (Family *Onagraceæ*.) [1]—For the principal kinds of Willow-herbs go on to No. **15**

---

[1] For more details as to the species of Willow-herbs reference must be made to more comprehensive Floras.

14
(following on 13).

⟳ Leaves coming to a point at the base (Fig. HM); flowers having a sweet perfume. → Dame's Hesperis (Dame's Violet) [*Hesperis matronalis*]—ornamental. ✿ (Family *Cruciferæ*.)

⟳ Leaves not pointed at the base but often shaped like an inverted heart (Fig. LB); flowers with no pronounced perfume.→Biennial Lunaria (Honesty) [*Lunaria biennis*] — ornamental. (Family *Cruciferæ*.)

15
(following on 13).

• Each flower measuring more than a centimetre and a half across when fully open 16

• Each flower measuring less than a centimetre and a half when fully open 17

16
(following on 15).

⊕ Leaves not surrounding the stalk at their base; flowers slightly irregular (Fig. ES). → Narrow - leaved Willow - herb (Rose - bay) [*Epilobium angustifolium*]—edible. ✿ (Family *Onagraceæ*.)

⊕ Leaves partially surrounding the stalk at their base; flowers regular (Fig. H). → Hairy Willow - herb (Codlins and Cream) [*Epilobium hirsutum*].—Shown in colour: 3, Plate 21. ✿ (Family *Onagraceæ*.)

17
(following on 15).

✠ Stalks with 2 or 4 angled sides, more or less sharply defined (see below, No. 18, Figs. T and R) 18

✠ Stalks not having well-defined angular sides 19

18
(following on 17).

§ Leaves without stalks (Fig. T). → Square - stalked Willow - herb [*Epilobium tetragonum*]. (Family *Onagraceæ*.)

§ Leaves having stalks (Fig. R). → Pale Rose Willow - herb [*Epilobium roseum*]. (Family *Onagraceæ*.)

19
(following on 17).

+ Leaves hairy (Fig. EP); stems very hairy. → Small - flowered Willow-herb [*Epilobium parviflorum*]. (Family *Onagraceæ*.)

+ Leaves only slightly hairy (Fig. M); stems almost without hairs, or with only very small woolly hairs on them. → **Mountain Willow - herb** [*Epilobium montanum*]. (Family *Onagraceæ*.)

20
(following on 10).

—• Leaves bristly, not spreading widely round the stalk at their base; flowers red, sometimes splashed with black. → **Common Poppy** (Corn Poppy, Corn Rose) [*Papaver Rhœas*]—medicinal; hurtful to animals.— Shown in colour: 1, Plate 5. (Family *Papaveraceæ*.)

—• Leaves without bristly hairs and spreading widely round the stalk at their base; flowers pink, purple, and only rarely red. → **Opium Poppy** [*Papaver somniferum*]— poisonous, medicinal, ornamental, and industrial.— Shown in colour: 2, Plate 5. (Family *Papaveraceæ*.)

21
(following on 9).

△ Leaves with their veins arranged in the shape of a fan, that is to say, when the principal veins spring from the very top of the leaf-stalk (Figs. GM, MS); leaves more or less cut up 22

△ Plants not having these characteristics 23

22
(following on 21).

✠ Petals entirely separated from one another down to the base (example: Fig. G, representing a flower the 5 separate petals detached from which are shown in PG). This flower has not got three small green leaves placed immediately below the green part (calyx) which surrounds the petals at their base. → **Crane's - bill** [*Geranium*].[1] (Family *Geraniaceæ*.)—For the principal kinds of Geraniums turn on to No. 94

✠ Petals joined together at their base (Fig. M). There are three little green leaves placed immediately below the green part (calyx) which surrounds the petals at their base (examples: MA, MM, which represent the calyx without the petals). → **Mallow** [*Malva*]. (Family *Malvaceæ*.)—For the principal kinds of Mallows turn on to No. 57

---

[1] This refers to the wild Geraniums, and not to those plants cultivated in gardens which are known, though often wrongly, under the name of Geraniums. These latter are in reality Pelargoniums, and came originally from the Cape of Good Hope. For more details as to the various species of Geraniums reference should be made to more comprehensive Floras.

23
(following on 21).

○ Plant fleshy, that is to say, with juicy and fleshy leaves; each flower has its petals sharply pointed at their tips (Fig. SR, enlarged). → **Orpine Stonecrop** (Live-long) [*Sedum Telephium*]—medicinal.—Shown in colour: 1, Plate 22. (Family *Crassulaceæ*.)

○ Plant not fleshy **24**

24
(following on 23).

— Flowers rosy purple, with no stalks, and in long clusters (Fig. LS). The green part which surrounds the petals

(calyx) has **8 to 12 toothed** points arranged in two rows (the 6 points of the outer row may be seen in Fig. SL). → **Willow-leaved Lythrum** (Purple Loosestrife) [*Lythrum Salicaria*] — medicinal. — Shown in colour: 4, Plate 21. (Family *Lythraceæ*.)

— Flowers **pink, reddish, greenish red, or pinky white**; plants not having the preceding characteristics..... **25**

25
(following on 24).

✳ Leaves all at the base of the plant; flowers all collected into a rounded mass at the top of the stem (Fig. PL). → **Seaside Thrift** [*Armeria maritima*]. (Family *Plumbaginaceæ*.)

✳ Leaves arranged along the stems; flowers not all collected into a rounded mass **26**

26
(following on 25).

═ Each leaf attached to the stem by a sheathing structure (examples: Figs. H, AV) **29**

═ Each leaf **not** attached to the stem by a sheathing structure **27**

27
(following on 26).

⊖ **There is a thick ring** within the flower at the base of its five parts (Fig. BT, enlarged—to be seen with a lens); flowers in elongated spikes (Fig. BV). → **Common Beet** (Beetroot) [*Beta vulgaris*]—food plant; industrial. (Family *Chenopodiaceæ*.)

⊖ **There is no thick ring** within the flower at the base of its five parts **28**

28
(following on 27).

× Leaves hairy; flowers in but slightly elongated clusters (Fig. P). → **Officinal Pellitory** (Pellitory of the wall) [*Parietaria officinalis*] — medicinal. — Represented in colour: **3**, Plate 48. (Family *Urticaceæ.*)

× Leaves without hairs or covered with a mealy powder; flowers in more or less elongated clusters (Figs. GL, U, BH). → **Goose-foot** [*Chenopodium*], **White Goose-foot**, and **Good-King-Henry Goose-foot** are represented in colour in Figs. 1 and 2 of Plate 46 (Family *Chenopodiaceæ.*) [1]

29
(following on 26).

☐ Leaves shaped like an arrow-head or an inverted heart (Fig. FG). → **Buckwheat Knot-grass** [*Polygonum Fagopyrum*] — food plant. ❀ — Represented in colour: **4**, Plate 46. (Family *Polygonaceæ.*)

☐ Leaves not arrow- or heart-shaped **30**

30
(following on 29).

✱ ✱ Flowers intermingled with the leaves along the leafy stems (Fig. AVI). → **Birds' Knot-grass** [*Polygonum aviculare*]. ❀ — Represented in colour: **5**, Plate 46. (Family *Polygonaceæ.*) [1]

✱ ✱ Flowers arranged in crowded spikes **31**

31
(following on 30).

☉ Leaves with a long stalk and more or less rounded at their base (Fig. A); plant often floating in water. → **Amphibious Knot-grass** [*Polygonum amphibium*]. (Family *Polygonaceæ.*)

☉ Leaves without a stalk or with a very short stalk and pointed at their bases (Fig. PC; see also Figs. PS and L, under No. 32, *infra*) **32**

32
(following on 31).

♥ The tube surrounding the base of the leaves is hairy and edged with long hairs (Fig. PS). → **Persicaria Knot-grass** [*Polygonum Persicaria*] — medicinal. (Family *Polygonaceæ.*)

♥ The tube surrounding the base of the leaves has few or no hairs and is edged with short hairs or is without hairs (Fig. L). → **Pale-flowered Knot-grass** [*Polygonum lapathifolium*]. (Family *Polygonaceæ.*)

[1] For the various species of Goose-foot reference should be made to more comprehensive Floras.

33 (following on 9).
⁂ Flowers all in one group ; the stalks of the flowers all spring from the same point at the top of the stem.... 40
⁂ Flowers not so arranged 34

34 (following on 33).
⊕ Flowers with 6 parts, rose colour; almost without stalks, in a very long cluster (Fig. LS).→**Willow-leaved Lythrum** (Purple Loosestrife) [*Lythrum Salicaria*]—medicinal.—Represented in colour : 4, Plate 21. (Family *Lythraceæ.*)

⊕ Flowers with 6 parts, white, tinged with pink at their bases; leaves shaped like an arrow-head (Fig. S).→**Arrowhead-leaved Sagittaria** (Arrow-head) [*Sagittaria sagittifolia*].—Represented in colour: 1 and 1 *bis*, Plate 52. (Family *Alismaceæ.*)

⊕ Flowers with 3 pinkish and 3 greenish parts; in each group of flowers the stalks are attached at the same point (Figs. PL and AF) 39

⊕ Flowers with 6 parts, reddish, brown, brownish, or greenish red 35

35 (following on 34).
✠ Flowers of a dry texture; leaves narrow and elongated, at least 15 times as long as they are broad, neither divided nor toothed 36
✠ Flowers not of a dry texture ; leaves less than 15 times as long as they are broad.→**Dock** (Sorrel) [*Rumex*].—For the chief species of *Rumex* go on to No. 152

36 (following on 35).
§ Leaves cylindric like the stems (Fig. J).→**Rush** [*Juncus*]

—industrial.—The **Spreading Rush** (Soft Rush) [*Juncus effusus*] is represented in colour: see 4, Plate 57.[1] (Family *Juncaceæ.*)

§ Leaves flat or folded lengthwise 37

37 (following on 36).
+ Leaves with rather long hairs scattered along their edges (Fig. LC). → **Wood-rush** [*Luzula*].[2] —The **Field Wood-rush** (*Luzula campestris*) is represented in colour: see 5, Plate 57. (Family *Juncaceæ.*)
+ Leaves without hairs 38

---

[1] For the numerous species of Rushes [*Juncus*] reference must be made to more comprehensive Floras.
[2] For the various species of Wood-rush [*Luzula*] reference must be made to more comprehensive Floras.

38
(following on 37).

—• **Flowers with 6 narrow divisions produced into long points** (Fig. B).→**Toad Rush** [*Juncus bufonius*]. Fig. BU represents the whole plant. (Family *Juncaceæ*.)

—• **Flowers with 6 oval divisions not with long points** (Fig. BB). →**Bulbous Rush** [*Juncus bulbosus*]. Fig. BL represents the top of a flowering stem. (Family *Juncaceæ*.)

39
(following on 34).

△ **Flowers arranged on very many branches;** each flower less than 5 millimetres across.→**Water-plantain Alisma** [*Alisma Plantago-aquatica*].—Represented in colour: 2 and 2 *bis*, Plate 52. (Family *Alismaceæ*.)

△ **Flowers arranged in 1 or 2 groups.**→**Ranunculus-like Alisma** [*Alisma ranunculoides*]. (Family *Alismaceæ*.)

40
(following on 33).

✠ **Flowers with 3 parts of a pinkish white and 3 green;** leaves flat.→**Ranunculus-like Alisma** [*Alisma ranunculoides*]. (Family *Alismaceæ*.)

✠ **Flowers with 6 parts all rose colour, pinkish white or streaked with green and rose colour;** leaves cylindric or semi-cylindric like the stems **41**

41
(following on 40).

○ **Each flower more than a centimetre across when open;** there are more than 2 small membranous leaves at the base of the collection of flowers (Fig. JF).→**Umbellate Butomus** (Flowering Rush) [*Butomus umbellatus*]. ✿ —Represented in colour: 3, Plate 52. (Family *Alismaceæ*.)

○ **Each flower less than a centimetre across;** there are only 1 or 2 membranous leaves at the base of the collection of flowers (Fig. A). →**Onions and Garlics** [*Allium*].[1]—For the chief species of *Allium* go on to No. **42**

---

[1] For details as to the various species of Onions, Garlic, etc. [*Allium*]. reference must be made to more comprehensive Floras.

42
(following on 41).

— The membranous leaf surrounding the flowers is prolonged into a point much longer than the flowers (Fig. O) ; flowers rose coloured mingled with green and red. → Cooking Allium (Field Garlic) [*Allium oleraceum*]. (Family *Liliaceæ*.)

— The membranous leaf surrounding the flowers is shorter than, or scarcely longer than, the flowers 43

43
(following on 42).

✳ Flowers pale pink; some of the flowers (such as those represented in Fig. VI) may be replaced by little oval bodies (Fig. V). → Vineyard Allium (Crow Garlic) [*Allium vineale*]. ❀—Represented in colour: 2, Plate 53. (Family *Liliaceæ*.)

✳ Flowers red, in a rounded mass (Fig. SM) ; none of the flowers replaced by a little tubercle. → Round-headed Allium [*Allium sphærocephalum*]. ❀ (Family *Liliaceæ*.)

44
(following on 9).

= Plant fleshy, with fleshy, thick, juicy leaves, forming rosettes at the base of the plant which resemble small artichokes (Fig. ST); petals pointed at their tips M. → Roof Sempervivum (House-leek) [*Sempervivum tectorum*]—medicinal. ❀—Represented in colour: 5 and 5 *bis*, Plate 22. (Family *Crassulaceæ*.)

= Plant not fleshy. (On examining the flower carefully, it will be seen that it is in reality a composite flower made up of a great number of little simple flowers crowded together and surrounded by a collarette of little leaves or scales.)—Go on to No. 771

45
(following on 8).

⊖ Plant climbing or trailing at length along the ground.. 46

⊖ Plant not climbing or trailing at any length 47

46
(following on 45).

✕ Plant without leaves, not green, attaching itself to other plants (Fig. CS). → Lesser Dodder [*Cuscuta Epithymum*]—harmful to crops. (Family *Convolvulaceæ*.)

✕ Plant with green leaves; flowers plaited, funnel shaped (Fig. LC). → Field Bindweed [*Convolvulus arvensis*]—medicinal. Represented in colour: 3, Plate 38. (Family *Convolvulaceæ*.)

47
(following on 45).

☐ Each flower with 6 parts (Fig. SU), pink or pinkish white; leaves very narrow and elongated. → Onions or Garlic [*Allium*]. — Refer back to No. 42

☐ Each flower with 6 parts, pink, united at their base in a long tube; leaves not developed.—Go on to No. ... 240

☐ Each flower having 6 teeth; leaves all at the base.. 244

☐ Each flower having 4 or 5 parts or 4 or 5 teeth 48

48
(following on 47).

✱✱ Stem with stiff hairs, harsh to the touch, sometimes prickly 49

✱✱ Stem with soft hairs, or without hairs 53

49
(following on 48).

⊙ Each flower spreading in a star-like manner (Fig. B): petals only united at their bases. → Officinal Borage [*Borago officinalis*] (There is a pink-flowered variety)—medicinal. ✿ —Represented in colour (with blue flowers): 4, Plate 39. (Family *Boraginaceæ*.)

⊙ Each flower having a tube of greater or less length at the base of its corolla (see Figs. P, C, and LA, at Nos. 50 and 52) 50

50
(following on 49).

♡ Flowers pink or reddish; on opening the flower from above, 5 little inner lobes are seen closing the tube of the corolla (example; Fig. P) 51

♡ Flowers first pink, then violet, then blue; on looking at the flower from the front, one does not see 5 little lobes closing the tube of the corolla (Fig. P represents the corolla). → Narrow-leaved Lungwort [*Pulmonaria angustifolia*]—medicinal. ✿ —Represented in colour: 2, Plate 39 (Family *Boraginaceæ*.)

51
(following on 50).

✳ Leaves prolonged at the base along the stem (Fig. SO); flowers hanging downwards (Fig. S). → Officinal Comfrey [*Symphytum officinale*]—medicinal. ✿ —Represented in colour: 3, Plate 39. (Family *Boraginaceæ*.)

✳ Leaves not prolonged along the stem 52

52
(following on 51).

⊕ Flowers of a purplish or brownish red, with a short tube (Fig. CY : the corolla detached). → Official Hound's - tongue [*Cynoglossum officinale*] — poisonous, medicinal. 🌑 (Family *Boraginaceæ*.)

⊕ Flowers pink with a long tube (Fig. LA : flower cut open lengthwise); upper leaves not surrounding the stem by their bases. → Corn Gromwell [*Lithospermum arvense*]. (Family *Boraginaceæ*.)

53
(following on 48).

✠ Flowers bell shaped, dark coloured, springing solitarily, or two together, from the axil of the leaves (Fig. B). → Belladonna Atropa (Deadly Night-shade) [*Atropa Belladonna*] — poisonous, medicinal. 🌑 (Family *Solanaceæ*.)

✠ Flowers not bell shaped, purplish or brownish red, with a short tube (see above, on the right, Fig. CY)......... 52

✠ Flowers not bell shaped, pink or rose red 54

✠ Flowers not bell shaped, with no tube at their base, reddish or reddish green.—Refer back to No......... 27

54
(following on 53).

§ Flowers all united in a rounded mass (Fig. AR) ; leaves narrow and elongated, all at the base of the plant. → Seaside Thrift [*Armeria maritima*]. (Family *Plumbaginaceæ*.)

§ Flowers in clusters, pinkish; each flower less than 8 millimetres across ; leaves of the shape of an inverted heart or of an arrow-head 520

§ Plant not having these characteristics........... 55

55
(following on 54).

+ Leaves more or less toothed or notched all round (examples:

Figs. MS, GO) : corolla not tubular (Fig. M)....... 56

+ Leaves neither notched nor toothed (Fig. IT) : corolla tubular at its base (Fig. MS, enlarged) ; flowers in a

cluster curving backward at the top (Fig. H). → Myosote (Scorpion-grass and Forget-me-not) [*Myosotis*]. (Family *Boraginaceæ*.) 261

56
(following on 55).

—. Leaves more or less hairy, but very green; there are 3 very small leaves or green scales attached immediately below the green part (calyx) which surrounds the petals at their base (see Figs. MR, MS, MM, MA, at Nos. 58 and 59, lower down on this page). → Mallows [*Malva*].—For the chief kinds of Mallow [*Malva*], go on to No. 57

—. Leaves very velvety, whitish; there are 6 to 9 very small leaves or green scales, more or less united together, and immediately below the greenish part (calyx) which surrounds the petals at their base (Fig. AO, representing the flower as seen from below). → Officinal Marsh-mallow [*Althæa officinalis*]—medicinal. (Family *Malvaceæ*.)

57
(following on 56).

△ Several flowers springing from the stem, in the axil of a single leaf (example: Fig. R) 58

△ A single flower springing from the stem, in the axil of a leaf (example : Fig. A) 59

58
(following on 57).

✠ Flowers pinkish white; the three very small green leaves which are immediately below the green calyx of the flower are very narrow (Fig. MR, representing the flower as seen from below) → Round-leaved Mallow (Dwarf Mallow) [*Malva rotundifolia*]—medicinal. ✿ (Family *Malvaceæ*.)

✠ Flowers of a purplish pink; the 3 very small green leaves which are immediately below the green calyx of the flower are oval (Fig. MS). → Common Mallow [*Malva sylvestris*]—medicinal. ✿ —Represented in colour : 4, Plate 10. (Family *Malvaceæ*.)

59
(following on 57).

○ The three very small green leaves which are immediately below the calyx of the flower are narrow (Fig. MM, representing a flower with the petals removed); plant giving off a smell of musk when dried. → Musk Mallow [*Malva moschata*]. (Family *Malvaceæ*.)

○ The three very small green leaves which are immediately below the calyx of the flower are oval; plant without the smell of musk when dried (Fig. MA). → Alcea Mallow [*Malva Alcea*].—Represented in colour: 5, Plate 10. (Family *Malvaceæ*.)

17

— Each flower has its petals separated from one another down to the base; that is to say, one of the petals (or parts of the flower coloured pink, red, or brown) can be removed whole down to its base without tearing the others. These petals, collectively, form the corolla (or coloured part) which surrounds the little threads and other organs situated in the centre of the flower; when the flower fades each petal (or coloured piece) falls or dries up separately. In some cases (Fig. Œ for example) it is necessary to tear the tube which encloses the petals at their base in order to see that the petals are separate from one another to the base (Fig. PŒ) [1] 61

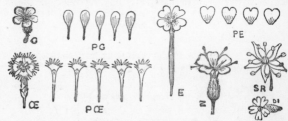

60 (following on 7).

Figs. G and Œ represent flowers with separate petals, the petals being shown detached in Figs. PG and PŒ; Fig. E represents a flower with separate petals, the detached petals being shown in PE; and Figs. N, SR, DI present various examples of flowers with separate petals.—In SR the petals are visibly separate to their base; in N and DI it is necessary to tear the green tube which encloses them in order to see that the petals are in reality separate from one another down to their bases.

— Each flower has its petals united to one another, at least at the base; that is to say, in trying to detach one of the parts of the flower which are coloured pink, red, or brown, one has to tear the corolla at least at its base; when the flower fades the corolla falls off or withers all in one piece 77

Fig. MC shows the corolla of a flower in which the petals are very slightly united; Fig. P represents the corolla of a flower the petals of which are united for a considerable distance, so that they are only distinct at the top and form a tube at the base of the corolla; the other figures give various examples of flowers with united petals.

N.B.—In some cases there may be a doubt as to whether a flower has its petals separated to the base or whether its petals are united at the base; such a difficulty will present itself when the petals are very slightly united, so that one can be removed without tearing the others. The name of the plant can be obtained which-ever question be chosen.

---

[1] In most flowers there is, outside the corolla, another covering to the flower, which is generally green and is called the *calyx*, and which encloses the base of the corolla. In some other cases it is difficult to distinguish the calyx and

✱ Flowers almost stalkless, in a long erect cluster (Fig. LS) ; the green part that encloses the base of the petals (calyx)

61
(following on 60).

is in the form of a tube with **8 or 12 teeth** at the top in two rows (Fig. S represents the calyx, 6 teeth of which are seen). → **Willow-leaved Lythrum** (Purple Loosestrife) [*Lythrum Salicaria*]—medicinal.—Represented in colour : 4, Plate 21. (Family *Lythraceæ*.)

✱ Plant not having all these characteristics together... **62**

62
(following on 61).

= Flowers having **2 petals,** each divided into two, but not down to their base, and 2 other parts red or greenish ; flowers in a cluster (Fig. C) ; leaves with a long stalk (Fig. CL). → **Mud-loving Circæa** (Enchanter's-Nightshade) [*Circæa lutetiana*]. (Family *Onagraceæ*.)

= Flowers having 4 or 8 petals, or pink or reddish parts **63**

= Flowers having 5 pink, red, or purple petals **64**

63
(following on 62).

⊖ Leaves with piercing hairs which sting the fingers.. **723**

⊖ Leaves not prickly, very small, narrow, crowded in 4 rows (Fig. C). → **Common Ling** (Heather) [*Calluna vulgaris*]. ❀ —Represented in colour : 2, Plate 36. (Family *Ericaceæ*.)

⊖ Leaves not prickly, **flat, not very crowded;** each flower has 4 pink spreading petals (Fig. H). → **Willow-herb** [*Epilobium*].—Refer back to No. **15**

64
(following on 62).

✕ Each petal divided into 4 narrow parts (Fig. FC) ; leaves without hairs on their surfaces. → **Cuckoo - flower Lychnis** (Ragged Robin) [*Lychnis Flos-cuculi*].—Represented in colour : 1, Plate 9. (Family *Caryophyllaceæ*.)

✕ Each petal not divided into 4 narrow parts (when the petals are much divided, it is into more than 4 parts) **65**

the corolla, they being more or less confounded together in a single floral envelope or covering. Lastly, some other flowers have actually only a single floral envelope which is coloured pink, reddish, or brown, like a corolla. We shall here use the names petals and corolla for those coloured parts, pink, red, or brown, which immediately surround the little threads or other organs that occupy the centre of the flower.

65
(following on 64).

☐ **Flower** with petals of a bluish rose colour, overtopped by the 5 green narrow parts from beneath (Fig. N); stems and leaves covered with tolerably long hairs. → **Corn-cockle Lychnis** [*Lychnis Githago*]—seeds dangerous. —Represented in colour: 4, Plate 8. (Family *Caryophyllaceæ.*)

☐ **Flower with petals of a deep rose colour, not overtopped by the reddish calyx;** stems and leaves covered with short hairs. → **Diœcious Lychnis** (Red Campion) [*Lychnis dioica*]. (Family *Caryophyllaceæ.*)

☐ Plant **not** having all these characteristics together...   66

66
(following on 65).

✱✱ **Leaves more or less notched at the edges** (example: Fig. GR) and with the veins arranged like a fan. → **Crane's-bill** [*Geranium*].[1]—For the chief kinds of Crane's-bills, go on to No.   94

✱✱ Leaves **not** notched or toothed   67

67
(following on 66).

☉ Each flower is **more than 1 inch across** when expanded   68

☉ Each flower is **less than** 1 inch across when expanded   69

68
(following on 67).

◝ The broadest leaves oval, less than 4 times as long as they are broad, with three well-marked veins from one end of the leaf to the other (Fig. SA); petals without teeth and not fringed at their edges (Fig. S). → **Officinal Soapwort** [*Saponaria officinalis*]—medicinal.—Represented in colour: 1, Plate 8. (Family *Caryophyllaceæ.*)

◝ The broadest leaves **elongated, more than 4 times as long as they are broad** (Fig. SE); petals toothed or fringed at their edges (Figs. Œ, CS). → **Pink** [*Dianthus*]—ornamental.[2] For the chief kinds of Pink go on to No.   70

---

[1] This refers to the wild Crane's-bills and not to the plants often grown in garden borders, which are often wrongly named Geraniums. These latter are in reality Pelargoniums, natives of the Cape of Good Hope. For fuller details as to the various species of Geranium reference must be made to more comprehensive Floras.

[2] For further details as to the various species of Pinks [*Dianthus*] reference must be made to more comprehensive Floras.

69
(following on 67).

❋ **Several small scales** or little leaves with tapering or abruptly pointed tips, situated immediately below each flower (see Figs. CM, A, P, OP, at Nos. 70 and 71). → Pink [*Dianthus*].—For the chief kinds of Pinks go on to No. **70**

❋ **No small scales** situated immediately below each flower **72**

70
(following on 69).

⊕ Flowers (Fig. CM) **purple** or a rather **dark rose colour**; leaves opposite and joined together at their bases by a tube which is about 4 times as long as it is broad. → The **Carthusians' Pink** [*Dianthus carthusianorum*].—Represented in colour: 2, Plate 8. (Family *Caryophyllaceæ*.)

⊕ Plant **not** having all these characteristics together **71**

71
(following on 70).

✠ Stems **hairy**; all the scales or small leaves which are underneath each flower ending in a **long point** (Fig. A). → **Deptford Pink** [*Dianthus Armeria*]. (Family *Caryophyllaceæ*.)

✠ Stems **not hairy**; the scales underneath each flower are oval (Figs. P and OP), the outer scales ending in a **very short** point. → **Proliferous Pink** [*Dianthus prolifer*]. (Family *Caryophyllaceæ*.)

72
(following on 69).

§ Petals rose coloured, red, or rosy pink and **longer than** the green calyx around them **73**

§ Petals rosy pink, **not** spreading much beyond the green calyx which surrounds them, and which is covered on the outside with numerous little hairs (Fig. RU represents a half-open flower, not a bud). It has some very small membranous scales at the base of the leaves. → **Red Sandwort-Spurrey** [*Spergularia rubra*]. (Family *Caryophyllaceæ*.)

73
(following on 72).

+ Flowers **scarlet, star shaped** (the petals are really slightly joined together at their base: Fig. MC represents the corolla detached); stems, for the most part, spread out over the soil; sometimes slightly erect; leaves oval (Fig. A). → **Field Pimpernel** (Scarlet Pimpernel, Poor Man's Weather-glass) [*Anagallis arvensis*]. —Represented in colour: 6, Plate 36.[1] (Family *Primulaceæ*.)

+ Flowers **pink, funnel shaped**; leaves rounded: plant growing in boggy ground (Fig. T). → **Bog Pimpernel** [*Anagallis tenella*]. (Family *Primulaceæ*.)

+ Plant **not** having all these characteristics together .. **74**

---

[1] The scarlet Field Pimpernel must not be confounded with the Chickweed-Starwort [*Stellaria media*]. This latter species is represented in colour: 4, Plate 9. (Family *Caryophyllaceæ*.)

74 (following on 73).

—• Petals pinkish white, notched at the edge (Fig. H): flowers all springing from the same point (Fig. HU). → **Umbelliferous Jagged-Chickweed** [*Holosteum umbellatum*]. (Family *Caryophyllaceæ*.)

—• **Plant not having all these characteristics together** 75

75 (following on 74).

△ Stems **very viscid** in the upper part; sticking to the finger; flowers more or less drooping (Fig. N). → **Nodding Silene** (Nottingham Catchfly) [*Silene nutans*]. (Family *Caryophyllaceæ*.)

△ Stems **not** viscid 76

76 (following on 75).

✠ Petals surrounded by a calyx which swells out at the

base and narrows in again towards the top (Figs. CN, CO). → **Conical Silene** [*Silene conica*].[1] (Family *Caryophyllaceæ*.)

✠ Petals surrounded by a calyx shrinking in at the base

(Fig. G, GY). → **Wall Gypsophila** [*Gypsophila muralis*]. 🌺 (Family *Caryophyllaceæ*.)

77 (following on 60).

○ Leaves **very small, narrow** and arranged in **4 rows** (Fig. C); stems **hard and woody**, except in the young twigs. → **Common Ling** (Heather) [*Calluna vulgaris*]. 🌺 —Represented in colour: 2, Plate 36. (Family *Ericaceæ*.)

○ Leaves **broad, with long stalks**; flowers having two parts much hollowed out, or indented, and two others sharply pointed, greenish or reddish 62

○ Plants without the above characteristics 78

---

[1] For further details as to the various species of Silene reference must be made to more comprehensive Floras.

78
(following on 77).

⊙ Petals entirely separated from each other down to the base. (Tear the calyx, which forms a tube or a sort of pitcher below the visible part of the petals so as to see the narrow part of the latter distinct one from the other down to their base.)—Refer back to....... 64

Figs. CS, LD, GI, S, D represent examples of flowers having petals separated entirely from one another down to their bases, which are concealed by the tube of the calyx.

Figs. SN, FC, V represent isolated petals of some of these flowers; petals which are detached down to their base.

⊙ Petals entirely joined together, at least at their base 79

(See further on Figs. MC, AC, VT, L, E, CA, M, TE, S from Nos. 80 to 87.)

79
(following on 78).

✳ Leaves giving out a **very fragrant** perfume when rubbed between the fingers 84

✳ Leaves **without any noticeable scent** when rubbed... 80

80
(following on 79).

= Flowers **scarlet**, having petals separated almost down to the base (Fig. MC); stems more or less spread out over the earth; leaves oval, not notched (Fig. A). → **Field Pimpernel** [*Anagallis arvensis*].—Represented in colour: 6, Plate 36. (See note indicated under No. 73.) (Family *Primulaceæ*.)

= Flowers rose coloured, purplish pink, or pinkish white; stems upright 81

81
(following on 80).

⊖ Leaves which towards the middle of the stem are attached to it with more than two at the same level. Flowers funnel shaped. → **Quinsy-wort** Asperula [*Asperula cynanchica*]—medicinal. (Family *Rubiaceæ*.)

⊖ Leaves all in opposite pairs 82

82
(following on
81).

× Stems prostrate on the ground with the exception of the flowering branches (Fig. O); flowers in elongated clusters. Each flower has 4 lobes of which one is larger than the three others (Fig. VT). → **Officinal Speedwell** [*Veronica officinalis*].—Represented in colour (with blue flowers): 3, Plate 42. (Family *Scrophulariaceæ*.)

× Stems upright; flowers not in elongated clusters .. **83**

83
(following on
82).

☐ Flowers white with red spots; leaves with very sharp notches, or much cut up (Fig. LY); flower slightly

irregular (Fig. L). → **Common Gipsy - wort** [*Lycopus europæus*]. 🌸 (Family *Labiatæ*.)

☐ Flowers pink; each flower more than 3 millimetres in width, and shaped like a long tube (Figs. E, EC). → **Common Centaury** [*Erythræa Centaurium*]—medicinal.[1]—Represented in colour: 1, Plate 38. (Family *Gentianaceæ*.)

☐ Flowers pinkish white; each flower less than 3 millimetres in width, arranged in groups at the tops of the branches (Fig. OL); flowers shaped like a tube rather wide at the mouth, and having 5 lobes not quite uniform (Fig. CA; examine it through a magnifying glass). → **Cooking Valerianella** (Common Corn Salad, Lamb's Lettuce) [*Valerianella olitoria*]—food plant.[2]—Represented in colour: 4, Plate 27. (Family *Valerianaceæ*.)

---

[1] For further details as to the various species of Centaury [*Erythræa*] reference must be made to more comprehensive Floras.
[2] For the various species of Valerianella reference must be made to more comprehensive Floras.

84
(following on 79).

** Leaves not notched, or only slightly so (Figs. OR, O); flowers surrounded by numerous small scales of purplish red colour; flowers slightly irregular, almost two lipped, that is to say, having two differently shaped parts one above the other. → **Common Marjoram** [*Origanum vulgare*]—medicinal. ✿ —Represented in colour: 3, Plate 43. (Family *Labiatæ*.)

** Leaves sharply notched; no numerous little purplish red scales surrounding the flowers; flowers almost irregular (Fig. M). → **Mint** [*Mentha*].—For the principal species of Mints see on to No. 169

85
(following on 7).

⊙ Flowers egg shaped (Figs. TE, EC); stems, except in the young twigs, hard and woody. → **Hoary Heath** (Fine-leafed Heath) [*Erica cinerea*]. ✿ —Represented in colour: 1, Plate 36. (Family *Ericaceæ*.) [1]

⊙ Flowers not egg shaped 86

86
(following on 85).

❧ Leaves arranged in threes at the same level on the stem; others in couples; others only attached separately

(Fig. LS); flowers of a deep rose purple standing erect in tall clusters. The green part which surrounds the petals at their base (calyx) is shaped like a tube, having 8 or 12 toothed notches arranged in two rows (the 6 teeth of the outer row may be seen in Fig. S, enlarged). → **Willow-leaved Lythrum** (Purple Loosestrife) [*Lythrum Salicaria*]—medicinal.—Represented in colour: 4, Plate 21. (Family *Lythraceæ*.)

❧ Leaves arranged in 4's, 5's, or 6's at the same level on the stem 87

87
(following on 86).

• Groups of flowers encircled at the base by a collarette of little leaves all joined together (Fig. SA); flowers lavender or white, having a narrow tube (Fig. S). → **Field Sherardia** (Field Madder) [*Sherardia arvensis*]. (Family *Rubiaceæ*.)

• Groups of flowers not thus encircled; the flower shaped like a funnel (Fig. AC). → **Quinsy-wort Asperula** [*Asperula cynanchica*]—medicinal. (Family *Rubiaceæ*.)

---

[1] For the various species of Heath [*Erica*] reference should be made to more comprehensive Floras.

⊕ **Opposite leaves** (those at the top of stems or branches
sometimes excepted), that is to say, leaves arranged in
pairs at the same height on the stems and facing one
another 89

The above figures represent examples of opposite leaves.

Note.—There will often be found developed in the axil of opposite
leaves small leafy branches, which might be supposed to be leaves
grouped in large numbers at the same level on the branch, and not
in opposite pairs only. On looking carefully, however, into such
groups of leaves, the two opposite ones are easily distinguishable.

⊕ **Whorled leaves**, at least towards the middle of the stem:
that is to say, 3, 4, 5 or even more leaves attached to the
stem at the same level, and arranged regularly round
it 104

The above figures represent examples of whorled leaves.

⊕ **Alternate leaves**, that is to say, leaves attached one by
one to the stem at different levels 107

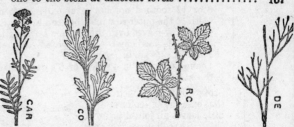

The above figures represent examples of alternate leaves.

⊕ **Leaves all at the base** of the plant 107

Fig. O represents an example of a plant
having all its leaves at the base.

Note.—If a plant has both alternate and opposite leaves (besides
those at the tips of the stems or branches), or, again, if the plant
have alternate or whorled leaves, either the one or the other question may be chosen. In both such cases the name of the plant will
be arrived at.

88
(follow-
ing on
6).

✠ Flowers bright red, with 4 petals (Fig. P) crumpled in the bud inside two green parts which fall off as the flower opens (Fig. PR). → **Common Poppy** (Corn Poppy, Corn Rose) [*Papaver Rhœas*]—medicinal ; harmful to cattle.—Represented in colour : 1, Plate 5. (Family *Papaveraceœ*.)

89
(following on 88).

✠ Flowers reddish forming 5 or 6 little tubes surrounded by a collarette made up of small scales crowded together (Fig. EC). (In reality, this is a composite flower made up of 5 or 6 tubular florets.) Flowers grouped together at the top of the stem (Fig. EV). → **Hemp Eupatorium** (Hemp Agrimony) [*Eupatorium cannabinum*]—medicinal. ✿ —Represented in colour : 1, Plate 31. (Family *Compositœ*.)

✠ Flowers pink, purple, rosy white, or white, but reddish outside, and not having the above characters 90

90
(following on 89).

§ **Flowers with 5 petals or with 5 lobes** 91

§ **Flowers with 4 or 8 pink or purple parts**; stems with the appearance and hardness of wood, except in their younger branches (the little branches with narrow leaves may be mistaken for compound leaves) (Fig. C). → **Common Ling** (Heather) [*Calluna vulgaris*]. ✿ —Represented in colour : 2, Plate 36. (Family *Ericaceœ*.)

91
(following on 90).

+ **Flowers white but reddish outside**, crowded together in a compact branched cluster (Fig. Y) ; leaves without hairs, deeply divided into from 7 to 11 segments. → **Dwarf Elder** (Dane-wort) [*Sambucus Ebulus*]—medicinal. ✿ —Represented in colour : 5, Plate 26. (Family *Caprifoliaceœ*.)

+ **Flowers pink or pinkish** 92

92
(following on 91).

—• **Each flower with petals separate from one another down to their bases**; that is to say, that one of the pink parts of the flower can be removed without tearing the others. (It may be necessary to tear the green or greenish part which encloses the base of the petals in order to see that they are completely separated down to the base.) Examples : Fig. G, the detached petals of which are shown in PG ; Fig. ER represents another flower with separate petals............. 93

—• **Each flower with petals united to one another so as to form a tube ending above in 5 lobes** (Figs. VO, V) 102

△ Leaves with from 7 to 13 segments arranged in **2 rows** (Fig. EC); flowers with 5 petals rather far apart (Fig. ER). → **Hemlock Stork's-bill** [*Erodium cicutarium*]. — medicinal. — Represented in colour: 2, Plate 11. (Family *Geraniaceæ*.)

93 (*following on 92*).

△ Leaves with their segments and veins arranged more or less like a fan (examples : Figs. RT, MA, GR). → **Crane's-bills** [*Geranium*].[1]—For the chief kinds of Crane's-bill go on to No. 94
—Herb-Robert **Crane's-bill** [*Geranium Robertianum*] is represented in colour : 1, Plate 11. (Family *Geraniaceæ*.)

94 (*following on 93*).

⊬ Petals **indented** at their tips (Figs. PY and M) 95

⊬ Petals **not** indented at their tips (Figs. R and L).. 101

95 (*following on 94*).

○ Petals **not projecting** beyond, or hardly projecting beyond, the five small green leaves of the calyx which surrounds them 96

○ Petals **distinctly projecting** beyond the five small green leaves of the calyx which surrounds them.......... 98

96 (*following on 95*).

✻ Leaves **without narrow divisions** (Fig. GR ; flower, Fig. P). → **Small-flowered Crane's-bill** [*Geranium pusillum*]. (Family *Geraniaceæ*.)

✻ Leaves **with narrow divisions** (Figs. DS and CL, below, under No. 97) 97

97 (*following on 96*).

= Flowers on stalks, the total length of which is **less** than that of the leaf in the axil of which they spring (Fig. DS). → **Jagged-leaved Crane's-bill** [*Geranium dissectum*]. (Family *Geraniaceæ*.)

= Flowers on stalks the total length of which is **more** than that of the leaf in the axil of which they spring (Fig. CL). → **Long-stalked Crane's-bill** [*Geranium columbinum*]. (Family *Geraniaceæ*.)

---

[1] The wild Crane's-bills here described must not be confounded with the garden plants generally, but wrongly, known as Geraniums. These latter are in reality Pelargoniums, natives of the Cape of Good Hope. For further details refer to more comprehensive Floras.

98
(following on 95).

⊖ Flowers 1 inch across, or even more; petals with wide indented outer edges (Fig. S); leaves much cut up (Fig. SAN). → **Bloody Crane's-bill** [*Geranium sanguineum*]. (Family *Geraniaceæ*.)

⊖ Flowers less than ½ inch wide **99**

99
(following on 98).

× Petals about 3 times as long as the green parts (calyx) which surround them (Fig. PY). → **Mountain Crane's-bill** [*Geranium pyrenaicum*]. 🌸 (Family *Geraniaceæ*.)

× Petals twice, or less than twice, as long as the 5 green parts (calyx) which surround them **100**

100
(following on 99).

☐ Petals very distinctly projecting beyond the 5 green parts (calyx) which surround them (Fig. M); leaves having, when bruised, a slight smell of Indian ink. → **Dove's-foot Crane's-bill** [*Geranium molle*]. (Family *Geraniaceæ*.)

☐ Petals projecting but little beyond the 5 green parts (calyx) which surround them (Fig. P); leaves without the smell of Indian ink. → **Small-flowered Crane's-bill** [*Geranium pusillum*]. (Family *Geraniaceæ*.)

101
(following on 94).

✱✱ Leaves cut at the most to half their width (Fig. GR). → **Round-leaved Crane's-bill** [*Geranium rotundifolium*]. (Family *Geraniaceæ*.)

✱✱ Leaves much divided (Fig. RT); flowers with elongated petals (Fig. GR). → **Herb - Robert Crane's - bill** [*Geranium Robertianum*]—medicinal.—Represented in colour: 1, Plate 11. (Family *Geraniaceæ*.)

102
(following on 92).

☉ Flowers arranged in long slender spikes; leaves more or less cut (Figs. VE and VER); flower with the tube of the calyx enclosing much of the length of the tube of the corolla (Fig. V). → **Officinal Vervain** (Common Vervain) [*Verbena officinalis*] — medicinal. 🌸 —Represented in colour: 5, Plate 45. (Family *Verbenaceæ*.)

☉ Flowers not arranged in long slender spikes; leaves completely cut into 7 to 21 divisions (see, at the top of the next page, Figs. O and D, under No. 103)... **103**

103 (following on 102).

⌇ Leaves on the middle part of the stem with 13 to 21 divisions (Fig. O); plant generally over 45 centimetres (1½ feet) high. → **Officinal Valerian** [*Valeriana officinalis*]—medicinal.—Represented in colour: 5 and 5 *bis*, Plate 27. (Family *Valerianaceæ*.)

⌇ Leaves on the middle part of the stem with 7 to 11 divisions (Fig. D); plant generally less than 45 centimetres (1½ feet) tall. → **Diœcious Valerian** (Marsh Valerian) [*Valeriana dioica*] —medicinal. (Family *Valerianaceæ*.)

104 (following on 88).

✳ Flowers **egg shaped** (Figs. EC and TE); stems with the appearance and hardness of wood, except the young shoots. (In reality the leaves are simple, but a young leafy branch is often mistaken for a compound leaf.) → **Hoary Heath** (Fine-leaved Heath) [*Erica cinerea*]. ❀—Represented in colour: 1, Plate 36. (Family *Ericaceæ*.)

✳ Flowers **not** egg shaped 105

105 (following on 104).

⊕ Flowers **grouped together at the top of the stem**; plant growing in the water; leaves with narrow segments arranged along their two sides like the barbs of a feather (Fig. H); some of the leaves are often whorled (example: Fig. HT). → **Marsh Hottonia** (Water Violet) [*Hottonia palustris*]. (Family *Primulaceæ*.)

⊕ **A single flower** at the top of the stem............. 106

106 (following on 105).

✠ Flowers **white or pinkish white**, less than 3 centimetres (1½ inches) long; 3 distinct leaves situated below the flower at one level (Fig. NV). → **Wood Anemone** (Wind-flower) [*Anemone nemorosa*] — poisonous. — Represented in colour: 4 Plate 1. (Family *Ranunculaceæ*.)

✠ Flower **reddish or deep pink or violet**, more than 3 centimetres long; the collarette below the flower is made up of leaves with narrow lobes (Fig. PL); the other leaves are at the base of the plant (Fig. PLS). → **Pasch Anemone** (Pasque-flower) [*Anemone Pulsatilla*] — poisonous; medicinal.—Represented in colour: 5 and 5 *bis*, Plate 1 (Family *Ranunculaceæ*.)

107
(following on 88).

§ Flowers in a compound umbel; that is to say, that their stalks all start from the same point like the rods supporting an umbrella; each principal stalk, spoke, or ray having at its top the rays of another umbel which each end in a flower (Figs. I, DC, and F show compound umbels: in I, O is the main umbel; *i, o,* and *f* are lesser or secondary umbels) 108

§ Flowers not in a compound umbel 112

108
(following on 107).

+ Flowers in an irregular umbel with 3, 4, or 5 principal rays (Fig. S); leaves with veins arranged like a fan (Fig. SE). → Wood Sanicle [*Sanicula europœa*] —medicinal. (Family *Umbelliferœ.*)

+ Flowers in a regular umbel with many principal rays; leaves much divided; veins not arranged in a fan. 109

109
(following on 108).

—• The small leaves which are immediately at the base of the principal rays are each deeply divided into narrow lobes (Figs. CT, DC); when the flowers are over, the rays of the umbel contract bending inwards towards one another. → Wild Carrot [*Daucus Carota*]—food-plant.—Represented in colour: 5, Plate 23. (Family *Umbelliferœ.*)

—• The small leaves at the base of the principal rays are not divided (Fig. O) 110

—• There are no small leaves at the base of the principal rays 110

110
(following on 109).

△ There are no small leaves immediately at the base of the secondary rays, that is to say, at the base of the small rays which each bear a flower (at *o* in Fig. A, where *s* is a secondary ray; *p,* a principal ray, the others having been cut away); leaves with leaflets in two rows (Figs. PM, PS). → Common Burnet-Saxifrage [*Pimpinella Saxifraga*]. (Family *Umbelliferœ.*)

△ There are small leaves at the base of the secondary rays (at *f,* Fig. B; *s,* a secondary ray; *p,* a principal ray, the others having been cut away); leaves divided into numerous narrow segments 111

111
(following on 110).

☩ Stems less than 80 centimetres (32 inches) high, as a rule; leaves with narrow erect lobes (Fig. SES). → **Mountain Seseli** [*Seseli montanum*]. (Family *Umbelliferæ*.)

☩ Stems more than 80 centimetres (32 inches) high, as a rule: leaves with narrow, spreading lobes (Fig. PR). → **Officinal Peucedanum** (Sulphurwort, Sea Hog's Fennel) [*Peucedanum officinale*]. (Family *Umbelliferæ*.)

112
(following on 107).

⊙ Leaves **all at the base of the plant** with the exception of a collarette of leaves divided into narrow lobes below the flower (Fig. PLS); **a solitary flower** deep violet or rose colour, more than 3 centimetres (1½ inches) across. → **Pasch Anemone** (Pasque-flower) [*Anemone Pulsatilla*]—poisonous: medicinal.—Represented in colour: 5 and 5 *bis*, Plate 1. (Family *Ranunculaceæ*.)

⊙ Leaves **arranged along the stem**, with numerous narrow thong-like segments (Fig. A) each less than 3 millimetres wide; flowers scarlet. → **Annual Pheasants-eye** [*Adonis annua*].—Represented in colour: 4. Plate 2. (Family *Ranunculaceæ*.)

⊙ Plant **not having the characteristics** of either of these two preceding plants 113

113
(following on 112).

♡ Each flower with **4 or 8 petals** (that is to say, 4 or 8 pink, red, or reddish parts) 114

♡ Each flower with **5 or 6 petals** (that is to say, 5 or 6 parts, pink, reddish, reddish green, or green edged with purple) 118

♡ Each flower having apparently **numerous petals or numerous tubes** coloured pink or purple. (In reality the flower is composite, being made up of numerous small flowers or florets without stalks, and either in the form of a tube or of a little tongue-like strap, the whole collection surrounded by a collarette of small leaves or scales.) Go on to No. 771

114
(following on 113).

✳ The collection of flowers **forms a reddish-green ball** (Fig. PS); leaves divided into 11- to 13-toothed leaflets. → **Bloody Burnet** (Salad Burnet) [*Poterium Sanguisorba*]—a salad plant.—Represented in colour: 6, Plate 19. (Family *Rosaceæ*.)

✳ Flowers **not** collected into balls 115

⊕ Petals **crumpled within the flower bud** (Fig. PR) when they are enclosed by two green parts which fall off as the flower opens PR. **116**

115 *(following on 114).*

⊕ Petals **not** crumpled in the bud, at which stage they are not enclosed by two green parts which fall off as the flower opens **117**

✠ Leaves **with hairs** and not surrounding the stem by a broad base (Fig. CO). → **Common Poppy** (Corn Poppy, Corn Rose) [*Papaver Rhœas*] — medicinal; harmful in crops.—Represented in colour: 1, Plate 5.[1] (Family *Papaveraceæ*.)

116 *(following on 115).*

✠ Leaves **without hairs**, embracing the stem with their broad bases (Fig. PV). → **Opium Poppy** (Garden Poppy) [*Papaver somniferum*] — poisonous: medicinal.—A variety of this plant is grown for industrial purposes.— Represented in colour: 2, Plate 5. (Family *Papaveraceæ*.)

§ Leaves **narrow, very small** (Fig. C), and arranged in 4 rows. (The small leafy branches have been mistaken for compound leaves.) → **Common Ling** (Heather) [*Calluna vulgaris*]. ❀ —Represented in colour: 2, Plate 36. (Family *Ericaceæ*.)

117 *(following on 115).*

§ Leaves **divided into lobes or leaflets** (Figs. P and CAR); stems **without hairs.** → Meadow Cardamine (Lady's

Smock, Cuckoo-flower) [*Cardamine pratensis*]—edible. ❀ —Represented in colour: 2, Plate 6. (Family *Cruciferæ*.)

§ Leaves **irregularly divided**; stems with hairs........ **292**

+ Each flower **with 5 green parts** edged with brownish purple; leaves with distinct long narrow lobes (Fig. HF). → **Stinking Hellebore** (Setterwort) [*Helleborus fœtidus*]—poisonous: medicinal. ❀ —Represented in colour: 2, Plate 3. (Family *Ranunculaceæ*.)

118 *(following on 113).*

+ Each flower **pink, pinkish, or purple**............. **119**

---

[1] For the various species of Poppy reference should be made to more comprehensive Floras.

119
(following on 118).

—• There are 3 small green leaves immediately below the green part (calyx) which surrounds the pink petals (examples: MA, MM, which show the calyx without the petals); petals united to one another at the base (Fig. M). → **Mallow** [*Malva*].—For the chief kinds of Mallow refer back to No. 57

—• There are not 3 small green leaves immediately below the green calyx 120

120
(following on 119).

△ Leaves with rough hairs and with leaflets in two rows, with some smaller lobes intercalated. Corolla covered with small hairs: petals united to one another; the corolla can be removed in one piece (Fig. BO, detached corolla, seen from below). → **Tuberous Nightshade** (Potato) [*Solanum tuberosum*] —food plant; medicinal.—Represented in colour: 4, Plate 40. (Family *Solanaceæ*.)

△ Plant not having all these characteristics together 121

121
(following on 120).

✠ Each leaf with 3 leaflets not toothed but notched at the top (Fig. OA); flowers with white petals, veined with purple, and yellow at the base; leaves all at the base of the plant. → **Sorrel Oxalis** (Wood Sorrel, Alleluia) [*Oxalis Acetosella*]—medicinal. (Family *Oxalidaceæ*.)

✠ Each leaf with 3- or 5-toothed leaflets, pointed at the top (Figs. RF and RC); a shrub with sharp prickles. → **Shrubby Bramble** (Blackberry) [*Rubus fruticosus*]—food plant; medicinal.—Represented in colour: 5, Plate 19. (Family *Rosaceæ*.)

✠ Plant not having these characteristics.............. 122

122
(following on 121)

⊙ Flowers pink or red; leaves either with their veins arranged like a fan, or with 7 to 13 leaflets. Refer back to No. 93

⊙ Flowers white, reddish outside; leaves with 23 to 41 leaflets (Fig. P); the principal leaflets have very small ones intercalated between them. → **Drop-wort Spiræa** [*Spiræa Filipendula*]—medicinal. (Family *Rosaceæ*.)

— Leaves **compound**; that is to say, that the whole leaf is made up by the union of secondary leaves known as *leaflets*, which are often mistaken for distinct leaves. The compound leaf as a whole is attached to the stem either by its base or by a stalk bearing all the leaflets; the base of a compound leaf never springs exactly from the axil of another leaf 200

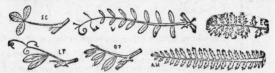

The above figures represent different types of compound leaves.

— Leaves **deeply divided** (except perhaps those leaves which are quite at the top of the stems), that is to say, that each leaf is cut in to an extent which is more than half its width 200

The above figures represent different types of deeply divided leaves.

— Leaves **simple**; that is to say, either not cut in more than half their width, or merely edged with teeth, or even without teeth on their edges 124

The above figures represent different types of simple leaves.

— Leaves **not developed** (see the figures under No. 125)   125

N.B.—If there is any doubt as between compound leaves and deeply divided leaves it is not important, since in either case the same number will be reached.

If there is any doubt as between deeply divided and simple leaves (as, for example, in the case of such a leaf as that represented in Fig. A), either question may be taken, and in either case the name of the plant will be reached. It will be the same thing if the plant has both simple leaves and compound or divided leaves (in addition to the few simple leaves which occur at the top of the flowering stems).

✳ Opposite leaves (except sometimes those at the top of a stem or branch) ; that is to say, leaves arranged in pairs, at the same height on the stem, and facing one another 165

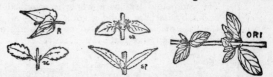

The above figures represent some examples of opposite leaves.

Note.—There will often be found developed in the axil of opposite leaves small leafy branches (see Fig. ORI above, to the right), which might easily be believed to be leaves grouped in large numbers at the same height on the stem, and not in opposite pairs only ; but by examining attentively the base of this group of leaves the two opposite leaves can easily be distinguished.

✳ Alternate leaves ; that is to say, leaves attached one by one to the stem at different levels 126

The above figures represent examples of plants having alternate leaves.

124
(*following on* 123).

✳ Grouped leaves ; that is to say, leaves attached to the stem in pairs, or greater numbers, at the same level, but arranged at this height on one side only of the stem (example : Fig. BE) 126

✳ Leaves all at the base of the plant (Fig. ME) 126

(Fig. ME represents an example of a plant having all its leaves at the base.)

Note.—If a plant possesses both alternate leaves (except those which are at the top of the stems) and opposite leaves at the same time (as, for example, Fig. PD), either question may be taken. In both cases the name of the plant will be reached.

If a plant has at the same time alternate and grouped leaves this is of no consequence, as in either case the same number (126) is indicated. It would be the same if, in the case of a plant having *nearly* all its leaves at the base, one were in any doubt between alternate leaves, and leaves *all* at the base of the plant.

— Flowers **without stalks** (Fig. O) ; the flower is more or less bell mouthed and terminates in two lips, of which the lower one has 3 lobes (Fig. OG). → Broom-rape [*Orobanche*]. Plants parasitic on green plants, injurious to crops. → Greater Broom - rape [*Orobanche major*] [1] is represented in colour ; 7, Plate 42. (Family *Orobanchaceæ*.)

125 *following on 123).*

= Flowers **having a short stalk** (Fig. NN) ; the flower is formed of 6 distinct and unequal parts placed above an oval mass. → Bird's-nest Neottia (Bird's-nest Orchid) [*Neottia Nidus-avis*] (Fig. N). — Represented in colour : 6, Plate 56. (Family *Orchidaceæ*.)

126 *(following on 124).*

⊖ Each flower is **made up of 6 distinct parts**; one of these parts has a very peculiar shape, and is at times lengthened out into that of a trumpet at its base (see figures in Nos. 127 to 137) 127

⊖ Each flower made up of **4 distinct parts** 20

⊖ Each flower **neither** made up of 4 nor 6 distinct parts 133

127 *following on 126).*

× Each of the **6 parts** of the flower is very **narrow, more than** ⅓ **of an inch in length,** and more or less **twisted or rolled** (see general view of the flowers, Fig. LO). → Goat Orchis (Lizard Orchis) [*Orchis hircina*].—Represented in colour : 6, Plate 55.

× One of the 6 parts of the flower has a peculiar shape, measures **less than** ⅓ **of an inch in length;** and is neither **twisted nor rolled** 128

128 *(following on 127).*

☐ Each flower is **extended at the base** by a **tube or horn,** more or less elongated and of the same colour as the corolla. → Orchis [*Orchis*].[2]—For the chief species of Orchis go on to No. 129

☐ Each flower **not** extended into a tube or horn 134

129 *(following on 128).*

✳ ✳ The little scale, or very small leaf (*b* Fig. PU), which is attached to the stem at the base of the flower is **3 to 8 times shorter** than what seems to be the twisted stalk of the flower (*o* Fig. PU) placed below the petals 130

✳ ✳ The little scale or small leaf attached to the base of the flower is **not 3 to 8 times shorter** than what seems to be the twisted stalk of the flower situated below the petals ; it is only a little shorter than the twisted part, or the same size, or bigger (see figures from Nos. 131 to 133) 131

---

[1] For the various species of Orobanche reference should be made to more comprehensive Floras.

[2] For further details as to the species of Orchis reference should be made to more comprehensive Floras.

130
(following on 129).

⊙ The largest petal with 3 lobes; the middle lobe is widened and slightly elongated at its base (Fig. P). → **Purple Orchis** (Old Lady Orchis) [*Orchis purpurea*].—Represented in colour; 1, Plate 55. (Family *Orchidaceæ*.)

⊙ The largest petal with 3 lobes; the middle lobe is widened and decidedly elongated at the base (Fig. MI). → **Military Orchis** [*Orchis militaris*]—medicinal. (Family *Orchidaceæ*.)

⊙ The largest petal with 3 lobes; the middle lobe is elongated and divided into two lobes which are as narrow as the two side lobes (Fig. S). → **Monkey Orchis** [*Orchis simia*].— Represented in colour: 5, Plate 55. (Family *Orchidaceæ*.)

131
(following on 129).

↷ The small scale or small leaf *b* which is attached to the stem at the base of the flower, is longer than the flower (Fig. LA). → **Broad-leaved Orchis** (Marsh Orchis) [*Orchis latifolia*] —medicinal.—Represented in colour: 3, Plate 55. (Family *Orchidaceæ*.)

↷ The small scale attached to the stem at the base of the flower is shorter than, or equal to, the flower (see Figs. PY, ML, and MR, under Nos. 132 and 133) 132

132
(following on 131).

✳ The largest petal bears two small projecting plates on its upper surface; the horn of the flower is elongated into a narrow tube which is longer than the base of the flower (the green part that is twisted on itself) (Fig. PY). → **Pyramidal Orchis** [*Orchis pyramidalis*]—medicinal.—Represented in colour: 4, Plate 55. (Family *Orchidaceæ*.)

✳ The largest petal does not bear two small plates; the horn of the flower is not longer than the base of the flower 133

133
(following on 132).

⊕ The flower has two petals spreading more or less right and left (Fig. ML); the horn which is at the base of the

flower is directed downward (Figs. ML and OT). → **Spotted Orchis** [*Orchis maculata*]—medicinal. (Family *Orchidaceæ*.)

⊕ The flower has not got two more or less spreading petals; except the largest petal, the 5 others are close together (Fig. MR); the horn which is at the base of the flower is directed to one side or upward (Figs. MR and OM). → **Helmet Orchis** [*Orchis Morio*]—medicinal. (Family *Orchidaceæ*.)

134
(follow-ing on 128).

✠ The petal with a peculiar form is **velvety above** and marked with patches which are not velvety; this petal is much more developed than the other petals (see the figures under Nos. 136 and 137). → Orchids [*Ophrys*].—For the chief kinds of Orchid go on to No. 135

✠ The petal with a peculiar form is **not** velvety; nor is this petal much more developed than the others (*l*, Fig. E). → Broad-leaved Epipactis [*Epipactis latifolia*]—medicinal.—Represented in colour: 7, Plate 56. (Family *Orchidaceæ.*)

135
(follow-ing on 134).

§ The largest petal is **scarcely at all notched** at the sides (see Figs. A and ART under No. 136) 136

§ The largest petal is **somewhat deeply notched** at the sides (see Figs. AP and MU under No. 137) 137

136
(follow-ing on 135).

+ The largest petal has a small yellowish tongue at its extremity and in the middle line, which is **recurved upwards** (*o*, Figs. A, AC). The large petal (Fig. ART) is purple with a greenish patch. → **Drone Orchid** [*Ophrys fuciflora*].—Represented in colour: 2, Plate 56. (Family *Orchidaceæ.*)

+ The largest petal has **not** got a small yellowish tongue at its extremity recurved upward in the middle line; there is sometimes at this spot merely a little tooth (*d*, Fig. AR and Fig. OA); the large petal (Fig. AF) is brown with 2 to 4 whitish or greenish lines. → **Spider Orchid** [*Ophrys sphegodes*].—Represented in colour: 1, Plate 56. (Family *Orchidaceæ.*)

137
(follow-ing on 135).

—• The large petal is **almost as broad as it is long**; this petal is recurved downwards at its extremity (Figs. AP, AF; the large petal is represented in APF). → **Bee Orchid** [*Ophrys apifera*].—Represented in colour; 3, Plate 56. (Family *Orchidaceæ.*)

—• The large petal is **a good deal longer than it is broad**; it is not recurved downwards (Figs. MU, MF; the large petal is represented by itself in Fig. MS). → **Fly Orchid** [*Ophrys muscifera*].—Represented in colour; 4, Plate 56. (Family *Orchidaceæ.*)

138
(following on 126).

△ Stems with stiff prickly hairs; flowers at first red, then blue or violet; corolla almost two lipped (Fig. EV) ; that is to say, it has an upper and a lower half. → **Common Viper's-Bugloss** [*Echium vulgare*]. 🌟 —Represented in colour : 1, Plate 39. (Family *Boraginaceæ*.)

△ Stems without stiff prickly hairs ; flowers not becoming blue or violet **139**

139
(following on 138).

✠ Each flower in the form of a mouth, having the lower lip inflated so as to touch the upper lip ; there is a hump at the base of the flower (see below, Figs. M and OR under No. 140). → **Snapdragon** [*Antirrhinum*].—For the chief kinds of Snapdragon [*Antirrhinum*] go on to No. ... **140**

✠ Each flower not in the form of a mouth and without a hump at the base **141**

140
(following on 139).

○ Flowers pink or red **with a yellow mouth**; corolla much longer than the green part (calyx) which surrounds it at the base (Fig. M). → **Greater Snapdragon** [*Antirrhinum majus*]—ornamental ; medicinal. 🌟 —Represented in colour : 1, Plate 41. (Family *Scrophulariaceæ*.)

○ Flowers pink or red **without a yellow mouth**; corolla scarcely longer, or not longer, than the calyx (Fig. OR). → **Lesser Snapdragon** [*Antirrhinum Orontium*]. (Family *Scrophulariaceæ*.)

141
(following on 139).

— Flower more than 1½ centimetres (⅗ inch) long; corolla in the form of a wide bell-mouthed tube, a little swollen beneath (Fig. PU). → **Purple Foxglove** [*Digitalis purpurea*]—poisonous ; medicinal. 🌟 —Represented in colour : 5, Plate 41. (Family *Scrophulariaceæ*.)

— Plant not having the above-mentioned characteristics together **142**

142
(following on 141).

✷ Corolla butterfly-like (see Fig. P); that is to say, made up of 5 unequal petals : one larger petal *e* above, two petals equal to one another (*a, a*) placed right and left, and two petals united to one another in the form of a boat (*cc*) placed below and to the front : flowers mingled with ordinary leaves (Fig. O). → **Creeping Rest-harrow** (Wild Liquorice) [*Ononis repens*]—medicinal ; dangerous for cattle.—Represented in colour : 1, Plate 15. (Family *Leguminosæ*.)

✷ Corolla not butterfly-like **143**

143
(following on 142).

— Each flower with 4 pink petals nearly equal (Fig. ES). Plant generally more than 45 centimetres (18 inches) high with flowers in a long erect cluster (Fig. EE). → **Narrow-leaved Willow-herb** (Rose-bay, French Willow-herb) [*Epilobium angustifolium*]. ✿ (Family *Onagraceæ*.)

= Each flower not having 4 pink petals nearly equal.. **144**

144
(following on 143).

⊖ Leaves surrounding the stem by their bases, few in number along the stem—and flower **with a horn or tube** at its base.—Go back to No. **129**

⊖ Leaves surrounding the stem by their bases, few in number along the stem—and flower **without a horn or tube** at its base.—Go back to No. **135**

⊖ Leaves not surrounding the stem by their bases, numerous along the stem **145**

145
(following on 144).

× Corolla enclosed by 2 small oval pink leaves (Figs. POL, PV). → **Common Milkwort** (Gangweed) [*Polygala vulgaris*]—medicinal.[1]—Represented in colour: 4, Plate 7. (Family *Polygalaceæ*.)

× Corolla not enclosed by 2 small oval pink leaves, but having two lips (Fig. R), that is to say, an upper part different from the lower half. → **Red Odontites** [*Odontites rubra*]. (Family *Scrophulariaceæ*.)

146
(following on 5).

☐ Leaves narrow, much elongated; lower leaves, at least, more than 10 times as long as they are broad; they are neither divided nor toothed **157**

☐ Leaves not developed **157**

☐ Plant not having the above characteristics....... **147**

147
(following on 146).

✱✱ Flowers enclosed in a large horn (Fig. AR), which is green, greenish, or of a whitish green; leaves triangular, with long stalks (Fig. M), all springing from the base of the plant. → **Spotted Arum** (Lords-and-ladies, Cuckoo-pint) [*Arum maculatum*]—medicinal.—Represented in colour: 2 and 2 *bis*, Plate 57 (Family *Araceæ*.)

✱✱ Flowers not enclosed in a large horn **148**

---

[1] For the various species of Polygala reference should be made to more comprehensive Floras.

148
(following on 147).

⊙ Leaves each divided into 11 to 19 toothed leaflets; flowers collected into rounded masses (Fig. PS). → **Bloody Burnet** (Salad Burnet) [*Poterium Sanguisorba*].—Represented in colour: 6, Plate 19. (Family *Rosaceæ*.)

⊙ Leaves not divided into 11 to 19 toothed leaflets　149

149
(following on 148).

♡ Flowers collected in a compact mass; leaves oval or elongatedly oval, all at the base of the plant.......　150

♡ Plant floating on water; flowers in spikes.........　721

♡ Plant not having these characteristics ....　151

150
(following on 149).

✳ Leaves elongated, narrowing gradually towards the base to form the stalk (Fig. PL). → **Lanceolate Plantain** [*Plantago lanceolata*]—medicinal—Represented in colour: 7, Plate 45. (Family *Plantaginaceæ*.)

✳ Leaves oval narrowing abruptly towards the base to form the stalk (Fig. MA) → **Greater Plantain** (Waybread) [*Plantago major*]—medicinal.—Represented in colours: 6, Plate 45. (Family *Plantaginaceæ*.)

151
(following on 149).

⊙ Plant from which a white milk flows when the stem is broken. A malformation or gall (Fig. G) at the top of the stem, produced by the puncture of a **Spurge** [*Euphorbia*] by an insect, has been mistaken for a flower.

⊙ No white milk when the stem is broken ....　152

152
(following on 151).

+ Leaves with two acute lobes, right and left of the base, either towards the base or about the middle.....　153

+ Leaves without these two acute lobes...........　154

153
(following on 152).

§ The two lobes of the leaf are directed more or less towards the base (Fig. A); plant over 50 centimetres (20 inches) high. → **Sorrel Dock** (Common Sorrel) [*Rumex Acetosa*][1] —edible; medicinal. ✿ —Represented in colour: 3, Plate 46. (Family *Polygonaceæ*.)

§ The two lobes of the leaf are spreading or directed upwards (Fig. AL); plant generally less than 50 centimetres (20 inches) high. → **Lesser-Sorrel Dock** (Sheep's Sorrel) [*Rumex Acetosella*]. (Family *Polygonaceæ*.)

---

[1] For further details as to the various species of Rumex reference should be made to more comprehensive Floras.

154
(following on 152).

+ Leaves at the base of the plant very large, 30 to 80 centimetres (12-32 inches) broad; the upper groups of flowers not intermingled with leaves (Fig. AQ). → **Great-Water Dock** [*Rumex Hydrolapathum*]. (Family *Polygonaceæ*.)

+ Leaves at the base much less than 30 centimetres (1 foot) broad 155

155
(following on 154).

—• Each leaf attached to the stem by a tubular structure (examples: Figs. H and L) 156

—• Each leaf not attached to the stem by a tubular structure.—Go back to No. 27

156
(following on 155).

△ Leaves crisped or waved (Fig. RCR). → **Curled Dock** [*Rumex crispus*]—medicinal. (Family *Polygonaceæ*.)

△ Leaves not crisped or waved (Fig. RCM). → **Clustered Dock** (Sharp Dock) [*Rumex conglomeratus*]. (Family *Polygonaceæ*.)

157
(following on 146).

✠ Leaves cylindric like the stem and not attached 4, 5 or more together at one level on the stem 158

✠ Leaves reduced to toothed membranous collarettes which are one above another—or leaves apparently cylindrical like the stem and attached 4, 5 or more together at the same level on the stem (see the figures under No. 1104). → **Horse-tail** [*Equisetum*].—Go on to No........ 1104

✠ Leaves neither cylindrical like the stems, nor reduced to toothed collarettes 159

158
(following on 157 or 146).

○ On a careful examination, each flower is seen to be made up of 6 parts regularly arranged (Fig. T). → **Rushes** [*Juncus*].—Go back to No.... 36

○ On a careful examination, the flowers are seen to be reduced to scales over-lapping one another (Figs. LT, LC). → **Lake Scirpus** (Common Rush, Club Rush, Pannier Rush) [*Scirpus lacustris*]—industrial.—Represented in colour: 2, Plate 58. (Family *Cyperaceæ*.)

○ On a careful examination, each flower is seen to be replaced by a small oval body (bulbil). → **Onion or Garlic** [*Allium*] with flowers transformed into bulbils (Fig. V).

159
(following on 157).

— Numerous very long hairs (Fig. A) of a brilliant white spring round the flowers which are reduced to blackish scales. → **Many - ranked Cotton - grass** [*Eriophorum polystachion*].—See coloured figure: 1, Plate 58.[1] (Family *Cyperaceæ*.)

— No numerous long hairs of a brilliant white springing round the flowers **160**

160
(following on 159).

✳ Leaves all at the base, with 3 or 5 strongly marked ribs or veins, the mid rib stronger than the others

(Figs. LA, PL); on a careful examination of the group of flowers which terminates the stem, each of them will be seen to have a brown corolla regularly divided into 4 parts. → **Lanceolate Plantain** [*Plantago lanceolata*] — medicinal.—Represented in colour: 7, Plate 45. (Family *Plantaginaceæ*.)

✳ Plant not having all these characteristics together.. **161**

161
(following on 160).

= Flowers which collectively form a long brown, velvety cylinder (Fig. A); above is another cylinder of a light brown, yellow, or yellowish colour. → **Reed-mace** (Cat's-tail, Bulrush) [*Typha*].—Go on to No. **162**

= Plant from which a white milk flows when the stem is broken. (A malformation or gall (Fig. G) at the top of the stem, produced by the puncture of a **Spurge** [*Euphorbia*] by an insect, has been mistaken for a flower.

= Plant not having these characteristics **163**

162
(following on 161).

⊖ The two cylinders of flowers are scarcely separated from one another (at *l*, Fig. L); leaves entirely flat. → **Broad-leaved Reed-mace** [*Typha latifolia*].—Represented in colour: 3, Plate 57. (Family *Typhaceæ*.)

⊖ The two cylinders of flowers are separated from one another by a tolerably long space (at I, Fig. A). → **Narrow-leaved Reed-mace** [*Typha angustifolia*]. (Family *Typhaceæ*.)

---

[1] For the various species of Cotton-sedge [*Eriophorum*] reference should be made to more comprehensive Floras.

163
(following on 161).

× On a careful examination each flower is seen to be made up of 6 parts arranged regularly (Figs. T, LZ, B).—Refer back to No. **37**

× On a careful examination the flowers are seen to be reduced to scales overlapping one another **164**

164
(following on 163).

☐ Leaves attached to the stem by a long sheath which is split lengthwise (F, *ft, g,* Fig. G) on the side opposite to the leaf; stem more or less cylindric (*t, t,* Fig. G); the leaf bears a small tongue (ligule) (*lg,* Fig. G) or a line of special hairs at the spot where it joins the stem, above the sheath of the leaf **1069**

☐ Leaves attached to the stem by a sheath which is **not split** lengthwise (F, *g,* Fig. C); stem with 3 angles (*t,* Fig. C), at least for some part of its length; the leaf does not bear either a tongue (ligule) or lines of special hairs at the spot where it joins the stem, above the sheath **1062**

165
(following on 124).

✱ ✱ Flower having apparently two lips (see figures below); the lower lip is sometimes very short (Fig. SC)... **173**

✱ ✱ Flowers with only one hanging lip, divided into 5 lobes, one larger than the rest (Fig. T); leaves rather leathery, strongly toothed (Fig. TC). → **Prostrate Germander (Wall Germander)** [*Teucrium Chamædrys*]—medicinal. ✿ —Represented in colour: 4, Plate 45. (Family *Labiatæ*.)

✱ ✱ Flowers not with two lips, nor with a single lip.. **166**

166
(following on 165).

⊙ Flower bearing at its base a long narrow acute horn (Fig. C); leaves rather thick and without hairs. → **Red Spur-valerian** [*Centranthus ruber*]—ornamental. (Family *Valerianaceæ*.)

⊙ Plant not having the above characteristics...... **167**

167
(following on 166).

♣ Leaves with a strong aromatic smell when bruised.. **168**

♤ Leaves with no special smell; stems erect; leaves with long stalks 62

♤ Leaves with no special smell; stems prostrate (Fig. O); leaves without a long stalk. → **Officinal Speedwell** [*Veronica officinalis*]—medicinal.—Represented in colour (with blue flowers): 3, Plate 42. (Family *Scrophulariaceæ*.)

168
(following on 167).

• Flowers surrounded by numerous red scales; leaves not toothed (Fig. OR, O); flowers almost two lipped. → **Common Marjoram** [*Origanum vulgare*]—medicinal. ⚘ —Represented in colour: 3, Plate 43. (Family *Labiatæ*.)

• Flowers not surrounded by numerous red scales; leaves more or less toothed; flowers almost regular. → Mints [*Mentha*].—Go on to No. **169**

169
(following on 168).

⊕ Flowers arranged in elongated masses (Fig. RON below) **170**

⊕ Flowers arranged in rounded masses (Figs. A, P, AQ, under Nos. 171 and 172) **171**

170
(following on 169).

✠ Leaves with rounded teeth; the green calyx, enclosing the corolla, has almost triangular teeth (Fig. RO). → **Round-leaved Mint** [*Mentha rotundifolia*]—medicinal. ⚘ —Represented in colour: 5, Plate 43. (Family *Labiatæ*.)

✠ Leaves with acute teeth; the calyx has 5 much elongated teeth (Fig. SI). → **Long-leaved Mint** (Horse Mint) [*Mentha longifolia*]. ⚘ —Represented in colour: 4, Plate 43. (Family *Labiatæ*.)

171
(following on 169).

§ Flowering stems with a bunch of small leaves at the top (Fig. A). → **Corn Mint** [*Mentha arvensis*]. ⚘ (Family *Labiatæ*.)

§ Flowering stems without a little bunch of leaves... **172**

172
(following on 171).

+ Leaves without stalks or almost without stalks, rounded masses of flowers mixed with leaves along the stems (Fig. P). → **Pennyroyal Mint** [*Mentha Pulegium*]—medicinal. ⚘ (Family *Labiatæ*.)

+ Leaves all with stalks more or less long; rounded masses of flowers only towards the top of the stem (Fig. AQ). → **Hairy Mint** (Capitate Mint, Water Mint) [*Mentha hirsuta*]. ⚘ (Family *Labiatæ*.)

173
(following on 165).

— • Plants **climbing** or **creeping** and of considerable length (Fig. LC) (the lower part of the stem will, on examination, be seen to have the look and hardness of wood); flowers yellowish or white streaked with pink. → **Common Honeysuckle (Woodbine)** [*Lonicera Periclymenum*]. — Represented in colour: 4, Plate 26. (Family *Caprifoliaceæ*.)

— • Plants **not** having all these characteristics **at the same** time **174**

174
(following on 173).

△ Flowers intermixed with numerous **red leaves,** each of which is divided into pointed lobes (Fig. AR); flowers with a long tube (Fig. A). → **Field Cowwheat** [*Melampyrum arvense*]—dangerous.—Represented in colour: 6, Plate 42. (Family *Scrophulariaceæ*.)

△ Flowers **not** intermixed with a number of red leaves with pointed lobes **175**

175
(following on 174).

✠ Flowers **more than** 2½ centimetres (1 inch) **in total length** (measure the flowers from base to tip); white splashed with pink or purple; leaves toothed (Fig. ME). → **Balm-leaved Melittis** (Bastard Balm) [*Mellitis Melissophyllum*] — medicinal; aromatic. — Represented in colour: 3, Plate 44. (Family *Labiatæ*.)

✠ Flowers from **7 to 22 millimetres** in total length **178**

✠ Flowers **less than 7 millimetres** in total length..... **176**

176
(following on 175).

○ Stems **prostrate** with upright branches; leaves generally less than 8 millimetres in width and not toothed (Fig. S). → **Wild Thyme** [*Thymus Serpyllum*] — medicinal. (Family *Labiatæ*.)

○ Stems **upright;** leaves usually more than 8 millimetres in width **177**

177
(following on 176)

— Flowers white dotted with red; leaves very sharply toothed (Fig. LY). → **Common Gipsy-wort** (*Lycopus europæus*]. (Family *Labiatæ*.)

— Flowers pink, leaves not toothed (Figs. O, OR). → **Common Marjoram** [*Origanum vulgare*]—medicinal. — Represented in colour: 3 Plate 43. (Family *Labiatæ*.)

178
(following on 175).

✳ The funnel-shaped part (calyx) which surrounds the base of the corolla has 5 teeth, each terminating in a sharp little spine (see below, Figs. T and LA). Inside, and at the top of the tube of the corolla, is found a ridge ending in a slight protuberance. → Hemp-nettle [*Galeopsis*].[1]—Go on to No. 179

✳ Plants not having the above characteristics together 180

179
(following on 178).

▬ Stems having **stiff prickly hairs and much swollen** at the spots whence spring the pairs of leaves ; calyx with long prickly teeth (Fig. T). → Common Hemp-nettle [*Galeopsis Tetrahit*]. ✿ (Family *Labiatæ*.)

═ Stem without prickly hairs, and slightly, or not at all, swollen at the parts from which the leaves spring (Fig. L); calyx has teeth with spinous tips only (Fig. LA). → Scented Hemp-nettle [*Galeopsis Ladanum*]. ✿ —Represented in colour : 2, Plate 44. (Family *Labiatæ*.)

180
(following on 178).

⊖ Flowers of a ruddy brown or brownish red; a little scale of the same colour as the corolla can be detected on the inside of the upper lip (*l*, Fig. SC and *e*, Fig. S ; this latter figure represents the corolla split open and unfolded). Leaves almost, or entirely, without hairs. → Figwort [*Scrophularia*].[2] For the principal kinds of Figworts go on to No. 181

⊖ Plants not having all the above characteristics together 182

181
(following on 180).

✕ Leaves pointed at the tip (Fig. N) and sharply toothed. The lower teeth of a leaf are larger than the upper ones ; stem having **4** angles, well marked, but not very sharp. → Knotted Figwort [*Scrophularia nodosa*]—medicinal. ✿ —Represented in colour : 4, Plate 41. (Family *Scrophulariaceæ*.)

✕ Leaves rounded at the tip (Fig. A) with scalloped edges. The lower scallops of the leaf are smaller than the upper ones ; stem has 4 angles very sharply edged. → Water Figwort [*Scrophularia aquatica*]. ✿ (Family *Scrophulariaceæ*.)

---

[1] For more details as to the various species of *Galeopsis* reference should be made to more comprehensive Floras.
[2] For more details as to the various species of Fig-wort [*Scrophularia*] reference should be made to more comprehensive Floras.

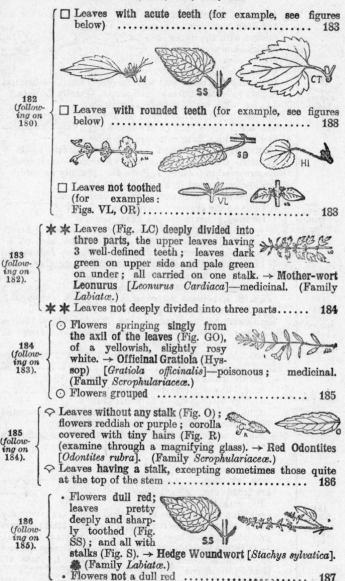

☐ Leaves **with acute teeth** (for example, see figures below) 183

182
(following on 180)

☐ Leaves **with rounded teeth** (for example, see figures below) 188

☐ Leaves **not toothed** (for examples: Figs. VL, OR) 188

183
(following on 182)

✳ ✳ Leaves (Fig. LC) deeply divided into three parts, the upper leaves having 3 well-defined teeth; leaves dark green on upper side and pale green on under; all carried on one stalk. → **Mother-wort Leonurus** [*Leonurus Cardiaca*]—medicinal. (Family *Labiatæ*.)

✳ ✳ Leaves not deeply divided into three parts...... **184**

184
(following on 183).

⊙ Flowers springing **singly from the axil of the leaves** (Fig. GO), of a yellowish, slightly rosy white. → **Officinal Gratiola** (Hyssop) [*Gratiola officinalis*]—poisonous; medicinal. (Family *Scrophulariaceæ*.)

⊙ Flowers grouped 185

185
(following on 184).

♡ Leaves without any stalk (Fig. O); flowers reddish or purple; corolla covered with tiny hairs (Fig. R) (examine through a magnifying glass). → **Red Odontites** [*Odontites rubra*]. (Family *Scrophulariaceæ*.)

♡ Leaves **having a stalk**, excepting sometimes those quite at the top of the stem **186**

186
(following on 185).

• Flowers dull red; leaves pretty deeply and sharply toothed (Fig. SS); and all with stalks (Fig. S). → **Hedge Woundwort** [*Stachys sylvatica*]. ❀ (Family *Labiatæ*.)

• Flowers **not a dull red** 187

187
(following on 186).

⊕ Leaves with rather sharp and deep teeth (Fig. CT); flowers with the upper lip straight and erect (Fig. N), either pink spotted with white or red, or white spotted with pink; plant with a disagreeable smell. → **Catmint Nepeta** [*Nepeta Cataria*]—medicinal. (Family *Labiatæ*.)

⊕ Leaves with teeth neither very acute nor deeply cut; flowers pink with only one small white spot on the middle of the lower lip; flowers in a rather loose cluster (Fig. C); plant having an aromatic smell. → **Officinal Calamint** [*Calamintha officinalis*]—medicinal.—Represented in colour: 1, Plate 43. (Family *Labiatæ*.)

188
(following on 182).

✠ Flowers grouped in 2's or 3's and all turned to the same side; stems in long trails on the ground; leaves rounded, reversedly heart shaped (Fig. GH). → **Ivy-like Nepeta** (Ground Ivy, Ale-hoof) [*Nepeta hederacea*]—medicinal. 🌸 —Represented in colour (with blue flowers): 4, Plate 44. (Family *Labiatæ*.)

✠ Plant not having all these characteristics together. **189**

189
(following on 188).

§ Upper lip of flower in profile has somewhat the form of a sickle (Figs. S, P); plant rather sticky, especially in the upper part where the flowers are. → **Meadow Sage** (Meadow Clary) [*Salvia pratensis*] — medicinal. 🌸 —Represented in colour: 7, Plate 43. (Family *Labiatæ*.)

§ Plant not having all these above-mentioned characteristics together **190**

190
(following on 189).

+ Flower stalks more than 3 millimetres long; flowers not very crowded in each group (Fig. C). → **Officinal Calamint** [*Calamintha officinalis*]—medicinal.—Represented in colour: 1, Plate 43. (Family *Labiatæ*.)

+ Flower stalks less than 2 millimetres long, or flowers without stalks; flowers very crowded in each group **191**

191
(following on 190).

—• Leaves about three times as long as they are broad (Fig. SB), with the exception of the leaves at the base which are reversedly heart shaped and are borne on a very long stalk; flowers grouped together towards the top of the stem (Fig. O). → **Officinal Woundwort** (Wood Betony) [*Stachys officinalis*]—medicinal.—Represented in colour: 1, Plate 44. (Family *Labiatæ*.)

—• Plant not having these characteristics together... **192**

192
(following on 191).

△ Plant having both pink or white flowers splashed with red or red splashed with white, and leaves rather cottony on the under surface **193**

△ Plant not having both these characteristics..... **194**

193
(following on 192).

⚔ Flowers white or pink, spotted with red ; leaves borne on a rather long stalk (Fig. CT). → **Catmint Nepeta** [*Nepeta Cataria*]—medicinal. (Family *Labiatæ*.)

⚔ Flowers pink or red, splashed with white towards the upper part of the tube of the corolla ; leaves without stalks (Fig. SP) or with short stalks ; the upper leaves surrounding the stem by their bases. → **Marsh Woundwort** [*Stachys palustris*]. ❀ (Family *Labiatæ*.)

194
(following on 192).

○ Leaves scarcely toothed or without teeth, greyish with hairs on their under surface; each group of flowers is surrounded by small acute scales more numerous than the flowers (Fig. CC). → **Foot-stool Calamint** (Wild Basil) [*Calamintha Clinopodium*]. ❀ —Represented in colour : 2, Plate 43. (Family *Labiatæ*.)

○ Leaves not greyish with hairs beneath, the lowest often distinctly toothed **195**

195
(following on 194).

— Flowers intermixed with broad, fringed, membranous, green scales, ending in an abrupt point (Fig. B), and surrounding the stem at their bases ; leaves with a stalk, except the two leaves at the base of the crowded group of flowers. → **Common Selfheal** [*Prunella vulgaris*]—medicinal. ❀ —Represented in colour : 6, Plate 43. (Family *Labiatæ*.)

— Plant not having all the above characteristics together **196**

196
(following on 195).

✻ Green funnel-shaped structure enclosing the base of the corolla (calyx) plaited lengthwise (Fig. BF), with 5 teeth at its top : each tooth is folded lengthwise. → **Black Horehound** [*Ballota nigra*]. — Represented in colour : 7, Plate 44. (Family *Labiatæ*.)

✻ Calyx not plaited, with teeth not folded lengthwise **197**

197
(following on 196).

= Corolla with two small lobes, very narrow and acute, on the two sides of the lower lip (Fig. M) ; tube of the corolla recurved towards the top. → **Spotted Dead-nettle** [*Lamium maculatum*]. (Family *Labiatæ*.)

= Plant not having these characteristics together..... **198**

198
(following on 197).

⊖ Leaves **alternate** on the upper part of the stem and on the branches; flowers in more or less elongated clusters; corolla covered externally with small hairs (Fig. R); leaves without stalks (Fig. O). → **Red Odontites** [*Odontites rubra*].[1] (Family *Scrophulariaceæ*.)

⊖ Leaves **all opposite**; flowers crowded in compact masses **199**

199
following on 198).

⊕ Upper leaves **rounded, entirely surrounding the stem** (Fig. AM); corolla with an elongated tube (Fig. LA represents the flower cut open lengthwise and enlarged). → **Amplexicaul Dead-nettle** (Hen-bit Dead-nettle) [*Lamium amplexicaule*].—Represented in colour: 5, Plate 44. (Family *Labiatæ*.)

⊕ Upper leaves **triangular-oval, not** entirely surrounding the stem (Fig. P); lower leaves with long stalks (Fig. PU). → **Red Dead-nettle** [*Lamium purpureum*]. (Family *Labiatæ*.)

200
(following on 123).

☐ Corolla **butterfly-like**, that is to say, with 5 unequal petals: an upper wider petal (*e* in the figures below), two petals, equal in size to one another, placed right and left (*a, a* in the figures below), and two lower petals united to one another (*cc*, figures below) in a boat-like form, in a few cases rolled together on themselves (Fig. PV, on the right) **212**

The above figures represent examples of butterfly-like (papilionaceous) flowers; in Fig. PS the five petals are detached, two, *cc*, being shown united to one another.

☐ Corolla **not butterfly-like**, that is to say, not presenting all the above-mentioned characteristics together **201**

The above figures represent some examples of flowers not papilionaceous.

---

[1] For the various species of *Odontites* reference should be made to more comprehensive Floras.

* * Leaves **opposite;** that is to say, leaves arranged in twos, and attached to the stem at the same level, facing one another on opposite sides of the stem **202**

The above figures represent examples of opposite leaves.

* * Leaves **alternate;** that is to say, leaves attached one by one on the stem at different levels (Fig. DE represents an example of alternate leaves) .. **206**

201
(following on 200).

⊙ Flowers **almost regular,** with 5 lobes (see below Figs. V and VO, under No. 203) **203**
⊙ Flowers **very irregular,** the corolla having apparently two lips, one upper, the other lower **204**

202
(following on 201).

⌔ Flowers arranged in long slender spikes; leaves more or less deeply cut (Figs. VE, VER); a large part of the tube of the corolla covered by the green tube which forms the calyx (Fig. V). → **Officinal Vervain** (Common Vervain) [*Verbena officinalis*] —medicinal. ※ —Represented in colour: **5, Plate 45.** (Family *Verbenaceæ.*)

⌔ Flowers arranged in **clusters that are not elongated,** and opening almost all at the same level; leaves completely cut up into 7 to 21 divisions (Fig. VAL); the tube of the corolla not covered by the calyx (Fig. VO). → **Valerian** [*Valeriana*].—For the chief kinds of Valerian refer back to No. **103**

⌔ Flowers **not very many** in each group; petals separated from one another down to their bases. — Refer to No. **211**

203
(following on 202).

• Flowers **pink or red;** lower leaves with **more than 20 divisions** (Fig. P); upper lip of the flower helmet shaped, slightly recurved (Fig. SI). → **Dwarf Red - Rattle** [*Pedicularis sylvatica*].[1] (Family *Scrophulariaceæ.*)

• Flowers **pink splashed with red,** or white splashed with red; lower leaves with 3 or 5 to 9 divisions...... **205**

204
(following on 202).

[1] For the various species of Red-Rattle [*Pedicularis*] reference should be made to more comprehensive Floras.

205
(following on 204).

⊕ **Leaves** deeply divided into 3 parts; upper leaves with 3 well-marked teeth (Fig. LC); flowers pink splashed with red. → **Motherwort Leonurus** [*Leonurus Cardiaca*]—medicinal (Family *Labiatæ.*)

⊕ Leaves more or less divided into unequal lobes (Fig. LY), upper leaves with many acute teeth; towards the base of the plant the leaves are deeply divided; flowers white spotted with red. → **Common Gipsywort** [*Lycopus europæus*]. (Family *Labiatæ.*)

206
(following on 201).

⊁ Flowers in a compound umbel, that is to say, that their stalks all start from the same point like the rods which support an umbrella; each principal ray, as these stalks are termed, bears at its summit other rays radiating in the same way and each ending in a flower (Fig. DC). **There is a collarette of small divided leaves** immediately below the umbel.................. 675

⊁ Flowers in a compound umbel, but **without the collarette of small leaves** below the umbel 687

⊁ Flowers not in a compound umbel............. 207

207
(following on 206).

§ Flowers nearly all arranged at the same level; leaves with more than 40 segments arranged in 2 rows (Fig. AM). On examining the plant carefully it will be seen that each flower is a composite flower of very small tubular flowers, surrounded by small strap-shaped flowers, and that round the whole there is a collarette of very small green scales. → **Milfoil Achillea** (Milfoil, Yarrow) [*Achillea Millefolium*]—medicinal.—Represented in colour (with white flowers): 6, Plate 31. (Family *Compositæ.*)

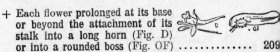

§ Plant not having all these characteristics together.. 208

208
(following on 207).

+ Each flower prolonged at its base or beyond the attachment of its stalk into a long horn (Fig. D) or into a rounded boss (Fig. OF) 209

+ Each flower not prolonged into a horn, into a tube, or into a rounded boss at its base 210

The above figures represent flowers with neither horn nor boss at their base.

209
(following on 208).

— Flowers more than a centimetre (½ inch) long, with 5 pink parts, one of which is produced into a long narrow horn (Fig. D);
leaves divided into very elongated lobes (Fig. DE). →
Consound Larkspur [*Delphinium Consolida*] — medicinal.
✱ — Represented in colour: 3, Plate 3.[1] (Family *Ranunculaceæ*.)

— Flowers less than a centimetre (½ inch) long, each produced beyond the attachment of its stalk into a short rounded boss (Fig. OF); leaves with many divisions which are not very long (Fig. FO). → Officinal
Fumitory [*Fumaria officinalis*]—medicinal.—Represented in colour: 4, Plate 5.[2] (Family *Fumariaceæ*.)

210
(following on 208).

△ Flowers with their corolla tubular below and two lipped, the upper lip helmet shaped (Fig. SI); leaves with divisions arranged in 2 rows (Fig. P). → **Dwarf Red-Rattle** [*Pedicularis sylvatica*].[3] (Family *Scrophulariaceæ*.)

△ Flowers with the corolla not tubular at the base and not with two lips of which the upper one is helmet shaped 211

211
(following on 210).

✠ Flowers red, with 4 petals, of which 2 are larger.... **116**

✠ Flowers red, with petals equal but irregularly arranged (Fig. AA); leaves with narrow divisions (Fig. A) less than 3 millimetres wide. → Annual Pheasants-eye [*Adonis annua*]. —Represented in colour (with regular flowers): 4, Plate 2. (Family *Ranunculaceæ*.)

✠ Flowers pink with 5 nearly equal petals (Fig. E); leaves with 7 to 13 toothed leaflets (Fig. EC). → Hemlock Stork's-bill [*Erodium cicutarium*].—Represented in colour: 2, Plate 11. (Family *Geraniaceæ*.)

---

[1] For the various species of Larkspur [*Delphinium*] reference should be made to more comprehensive Floras.
[2] For the various species of Fumitory [*Fumaria*] reference should be made to more comprehensive Floras.
[3] For the various species of Red-Rattle [*Pedicularis*] reference should be made to more comprehensive Floras.

○ Leaves ending in a thread more or less coiled up.. 213

The above figures represent examples of leaves ending in a coiled-up thread.

○ Leaves ending in a **short thread which is not coiled** (Fig. OT); flowers of a purplish pink, afterwards bluish. → **Tuberous Bitter-Vetch** (Wood Pea) [*Orobus tuberosus*].—Represented in colour: 4, Plate 16. (Family *Leguminosæ*.)

212 (*following on* 200).

○ Leaves **not ending in a thread** 218

The above figures represent examples of leaves not ending in a thread.

213 (*following on* 212).

— The 2 leaflets attached to the stem at the base of each leaf are **larger** than the leaflets of the leaf (Fig. P); flowers reddish. → **Field Pea** [*Pisum arvense*]—fodder plant. ❀ (Family *Leguminosæ*.)

— The 2 leaflets attached to the stem at the base of each leaf are **smaller** than the leaflets of the leaf (Fig. V), or at most are equal to them 214

214 (*following on* 213).

✱ Leaves with **less than 6 leaflets** (without counting the two small leaflets attached to the stem at the base of the leaf) 217

✱ Leaves with **6 or more leaflets**, in addition to the two small leaflets attached to the stem. → **Vetch** [*Vicia*].[1]— For the chief kinds of *Vicia*, go on to No........ 215

215 (*following on* 214).

= Flowers **in groups of two or isolated** (Fig. VS). → **Cultivated Vetch** (Common Vetch) [*Vicia sativa*] — fodder plant. ❀ —Represented in colour: 5, Plate 17. (Family *Leguminosæ*.)

= Flowers **in groups of more than two**.............. 216

---

[1] For further details as to the species of *Vicia* reference should be made to more comprehensive Floras.

216 (following on 215).

⊖ Clusters of less than 8 pinkish or bluish flowers; the stalk of the cluster is much shorter than the leaf in the axil of which it is attached (Fig. S). → **Bush Vetch** [*Vicia sepium*]. 🐝 —Represented in colour: 6, Plate 17. (Family *Leguminosæ*.)

⊖ Clusters of more than 8 violet flowers, the stalk of the cluster is as long or nearly as long as the leaf in the axil of which it is attached (Fig. CR). → **Tufted Vetch** [*Vicia Cracca*]. 🐝 —Represented in colour: 7, Plate 17. (Family *Leguminosæ*.)

217 (following on 214).

× Flowers **pink**; stems with flat flanges along their whole length and flowers in groups of more than 3; leaflets very acute (Fig. LS). → **Wood Vetchling** (Narrow-leaved Everlasting Pea) [*Lathyrus sylvestris*]—fodder plant. 🐝 —Represented in colour: 3, Plate 17. (Family *Leguminosæ*.)

× Flowers **pinkish blue**; stems with flat flanges along their whole length, flowers solitary (Fig. LH) or in groups of 2 or 3; leaflets oval, acute (Fig. LH). → **Rough-podded Vetchling** [*Lathyrus hirsutus*]. (Family *Leguminosæ*.)

× Flowers **red**; stems without the flat flanges along their whole length; **flowers in groups of more than 3**; leaflets acute (Fig. LT). → **Tuberous Vetchling** (Peas Earth-nut) [*Lathyrus tuberosus*]—edible. (Family *Leguminosæ*.)

218 (following on 212).

☐ Lower leaves having their terminal leaflet much larger than the other leaflets (Fig. AV); at the base of the

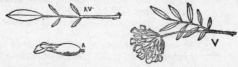

flowers there are small leaves in the form of a fan (Fig. V); the calyx, enclosing the base of the petals, is more or less inflated (Fig. A). → **Healing Anthyllis** (Kidney Vetch, Lady's Fingers) [*Anthyllis Vulneraria*] —medicinal. (Family *Leguminosæ*.)

☐ Plant not having all these characteristics together **219**

⁕ ⁕ Leaves having 3 leaflets (without counting the two small leaflets attached to the stem at the base of the leaf) 220

The above figures represent examples of leaves having 3 leaflets.

219
(following on 218).

⁕ ⁕ Leaves having the appearance of 5 leaflets; the leaflets attached to the stem resembling more or less the three leaflets belonging to the leaf (Fig. LO). → Bird's-foot Lotus (Butter-and-eggs, Shoes-and-stockings) [*Lotus corniculatus*]. ☙ —Represented in colour: 1, Plate 14. (Family *Leguminosæ*.)

⁕ ⁕ Leaves with more than 5 leaflets.............. 226

220
(following on 219).

⊙ **Climbing plants;** flowers bright scarlet, having the lower petals curled over on themselves (Fig. P); leaves having 3 pointed leaflets (Fig. H). → **Many-flowered Haricot** (Scarlet Runner) [*Phaseolus multiflorus*]— ornamental. (Family *Leguminosæ*.)

⊙ **Non-climbing plants** 221

221
(following on 220).

♥ Flowers intermixed with ordinary leaves (Fig. RE) and not united in a crowded head at the top of the branches. → Creeping **Rest-harrow** (Wild Liquorice) [*Ononis repens*]—medicinal; dangerous.—Shown in colour: 1, Plate 15. (Family *Leguminosæ*.)

♥ Flowers all united in a crowded head at the end of the branches (see figures under Nos. 222 to 225) 222

222
(following on 221).

• Stems **prostrate** and bearing roots here and there (Fig. R); flowers white; pale pink underneath. → **Creeping Trefoil** (White Clover, Dutch Clover) [*Trifolium repens*]—fodder plant. ☙ —Represented in colour: 3, Plate 14. (Family *Leguminosæ*.)

• Plant **not having these characteristics** 223

223
(follow-ing on 222).

⊕ Each of the flower heads is elongated in shape and from 4 to 6 centimetres in length ; flowers crimson or of a bright purple. → Crimson Trefoil [*Trifolium incarnatum*]—fodder plant. ❀ —Represented in colour: 5, Plate 14. (Family *Legu-minosæ*.)

⊕ Each of the flower heads is elongated or rounded, but is less than 3 centimetres in length 224

224
(follow-ing on 223).

✠ Each of the flower heads is softly hairy, and in length more than twice its width (Fig. A) ; flowers of a pinkish white. → Field Trefoil (Hare's-foot Trefoil) [*Trifolium arvense*]. (Family *Leguminosæ*.)

✠ Plants not having these characteristics together.. 225

225
(follow-ing on 224).

§ Each of the heads of flowers becomes swollen, solid, the flowers crowded together in a round head (Fig. F). → Strawberry-headed Trefoil [*Trifolium fragiferum*]. (Family *Legu-minosæ*.)

§ None of the flower heads become swollen or solid, and the flowers remain separated from each other. → Meadow Trefoil (Red Clover) [*Trifolium pratense*]—fodder plant. —Represented in colour: 4, Plate 14 (Family *Leguminosæ*.)

226
(follow-ing on 219).

—• Each flower is less than 6 millimetres in length ; flowers whitish, veined with pink—flesh colour. There is often a small leaf immediately below the groups of flowers (Fig. OP). → Common Bird's-foot [*Ornithopus perpusillus*]. ❀ (Family *Leguminosæ*.)

—• Each flower more than 6 millimetres in length.. 227

227
(follow-ing on 226).

△ Flowers arranged in clusters more or less lengthy (Fig. OS) ; stems upright. → Cultivated Sainfoin (Cock's Head) [*Onobrychis sativa*] —fodder plant. ❀ —Represented in colour: 3, Plate 16. (Family *Leguminosæ*.)

△ Flowers arranged like a crown at the top of the stalks (Fig. V) ; stems more or less prostrate or trailing.→Variegated Coronilla [*Coronilla varia*]—medicinal. ❀ —Repre-sented in colour: 1, Plate 16. (Family *Leguminosæ*.)

✠ Each flower **regular;** that is to say, that the similar parts of the flower, blue, lilac, or violet in colour, are arranged regularly round the centre of the flower, and are obviously similar to one another 229

The above figures represent some examples of regular flowers.

✠ Each flower **irregular;** that is to say, when the flowers do not answer to the description given above 297

228
(follow-
ing on
4).

✠ Each flower reduced to **little bluish or purplish scales,** or surrounded by a large purple sheath or spathe.... 352

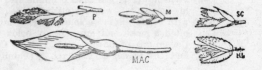

The figures above represent some examples of flowers reduced to scales.—Fig. MAC represents a large sheath surrounding the very reduced flowers.

N.B.—If there is any doubt as to whether a flower is regular or irregular, as, for example, in the flowers represented by Figs. VT, M, and AR, either one or other of the numbers referred to may be taken. In both cases the name of the plant will be reached.

There may also be some doubt as to flowers reduced to scales and regular flowers, as certain flowers, although regular, are formed of membranous parts, and look as if they were reduced to scales. Here also either of the numbers to which one has been referred may be chosen. The name of the plant will be reached in both cases.

○ Leaves **compound**; that is to say, that the whole leaf is made up of secondary leaves, or *leaflets*, which are each often mistaken for a leaf ; the compound leaf is attached to the stem by its base or by a stalk which bears all the leaflets. The base of a compound leaf is never situated exactly in the axil of another leaf 284

The above figures represent examples of compound leaves.

○ Leaves **deeply divided** (except sometimes those leaves which are quite at the top of the stems) ; that is to say, that each leaf is, as it were, cut in to the extent of more than half its breadth 284

The above figures represent examples of divided leaves.

229 *(following on 228).*

○ Leaves **simple**; that is to say, either not cut in to the extent of half their breadth, or merely edged with teeth or even without teeth on their edges 230

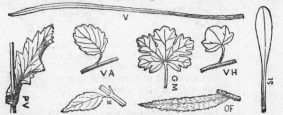

The above figures represent examples of simple leaves.

○ Leaves **not developed** 231

N.B.—It is of no consequence if some doubt exists as between compound and deeply divided leaves, since in either case one is referred to the same number (284).

So, too, if there is any hesitation as between deeply divided and simple leaves, either question may be taken, and in either case the name of the plant will be reached. So, too, if the plant happens to have both simple and compound or divided leaves (apart from the few simple leaves which may occur quite at the top of the flowering stems).

— Leaves **opposite** (except sometimes at the upper part of the stems or branches); that is to say, leaves arranged in twos, attached to the stem at the same level, on opposite sides of the stem to one another 267

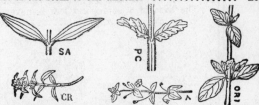

The above figures represent examples of opposite leaves.

N.B.—In the axils of opposite leaves little leafy branches are tolerably often formed (as in Fig. ORI, above, on the right). These may lead to the belief that the leaves are grouped many together at the same level on the stem and not merely in opposite pairs; but if the base of such a group of leaves be carefully examined, the two opposite leaves will be readily distinguished.

— Leaves **whorled**, at least towards the middle region of the stems; that is to say, leaves attached at the same level on the stem by 3's, 4's, 5's, or even more, and arranged regularly round the stem 267

230 (following on 229).

The above figures represent examples of whorled leaves.

— Leaves **alternate**; that is to say, leaves attached one by one on the stem at different levels (examples: Figs. GA, HM) 231

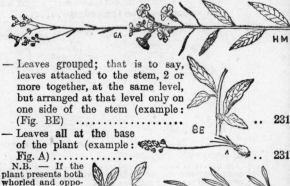

— Leaves **grouped**; that is to say, leaves attached to the stem, 2 or more together, at the same level, but arranged at that level only on one side of the stem (example: (Fig. BE) 231

— Leaves **all at the base** of the plant (example: Fig. A) 231

N.B. — If the plant presents both whorled and opposite leaves (as, for example, Fig. P), or both alternate and whorled leaves (as, for example, Fig. LS), either question may be followed up and the name of the plant will be reached.

✳ Each flower has its petals separated from one another down to their bases; that is to say, that one of the petals (or parts of the flower coloured blue, violet, or lilac) may be removed down to its base without tearing the others. This refers to those parts of the flower that, collectively, constitute the corolla or coloured structure surrounding the threads and other organs that occupy the centre of the flower; when the flower fades each petal (or coloured piece) falls or shrivels up separately.[1] 232

231
(follow-
ing on
230).

Fig. E (above, on the right) represents a flower with distinct petals, in which case the 6 petals (or parts coloured blue) may be seen detached.—The other figures represent other examples of flowers with separate petals. In Fig. N the petals (or parts coloured blue) appear to be united; but it is only necessary to detach one of the 6 pieces of the flower to realise that it is free down to its base (as is seen in Fig. E above).

✳ Each flower with petals united to one another, at least at the base; that is to say, that in trying to detach one of the parts of the flower coloured blue, violet, or lilac one has to tear the corolla, at least at its base. When the flower fades the corolla falls off or withers in one piece......... 242

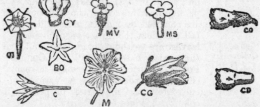

The petals are united to one another at very varying heights in different flowers. Fig. M represents the corolla of a flower the petals of which are very little united to one another at their bases; in the corolla BO, the petals are more united, and still more in CY, MV, MS, and C, which are in the form of a tube at their bases; in the flower CG the petals are only separated at their tips where they form five teeth; and lastly, in the flower S, the petals are united to one another almost to their tips.—Fig. CD represents the corolla of the flower CO detached.

---

[1] In most flowers there is, outside the corolla, another covering to the flower, generally green, known as the *calyx*, which surrounds the base of the corolla. In other flowers it is difficult to distinguish the calyx and the corolla, they being more or less combined in a single floral envelope. Other flowers, lastly, have actually only a single envelope coloured blue, lilac, or violet, like a corolla. We shall understand here, therefore, under the names petal and corolla, those pieces, coloured blue, lilac, or violet, which immediately surround the little threads and other organs that occupy the centre of the flower.

232
(following on 231).

= Flowers rose lilac, almost without stalks, arranged in a long cluster (Fig. LS). The green part which encloses

the petals at their bases (calyx) is in the form of a tube bearing 8 to 12 teeth arranged in 2 rows (6 teeth of the outer row are visible in Fig. SI) ; some of the leaves are alternate, some opposite, and some whorled. → **Willow-leaved Lythrum** (Purple Loosestrife) [*Lythrum Salicaria*] —medicinal.—Represented in colour: 4, Plate 21. (Family *Lythraceæ*.)

= Plant not having all these characteristics together **233**

233
(following on 232).

⊖ Each flower with **4 petals** or 4 parts similar to one another, coloured blue, lilac, or violet **234**

⊖ Each flower with **5 petals** or 5 parts similar to one another, coloured blue, lilac, or violet **237**

⊖ Each flower with **3, 6, or 9 petals**, or 3, 6, or 9 parts similar to one another, coloured blue, lilac, or violet **240**

⊖ Each flower having **apparently numerous petals**. On examining the flower carefully it will be seen that it is in reality a composite flower made up of very many small flowers in the form of tubes or of straps which are surrounded by a collarette of numerous small leaves or scales.—Go on to No. **810**

234
(following on 233).

× Each flower **more than 5 centimetres (2 inches) across**; the four petals are crumpled in the bud and are enclosed by 2 green parts which fall off when the flower opens ; the leaves are without hairs and embrace the stem by their wide base (Fig. PV). → **Opium Poppy** (Garden Poppy) [*Papaver somniferum*]—medicinal ; ornamental. (Family *Papaveraceæ*.) A variety of this plant is cultivated for industrial purposes.—Represented in colour: 2, Plate 5.

× Each flower **less than 5** centimetres (2 inches) across **235**

235
(following on 234).

☐ The lower leaves are **deeply divided** (Fig. NG), the others more or less divided or toothed ; flowers with lilac petals **having dark veins** (Fig. RR). → **Wild Radish** (White Charlock) [*Raphanus Raphanistrum*]. ✿ (Family *Cruciferæ*.) A related species (*Raphanus sativus*), the Garden Radish, is grown for the sake of its enlarged edible roots.

☐ Plant not having these characteristics **236**

236 (following on 235).

✱✱ Leaves acute at the base (Fig. HM); flowers sweet scented.→ **Dame's Hesperis** (Dame's Violet) [*Hesperis matronalis*]--ornamental. (Family *Cruciferæ.*)

✱✱ Leaves **not** acute at the base, often reversedly heart shaped (Fig. LB); flowers without any decided smell. → **Biennial Lunaria** (Honesty) [*Lunaria biennis*]—ornamental. ❀ (Family *Cruciferæ.*)

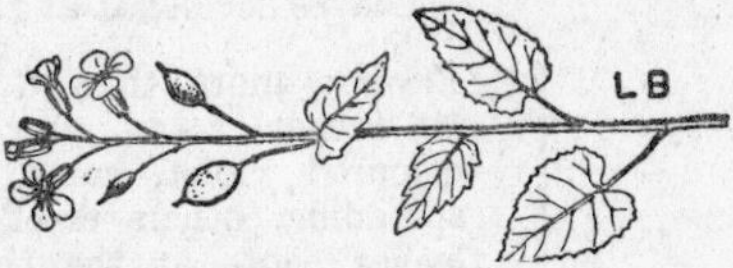

237 (following 233).

⊙ Leaves **toothed and more or less cut**............ 238

⊙ Leaves **not both** toothed and cut................ 239

238 (following on 237).

♤ Leaves **more or less hairy, but very green; there are 3 very small leaves** or green scales below the green part (calyx) which surrounds the petals at their base (Figs. MM, MA (calyxes only) and MS, entire flower). → **Mallows** [*Malva*].—For the chief kinds of Mallow refer back to No... 57

♤ Leaves (Fig. GO), **very velvety, whitish;** there are **6 to 9 very small leaves** or green scales below the green calyx which surrounds the petals at their base (Fig. AO). → **Officinal Marsh-mallow** [*Althæa officinalis*]—medicinal. ❀ (Family *Malvaceæ.*)

239 (following on 237).

• Flowers **violet** (the petals are in reality united to one another at their bases); each of the petals has near its base two green spots edged with white; leaves rather broad, sometimes divided (Fig. DU). → **Bittersweet Nightshade** (Woody Nightshade) [*Solanum Dulcamara*]—poisonous; medicinal.—Represented in colour: 2 and 2 *bis*, Plate 40. (Family *Solanaceæ.*)

• Flowers **blue;** leaves long, narrow (Fig. L), with smooth edges. → **Cultivated Flax** (Common Flax) [*Linum usitatissimum*] — industrial; medicinal. — Represented in colour: 1 and 1 *bis*, Plate 10. (Family *Linaceæ.*)

• Flowers **lilac or lilac pink;** leaves long, narrow, a little rough along their edges. → **Slender-leaved Flax** [*Linum tenuifolium*].—Represented in colour: 2, Plate 10. (Family *Linaceæ.*)

240
(following on 233).

⊖ **Leaves not developed** when the plant flowers; flower funnel shaped (Fig. CO). (The parts coloured lilac or violet are in reality united at their base in a long tube. → **Autumn Colchicum** (Meadow Saffron) [*Colchicum autumnale*]—poisonous; medicinal.—Represented in colour: 4, Plate 52. (Family *Liliaceæ*.)

⊖ Leaves **developed** at the same time as the flowers **241**

241
(following on 240).

⟳ Flowers **more than 3 centimetres (1¼ inches) across,** having 9 parts coloured violet, some reflexed or spreading, others erect (Fig. IA); leaves acute at the tip, arranged along the stem and at the base of the plant. → **German Iris** (Common Flag) [*Iris germanica*]—ornamental. (Family *Iridaceæ*.)

⟳ Flowers **less than 3** centimetres (1¼ inches) across, arranged in a cluster and having 6 parts recurved at their tips (Fig. N); plant less than 46 centimetres (18 inches) high; leaves all at the base of the plant. → **Uninscribed Hyacinth** (Blue-bell, Wild Hyacinth) [*Endymion nonscriptum*].—Represented in colour: 5, Plate 53. (Family *Liliaceæ*.)

⟳ Flowers less than 3 centimetres, with 6 parts arranged in a star **259**

242
(following on 231).

• Each flower shaped like a **bell, a rattle, a tube, or a funnel.** (Remove the corolla of the flower in order to see its form.) **243**

The above figures represent examples of bell-shaped, rattle-shaped, tubular- or funnel-shaped flowers.

• Each flower spreading into a **wide cup or into a star** (examples) **257**

The above figures represent examples of cup-shaped or star-shaped flowers.

243
(following on 242).

⊕ Each flower with 6 parts deeply separated but uniting at their base into a **long tube** (Fig. CO) ; leaves not developed when the plant flowers.—Refer back to No. **240**

⊕ Each flower with 6 parts separated almost to their base and **without a long tube.**—Refer back to No. **241**

⊕ Each flower with 6 short teeth; leaves all at the base **244**

⊕ Each flower with **5 divisions** **245**

244
(following on 243).

⋈ Flowers **in a very elongated cluster** (Fig. C), more than 3 times longer than it is broad ; upper flowers in an erect tuft. → **Hairy Grape-hyacinth** [*Muscari comosum*].— Represented in colour : 3, Plate 53. (Family *Liliaceæ*.)

⋈ Flowers **in a short cluster** (Fig. R), less than 3 times as long as it is broad ; upper flowers not in an erect tuft. → **Common Grape-hyacinth** (Starch Hyacinth) [*Muscari racemosum*]. (Family *Liliaceæ*.)

245
(following on 243).

① Flowers **less than 8 millimetres** (⅓ inch) across and all crowded into a single very compact mass at the top of the stem (see Figs. I and PS under No. 826)......... **826**

① Plant **not having these characteristics** together.... **246**

246
(following on 245).

+ Flowers **of a dark violet purple or reddish**; upper leaves grouped in twos at the same level on the stem (Fig. B). → **Belladonna Atropa** (Deadly Nightshade) [*Atropa Belladonna*]—medicinal ; poisonous. ✿ (Family *Solanaceæ*.)

+ Plant not having the above characteristics together **247**

247
(following on 246).

─• Flowers **without stalks**; flowers crowded at the top (Fig. CA). → **Clustered Bell-flower** [*Campanula glomerata*].—Represented in colour : 2, Plate 35. (Family *Campanulaceæ*.)

─• Flowers **borne on a stalk**, sometimes rather short **248**

248
(following on 247).

§ The corolla of each flower **can be detached in one piece** and ends in 5 lobes more or less spreading or curved outwards (see the figures under Nos. 253 and 256) .. **253**

§ The corolla of each flower **cannot be detached in one piece** without tearing it at least at its base, and ends in 5 erect lobes (see the figures under Nos. 247 and 251) ... **249**

249
(following on 248).

△ Leaves rough to the touch, very hairy ; the 5 green parts which surround the corolla are covered with rough hairs 250

△ Leaves usually **not rough** to the touch, with fine hairs or without hairs ; the 5 green parts which surround the corolla are without hairs or have hairs that are **not** rough 251

250
(following on 249).

⊞ The 5 green parts (calyx) which surround the corolla are bent back (Fig. RO) when the flower withers. → **Rampion-like Bell-flower** [*Campanula rapunculoides*]. (Family *Campanulaceæ*.)

⊞ The 5 green parts (calyx) which surround the corolla are erect (Figs. T, CG) even when the flower withers. → **Nettle-leaved Bell-flower** (Canterbury Bells) [*Campanula Trachelium*]—medicinal.—Represented in colour: 4, Plate 35. (Family *Campanulaceæ*.)

251
(following on 249).

○ Flowers more than 2 centimetres (⅘ inch) across; the 5 lobes at the top of the corolla more or less rounded (Fig. P). → **Peach-leaved Bell-flower** [*Campanula persicæfolia*]. (Family *Campanulaceæ*.)

○ Flowers less than 2 centimetres across; the 5 lobes at the top of the corolla more or less acute 252

252
(following on 251).

— Flowers arranged in an erect, elongated cluster (Fig. CRP) ; the stalks of the flowers all erect, even of those entirely withered. → **Rampion Bell-flower** [*Campanula Rapunculus*]—food plant.—Represented in colour: 3, Plate 35. (Family *Campanulaceæ*.)

— Flowers arranged in a more or less spreading cluster (Fig. CRD) ; stalks of the flowers curving downwards when the flowers are completely over.[1] → **Round-leaved Bell-flower** (Harebell, Blue-bell of Scotland) [*Campanula rotundifolia*].—Represented in colour: 5, Plate 35. (Family *Campanulaceæ*.)

---

[1] When the plant is young, it produces at its base branches with rounded leaves ; but these have generally disappeared by the time the plant flowers.

253
(following on 248).

= Flowers at first red, then violet, then blue; leaves often spotted with white on their upper surfaces; flowers with 5 deep lobes (Fig. P; Fig. O represents a flower cut lengthwise). → **Narrow-leaved Lungwort** [*Pulmonaria angustifolia*]—medicinal.—Represented in colour: 2, Plate 39. (Family *Boraginaceæ*.)

= Flowers violet or rosy; leaves prolonged at their base along the stem (Figs. SO, S); flowers with 5 small lobes recurved outwards (Fig. CO). → **Officinal Comfrey** [*Symphytum officinale*]—medicinal. ✿ —Represented in colour: 3, Plate 39. (Family *Boraginaceæ*.)

= Flowers of a purplish or red brown; upper leaves surrounding the stem by their bases; flowers with a short tube and 5 deep lobes (Fig. CY representing the corolla detached). → **Officinal Hound's-tongue** [*Cynoglossum officinale*] — poisonous; medicinal. ✿ (Family *Boraginaceæ*.)

= Flowers blue, red, or a bluish white, less than 7 millimetres (¼ inch) across or, at most, 7 millimetres 254

254
(following on 253).

⊖ Plant with pricking hairs; on removing the corolla, the tube of the corolla is seen to be, as it were, slightly bent (Fig. AR). → **Field Bugloss** [*Lycopsis arvensis*].—Represented in colour: 5, Plate 39. (Family *Boraginaceæ*.)

⊖ Plant with hairs that are not pricking 255

255
(following on 254).

× With a small leaf on the stem immediately below each flower (Fig. EC). → **Bardanette Echinospermum** [*Echinospermum Lappula*]. (Family *Boraginaceæ*.)

× No small leaf on the stem immediately below each flower 256

256
(following on 255).

☐ Flower bluish white, in much recurved clusters (Fig. H); tube of the corolla not closed at the top by 5 small scales. → **European Heliotrope** [*Heliotropium europæum*]. (Family *Boraginaceæ*.)

☐ Flowers blue, in clusters recurved at the top; tube of the corolla bordered at the mouth or closed by 5 small scales (Fig. P); flowers bending apart from one another as they wither. → **Myosote** (Scorpion-grass) [*Myosotis*]. —For the various kinds of Scorpion-grass [*Myosotis*] go on to No. 261

257
(following on 242).

✳ ✳ Each flower with **6 parts, blue or violet. →** Squill [*Scilla*].—For the chief kinds of Squills [*Scilla*] go on to No. 259

✳ ✳ Each flower with **5 parts or 5 lobes, blue or violet** 258

✳ ✳ Each flower with **4 (sometimes 5) parts, rather unequal (Fig. VT), coloured blue or lilac. →** **Speedwells** [*Veronica*].—For the chief kinds of Speedwell [*Veronica*] go on to No. 315

258
(following on 257).

☉ **Corolla violet with two green spots bordered with white at the base of each** petal ; stems with the appearance and hardness of wood, except in the young portions ; leaves sometimes divided (Fig. DU). → **Bittersweet Nightshade (Woody Nightshade)** [*Solanum Dulcamara*]—medicinal ; poisonous.—Represented in colour: 2 and 2 *bis*, Plate 40. (Family *Solanaceæ*.)

☉ **Flowers all crowded into a compact mass at the top of** the stem (see Figs. I and PS under No. 826)..... 826

☉ Plant not having these characteristics together.. 260

259
(following on 257).

♡ Flowers with a stalk longer than the expanded flower ; leaves **much shorter** than the stem (Fig. A). → **Autumnal Squill** [*Scilla autumnalis*]. (Family *Liliaceæ*.)

♡ Flowers with a stalk about as long as the expanded flower ; leaves nearly as long as the flowering stem (Fig. B). → **Two-leaved Squill** [*Scilla bifolia*].—Represented in colour: 4, Plate 53. (Family *Liliaceæ*.)

260
(following on 258).

• Flowers more than 7 millimetres across 264

• Flowers less than 7 millimetres across, with the tube yellow on the inside. → **Myosote (Scorpion-grass)** [*Myosotis*].[1]—For the chief kinds of Myosote [*Myosotis*] go on to No. 261

261
(following on 260).

⊕ The green calyx which encloses the tube of the corolla is covered with hairs lying flat (Fig. PA), **not hooked** (examine with a lens) ; plant growing in damp places. → **Scorpioid Myosote (Forget-me-not)** [*Myosotis scorpioides*].—Represented in colour: 6, Plate 39. (Family *Boraginaceæ*.)

⊕ The calyx is covered with hooked hairs (Fig. MI), especially on its lower half (examine with a lens) 262

[1] For further details as to the various species of *Myosotis* reference should be made to more comprehensive Floras.

262
(following on 261).

⚜ Flowers yellow, then whitish, then reddish, then blue; corolla with a tube longer than the calyx which surrounds it (Figs MV and V). → Colour-changing Myosote [*Myosotis versicolor*]. (Family *Boraginaceæ*.)

⚜ Flowers blue with a yellow throat; corolla with a tube not longer than the calyx (Fig. MI) 263

263
(following on 262).

§ The lowest flowers when withered each borne on a stalk about twice as long as the flower (Fig. I). → Field Myosote [*Myosotis arvensis*]. (Family *Boraginaceæ*.)

§ The lowest flowers when withered each borne on a stalk about the same length as the flower (Fig. H). → Hill Myosote [*Myosotis collina*]. (Family *Boraginaceæ*.)

264
(following on 260).

+ Flowers a pink lilac; below the green calyx which surrounds the petals at their base, there are 3 to 9 small leaves or green scales (Figs. MR, MA, MM, O, below, under No. 265) 265

+ Flowers blue or a blue violet 266

265
(following on 264).

—• Leaves more or less hairy but very green; there are 3 small leaves or green scales below the green calyx of the flower (Fig. MR, whole flower seen from below; Figs. MA, MM only show the calyx and the three small leaves or green scales below it). → Mallows [*Malva*].—For the chief kinds of Mallows [*Malva*] refer back to No. 57

—• Leaves very velvety, whitish; there are 6 to 9 small leaves or green scales below the calyx (Fig. O). → Common Marsh - Mallow [*Althæa officinalis*]—medicinal. ✿ (Family *Malvaceæ*.)

266
(following on 264).

△ Plant with pricking hairs; stalks of the flowers curving downwards; petals deeply separated (Fig. B). → Officinal Borage [*Borago officinalis*] —medicinal. ✿ —Represented in colour: 4, Plate 39. (Family *Boraginaceæ*.)

△ Plants without hairs or with pricking hairs; stalks of the flowers always erect; petals hardly separated, forming collectively a 5-angled corolla (Fig. S). → Looking - glass Specularia (Venus' Looking-glass) [*Specularia Speculum*].—Represented in colour: 6, Plate 35. (Family *Campanulaceæ*.)

✠ Each flower has its **petals separated from one another down to their bases;** that is to say, that one petal (or part coloured blue, lilac, or violet) can be removed down to its base without tearing the others. This refers to those parts of the flowers which, collectively, form the corolla or coloured structure surrounding the little threads and other organs that occupy the centre of the flower; when the flower withers each petal (or coloured piece) falls off or shrivels up separately [1] 268

In some cases (Figs. S, N, OP, below, for example) it is necessary to tear the green or brownish tube which encloses the petals in order to see that **the petals are distinct from one another down to their bases.**

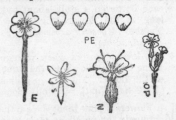

PE

267
(following on
230).

Fig. E shows a flower with distinct petals, the 4 petals being shown separate in Fig. PE.—The other figures (S, N OP) represent other examples of flowers with separate petals.

✠ Each flower has its **petals united to one another, at least at the base;** that is to say, that in trying to detach one of the parts of the flower coloured blue, lilac, or violet, one is obliged to tear the corolla at least at its base; when the flower fades the corolla falls off or withers all in one piece 271

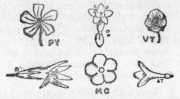

The petals are united to one another up to very different heights in different flowers. Figs. MC, VT represent the corolla of a flower (MC) or a flower (VT) the petals of which are very slightly united at their base: the flowers shown in Figs. PY, CA, G, AT have their petals united through a greater or lesser length into a tube or funnel.

---

[1] In most flowers, outside the corolla, another floral covering or envelope is found, which is generally green and is called the *calyx*, and which surrounds the base of the corolla. In other flowers it is difficult to distinguish the calyx and the corolla, which are more or less blended into a single floral envelope. Lastly, some other flowers have really only a single floral envelope coloured blue, lilac, or violet like a corolla. Under the names petal and corolla, we shall here include those parts of the flower coloured blue, lilac, or violet, which immediately surround the little threads and other organs that occupy the centre of the flower.

○ Each flower **almost without a stalk**; flowers arranged in a long cluster (Fig. LS). The green part which

268
(following on 267).

encloses the petals at their bases (calyx) forms a tube bearing 8 to 12 teeth arranged in 2 rows (in Fig. SI, 6 teeth of the outer row are shown, enlarged). → **Willow-leaved Lythrum** (Purple Loosestrife) [*Lythrum Salicaria*]—medicinal.—Represented in colour: 4, Plate 21. (Family *Lythraceæ*.)

○ Plant **not having the above-mentioned characteristics** together 269

269
(following on 268).

— Flower with **8 divisions of a greenish violet**; the inner divisions are narrower than the outer ones; leaves 4 (Fig. PA), or sometimes 5, in a whorl. → **Four-leaved Paris** (Herb Paris) [*Paris quadrifolia*]. (Family *Liliaceæ*.)

— Each flower with **4 or 8 divisions of a pink lilac** and stems hard like wood, except in the young branches.—Refer back to No. 117

— Each flower with **5 lilac or violet** petals 270

— Each flower with **4 pink or red** petals (Fig. E); stems not hard like wood. → **Willow-herbs** [*Epilobium*]. —For the chief kinds of Willow-herbs [*Epilobium*] refer back to No. 15

270
(following on 269).

✳ Flowers **rose pink** and each less than a centimetre (⅖ inch) across; flowers surrounded by membranous scales with a very small point at their tips (Figs. OP and P). → **Proliferous Pink** [*Dianthus prolifer*]. (Family *Caryophyllaceæ*.)

✳ Flowers **pink** and each more than a centimetre (⅖ inch) across; leaves oval (Fig. SA) with a few hairs; calyx surrounding the petals with 4 teeth shorter than the petals (Fig. S shows a flower). → **Officinal Soapwort** [*Saponaria officinalis*]—medicinal; industrial.—Represented in colour: 1, Plate 8. (Family *Caryophyllaceæ*.)

✳ Flowers of a **bluish red** and each more than 2 centimetres (⅘ inch) across; leaves very elongated, very hairy; calyx with 5 green divisions longer than the petals (Fig. N). → **Corn-cockle Lychnis** [*Lychnis Githago*]—poisonous; harmful to crops.—Represented in colour: 4, Plate 8. (Family *Caryophyllaceæ*.)

271
(following on 267).

= **Leaves in whorls of 4, or more than 4** (Fig. SA); that is to say, arranged regularly by fours or more attached at the same level on the stem **272**

= Leaves **opposite, or in whorls of 3,** that is to say, arranged two by two, attached at the same point to the stem, facing one another on opposite sides of the stem, or more rarely attached **three** together at one point on the stem **274**

272
(following on 271).

⊖ Flowers **rose colour and shaped like an elongated child's rattle;** leaves small and very narrow; stems hard like wood, except in the young branches. → **Hoary Heath** (Fine-leaved Heath) [*Erica cinerea*].[1]—Represented in colour: 2, Plate 36. (Family *Ericaceæ.*)

⊖ Plant **not having the above-mentioned characteristics** together **273**

273
(following on 272).

× Flowers **lilac with a straight tube** (Fig. S); leaves with numerous hairs over the whole of the upper surface (examine with a lens). → **Field Sherardia** (Field Madder) [*Sherardia arvensis*]. (Family *Rubiaceæ.*)

× Flowers **blue;** leaves fringed along their edges and the chief veins (Fig. A). → **Field Asperula** [*Asperula arvensis*]. (Family *Rubiaceæ.*)

274
(following on 271).

☐ Flowers **of a bluish white** shaped like a little funnel with 5 lobes (Fig. CA); each flower less than 3 millimetres across: flowers crowded in groups (Fig. OL). → **Cooking Valerianella** (Lamb's Lettuce, Corn-Salad) [*Valerianella olitoria*]—food plant.[2]—Represented in colour: 4, Plate 27. (Family *Valerianaceæ.*)

☐ Plant not having the above-mentioned characteristics together **275**

275
(following on 274).

✳✳ Petals in reality **separated from one another down to their bases.** Tear the calyx of the flower, which forms a tube below the petals, in order to see the narrow bases of the petals distinct from one another.—Refer back to No. **270**

✳✳ Petals in reality **united to one another at least at their bases** **276**

---

[1] For the various species of Heath [*Erica*] reference should be made to more comprehensive Floras.
[2] For the various species of *Valerianella* reference should be made to more comprehensive Floras.

276
(following on 275).

⊙ The 4 or 5 lobes of the flower are quite equal to one another 277

⊙ The 4 or 5 lobes of the flower are not quite equal to one another (Figs. VT, V, for example).... .. 281

277
(following on 276).

⌢ Stems prostrate on the ground, then rising erect, and flowers with 5 very spreading petals, in the axils of ordinary leaves 280

⌢ Plant not having all these characteristics together. → Gentian [*Gentiana*].[1]—For the chief kinds of Gentian [*Gentiana*] go on to No. 278

278
(following on 277).

• Each flower without a stalk; flowers grouped in the axils of the leaves (Fig. CR). → Cross-leaved Gentian [*Gentiana Cruciata*]—medicinal.—Represented in colour: 2, Plate 38. (Family *Gentianaceæ*.)

• Each flower with a stalk; flowers solitary...... 279

279
(following on 278).

⊕ Each flower violet, bearded inside, with 5 elongated lobes (Fig. G). → German Gentian [*Gentiana germanica*]. (Family *Gentianaceæ*.)

⊕ Each flower of a beautiful blue, not bearded inside, with 5 short lobes (Fig. PN). → Marsh Gentian [*Gentiana Pneumonanthe*]. (Family *Gentianaceæ*.)

280
(following on 277).

✠ Flowers more than a centimetre and a half across; corolla with its tube ending in 5 spreading lobes slightly curved and, as it were, cut off obliquely at their tips (Fig. PY); leaves sometimes apparently in whorls of three (Fig. P). → Lesser Periwinkle [*Vinca minor*]—medicinal.[2]—Represented in colour: 4, Plate 37. (Family *Apocynaceæ*.)

✠ Flowers less than a centimetre and a half across; corolla with a very short tube, ending in 5 rounded lobes (Figs. MC and A). → Blue Pimpernel [*Anagallis cærulea*].—Represented in colour: 6 *bis*, Plate 36. (See note 1 under No. 73.) (Family *Primulaceæ*.)

281
(following on 276).

§ Each flower with 5 lobes 282

§ Each flower with 4 lobes 283

---

[1] For further details as to the various species of Gentian [*Gentiana*] reference should be made to more comprehensive Floras.

[2] The Greater Periwinkle [*Vinca major*], with larger blossoms, is grown in gardens.

282
(following on 281).

+ **Leaves strongly toothed or divided** (Fig. VE) ; flowers arranged in elongated slender spikes ; flowers with 5 slightly unequal lobes (Fig. V). → **Officinal Vervain** (Common Vervain) [*Verbena officinalis*]—medicinal. ❀ —Represented in colour : 5, Plate 45. (Family *Verbenaceæ*.)

+ **Leaves scarcely toothed or without teeth;** flowers in compact groups (Fig. O) ; each flower rather irregular. → **Common Marjoram** [*Origanum vulgare*]—medicinal. ❀ — Represented in colour : 3, Plate 43. (Family *Labiatæ*.)

283
(following on 281).

• **Leaves with a strong aromatic scent** (the well-known scent of mint) ; each flower with lobes not spreading (Fig. M). → **Mints** [*Mentha*].—For the chief kinds of Mints [*Mentha*] refer back to No. 169

• **Leaves without a strong aromatic scent**, each flower (Fig. VT) with petals united at their base into a very short tube. → **Speedwells** [*Veronica*].—For the chief kinds of Speedwell [*Veronica*] go on to No. 315

284
(following on 229).

△ **Each flower shaped like an elongated rattle** (Fig. EC) ; (twigs with simple leaves have been mistaken for compound leaves) (Fig. EC). → **Hoary Heath** (Fine-leaved Heath, Crimson Heather) [*Erica cinerea*]. ❀ —Represented in colour : 1, Plate 36. (Family *Ericaceæ*.)

△ Each flower **not rattle shaped** 285

285
(following on 284).

✠ **Leaves opposite** (at least those towards the base of the plant), that is to say, the leaves are arranged in pairs, attached to the stem two at the same level, on opposite sides of it to one another (examples : Figs. SAN, VER) 287

✠ **Leaves whorled**, that is to say, leaves attached 3 or 4 together at the same level on the stem and arranged regularly round it (example : Fig. HT) 236

✠ **Leaves all alternate**, that is to say, leaves attached one by one to the stem at different levels (example : Fig. DU) 289

✠ **Leaves grouped**, that is to say, leaves attached, 2 or more together at the same level on the stem, but arranged at that level on one side only of the stem 289

✠ **Leaves all at the base of the plant** (example : Fig. PLS) 286

286
(following on 285).

○ Leaves all at the base of the plant, except a collarette of leaves with narrow divisions situated below the flower (Fig. PL, and Fig. PLS at the foot of the preceding page); flowers of a violet purple. → **Pasch Anemone** (Pasque-flower) [*Anemone Pulsatilla*] — poisonous; medicinal. — Represented in colour: 5 and 5 *bis*, Plate 1. (Family *Ranunculaceæ*.)

○ Leaves whorled in groups along the stem, with narrow divisions in 2 rows (Fig. H); flowers of a pale lilac; plant growing in water or in flooded ground. → **Marsh Hottonia** (Water Violet) [*Hottonia palustris*]. (Family *Primulaceæ*.)

287
(following on 285).

— Flowers with 5 petals completely separated from one another down to the base (Fig. G; at PG the 5 detached petals are shown); that is to say, that one of the rose-coloured petals can be removed down to its base without tearing the other petals, even at their bases; leaves with their veins arranged like a fan. → **Crane's-bills** [*Geranium*]. —Refer back to No. **94**

— Flowers with 4 or 5 lobes united together at the base so as to form a tube, sometimes very short (the corolla can be detached all in one piece) **288**

288
(following on 287).

✳ Flowers with 4 lobes (Fig. VT) of a dark blue; upper leaves alternate and divided into 3 lobes (Fig. TR). → **Finger-leaved Speedwell** [*Veronica triphyllos*]. (Family *Scrophulariaceæ*.)

✳ Flowers with 5 lobes (Fig. V) of a pale lilac; leaves all opposite (Fig. VER). → **Officinal Vervain** (Common Vervain) [*Verbena officinalis*]—medicinal. ✿ —Represented in colour: 5, Plate 45. (Family *Verbenaceæ*.)

289
(following on 285).

= Flowers in which 5 out of 10 parts coloured blue or violet are prolonged downwards into a recurved horn (Fig. AV); leaves much divided (Fig. AN shows a fragment of a large leaf). → **Common Columbine** (Culverkeys) [*Aquilegia vulgaris*]—ornamental. ✿ —Represented in colour: 4 and 4 *bis*, Plate 3. (Family *Ranunculaceæ*.)

= Flowers not having these characteristics.......... **290**

290
(following on 289)

⬤ Flowers with 4 petals or parts coloured lilac or some shade of violet 291

⊖ Flowers with 5 petals or parts coloured lilac, violet, or blue 293

⊖ Flowers with numerous petals, straps, or tubes coloured blue, violet, or lilac. On examining it with care, this flower is seen to be in reality a composite flower made up of numerous little strap-shaped or tubular flowers surrounded by a collarette of numerous little leaves or scales.—Go on to No. 810

291
(following on 290).

✕ Petals **crumpled in the bud** of the flower (Fig. PR) and enclosed by two green parts that fall off as the flower opens; leaves without hairs, embracing the stem by their bases (Fig. PV); flowers lilac or more or less violet. → Opium Poppy (Garden Poppy) [*Papaver somniferum*]—poisonous; medicinal. (A variety of this plant is grown for industrial purposes.)—Represented in colour: 2, Plate 5. (Family *Papaveraceæ*.)

✕ Plant **not having all these characteristics together**.. 292

292
(following on 291).

☐ Stems **without hairs;** upper leaves very deeply divided (Fig. PR), those at the base with rounded leaflets (Fig. P); flower slightly elongated below the spreading of the petals (Fig. C). → Meadow **Cardamine** (Lady's Smock, Cuckoo flower) [*Cardamine pratensis*]—edible. ❀—Represented in colour: 2, Plate 6. (Family *Cruciferæ*.)

☐ Stems **with hairs;** upper leaves not divided or rather irregularly cut (Fig. R); flower rather elongated below the spreading of the petals (Fig. RR). → **Wild Radish** (White Charlock) [*Raphanus Raphanistrum*]. ❀ (Family *Cruciferæ*.)

293
(following on 290).

✳✳ Leaves with their **veins arranged like a fan;** flowers lilac or rose colour 294

✳✳ Plant **not having these characteristics together**.. 295

294
(following on 293).

⊙ **Petals united to one another quite at the base** (Fig. M) ; there are three very small leaves or green scales immediately below the green calyx which surrounds the lilac petals. → Mallows [*Malva*].—For the chief kinds of Mallow [*Malva*] refer back to No. 57

⊙ **Petals free from one another down to the base;** that is to say, that one of the lilac or rose-colour petals can be removed down to its base without tearing the other petals even at their bases (example: Fig. PG shows the 5 petals of the flower shown in Fig. G detached). → Crane's-bills [*Geranium*].[1]—For the chief kinds of Crane's-bill refer back to No. ... 94

295
(following on 293).

♢ **Leaves with numerous very narrow divisions** (Fig. NG) ; the divisions are each less than 3 millimetres wide ; flowers (Fig. N) of a light or whitish blue, veined with blue. → **Field Love-in-a-mist** (Fennel-flower) [*Nigella arvensis*] —medicinal. ❀—Represented in colour: 5, Plate 2. (Family *Ranunculaceæ*.)

♢ **Leaves not** with narrow divisions ; flowers with their petals united, at least at the base (Fig. N) 296

296
(following on 295).

✳ **Flowers each division of which has at its base two green spots bordered with white;** stems with the appearance and hardness of wood towards the base of the plant ; leaves sometimes divided (Fig. DU) ; plant climbing or supporting itself on other plants. → **Bittersweet Nightshade** (Woody Nightshade) [*Solanum Dulcamara*]—medicinal ; poisonous.—Represented in colour: 2 and 2 *bis*, Plate 40. (Family *Solanaceæ*.)

✳ **Flowers the divisions of which have not got two green spots bordered with white** at their bases ; stems having neither the appearance nor the hardness of wood even at the base of the plant ; leaves made up of leaflets (Fig. P) ; stems erect, not climbing ; the underground stems form swollen tubercles. → **Tuberous Nightshade** (Potato) [*Solanum tuberosum*]—food plant ; medicinal.—Represented in colour: 4, Plate 40. (Family *Solanaceæ*.)

---

[1] The wild Crane's-bills must not be confused with the garden plants commonly, but inaccurately, known as Geraniums. These latter are in reality Pelargoniums, natives of the Cape of Good Hope.

⊕ Leaves **compound**; that is to say, that the leaf as a whole is made up of secondary leaves known as *leaflets* which are each often mistaken for a leaf; the whole leaf is attached to the stem by its base, or by a stalk which bears all the leaflets; the base of the compound leaf is not attached in the axil of another leaf 340

The above figures show some examples of compound leaves.

⊕ Leaves **deeply divided** (except sometimes the leaves which are quite at the upper part of the stems), that is to say, that each leaf is, as it were, cut to the extent of more than half its breadth 340

297
(*following on* 228).

The above figures show examples of divided leaves.

⊕ Leaves **simple**; that is to say, either not cut to the extent of more than half the breadth of the leaf, or merely edged with teeth, or even without teeth on its edges..... 298

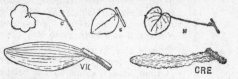

The above figures show examples of simple leaves.

N.B.—It is of no consequence if there is some doubt in deciding between compound leaves and leaves deeply divided, since in both cases the reference is to the same number (340).
If there is a doubt as between leaves deeply divided and simple leaves (Fig. A, for example) either question may be followed, and in either case the name of the plant will be reached. The same result will follow if the plant has both simple leaves and compound or divided leaves at the same time (in addition to the simple leaves which may occur at the top of the flowering stems).

✠ Leaves **opposite** (except sometimes on the upper part of the stems or branches); that is to say, leaves arranged in pairs, attached to the stem at the same level, opposite to one another 324

The above figures show examples of opposite leaves.

N.B.—Little leafy branches are often formed in the axils of opposite leaves (as in Fig. ORI, above, to the right), and may lead to the belief that the leaves are grouped in a large number at the same level on the stem, and not only in an opposite pair; but on careful examination at the base of this group of leaves, the two opposite leaves will be readily made out.

✠ Leaves **whorled**, at least in the middle region of the stems; that is to say, leaves attached at the same level on the stem 3 or 4 together, and arranged regularly round the stem (example: Fig. LS) 310

298
(following on 297).

✠ Leaves **alternate**; that is to say, leaves attached one by one to the stem at different levels 299

The above figures show examples of alternate leaves.

✠ Leaves **grouped**; that is to say, leaves attached to the stem, 2 or more together at the same level, but arranged, at that level, on one side only of the stem 299

✠ Leaves **all at the base of the plant** 299

Fig. VP represents an example of a plant with all its leaves at the base.

N.B.—If the plant presents alternate leaves and opposite leaves at the same time (as, for example, in Fig. LM), or alternate and whorled leaves at the same time, either question may be followed up and will lead to the name of the plant.

§ Each flower has its petals separated from each other down
to the base; that is to say, that one of the petals (or parts
coloured blue, lilac, or violet) may be removed down to
the base without tearing the others. This refers to those
coloured parts of the flower which, collectively, form the
corolla (or coloured part) and surround the little threads
and other organs that occupy the centre of the flower ;
when the flower fades each petal (or coloured piece) falls
off or withers separately.[1] 300

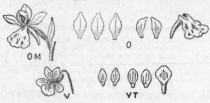

Fig. OM shows a flower with separate petals, Fig. O showing the
6 petals detached. Fig. V shows a flower with separate petals,
and Fig. VT its 5 petals detached.

299
*(follow-
ing on
298).*

§ Each flower has its petals united together, at least at their
base; that is to say, that on trying to detach one of the
parts of the flower coloured blue, lilac, or violet one has
to tear the corolla, at least at its base ; when the flower
fades, the corolla falls off or withers all in one piece   307

The petals are united to one another at very different heights
in different flowers. Fig. VT shows the corolla of a flower the
petals of which are very slightly united to one another at the base ;
in the other figures the petals are more united so that the corolla
forms a tube at its base.

N.B.—If there is any doubt as between the flower
having its petals separated from one another to the base,
or having its petals united to one another at least at the
base (as, for example, in the case of the flower shown in
Fig. POL), either question may be followed up and will
lead in either case to the name of the plant.

---

[1] In most flowers there is, outside the corolla, another covering to the
flower, generally green, known as the *calyx*, which surrounds the base of the
corolla. In other flowers it is difficult to distinguish the calyx and corolla,
they being more or less blended into a single floral envelope. Lastly, in some
other flowers there is really only one floral envelope coloured blue, lilac, or
violet, like a corolla. The names petal and corolla will here be used for those
pieces coloured blue, lilac, or violet, which immediately surround the little
threads or other organs occupying the centre of the flower.

300
(following on
299).

— Each flower having one petal prolonged at its base into a horn or closed tube (see Figs. V and MR under Nos. 301 and 306); 5 or 6 petals separate from one another to their bases...................... 301

— Each flower without a petal prolonged into a horn or tube at its base: there are two little oval parts, violet or lilac, distinct from the rest of the flower (Fig. POL). → Common Milkwort [Polygala vulgaris]—medicinal.[1]—Represented in colour: 4, Plate 7. (Family Polygalaceæ.)

— Each flower without a petal prolonged at the base into a horn or tube, with 6 petals, one larger than the rest.—Refer back to No. 135

301
(following on
300).

⊖ Each flower having 5 petals (Figs. V and T); leaves with veins more or less branched (hold the leaf up to the light). → Violets (including the Pansies and the Violets properly so called) [Viola].—Go on to No. 302

⊖ Each flower having 6 petals of which one has a peculiar form: leaves with veins not branched 306

302
(following on
301).

× The 4 upper petals erect (see the right hand Fig. T, under No. 301). → Tricolor Viola (Pansy, Hearts-ease) [Viola tricolor]—ornamental; medicinal.—Represented in colour (with yellow flower): 2, Plate 7. (Family Violaceæ.)

× Only the 2 upper petals erect (see the left hand Fig. V, above, under No. 301) 303

303
(following on
302).

☐ Flowers strongly scented; stem bearing branches which lie on the ground and give out roots here and there; petals not sloped at the top (Fig. O). → Sweet Viola (Violet) [Viola odorata]—medicinal. —Represented in colour: 3, Plate 7. (Family Violaceæ.)

☐ Flowers without any pronounced perfume 304

304
(following on
303).

✳ ✳ Leaves all at the base of the plant; petals sloped at the top (Fig. H). → Hairy Viola [Viola hirta]. (Family Violaceæ.)

✳ ✳ Leaves at the base and also along the flowering stems 305

305
(following on
304).

⊙ The two little scales which are attached to the stem at the right and left of the base of each leaf-stalk have hairs nearly as long as the scale is wide (Fig. S). → Wood Viola [Viola sylvestris]. (Family Violaceæ.)

⊙ The two little scales which are attached to the stem at the right and left of the base of each leaf-stalk have hairs shorter than the width of each scale (Fig. C). → Dog Viola [Viola canina]. (Family Violaceæ.)

---

[1] For the various species of Milkwort [Polygala] reference should be made to more comprehensive Floras.

306
(following on 301).

♀ Flowers **pink or dark rose colour;** the horn or long tube into which the flower is prolonged below is directed upwards or across (Figs. MR and OM). → Helmet Orchis [*Orchis morio*]—medicinal. (Family *Orchidaceæ*.)

♀ Flowers **white, veined, and spotted with lilac;** the horn of the flower is directed downward (Figs. ML and OT). → Spotted Orchis [*Orchis maculata*]—medicinal. (Family *Orchidaceæ*.)

307
(following on 299).

• Each flower **in the form of a mouth,** that is to say, with a lower lip inflated and touching the upper lip, prolonged towards the base into a **horn-like swelling or a tube** more or less long (examples: Figs. PE, ST) .. **308**

• Each flower **not in the shape of a mouth** and with neither horn nor tube at its base **311**

308
(following on 307).

△ Leaves supported by a stalk **distinct** but sometimes very short; stems more or less prostrate or hanging .. **309**

△ Leaves **without stalks;** stems erect **310**

309
(following on 308).

✠ Flowers **yellow,** but purple on the inside of the upper lip; plant hairy; leaves with a very short stalk (Fig. S). → False Toad-flax (Male Fluellen) [*Linaria spuria*]. (Family *Scrophulariaceæ*.)

✠ Flowers (Fig. CY) **lilac or a bluish rose colour;** plant without hairs; leaves with a tolerably long stalk (Fig. C). → Ivy-leaved Toad-flax (Mother of Thousands) [*Linaria Cymbalaria*]—ornamental. —Represented in colour: 2, Plate 41. (Family *Scrophulariaceæ*.)

310
(following on 308).

○ Plant **without hairs;** leaves sometimes 3 or 4 together at the same level on the stem (Fig. LS); flowers with a short horn at the base (Fig. ST). → Creeping Toad-flax [*Linaria repens*]. ✿ (Family *Scrophulariaceæ*.)

○ Plant **with hairs;** lower leaves in pairs at one level on the stem (Fig. LM); flowers with a tolerably long and acute horn at their base (Fig. MI). → Least Toad-flax [*Linaria minor*]. (Family *Scrophulariaceæ*.)

311
(following on 307).
{
— Stems with stiff, pricking hairs................. 312
— Stems with soft, not pricking hairs, or stems without hairs 313
}

312
(following on 311).
✻ Flowers less than 9 millimetres long, with a corolla almost regular; on detaching the corolla carefully, it will be seen that the tube of the corolla is slightly bent about the middle (Fig. AR, enlarged). → Field Bugloss [*Lycopsis arvensis*]. —Represented in colour: 5, Plate 39. (Family *Boraginaceæ*.)

✻ Flowers more than 9 millimetres long, with a distinctly irregular corolla (Fig. EV). → Common Viper's-bugloss [*Echium vulgare*]. —Represented in colour: 1, Plate 39. (Family *Boraginaceæ*.)

313
(following on 311)
{
⊖ Each flower distinctly two-lipped, that is to say, with an upper division different from the lower division (Fig. E); flowers white, striped with violet and yellow inside the upper part of the tube of the corolla; leaves toothed at their edges (Fig. O shows the whole plant). → Common Eye-bright [*Euphrasia officinalis*]—medicinal. (Family *Scrophulariaceæ*.)

⊖ Plant not having all these characteristics together 314
}

314
(following on 313).
= Each flower with two oval pieces, free to their bases (Figs. POL, PV) and blue or pink in colour. → Common Milkwort [*Polygala vulgaris*]—medicinal.[1]—Represented in colour: 4, Plate 7. (Family *Polygalaceæ*.)

= Each flower with 5 rather unequal lobes; flowers yellowish veined with purple, more than a centimetre and a half (⅜ inch) across; flowers in a recurved cluster (Fig. HN). → Black Henbane [*Hyoscyamus niger*]—poisonous; medicinal. —Represented in colour: 1, Plate 40. (Family *Solanaceæ*.)

= Each flower with 4 rather unequal lobes (Fig. VT); flowers blue, violet, or white, veined sometimes with violet, sometimes with blue. → Speedwells [*Veronica*].[2]—For the chief kinds of Speedwell [*Veronica*] go on to No. 315

---

[1] For the various species of Milkwort [*Polygala*] reference should be made to more comprehensive Floras.
[2] For the various species of Speedwell [*Veronica*] reference should be made to more comprehensive Floras.

315
(following on 314).

× Leaves all opposite 316

× Leaves alternate, at least on the upper part of the stems 320

316
(following on 315).

☐ Leaves without hairs (examine them with a lens) 317

☐ Leaves with hairs 318

317
(following on 316).

✳ ✳ Flowers of a beautiful blue; leaves (at least the lower ones) more or less rounded at the tip, with a stalk of more or less length (Fig. B), not embracing the stem by its base; stems cylindrical. → Brooklime Speedwell [*Veronica Beccabunga*]—edible; medicinal. (Family *Scrophulariaceæ*.)

✳ ✳ Flowers lilac or of a pale blue; leaves acute at the tip, all without stalks (Fig. AN), more or less embracing the stem by their bases; stems almost 4-angled. → Water - Pimpernel Speedwell [*Veronica Anagallis-aquatica*]. (Family *Scrophulariaceæ*.)

318
(following on 316).

⊙ Stems with two lines of hairs down opposite sides (Fig. PC); flowers rather separated from one another. → Germander Speedwell (Angel's-eye) [*Veronica Chamædrys*]. — medicinal.—Represented in colour: 2, Plate 42. (Family *Scrophulariaceæ*.)

⊙ Stems with hairs all round them; flowers near together 319

319
(following on 318).

↶ Flowers of a pale blue or pinkish; stems prostrate on the ground, with the exception of the flowering branches (Fig. O). → Officinal Speedwell [*Veronica officinalis*]—medicinal.—Represented in colour: 3, Plate 42. (Family *Scrophulariaceæ*.)

↶ Flowers of a beautiful blue; stems more or less erect; leaves toothed or without teeth (Figs. TE, P). → Female Speedwell [*Veronica Teucrium*]—medicinal.—Represented in colour: 1, Plate 42. (Family *Scrophulariaceæ*.)

320
(following on 315).

• Leaves glossy, without hairs (examine them with the lens); the leaves are oval (Fig. SP). → Thyme-leaved Speedwell [*Veronica serpyllifolia*]. (Family *Scrophulariaceæ*.)

• Leaves with hairs 321

321
(follow-ing on 320).

⊕ **Leaves with 3 or 4 divisions** (Fig. TR), cut to an extent of more than half the breadth of the leaf. → **Finger-leaved Speedwell** [*Veronica triphyllos*]. (Family *Scrophulariaceæ*.)

⊕ **Leaves not deeply divided** 322

322
(follow-ing on 321).

⯒ Stems **erect**; each flower on expansion having a stalk shorter than the breadth of the flower (Fig. A). → **Field Speedwell** [*Veronica arvensis*]. (Family *Scrophulariaceæ*.)

⯒ Stems **prostrate or hanging**; each flower on expansion having a stalk longer than the breadth of the flower 323

323
(follow-ing on 322).

§ Each leaf **with a middle lobe bigger** than the other lobes (Figs. VH and H); flowers of a pale blue. → **Ivy-leaved Speedwell** [*Veronica hederæfolia*]. (Family *Scrophulariaceæ*.)

§ Each leaf with a middle lobe **not** perceptibly bigger than the other lobes (Figs. VA and AG); flowers of a beautiful blue. → **Greenfield Speedwell** [*Veronica agrestis*]. (Family *Scrophulariaceæ*.)

—
324
(follow-ing on 298).

+ Flowers **two-lipped**, that is to say, with two divisions different from one another, one upper and the other lower (examples : Figs. S, E, AL) 325

+ Flowers with only one hanging lip with 3 lobes, of which the middle one is the largest (example : Fig. A) 336

+ Flowers slightly irregular in appearance, with 4 or 5 lobes (examples : Figs. M, V, CA, VT, above ... 337

325
(follow-ing on 324).

—• The upper lip of each flower, seen from the side, has the form of a sickle which has been, as it were, cut across at the tip (Figs. S and P); plant more or less sticky, clinging a little to the fingers in its upper portion. → **Meadow Sage** (Meadow Clary) [*Salvia pratensis*]—medicinal. ✿—Represented in colour: 7, Plate 43. (Family *Labiatæ*.)

—• Plant not having these characteristics 326

326
(following on 325).

△ Flowers grouped in a crowded mass on the top of the stems or branches (see below Nos. 327 to 331, Figs. S, V, OL, HY, O) 327

△ Flowers not in crowded groups, or flowers distributed more or less along the length of the stalk; flowers, or groups of flowers, intermingled with ordinary leaves (see further on Nos. 332 to 335, Figs. ME, GH, O, GA, AC) 332

327
(following on 326).

✠ Stems prostrate with upright shoots; leaves less than half a centimetre in width; shape an elongated oval (Fig. S). → Wild Thyme [*Thymus Serpyllum*]—medicinal. ❀ (Family *Labiatæ*.) There is a related species often cultivated in gardens, Common Thyme [*Thymus vulgaris*], which grows wild in the region of the Mediterranean, and which is an edible plant.

✠ Plant not having these characteristics together 328

328
(following on 327).

○ Flowers intermingled with broad, membranous scales green and fringed, ending abruptly in a point and encircling the stem at their base (Fig. B; Fig. V represents a flowering stem). → Common Self-heal [*Prunella vulgaris*]—medicinal. ❀ —Represented in colour: 6, Plate 43. (Family *Labiatæ*.)

○ Plant not having these characteristics 329

329
(following on 328).

— Leaves having a strong aromatic odour when rubbed between the fingers 330

— Leaves without any special aromatic odour (Figs. CA and OL represent a flower (enlarged) and a flowering stem). → Cooking Valerianella (Corn-salad, Lamb's Lettuce) [*Valerianella olitoria*]—food plant.[1]—Represented in colour: 4, Plate 27. (Family *Valerianaceæ*.)

330
(following on 329).

✻ Flowers blue; leaves narrow and elongated (Fig. HY); without, or almost without, hairs. → Officinal Hyssop [*Hyssopus officinalis*]—medicinal; condiment. ❀ (Family *Labiatæ*.)

✻ Flowers lilac, or of a pinkish lilac; leaves oval or rounded 331

---

[1] For the various species of *Valerianella* reference should be made to more comprehensive Floras.

331
(following on 330).

= Flowers surrounded by numerous deep red scales; leaves very slightly toothed or not at all (Figs. OR and O); each flower is almost two-lipped. → Common Marjoram [*Origanum vulgare*]—medicinal. ❀ —Represented in colour: 3, Plate 43. (Family *Labiatæ*.)

= Flowers **not** surrounded by numerous dark red scales; leaves more or less toothed along their edges; each flower almost regular (Fig. M). → Mint [*Mentha*].—For the principal kinds of Mints [*Mentha*] refer back to No. ... 169

332
(following on 326).

⊖ Flowering stems ending in leaves; each flower more than 2 centimetres in length; flowers white, MM spotted with crimson on the under lip (Figs. ME and MM). → Balm-leaved Melittis (Bastard Balm) [*Melittis melissophyllum*]—medicinal.—Represented in colour: 3, Plate 44. (Family *Labiatæ*.)

⊖ Flowering stems ending in leaves; each flower less than 2 centimetres in length; plant with prostrate stems becoming upright; leaves rounded and reversedly heart-shaped, each one springing from a somewhat elongated stalk (Fig. GH). → Ivy-leaved Nepeta (Ground Ivy, Ale-hoof) [*Nepeta hederacea*]—medicinal. ❀ —Represented in colour: 4, Plate 44. (Family *Labiatæ*.)

⊖ Plants not having these characteristics 333

333
(following on 332).

✕ Flowers white or bluish with violet streaks and yellow inside; with E two very unequal lips (Fig. E); leaves oval (Fig. O) and sharply toothed. → Common Eyebright [*Euphrasia officinalis*]—medicinal. (Family *Scrophulariaceæ*.)

✕ Flowers bluish, lilac, or purplish; leaves either not sharply toothed, or not toothed at all 334

334
(following on 333).

☐ Flowers attached singly in the axil of the leaves (Fig. GA); corolla has a bent tube. → Greater Skull-cap [*Scutellaria galericulata*]—medicinal.[1]

☐ Flowers grouped in pairs or more than two together in the axil of the leaf. (Family *Labiatæ*.)......... 335

---

[1] For the various species of Skull-cap [*Scutellaria*] reference should be made to more comprehensive Floras.

335
(following on 334).

✻ ✻ Each flower almost regular; flowers crowded together in large numbers. → Mint [*Mentha*].—Refer back to No. 169

✻ ✻ Each flower very irregular, and with 2 well-defined lips (Fig. ACI); flowers grouped together in twos or threes (Fig. AC). → Basil Calamint (Basil Thyme) [*Calamintha Acinos*] (Family *Labiatæ*.)

336
(following on 324).

✻ Stem hairy on two sides only (Fig. AR); plant producing at its base creeping branches without flowers (Fig. RE). → Creeping Bugle (Common Bugle) [*Ajuga reptans*]. ✿ — Represented in colour: 2, Plate 45. (Family *Labiatæ*.)

✻ Stem hairy on all 4 sides (Fig. G); plant not producing at its base creeping branches without flowers. → Genevan Bugle [*Ajuga genevensis*].—Represented in colour: 1, Plate 45. (Family *Labiatæ*.)

337
(following on 324).

⌒ Each flower has 4 lobes more or less spread out (Fig. VT) above a very short tube. → Speedwell [*Veronica*].—For the principal kinds of Speedwell [*Veronica*] refer back to No. 315

⌒ Each flower has 5 lobes 338

338
(following on 337).

• Leaves more or less divided (Fig. VER), except those at the top of the stems (Fig. VE); flowers in long tapering spikes; corolla has 5 lobes well spread out (Fig. V). → Officinal Vervain (Common Vervain) [*Verbena officinalis*].—Represented in colour: 5, Plate 45. (Family *Verbenaceæ*.)

• Leaves not divided; flowers arranged in crowded groups 339

339
(following on 338).

⊕ Leaves with a strong aromatic odour when rubbed between the fingers. → Mint [*Mentha*].—Refer back to No. 169

⊕ Leaves without any aromatic odour; flowers crowded in little groups at the tops of the upper stalks (Fig. OL). → Cooking Valerianella (Corn-salad, Lamb's Lettuce) [*Valerianella olitoria*]—food plant.[1]—Represented in colour: 4, Plate 27. (Family *Valerianaceæ*.)

---

[1] For the various species of *Valerianella* reference should be made to more comprehensive Floras.

✠ Flowers butterfly-like, that is to say, with **5** unequal petals : one upper broader petal (*e* in the figures below), two petals equal to one another, placed right and left (*a, a* in the figures below), and two lower petals (*cc*) united together in the form of the underpart of a boat (Fig. PS below, on the right, shows the petals of a *papilionaceous* or butterfly-like corolla detached) ; the two lower petals are less commonly rolled together on themselves (Fig. PH) 341

340 (following on 297).

✠ Flowers not butterfly-like 349

The Figs. V, A, D, AG show some examples of flowers which are not papilionaceous.

§ Leaves ending in a thread rolled up or branched (see Figs. P and V below) 342

341 (following on 340).

§ Leaves ending in a short thread, neither rolled up nor branched (Fig. OT). → Tuberous Bitter-vetch (Wood Pea, Cormeille) [*Orobus tuberosus*].—Represented in colour : 4, Plate 16. (Family *Leguminosæ*.)

§ Leaves not ending in a thread and with distinct leaflets 345

§ Leaves not ending in a thread and deeply divided but without distinct leaflets (see Fig. AN under No. 351) 351

342 (following on 341).

+ Flowers less than half a centimetre (½ inch) long.. 343
+ Flowers more than half a centimetre long 344

343 (following on 342).

—• The two small leaves attached to the stem right and left of the base of each leaf near the middle part of the stem are shaped like an arrow-head. → Four - seeded Vetch (Smooth Tare) [*Vicia tetrasperma*] (Fig. TE)—fodder plant. (Family *Leguminosæ*.)

—• The two small leaves attached to the stem at the base of each leaf near the middle part of the stem are oval and not toothed. → Lentil Vetch [*Vicia Lens*] (Fig. LE)—food plant. (Family *Leguminosæ*.)

344
(following on 342).

△ The two leaflets at the base of each leaf are larger than the leaflets of the leaf (Fig. P); flowers of a purplish red. → Field Pea [*Pisum arvense*]—fodder plant. 🌸 (Family *Leguminosæ*.)

△ The two leaflets at the base of each leaf are smaller than the leaflets of the leaf (Fig. V, for example). → Vetch [*Vicia*].—For the chief kinds of Vetch [*Vicia*] refer back to No. 215

345
(following on 341).

⚥ Leaves with 3 leaflets (not counting the two little leaflets attached to the stem at the base of the leaf) 346

⚥ Leaves with 5 to 9 leaflets arranged like a fan (Fig. H). → Variable Lupine [*Lupinus varius*]—food plant. (Family *Leguminosæ*.)

⚥ Leaves with 11 to 25 leaflets (except the leaves on the upper part of the stem); plant with hanging or spreading stems; flowers in a coronet (Fig. V). → Variegated Coronilla [*Coronilla varia*]—medicinal. 🌸 —Represented in colour: 1, Plate 16. (Family *Leguminosæ*.)

346
(following on 345).

○ Stems twisting themselves round other plants; each flower more than a centimetre (⅖ inch) across, with petals rolled up over one another (Fig. P); leaves with broad leaflets acute at their tips (Fig. H). → Common Haricot (French Bean, Haricot Bean) [*Phaseolus vulgaris*]—food plant. 🌸 —Represented in colour (with white flowers): 2, Plate 14. (Family *Leguminosæ*.)

○ Plant not having these characteristics 347

347
(following on 346).

— Flowers violet or bluish, less commonly with a mixture of yellow; at the base of the short stalk, which supports each flower, is a very small narrow and acute scale (Fig. SA). → Cultivated Medick (Lucerne) [*Medicago sativa*]—fodder plant. 🌸 — Represented in colour: 2, Plate 15. (Family *Leguminosæ*.)

— Flowers of a lilac pink or a pale lilac 348

348
(following on 347).

• The collection of flowers form a downy head distinctly longer than it is broad (Fig. A); leaves with narrow leaflets. → Field Trefoil (Hare's-foot Trefoil) [*Trifolium arvense*]. (Family *Leguminosæ*.)

• The collection of flowers does not form a downy head and is almost round (Fig. TP); leaves with oval leaflets. → Meadow Trefoil (Red Clover) [*Trifolium pratense*] —fodder plant.—Represented in colour: 4, Plate 14. (Family *Leguminosæ*.)

349
(following on 340).

+ Flowers **in a compound umbel** (Fig. ANG), that is to say, that the stalks which bear the groups of flowers all start exactly from the same point, like the spokes which support an umbrella, and that these principal *rays* them-  selves support secondary rays, which also start all from one point and each end in a flower; the stems are hollow inside and have, when broken, the well-known smell of Angelica. → **Wood Angelica** [*Angelica sylvestris*]—medicinal. ✿ —Represented in colour: 1, Plate 25. (Family *Umbelliferæ*.)

+ Flowers **not in a compound umbel** **350**

350
(following on 349).

○ Flowers **almost regular**, with 5 lobes (Fig. V) less than half a centimetre across; leaves more or less divided (Figs. VE, VER). → **Officinal Vervain** (Common Vervain) [*Verbena officinalis*]—medicinal. ✿ —Represented in colour: 5, Plate 45. (Family *Verbenaceæ*.)

○ Flowers **almost regular, with 4 lobes** (Fig. VT) less than half a centimetre across; leaves with 3 lobes (Fig. TR). → **Finger-leaved Speedwell** [*Veronica triphyllos*]. (Family *Scrophulariaceæ*.)

○ Flowers **very irregular** (see Figs. D and A, below, under No. 351) more than a centimetre across........ **351**

351
(following on 350).

— Flower **prolonged at its base** by a long horn or tube closed at the end (Fig. D); leaves with very narrow and elongated lobes (Fig. DE). → **Consound Larkspur** [*Delphinium Consolida*]—medicinal. ✿ —Represented in colour: 3, Plate 3. (Family *Ranunculaceæ*.)

— Flower **not prolonged at its base** by a long horn or closed tube; upper piece of the flower in the form of a hood (Fig. A); leaves with veins arranged like a fan (Fig. AN). → **Monkshood Aconite** (Monk's - hood, Wolf's - bane) [*Aconitum Napellus*] — poisonous; medicinal. ✿ —Represented in colour: 1, Plate 3. (Family *Ranunculaceæ*.)

352
(following on 228).

✳ Group of flowers enclosed in a great horn (Fig. MAC), green, yellowish, or of a whitish green, sometimes purplish at its edges; this group of flowers end in a sort of purple club; the flowers are reduced to very small yellowish, reddish, or purplish masses crowded together in the interior of the horn. → Spotted Arum (Lord-and-Ladies, Cuckoopint) [*Arum maculatum*]—medicinal.—Represented in colour: 2 and 2 *bis*, Plate 57. (Family *Araceæ*.)

✳ Plant not having all the above-mentioned characteristics together 353

353
(following on 352).

= Leaves attached to the stem by a **sheath which is split length-wise** down the side opposite to the leaf (*ft*, Fig. G); stem more or less cylindric (*tt*, Fig. G); the leaf F bears a little tongue (*lg*, Fig. G) or a row of special hairs at the spot where it adjoins the stem above the sheath of the leaf 1069

= Leaves attached to the stem by a sheath which is **not split length-wise** (*f, g,* Fig. C); stem 3 angled, at least for a part of its length; the leaf (Fig. C) has neither tongue nor row of special hairs at the spot where it approaches the stem above the sheath of the leaf 1062

354
(following on 4).

⊖ Flowers **in a compound umbel**, that is to say, that all the stalks that bear the groups of flowers start exactly from one and the same point, like the spokes which support an umbrella, and themselves bear stalks starting from one point and each ending in a flower (see the figures below) 374

Fig. C shows the construction of a compound umbel: IO, the principal umbel bearing the principal rays; *o, i* or *bf*, secondary umbels bearing the secondary rays. Figs. PS, B, and F show examples of flowers arranged in compound umbels.

⊖ Flowers **not** in a compound umbel 355

No. 355

× Each flower regular, that is to say, that the similar parts of the flower which are yellow or yellowish in colour are regularly arranged round the centre of the flower, and are obviously equal to one another 356

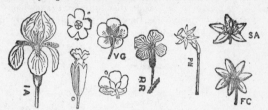

The above figures represent examples of regular flowers.

× Each flower irregular, that is to say, that the flowers are not arranged as described above 455

N.B.—Those flowers which only have a right half similar to the left half must not be looked upon as regular.

355
(follow-
ing on
354).

The above figures represent some examples of irregular flowers.

× Each flower reduced to little scales which are yellow or yellowish, or flowers enclosed in a horn (Fig. MAC) more than 6 centimetres (2¼ inches) long and not yellow 502

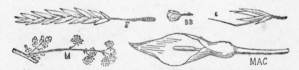

The above figures represent some examples of flowers, or groups of flowers, reduced to scales.

N.B.—If there is any doubt as to a flower being regular or irregular, as, for example, the flower represented by Fig. ML, either one or the other question may be followed up and the name of the flower will in either case be reached.   There may also be some doubt as between flowers reduced to scales and regular flowers, because some flowers, although regular, are made up of membranous parts and so seem reduced to scales, as, for example, the flower represented in Fig. SI, or the group of flowers in Fig. M above.   Here again either question may be chosen and in either case the name of the plant will be reached.

95

☐ Leaves **compound;** that is to say, that the leaf, as a whole, is made up by the union of secondary leaves, known as *leaflets*, each of which is often mistaken for a leaf; the compound leaf, as a whole, is attached to the stem by its base or by a stalk that bears all the leaflets; the base of a compound leaf is never situated precisely in the axil of another leaf **416**

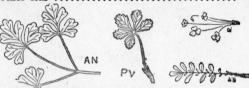

The above figures represent some examples of compound leaves.

☐ Leaves **deeply divided** (except sometimes those leaves that are quite at the upper part of the stems); that is to say, that each leaf is, as it were, cut to an extent which is more than half the breadth of the leaf **416**

356
(following on 355).

The above figures represent examples of divided leaves.

☐ Leaves **simple;** that is to say, either not cut to the extent of more than half the breadth of the leaf, or merely edged with teeth, or even without teeth on their edges .. **357**

The above figures represent examples of simple leaves.

☐ Leaves **not developed, or reduced to scales** (see the figures under Nos. 359 and 360) **359**

N.B.—It is of no consequence if there is a doubt as between compound and deeply divided leaves.
If there is any hesitation as between deeply divided and simple leaves (as, for example, Fig. A) either question may be followed up, and in either case the name of the plant will be reached. So, **too,** if the plant has both simple and compound or deeply divided **leaves** (in addition to the few simple leaves which may occur at the top of the flowering stems).

✱ ✱ **Leaves opposite** (except sometimes at the upper part
of the stems or branches); that is to say, leaves
arranged in pairs, attached to the stem at the same
level, on opposite sides of it 397

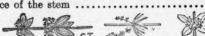

The above figures represent examples of opposite leaves.

N.B.—There often occur in the axils of opposite leaves little
leafy shoots which might be supposed to be leaves grouped in a
large number at the upper part of the stem, and not merely in an
opposite pair ; but on careful examination of the base of such a
group of leaves, the two opposite leaves will be readily distinguished.

✱ ✱ **Leaves whorled;** that is to say, leaves attached to
the stem, 3, 4, 5 or even more together at the same
level, and arranged regularly round the whole circumference of the stem 397

The above figures represent examples of whorled leaves.

✱ ✱ **Leaves alternate;** that is to say, leaves attached to
the stem one by one at different levels 358

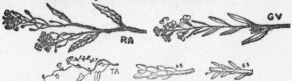

357
follow-
ing on
356).

The above figures represent plants with alternate leaves.

✱ ✱ **Leaves grouped;** that is to
say, leaves attached to the stem
2 or more together at the same
level, but arranged, at that
level, on one side of the stem
only (example : Fig. BE) ....  .. 353

✱ ✱ **Leaves all at the base of the plant** 358

Figs. VI and P represent examples of plants with all their leaves
at the base.

N.B.—If the plant has alternate and opposite leaves at the same
time (without counting those at the upper part of the stem), or has
both alternate and whorled leaves, either question may be followed
up, and in either case the name of the plant will be reached.

⊙ Each flower with petals separated from one another **down to their bases**; that is to say, that one of the petals (or parts coloured yellow or yellowish) can be removed down to its base without tearing the others. This refers to those parts of the flower which, collectively, make up the corolla (or coloured structure surrounding the little threads and other organs in the centre of the flower); when the flower fades each petal (or coloured piece) falls off or withers separately [1] 361

358 *(following on 357).*

Fig. HE represents a flower with separate petals, its 5 petals being shown detached in Fig. HL. The other figures represent examples of flowers with separate petals as seen from above, from the side and from below.

⊙ Each flower with petals united to one another, **at least at the base**; that is to say, that on trying to detach one of the yellow or yellowish parts of the flower, one is obliged to tear the corolla, at least at its base; when the flower fades the corolla falls off, or withers, all in one piece 386

The petals are united together at very different heights in different flowers. Fig. ML represents the corolla of a flower with the petals very slightly united together at the base. In the flowers represented in the other figures, the corolla is made up of petals united together in a tube of greater or less length, except at their tips where they form spreading or erect lobes.

359 *(following on 356).*

Climbing plant, twisted round other plants to which it attachs itself by little suckers (Fig. CS); stems very slender, of a yellow colour; plant parasitic on Lucerne; flowers scented. → Scented Dodder (Lucerne Dodder) [*Cuscuta suaveolens*]—harmful to crops. (Family *Convolvulaceæ*.)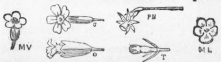

Plant not climbing 360

---

[1] In most flowers there is, outside the corolla, another covering to the flower, generally green, which is known as the *calyx* and encloses the base of the corolla. In other flowers it is difficult to distinguish the calyx and corolla, which are more or less blended into a single floral envelope (Figs. L, PN, for example). Lastly, in other flowers there is in reality only a single floral envelope, which is coloured yellow or yellowish like a corolla. Under the names petal and corolla we shall here include those yellow or yellowish pieces, which immediately surround the little threads or other organs which occupy the centre of the flower.

360
(follow-ing on 359).

＊ Leaves yellowish; flowers yellow-ish, all turned towards one side (Fig. M); flowering stem curved at its top. → Pine Bird's-nest (Fir-rape) [*Monotropa Hypopitys*]. (Family *Ericaceæ*.)

＊ Leaves green; flowers yellow, solitary at the top of the stem (Fig. F) (in reality the flower is a composite one made up of a number of very little flowers without stalks and crowded together). → Colt's-foot Tussilago (Colt's-foot) [*Tussilago Farfara*] — medicinal. ❀ —Represented in colour : 2, Plate 31. (Family *Compositæ*.)

361
(follow-ing on 358).

⊕ Plant which yields a white milk 396

⊕ Plant without white milk 362

362
(follow-ing on 361).

✣ Plant fleshy, with thick, fleshy, juicy leaves.... 384

✣ Plant not fleshy 363

363
(follow-ing on 362).

§ Each yellow petal has at its base a little yellow scale (*e*, Fig. R) or a little hollow (remove care-fully one of the petals and examine the base of it on the side turned towards the centre of the flower). → Crowfoot (Buttercup) [*Ranunculus*].[1]—For the chief kinds of Buttercups [*Ranunculus*] go on to No. 442

§ No little yellow scale nor little hollow at the inside of the base of the petals 364

364
(follow-ing on 363).

—• Each flower with 4 petals (that is to say, 4 parts coloured yellow or yellowish) 365

—• Each flower with 5 petals (that is to say, 5 parts coloured yellow or yellowish) 378

—• Each flower with more than 5 petals (or parts coloured yellow or yellowish) or with a number of little yellow tubes 380

365
(follow-ing on 364).

△ There is a small leaf on the stem at the point where each flower is attached; yellow flower - buds pointed at the tip (Fig. OB). → Biennial Œnothera (Evening Primrose) [*Œnothera biennis*] — ornamental. ❀ — Represented in colour : 2, Plate 21. (Family *Onagraceæ*.)

△ There is no small leaf on the stem at the point where each flower is attached 366

---

[1] For further details as to the various species of Crowfoot [*Ranunculus*] reference should be made to more comprehensive Floras.

366
(following on 365).

✠ Leaves without hairs (examine with a lens) 367
✠ Leaves with hairs 370

367
(following on 366).

○ Each flower more than 12 millimetres across when it is fully open 368
○ Each flower less than 12 millimetres across when fully open 369

368
(following on 367).

— Leaves all narrowing to the base into a very short stalk (Figs. GV, G); flowers sweet-scented. → Common Wallflower (Gilliflower) [*Cheiranthus Cheiri*] —ornamental. ✿ —Represented in colour: 1, Plate 6. (Family *Cruciferæ*.)—A variety of this plant with the flowers veined and variegated with brown is commonly grown for ornament.

— Plant not having both these two characteristics.. 373

369
(following on 367).

✶ Leaves embracing the stem by means of two narrow ear-like lobes (Fig. P); plant growing in dry spots. → Dyers' Woad [*Isatis tinctoria*]—industrial. ✿ (Family *Cruciferæ*.)

✶ Leaves in the middle region of the stem not embracing the stem by two narrow ear-like lobes (Figs. RA and AM);

plant growing in wet places. → Amphibious Yellow-cress [*Armoracia amphibia*]. (Family *Cruciferæ*.)

370
(following on 366).

= Flowers yellow or yellowish brown, sweet-scented; with leaves neither divided nor toothed (Fig. GV); each flower more than 2 centimetres across when fully open. → Common Wallflower (Gilliflower) [*Cheiranthus Cheiri*]—ornamental. ✿ —Represented in colour: 1, Plate 6. (Family *Cruciferæ*.)—A variety of this plant with flowers veined and variegated with brown is grown for ornament.

= Plant not having all these three characteristics.. 371

371
(following on 370).

⊖ Flowers yellowish, turning white as they fade; flowers less than 3 millimetres across; leaves without any teeth; plant with small leaves (Fig. AC), all covered with little star-shaped hairs (examine with the lens). → **Yellow Alysson** [*Alyssum calycinum*]. (Family *Cruciferæ*.)

⊖ Flowers yellowish veined with violet (Fig. RR). → **Wild Radish (White Charlock)** [*Raphanus Raphanistrum*]. 🌸 (Family *Cruciferæ*.)

⊖ Flowers yellow **372**

372
(following on 371).

× The four small green or yellowish parts (calyx) which surround the base of each flower are spreading when the flower is fully out (Fig. AR).—Go on to No. **436**

× The four small green parts of the calyx are always erect (Fig. ES); none of the leaves are divided (Fig. VF). → **Worm-seed Treacle-mustard** [*Erysimum cheiranthoides*]. 🌸 (Family *Cruciferæ*.)

373
(following on 368).

☐ The four small green or yellowish parts (calyx) which immediately surround the base of flower are spreading when the flower is fully out (Fig. AR); leaves on the middle of the stem not divided and embracing the stem at their base (Fig. CN). → **Rape Cabbage (Cole-seed)** [*Brassica Napus*]—food plant. 🌸 (Family *Cruciferæ*.)—A variety of this plant is also cultivated, under the name of Colza, for industrial purposes.

☐ The four green or yellowish parts are erect (Fig. LI).—Go on to No..... **433**

374
(following on 354).

✱ ✱ Leaves neither divided nor toothed (Fig. F); not yielding white milk when the stem is cut. → **Sickle-leaved Buplever or Hare's-ear** [*Bupleurum falcatum*]—medicinal. 🌸 (Family *Umbelliferæ*.)

✱ ✱ Leaves not divided; yielding white milk when the stem is cut **706**

✱ ✱ Leaves deeply divided (see Figs. PC, PA, AF, SI, under Nos. 375, 376, and 377) **375**

375
(following on 374).

⊙ Plant with the well-known smell of parsley; flowers of a yellowish green; leaves glossy with lobes divided in threes (Fig. PC). → **Cultivated Parsley** [*Petroselinum sativum*]—condiment; medicinal. (Family *Umbelliferæ*.)

⊙ Plant not having these characteristics **376**

376
(following on 375).

◇ Leaves with divisions the broadest of which are at least a centimetre across; with divisions arranged in two rows opposite one another (Fig. PA). → Cultivated Parsnip [*Pastinaca sativa*]—food plant. 🌸 — Represented in colour: 3, Plate 24. (Family *Umbelliferæ*.)

◇ Leaves with divisions, the broadest of which are less than half a centimetre across, the divisions being themselves divided (see Figs. AF and SI, below, under No. 377.................................. 377

377
(following on 376).

• Divisions of the leaves less than 2 millimetres across, forming elongated threads (Fig. AF). → Common Fennel [*Fœniculum officinale*]—medicinal; condiment. 🌸 —Represented in colour: 1 and 1 *bis*, Plate 24. (Family *Umbelliferæ*.)

• Divisions of the leaves more than 2 millimetres across, not being more than 8 times as long as they are broad (Fig. SI). → Yellow Pepper-Saxifrage (Sulphur-wort) [*Silaus flavescens*]. (Family *Umbelliferæ*.)

378
(following on 364).

⊕ On looking at the flower from below, 5 very small leaves, or green, greenish, or brownish scales, will be seen, 3 larger and 2 smaller, placed immediately below the 5 yellow petals (Fig. VG; Fig. V represents the calyx only, seen from below). → Rock-rose [*Helianthemum*].—For the chief kinds of Rock-rose [*Helianthemum*] go on to No. 379

⊕ On looking at the flower from below, no small leaf or scale is to be seen immediately below the 5 yellow parts of the flower (Fig. PP). → Marsh Caltha (Marsh Marigold, Water-blobs, King-cups) [*Caltha palustris*] — poisonous. 🌸 —Represented in colour: 3, Plate 2. (Family *Ranunculaceæ*.)

379
(following on 378).

⊬ Flowers yellow with a brown spot on each petal (Fig. G); there is no little leaf at the base of the stalk of each flower (Fig. G). → Spotted Rock-rose [*Helianthemum guttatum*]. 🌸 (Family *Cistaceæ*.)

⊬ Flowers yellow without a brown spot (Fig. HE); there is a little leaf at the base of the stalk of each flower (Fig. VUL). → Common Rock-rose [*Helianthemum vulgare*]—medicinal.—Represented in colour: 1, Plate 7. (Family *Cistaceæ*.)

380
(following on 364).

§ Similar parts of the flower arranged in 3's (Fig. IP) ; leaves acute with unbranched veins. → **Acorus-like Iris** (Corn Flag, Yellow Iris) [*Iris Pseudacorus*]—medicinal. — Represented in colour : 5, Plate 54. (Family *Iridaceæ*.)

§ Flower with 6 yellowish parts; branches slender, green, in groups, resembling **very narrow leaves** 557

§ Plant **not having the above characteristics** 381

381
(following on 380).

+ Leaves cylindrical like the stems (Fig. J) ; flowers **of a dry texture**. → **Spreading Rush** (Rush, Soft Rush) [*Juncus effusus*]—industrial.—Represented in colour : 4, Plate 57. (Family *Juncaceæ*.)

+ Leaves **not cylindrical** like the stems 382

382
(following on 381).

—• Plant **submerged in water**, with large floating leaves ; flowers solitary, opening at the surface of the water (Fig. NL represents the flower cut lengthwise). → **Yellow Nuphar** (Yellow Water-lily, Brandy-bottle) [*Nuphar luteum*].—Represented in colour : 1, 1 *bis* and 1 *ter*, Plate 4. (Family *Nymphæaceæ*.)

—• Plant **not submerged** in water 383

383
(following on 382).

△ Each flower with 6 to 9 yellow petals surrounded at their base by 3 small leaves or greenish or yellowish scales (Fig. FC) ; plant without hairs, with leaves reversedly heart-shaped (Fig. F). → **Fig-wort Crowfoot** (Lesser Celandine, Figwort, Pilewort) [*Ranunculus Ficaria*]—poisonous; medicinal.—Represented in colour : 2, Plate 2. (Family *Ranunculaceæ*.)

△ Each flower with 6 to 9 petals but without 3 small leaves or greenish or yellowish scales beneath 378

△ Each flower apparently having **numerous petals** or numerous little yellow tubes. On examining the flower carefully, it is seen to be in reality a composite flower made up of numerous little strap-shaped or tubular flowers, the whole surrounded by a large number of little leaves or scales forming a collarette.—Go on to No. 828

384
(following on 362).

✠ Lower leaves in **opposite** pairs, more or less flat ; leaves on the twigs alternate or grouped at the top of the twigs (Fig. O). → **Cooking Purslane** [*Portulaca oleracea*]— food plant ; medicinal. (Family *Portulacaceæ*.)

✠ Leaves all **alternate**; leaves in the form of oval grains or of cylinders ; petals pointed at their tips 385

385
(following on 384).

○ Leaves in the shape of grains rounded at their tips (Fig. AC); each flower with 4 or 5 petals (Fig. SA). → Biting Stonecrop (Wall - Pepper) [*Sedum acre*]—poisonous; medicinal. —Represented in colour: 3, Plate 22. (Family *Crassulaceæ*.)

○ Leaves cylindrical, pointed at their tips (Fig. R); each flower generally with 6, 7, or 8 petals (Fig. SR). → Recurved Stonecrop [*Sedum reflexum*]—medicinal.—Represented in colour: 2, Plate 22. (Family *Crassulaceæ*.)

386
(following on 358).

— Leaves all at the base of the plant **387**
— Leaves arranged along the stem **391**

387
(following on 386).

✻ Each flower with 5 yellow lobes (Figs. O and G); stalks of the flowers all starting from the same point; leaves with branch-veins. → Primroses [*Primula*].[1]—For the chief kinds of Primrose [*Primula*] go on to No. **388**

✻ Each flower with 6 yellow or yellowish parts **390**

388
(following on 387).

⚌ Flowers of a deep yellow, often with orange spots; the greenish part which encloses the tube of the corolla is inflated, very open, with wide lobes (Fig. O). → Officinal Primula (Cowslip, Paigle) [*Primula officinalis*]—medicinal.—Represented in colour: 4, Plate 36. (Family *Primulaceæ*.)

⚌ Flowers of a pale yellow; the tube of the corolla is enclosed by a narrow calyx with pointed lobes (Fig. G) **389**

389
(following on 388).

⊖ Flowers with stalks all starting from the top of an elongated stem; leaves abruptly narrowed towards the base (Fig. E). → Taller Primula (Oxslip) [*Primula elatior*]. (Family *Primulaceæ*.)

⊖ Flowers with stalks all starting from the base of the plant; leaves tapering gradually towards the base (Fig. PG). → Common Primula (Primrose) [*Primula vulgaris*]—ornamental.—Represented in colour: 3, Plate 36. (Family *Primulaceæ*.)

[1] For further details as to the various species of *Primula* reference should be made to more comprehensive Floras.

× **Each flower more than 3 centimetres across;** within the six divisions of the flower (Fig. PN) is a sort of crown or cup of a less pale yellow with rounded or slightly marked lobes on its margin. → **False Narcis** (Daffodil, Lent Lily) [*Narcissus Pseudo-Narcissus*]—ornamental; poisonous; medicinal.—Represented in colour: 4, Plate 54. (Family *Amaryllidaceæ*.)

390 (following on 387).

× **Each flower less than 3 centimetres across;** there is neither crown nor cup within the six divisions of the flower; flowers in a cluster (Fig. PY); flowers yellowish or of a slightly greenish yellow. → **Mountain Star-of-Bethlehem** [*Ornithogalum pyrenaicum*]. (Family *Liliaceæ*.)

391 (following on 386).

☐ **Plant climbing,** either by means of long threads rolled up on themselves, or by twining themselves round other stems 395

☐ Plant not climbing 392

392 (following on 391).

✳ ✳ **Flowers yellowish veined with brown or blackish lines** arranged in a network; lower leaves deeply divided; plant covered with hairs, slightly sticky (Fig. HN represents the upper part of the plant). → **Black Henbane** [*Hyoscyamus niger*]—poisonous; medicinal.—Represented in colour: 1, Plate 40. (Family *Solanaceæ*.)

✳ ✳ Flowers not both yellowish and veined with brown or blackish lines 393

393 (following on 392).

⊙ **Each flower with 5 slightly unequal divisions** (Fig. ML); leaves prolonged at their bases down the stem. → **Great Mullein** (Hag-taper) [*Verbascum Thapsus*]—medicinal.—Represented in colour: 5, Plate 40.[1] (Family *Scrophulariaceæ*.)

⊙ Each flower with 5 equal divisions or 5 lobes equal to one another; leaves not prolonged down the stem at their bases 394

---

[1] For the various species of Mullein [*Verbascum*] reference should be made to more comprehensive Floras.

394
(following on 393).

♀ Flowers yellowish, with 5 greenish lobes outside; leaves very narrow (Figs. T and TH); flowers in clusters (Fig. TH). → **Prostrate Bastardtoadflax** [*Thesium humifusum*]. (Family *Santalaceæ*.)

♀ Flowers at first yellow, then yellowish, then pink, then blue (flowers of these various colours can be seen on the same plant); corolla with an elongated tube ending in 5 spreading lobes (Figs. MV and V). → **Colour-changing Myosote** [*Myosotis versicolor*]. (Family *Boraginaceæ*.)

♀ Flowers yellow; plant with both alternate and opposite leaves and sometimes whorls of 3 or 4 (Fig. VUL). → **Common Loosestrife** [*Lysimachia vulgaris*]. (Family *Primulaceæ*.)

395
(following on 391).

✱ Plant clinging to other plants by slender threads rolled upon themselves (Fig. BR); each flower with 5 divisions. → **Diœcious Bryony** (White Bryony) [*Bryonia dioica*]—poisonous; medicinal. 🌿—Represented in colour: 1 and 1 *bis*, Plate 21. (Family *Cucurbitaceæ*.)

✱ Plant twining itself round other plants by its stems (Fig. TA); each flower with **6 divisions**. → **Common Tamus** (Black Bryony) [*Tamus communis*]. (Family *Dioscoreaceæ*.)

396
(following on 361).

⊕ Each flower having apparently **numerous yellow petals**. On examining a flower carefully, it will be seen that it is in reality a composite flower made up of very numerous little strap-shaped flowers, the whole surrounded by a collarette of little leaves or scales.— Go on to No. 828

⊕ Each flower with 2 or 4 yellow or yellowish parts; the stalks that bear the groups of flowers, towards the upper part of the plant, all spring from the stem at the same point (see, for example, the figures below). → **Spurges** [*Euphorbia*].—Go on to No. 706

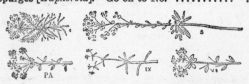

✠ Each flower with its petals separated from one another down to their bases; that is to say, that one of the petals (or parts of the flower coloured yellow or yellowish) can be removed down to its base without tearing the others. This refers to those parts of the flower which, collectively, make up the corolla or coloured structure surrounding the little threads and other organs occupying the centre of the flower; when the flower fades each petal (or coloured piece) falls off or withers separately [1] **398**

397
(following on 357).

Figs. FC, H, and T represent some examples of flowers with separated petals.

✠ Each flower with its petals united to one another, at least at their bases; that is to say, that in trying to detach one of the parts of the flower coloured yellow or yellowish, one is obliged to tear the corolla at least at its base; when the flower fades the corolla falls off, or withers, all in one piece (examples: Figs. MC, GM, and VC) **410**

398
(following on 397).

§ Plant climbing, with stems which twine themselves round other plants or round supports; leaves rough beneath, more or less deeply cut (Fig. H). → Rough Hop [*Humulus Lupulus*]—industrial; medicinal. 🌸 —Represented in colour: 1 and 1 *bis*, Plate 48. (Family *Urticaceæ*.)

§ Plant not climbing; leaves not cut **399**

399
(following on 398).

+ Plant attached to the branches of trees; stems hard, but green; twigs arranged in a succession of forkings, sometimes 3 or more; leaves not toothed (Fig. VI). → White Mistletoe [*Viscum album*]—medicinal. 🌸 —Represented in colour: 3 and 3 *bis*, Plate 26. (Family *Loranthaceæ*.)

+ Plant not attached to the branches of trees........ **400**

400
(following on 399).

—• Plant fleshy, with leaves thick, fleshy; flowers without stalks; leaves alternate or grouped on the shoots (Fig. O). → Cooking Purslane [*Portulaca oleracea*]—food plant; medicinal. (Family *Portulacaceæ*.)

—• Plant not fleshy; flowers borne by a stalk of greater or less length **401**

---

[1] In the majority of flowers there is, outside the corolla, another covering to the flower, generally green, known as the *calyx*, which surrounds the base of the corolla. In other flowers it is difficult to distinguish the calyx and corolla, which are more or less blended into a single floral envelope. In other flowers, again, there is really only a single floral envelope coloured yellow or yellowish like a corolla. Under the names petals and corolla we shall here include the pieces coloured yellow or yellowish, which immediately surround the little threads or other organs that occupy the centre of the flower.

△ Each flower with 4 petals or 4 divisions.......... 402

△ Each flower with 5 petals 404

401
(following on 400).

△ Each flower with 6 to 9 petals (Fig. FC, flower seen from below); plant without hairs, with leaves reversedly heart-shaped (Fig. F). → Fig-wort Crowfoot (Lesser Celandine, Figwort, Pilewort) [*Ranunculus Ficaria*]—poisonous; medicinal. — Represented in colour: 2, Plate 2. (Family *Ranunculaceæ*.)

△ Each flower with more than 9 petals or with numerous little yellow tubes. On examining the flower carefully, it is seen to be a composite flower made up of numerous little flowers either strap-shaped or tubular, the whole surrounded by a collarette of scales or small leaves.. 828

402
(following on 401).

✠ Leaves toothed or divided, attached one by one to the stem at different heights, seldom in opposite pairs (as in Fig. T); at the base of the leaves are two little leaflets attached to the stem (Fig. TO). → Tormentil Potentil (Tormentil) [*Potentilla Tormentilla*] — medicinal. — Represented in colour: 1, Plate 19. (Family *Rosaceæ*.)

✠ Leaves neither toothed nor divided, attached from 4 to 12 together at the same point on the stem, and arranged regularly round its whole circumference........ 403

403
(following on 402).

○ Leaves oval, attached in 4's at the same level on the stem (Figs. GC and CT); groups of flowers between the ordinary leaves. → Cross-wort Bedstraw [*Galium Cruciata*].— Represented in colour: 2, Plate 27. (Family *Rubiaceæ*.)

○ Leaves elongated and narrow, attached from 6 to 12 together at the same level on the stem (Fig. V); groups of flowers towards the top of the stem, above the ordinary leaves. → True Bedstraw (Lady's Bedstraw, Yellow Bedstraw) [*Galium verum*]—industrial; medicinal.—Represented in colour: 1, Plate 27. (Family *Rubiaceæ*.)

404
(following on 401).

— On examining a flower with care, it is seen that the petals are in reality united together at their bases (as in Fig. MC). → Loosestrife [*Lysimachia*].—Go on to No. 415

— Petals really separated from one another down to their bases 405

405
(following on 404).

✱ In looking at the flower from below, 5 very small leaves or green scales (calyx) are seen which are equal to one another; the yellow petals are edged with very small black glands (examine with the lens). → St. John's-wort [*Hypericum*].[1]—For the chief kinds of St. John's-wort [*Hypericum*] go on to No. 406

✱ In looking at the flower from below, 5 very small leaflets or greenish or brownish scales are seen, of which 3 are larger and 2 smaller (Fig. VG; Fig. P represents the calyx only); the yellow petals are not edged with very small black glands. → Rock-roses [*Helianthemum*].—For the chief kinds of Rock-roses [*Helianthemum*] refer back to No. 379

406
(following on 405).

= Flowers when fully open less than a centimetre across; stems more or less prostrate on the ground (Fig. HU). → Trailing St. John's-wort [*Hypericum humifusum*]. (Family *Hypericaceæ*.)

= Plant not having these characteristics together... 407

407
(following on 406).

⊖ Stems with 2 more or less projecting lines down their sides (Fig. PE shows the traces of these two lines as seen in a cross-section of the stem). On looking at the leaves against the light, it will be seen that they appear to be pierced with little holes; this appearance is due to little oil glands which are more transparent than the rest of the leaf. → Perforate St. John's-wort [*Hypericum perforatum*]—medicinal. — Represented in colour: 3, Plate 11. (Family *Hypericaceæ*.)

⊖ Stems with 4 more or less projecting lines down their sides (Figs. Q and T show the 4 lines as seen in a cross-section of the stem) 408

⊖ Stems without projecting lines down their sides.... 409

408
(following on 407).

✕ The yellow petals are covered with very small black glands (Fig. HQ, enlarged) (examine with the lens); stems with 4 slightly projecting lines. → Four-angled St. John's-wort [*Hypericum quadrangulum*]. (Family *Hypericaceæ*.)

✕ The yellow petals only have the very small black glands on their edges (Fig. TE, enlarged); stems with 4 very prominent flanges. → Four-winged St. John's-wort [*Hypericum tetrapterum*]. (Family *Hypericaceæ*.)

---

[1] For further details as to the various species of St. John's-wort [*Hypericum*] reference should be made to more comprehensive Floras.

409
(following on 407).

☐ Stems **without hairs;** leaves encircling the stem at their base (Fig. MO). → Mountain St. John's-wort (*Hypericum montanum*]. (Family *Hypericaceæ*.)

☐ Stems **hairy;** leaves not encircling the stem at their base (Fig. HI). → Hairy St. John's-wort [*Hypericum hirsutum*]. (Family *Hypericaceæ*.)

410
(following on 397).

✳ ✳ Leaves whorled; that is to say, attached in 3's or more to the stem at exactly the same level and arranged regularly around it (example: Fig. GA) **411**

✳ ✳ Leaves opposite; that is to say, attached in pairs to the stem at the same level and opposite to one another (example: Fig. DV). Sometimes the leaves are attached singly to the branches, or arranged in irregular groups (example: Fig. O, No. 413) **413**

N.B.—If the plant has both whorled and opposite leaves (as in Fig. VUL below) either question may be taken. In both cases the name of the plant will be reached.

411
(following on 410).

☉ Each flower more than 8 millimetres across, and having 5 yellow divisions; some of the leaves are whorled, others opposite (Fig. VUL). → **Common Loosestrife** [*Lysimachia vulgaris*]. (Family *Primulaceæ*.)

☉ Each flower less than 8 millimetres across; all the leaves whorled **412**

412
(following on 411).

♤ Flowers **yellowish white;** leaves edged with very small, sharp bristles (Fig. RP). → Wild Madder [*Rubia peregrina*]. —Dyers' Madder [*Rubia tinctorum*] is sometimes cultivated as an industrial plant. (Family *Rubiaceæ*.)

♤ Flowers **yellow;** leaves without small bristles.—Refer back to **403**

413
(following on 410).

• Plant **fleshy,** with thick, fleshy leaves, flowers having **no stalks;** leaves either alternate or grouped on the stems (Fig. O). → **Cooking Purslane** [*Portulaca oleracea*]— food plant; medicinal. (Family *Portulacaceæ*.)

• Plant slightly **fleshy, erect, grey-green,** without hairs; leaves united at their base; flowers **on stalks,** large, with pointed petals (Fig. P). → Perfoliate Yellow-wort [*Blackstonia perfoliata*]. (Family *Gentianaceæ*.)

• Plant not fleshy or grey-green **414**

414
(following on 413).

⊕ Flowers whitish yellow; leaves having their secondary veins recurved (Fig. D); stem with 2 lines of hairs along its length (see above Fig. DV at No. 410).
→ **Officinal Swallow-wort** (Tame-poison) [*Vincetoxicum officinale*]—poisonous; medicinal.—Represented in colour: 5, Plate 37. (Family *Asclepiadaceæ*.)

⊕ Flowers bright yellow. → **Loosestrife** [*Lysimachia*].[1]— For the principal kinds of Loosestrife see on to... **415**

415
(following on 414).

✠ Stems **upright;** some leaves opposite, others whorled, sometimes alternate (Fig. VUL). → **Common Loosestrife** [*Lysimachia vulgaris*]. (Family *Primulaceæ*.)

✠ Stems **prostrate;** all the leaves opposite; flowers **rather large, cup-shaped;** sepals reversedly heart-shaped (Fig. LN). → **Money-wort Loosestrife** (Herb Twopence, Creeping Jenny) [*Lysimachia Nummularia*]—medicinal.—Represented in colour: 5, Plate 36. (Family *Primulaceæ*.)

✠ Stems **prostrate;** leaves opposite; flowers small, star-shaped; sepals not reversedly heart-shaped (Fig. NE); leaves oval (Fig. NM). → **Wood Loosestrife** (Yellow Pimpernel) [*Lysimachia nemorum*]. (Family *Primulaceæ*.)

416
(following on 356).

§ Flowers **yellow** **422**

§ Flowers **yellowish,** veined with **brown, dark purple,** or **blackish** lines **417**

§ Flowers **yellowish,** not veined with **dark** lines, or **greenish yellow** or **whitish yellow** **418**

417
(following on 416).

+ Flowers more than a centimetre and a half (⅔ inch) across; corolla having its petals united at the base and coming away in one piece with 5 divisions (the top of the plant is shown in HN); leaves more or less divided. → **Black Henbane** [*Hyoscyamus niger*]—poisonous; medicinal.—Represented in colour: 1, Plate 40. (Family *Solanaceæ*.)

+ Flowers less than a centimetre and a half across; corolla having **4** petals separated from one another right down to the base (Fig. RR). → **Wild Radish** (White Charlock) [*Raphanus Raphanistrum*]. (Family *Cruciferæ*.)

---

[1] For the various species of Loosestrife [*Lysimachia*] reference should be made to more comprehensive Floras.

418
(following on 416).

—• Plant climbing, with twining stems; leaves arranged in pairs, and each one divided into 3 lobes (Fig. H) or 5 lobes. → **Rough Hop** [*Humulus Lupulus*]—industrial; medicinal. 🌸 —Represented in colour: 1, Plate 48. (Family *Urticaceœ*.)

—• Plant climbing, with leaves attached one by one to the stem; each flower having 5 petals 395

—• Plant not climbing 419

419
(following on 418).

△ Leaves divided into very numerous leaflets (example: Fig. CH). → **Meadow-rue** [*Thalictrum*].[1]—For the principal kinds of Meadow-rue [*Thalictrum*] go on to 421

△ Leaves not divided into numerous leaflets 420

420
(following on 419).

✠ On examining it with care, this flower will be seen in reality to be a composite flower made up of numerous exceedingly small tubular flowers, the whole surrounded by a collarette of very small scales.—Refer on to 828

✠ Flowers not composite (Fig. AU). → **Goldilocks Crowfoot** [*Ranunculus auricomus*]. (Family *Ranunculaceœ*.)

421
(following on 419).

○ Flowers upright and united in compact masses (Fig. F) at the top of the branch. → **Yellow Meadow-rue** (Meadow Rhubarb) [*Thalictrum flavum*].—Represented in colour: 1, Plate 2. (Family *Ranunculaceœ*.)

○ Flowers drooping and more or less isolated from one another even at the top of the branches (Fig. M). → **Lesser Meadow-rue** [*Thalictrum minus*]. (Family *Ranunculaceœ*.)

422
(following on 416).

— Each flower has **4 petals** (or 4 coloured parts), yellow 423

— Each flower has 5 to 10 petals (or 5 to 10 coloured parts), yellow 438

— Each flower has apparently more than 10 yellow petals or more than 10 parts shaped like tubes, yellow. On examining it with care, however, it will be seen that it is in reality a flower made up of a number of little flowers without stalks and shaped like little straps or tubes, the whole being surrounded by a collarette of tiny leaves or scales.—Refer on to 828

---

[1] For further details as to the various species of Meadow-rue [*Thalictrum*] reference should be made to more comprehensive Floras.

423
(following on 422).

✱ A yellow juice exudes from the stem when it is broken or cut; the 4 yellow petals are surrounded in the flower bud by 2 green or yellowish green parts which fall when the flower opens (Fig. C represents the top of a flowering stem). → **Greater Celandine** (Fellonwort) (*Chelidonium majus*]—poisonous; medicinal.—Represented in colour: 3, Plate 5. (Family *Papaveraceæ*.)

✱ No yellow juice exudes when the stem is broken... **424**

424
(following on 423).

= Leaves having 3, 5, or 7 leaflets arranged in fan shape; the 2 leaflets to right and left of the base of each leaf, but attached to the stem resemble more or less the leaflets belonging to the leaf. → **Tormentil Potentil** (Tormentil) [*Potentilla Tormentilla*]—medicinal.—Represented in colour: 1, Plate 19. (Family *Rosaceæ*.)

= Leaves not shaped like the preceding ones (see, for example, the shapes of the leaves represented in the figures of No. 427, or, again, in those of Nos. 433 and 435) **425**

425
(following on 424).

⊖ Each flower less than 6 millimetres in length **426**

⊖ Each flower more than 6 millimetres in length..... **429**

426
(following on 425).

✕ Leaves attached towards the middle of the stem have 11 or more than 11 divisions (the leaves above these have a smaller number of divisions)............ **427**

✕ Leaves attached towards middle of the stem have less than 11 divisions................................. **428**

427
(following on 426).

☐ Yellow petals shorter than the 4 little green or greenish parts of the calyx; stem erect from its base; leaves with very narrow divisions (Fig. SF). → **Flixweed Hedge-Mustard** [*Sisymbrium Sophia*]—medicinal. (Family *Cruciferæ*.)

☐ Yellow petals longer than the 4 little green or greenish parts of the calyx which surrounds them; stems prostrate, spreading, or erect; leaves divided, not very narrowly (Fig. CS). → **Wood Watercress** [*Nasturtium sylvestre*]—medicinal. (Family *Cruciferæ*.)

428
(following on 426).

✳ ✳ Stem hairy, rather rough; leaves midway up the stem have lobes projecting from their lower part (Fig. OFF; Fig. OF represents the top of a flowering stem). → Officinal Hedge-Mustard [*Sisymbrium officinale*]—medicinal. (Family *Cruciferæ*.)

✳ ✳ Stems hairless, or almost hairless; leaves pointed at the tip with outspread lobes (Fig. SI). → Rocket Hedge-Mustard (London Rocket) [*Sisymbrium Irio*]. (Family *Cruciferæ*.)

✳ ✳ Stems and leaves without hairs; leaves in the middle of the stem with a very large upper lobe rounded at the end 433

429
(following on 425).

☉ Leaves without hairs (examine with a magnifying glass) 430

☉ Leaves with hairs 436

430
(following on 429).

♡ The 4 green or yellowish parts (calyx) which surround the base of the 4 yellow petals spread out widely (Fig. AR) when the flower is fully open 431

♡ The 4 green or yellowish parts (calyx) which surround the base of the 4 yellow petals are upright and pressed against the lower part of the petals (Fig. LI) when the flower is fully open 433

431
(following on 430).

• Leaves towards the middle of the stem neither divided nor toothed (Fig. CN); the root having the well-known odour of the turnip. → Rape Cabbage (Coleseed) [*Brassica Napus*]—food plant. A variety of this plant is cultivated for industrial purposes under the name of Colza. (Family *Cruciferæ*.)

• Leaves towards the middle of the stem more or less divided; root with no smell of the turnip 432

432
(following on 431).

⊕ Leaves all very deeply divided (Fig. CS). → Wood Water-Cress [*Nasturtium sylvestre*]—medicinal. (Family *Cruciferæ*.)

⊕ Upper leaves toothed (Figs. AM, RA). → Amphibious

Yellow-cress [*Armoracia amphibia*]. (Family *Cruciferæ*.)

433
(following on 430).

⊞ Leaves clasping the stem at their base as if by two little ears (Fig. BAR). → Common Winter-Cress [*Barbarea vulgaris*]—medicinal. (Family *Cruciferæ*.)

⊞ Leaves not clasping the stem as if with two little ears, but sometimes half clasping it **434**

434
(following on 433).

§ The 4 green or yellowish parts which surround the petals (and which together form the calyx) remain upright even when the flower is fully open (Fig. ES). The leaves at the middle of the stem have no stalks. → Cooking Cabbage [*Brassica oleracea*]—food plant. 🌸 —Represented in colour: 6, Plate 5. (Family *Cruciferæ*.)

§ The 4 green or yellowish parts of the calyx spread out slightly when the flower is fully open (Fig. T); the leaves at the middle of the stem have a stalk more or less long **435**

435
(following on 434).

+ Flower-stalk 2 to 4 times the length of the full-blown flower (Fig. DTE). → Slender-leaved Wall-Rocket [*Diplotaxis tenuifolia*]. 🌸 (Family *Cruciferæ*.)

+ Flower-stalk shorter than the full-blown flower (Fig. NO). → Black Mustard [*Sinapis nigra*]—medicinal. (Family *Cruciferæ*.)

436
(following on 429).

—• Leaves all with stalks more or less long......... **435**

—• Upper leaves without stalks (see below Figs. MB and MC at No. 437) **437**

437
(following on 436).

△ The 4 green or yellowish parts that surround the petals are upright and pressed against the petals **417**

△ The 4 parts which are at the base of the petals are spread out; upper leaves more or less divided (Fig. MB). → White Mustard [*Sinapis alba*]—medicinal. 🌸 (Family *Cruciferæ*.)

△ The 4 parts which are at the base of the petals are spread out; upper leaves not divided (Fig. MC). → Field Mustard (Charlock) [*Sinapis arvensis*]—harmful to crops. 🌸 —Represented in colour: 5, Plate 5. (Family *Cruciferæ*.)

438
(following on 422).

⊬ Leaves having narrow and elongated divisions (Fig. A), each division being everywhere less than 3 millimetres across; flowers having 5 to 10 yellow petals without a little scale on the inside at the base of each petal. → **Annual Pheasants Eye** [*Adonis annua*].—Represented in colour (with red flowers) : 4, Plate 2. (Family *Ranunculaceæ*.)

⊬ Leaves not having the above characteristics together   **439**

439
(following on 438).

○ Flowers arranged in a long upright spike (Fig. AF) ; below the 5 yellow petals will be found a green part covered with little hooked spines (Fig. A represents the flower cut lengthwise) ; each leaf has numerous divisions in two opposite rows. → **Eupator's Agrimony** (Agrimony) [*Agrimonia Eupatoria*] — medicinal. — Represented in colour : 3, Plate 19. (Family *Rosaceæ*.)

○ Flowers not arranged in a long upright spike, and with no little hooked spines below the petals **440**

440
(following on 439).

— **A white milk exudes from the** stem when broken or cut ; each of the 5 yellow parts of the flower (Fig. P) has 5 little teeth at its tip (Fig. PH). In reality, what is called the flower is one made up of 5 little strap-shaped flowers. → **Wall Lettuce** (Ivy-leaved Lettuce) [*Lactuca muralis*]. (Family *Compositæ*.)

— **No white milk exudes when the stem is broken or cut ;** none of the yellow petals of the flower have 5 little teeth at their tips **441**

441
(following on 440).

✳ Each petal has at its base on the inside a small scale or little hollow (*e*, Fig. R). → **Crowfoot** [*Ranunculus*].[1]—For the principal kinds of Crowfoot [*Ranunculus*] see on to No. **442**

✳ Petals without a small scale or little hollow at their base on the inside **449**

442
(following on 441).

⊖ Leaves reversedly heart-shaped; flowers having 6 to 9 oval and elongated petals.—Refer to No. **383**

⊖ Leaves not in the least cut; flowers with petals more or less rounded **448**

⊖ Leaves more or less deeply cut **443**

---

[1] For further details as to the various species of Crowfoot [*Ranunculus*] reference should be made to more comprehensive Floras.

443
(following on 442).

= The 5 green or yellowish parts (which collectively form the calyx), and which enclose the bases of the 5 yellow petals, are erect or spreading, even when the flower is fully open (Fig. A) **444**

= The 5 green or yellowish parts of the calyx are bent downwards when the flower is fully open (Fig. BU) **447**

444
(following on 443).

× Flowers of a slightly greenish yellow, veined, not exceeding a centimetre in breadth; leaves with rather elongated divisions (Fig.  RAR). → **Field Crowfoot** (Hedgehog) [*Ranunculus arvensis*].—Represented in colour: 2, Plate 1. (Family *Ranunculaceæ*.)

× Flowers of a beautiful shining yellow **445**

445
(following on 444).

☐ The middle lobe of the leaf is itself borne by a small stalk which  is a prolongation of the stalk of the leaf (Fig. RP); stems often trailing and giving out roots (Fig. RE). → **Creeping Crowfoot** (Creeping Buttercup) [*Ranunculus repens*]. (Family *Ranunculaceæ*.)

☐ The middle lobe of the leaf is **not** borne by a small stalk **446**

446
(following on 445).

✱✱ Stems and leaves covered with more or less fine hairs; leaves with veins arranged like a fan (Figs.

ACR, RAC). → **Bitter Crowfoot** (Common Buttercup) [*Ranunculus acris*]. (Family *Ranunculaceæ*.)

✱✱ Stems and leaves without hairs, or almost without hairs. → **Goldilocks Crowfoot** [*Ranunculus auricomus*]. (Family *Ranunculaceæ*.)

E

447
(following on 443.)

⊙ Leaves **without hairs**; the 5 yellow petals (Fig. SC) are not longer, or are scarcely longer, than the 5 green parts that surround them. → **Celery-leaved Crowfoot** [*Ranunculus sceleratus*]—poisonous. (Family *Ranunculaceæ*.)

⊙ Leaves **with hairs**; the 5 yellow petals are distinctly longer than the 5 green or yellowish parts that surround them (Fig. BU). → **Bulbous Crowfoot** (Buttercup) [*Ranunculus bulbosus*]—poisonous; medicinal.—Represented in colour: 1, Plate 1. (Family *Ranunculaceæ*.)

448
(following on 442).

↬ Flowers less than a centimetre and a half (⅗ inch) across; the leaves that are attached about the middle of the stem taper into a tolerably long stalk (Fig. F). → **Lesser-Spearwort Crowfoot** [*Ranunculus Flammula*]—dangerous. (Family *Ranunculaceæ*.)

↬ Flowers more than a centimetre and a half across; the leaves that are attached about the middle of the stem have no stalk (Fig. L). → **Great-Spearwort Crowfoot** [*Ranunculus Lingua*]—dangerous. (Family *Ranunculaceæ*.)

449
(following on 441).

• Leaves with 3 leaflets **not toothed** (Fig. OS); petals yellow, whitish at their base (Fig. S represents the top of a flowering shoot). → **Upright Oxalis** [*Oxalis stricta*]. (Family *Oxalidaceæ*.)

• Leaves with leaflets **toothed** along their edges; petals yellow, not whitish, at their base 450

450
(following on 449).

⊕ Upper leaves not divided or with 3 lobes (Fig. B) (not counting the two leaflets attached to the stem and placed right and left of the base of each leaf); those attached lower down have 3 leaflets (Fig. B); the 5 green parts on which the 5 petals are attached have on their inside a narrow cottony edging (examine with the lens). → **Common Avens** (Herb Benet) [*Geum urbanum*] —medicinal. (Family *Rosaceæ*.)

⊕ Plant not having these characteristics together. → Potentils [*Potentilla*].[1]—For the chief kinds of Potentil [*Potentilla*] go on to No. 451

---

[1] For further details as to the various species of Potentil [*Potentilla*] reference should be made to more comprehensive Floras.

451
(following on 450).

✠ Each leaf with leaflets arranged in two rows, alternating with smaller leaflets (Fig. AN), green above and silky and silvery underneath. → **Goose-grass Potentil** (Silver-weed) [*Potentilla Anserina*]—medicinal. (Family *Rosaceæ*.)

✠ Each leaf with its leaflets arranged like a fan and all springing from the same point **452**

452
(following on 451).

§ Leaves white on the under surface (Fig. PA). → **Silver Potentil** [*Potentilla argentea*]. (Family *Rosaceæ*.)

§ Leaves green on both surfaces **453**

453
(following on 452).

+ The two leaflets which are attached to the stem, to the right and left of the base of the stalk of each leaf, are somewhat similar to the leaflets of the leaf (Figs. TO and T); stems more or less erect; each flower with 4 yellow petals, less commonly 5 petals. → **Tormentil Potentil** (Tormentil) [*Potentilla Tormentilla*] — medicinal. — Represented in colour: 1, Plate 19. (Family *Rosaceæ*.)

+ The two little leaflets which are attached to the stem, at the base of each leaf, are very different from the leaflets of the leaf (example: Fig. PR); stems prostrate on the ground, for at least a great part of their length **454**

454
(following on 453).

—• Leaves without hairs or only finely hairy on the under surface; stems giving out roots below at the points where the leaves are attached (Fig. RE and Fig. PR above). → **Creeping Potentil** (Cinquefoil) [*Potentilla reptans*] —medicinal.—Represented in colour: 2, Plate 19. (Family *Rosaceæ*.)

—• Leaves finely hairy on both surfaces (examine with the lens) and hairy along their edges; stems not giving out roots below at the points where the leaves are attached (Figs. V and AP); the stems are often less elongated than the one here represented. → **Spring Potentil** [*Potentilla verna*]. (Family *Rosaceæ*.)

△ Leaves **compound**; that is to say, that the leaf, as a whole, is made up of the union of secondary leaves, known as *leaflets*, each of which is often mistaken for a leaf; the whole compound leaf is attached to the stem by its base or by a stalk which bears all the leaflets. The base of the compound leaf or of its stalk is not situated just at the same point as and above another leaf 456

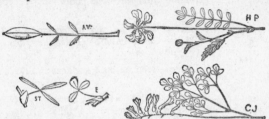

The above figures represent some examples of compound leaves or of plants with compound leaves.

455 *(following on 355).*

△ Leaves **deeply divided** (except sometimes the leaves quite at the upper part of the stem); that is to say, that each leaf is, as it were, cut to the extent of more than half its breadth 456

The above figures represent examples of plants with deeply divided leaves.

△ Leaves **simple**; that is to say, either not cut to the extent of more than half the width of the leaf, or merely edged with teeth, or even without teeth on their edges... 470

The above figures represent examples of simple leaves.

△ Leaves reduced to scales 470

N.B.—It is of no consequence if there is a doubt as between compound and deeply divided leaves, since in both cases the reference is to the same number (456). If there is any hesitation between deeply divided and simple leaves either question may be followed up, and in either case the name of the plant will be reached. So, too, if the plant has both simple and compound or divided leaves (not counting the few simple leaves which may occur quite at the top of the flowering stems).

456
(following on 455).

⚓ Flowers butterfly-like, that is to say, with 5 unequal petals, one upper larger petal, two petals equal to one another (*a, a*), placed right and left, and two lower petals (*cc*) united to one another in the form of a boat (see the figures below) 462

⚓ Flowers **not** butterfly-like 457

457
(following on 456).

◯ Leaves divided into very narrow elongated lobes (Fig. V); flower in the form of a mouth, with the lower lip inflated (Fig. UV); plant floating in water. → Common **Bladderwort** [*Utricularia vulgaris*]. (Family *Lentibulariaceæ*.)

◯ Flowers in elongated clusters, each flower less than 7 millimetres across; petals very much divided (examine with the lens) 497

◯ Plant **not** having the above-mentioned characteristics 458

458
(following on 457).

— Flowers almost regular, yellowish, veined with dark violet or brown; upper leaves often slightly divided (Fig. N).— Go on to No. 500

— Flowers **very irregular**, yellow, not veined 459

459
(following on 458).

✳ Leaves in **opposite** pairs, each with 3 deep divisions (Fig. O; Fig. AP represents a flower); a solitary flower in the axil of the leaves. → Ground-Pine **Bugle** [*Ajuga Chamæpitys*] —medicinal. (Family *Labiatæ*.)

✳ Leaves **not** opposite 460

460
(following on 459).

= Flowers apparently with **numerous** petals not regularly arranged. In reality, what is taken for a flower is **a** composite flower made up of numerous little tubular or strap-shaped flowers surrounded by a collarette of very small leaves or scales.—Go on to No. 828

= Flowers **not** having these characteristics 461

461
(following on 460).

⊖ Flowers in clusters; leaves divided into a great number of leaflets (Fig. CJ). → Yellow **Corydalis** [*Corydalis lutea*]—ornamental. (Family *Fumariaceæ*.)

⊖ Flowers **not** in clusters (Fig. AU); leaves with not many divisions cut or toothed. → **Goldilocks** Crowfoot [*Ranunculus auricomus*]. (Family *Ranunculaceæ*.)

× Flowers crowded together in more or less rounded heads 463

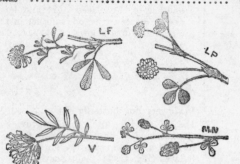

462 (following on 456).

The above figures represent examples of plants with their flowers crowded into more or less crowded heads.

× Flowers in clusters, in circlets, or solitary, not all crowded together and in more or less rounded heads..... 466

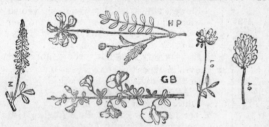

The above figures represent examples of plants with their flowers in clusters, in circlets, or solitary.

463 (following on 462).

☐ The leaves that are towards the base of the plant have the leaflet at their

tips decidedly larger than the other leaflets (Fig. AV); calyx slightly swollen (Fig. V); under the flowers there are little fan-shaped leaves (Fig. VU). → Healing Anthyllis (Kidney Vetch, Lady's Fingers) [*Anthyllis Vulneraria*]—medicinal. (Family *Leguminosæ*.)

☐ Plant not having all these characteristics together.. 464

464
(following on 463).

✱✱ Each flower more than 6 millimetres in total length, and with leaves of three elongated leaflets (Fig. LF). → **Sickle Medick** (Wild Lucerne) [*Medicago falcata*] —fodder plant. (Family *Leguminosæ*.)

✱✱ Plant **not having both these two characteristics** 465

465
(following on 464).

⊙ Leaves with little hairs lying flat over all the under-surface of the three leaflets (examine with the lens); the yellow petals of the flowers falling off when the flowers are withered (Fig. MN). → **Hop Medick** (Hop Trefoil, Nonsuch) [*Medicago lupulina*]—fodder plant. ✿ —Represented in colour: 3, Plate 15. (Family *Leguminosæ*.)

⊙ Leaves **not having small hairs lying flat** on the under surface of the leaflets, except on the principal **vein** of each leaflet (examine with the lens); the yellow petals of the flowers not falling off when the flowers are withered (Fig. P), but becoming membranous and yellowish or russet while hanging on the plant.→ **Procumbent Trefoil** (Hop Trefoil) [*Trifolium procumbens*]—fodder plant.[1] (Family *Leguminosæ*.)

466
(following on 462).

✠ Each leaf with 2 **leaflets** (without counting the 2 little leaflets at the base, attached to the stem) (Fig. L). → **Meadow Vetchling** [*Lathyrus pratensis*].—Represented in colour: 4, Plate 17. (Family *Leguminosæ*.)

✠ Each leaf with 3 **leaflets** **467**

✠ Each leaf with apparently **5 leaflets** (the 2 leaflets which are at the base of the leaf and attached to the stem being nearly similar to the 3 leaflets of the leaf) (Fig. LO); flowers more or less in a circlet. → **Bird's-foot Lotus** (Butter-and-eggs, Shoes-and-stockings) [*Lotus corniculatus*]. ✿ —Represented in colour: 1, **Plate 14.** (Family *Leguminosæ*.)

✠ Each leaf with more than 5 leaflets arranged right and left in two rows, with a leaflet at the tip of the leaf (example: Fig. GLY) 469

---

[1] For the various species of yellow-flowered Trefoils reference should be made to more comprehensive Floras.

467
(following on 466).

§ The lower part of the fully-open flower is more or less hanging below the rest of the flower (Fig. GB); the part which immediately surrounds the base of the petals (calyx) has a membranous texture; stems with the hardness of wood, except in the young shoots. → **Common Broom** [*Sarothamnus scoparius*]—industrial; poisonous; medicinal. ❀ —Represented in colour: 2, Plate 13. (Family *Leguminosæ*.)

§ Plant not having the above-mentioned characteristics together 468

468
(following on 467).

△ Flowers in very long clusters (Fig. M); the flowers are not mixed with ordinary leaves. → **Yellow Melilot** [*Melilotus altissima*]—medicinal. ❀ —Represented in colour: 4, Plate 15.[1] (Family *Leguminosæ*.)

△ Flowers in clusters not very long; the flowers are mixed with leaves (flower: Fig. N). → **Yellow Restharrow** [*Ononis Natrix*]. (Family *Leguminosæ*.)

469
(following on 466).

•— Flowers yellow, arranged in circlets or grouped in 2's or 3's; each group of flowers is borne on a stalk longer than the leaf at its base (Fig. HP). → **Tufted Horseshoe-vetch** [*Hippocrepis comosa*]. (Family *Leguminosæ*.)

•— Flowers of a greenish yellow, arranged in clusters (Fig. AG); each cluster is borne on a stalk shorter than the leaf at its base. → **Sweet Milk-vetch** [*Astragalus glycyphyllos*]. (Family *Leguminosæ*.)

470
(following on 455).

⟅ Flowers butterfly-like, that is to say, with 5 unequal petals: one upper petal larger (*e*), two petals equal to one another (*a, a*), placed right and left, and two lower petals (*cc*) united together in a boat-like shape (see the figures below) 471

⟅ Flowers not butterfly-like 478

---

[1] For the various species of Melilot [*Melilotus*] reference should be made to more comprehensive Floras.

471
(following on 470).

- Leaves each having the form of a thread more or less elongated; to the right and left of this thread, attached to the stem, are two leaflets resembling leaves (Fig. A); flowers attached singly to the stem. → **Aphaca Vetchling** (Yellow Vetchling) [*Lathyrus Aphaca*].—Represented in colour: 2, Plate 17. (Family *Leguminosæ*.)
- Leaves not having that form **472**

472
(following on 471).

⊕ Group of flowers with little fan-shaped leaves at their base. The part which encloses the base of the petals (calyx) is rather inflated (Fig. V). → **Healing Anthyllis** (Kidney Vetch, Lady's Fingers) [*Anthyllis Vulneraria*]—medicinal. (Family *Leguminosæ*.)

⊕ Plant not having these characteristics together.. **473**

473
(following on 472).

⊠ Leaves toothed at the edges in their upper part (flower: Fig. N); plant rather sticky, especially at its upper part. → **Yellow Rest-harrow** [*Ononis Natrix*]. (Family *Leguminosæ*.)

⊠ Leaves without teeth at their edges **474**

474
(following on 473).

§ Each fully open flower having the 2 petals which are united like a boat hanging below the rest of the flower (Fig. S); the part that immediately surrounds the base of the petals (calyx) has a membranous texture. → **Common Broom** [*Sarothamnus scoparius*] —medicinal; industrial. 🏵 — Represented in colour: 2, Plate 13.

§ Plant not having these characteristics together. → *Genista.* — For the chief kinds of *Genista* go on to No. **475**

475
(following on 474).

+ Stems having broad green flanges in the direction of their length (Fig. GS). → **Winged Greenweed** [*Genista sagittalis*]. (Family *Leguminosæ*.)

+ Stems without green flanges **476**

476
(following on 475).

—• Plant with spinous branches, except the little twigs that bear the flowers (Figs. AN and GA). → **English Greenweed** (Petty Whin, Needle Whin) [*Genista anglica*]. (Family *Leguminosæ*.)

—• Plant without spinous branches **477**

477
(following on 476).

△ Flowers hairy (examine with the lens) (Fig. GP), not exceeding, as a rule, a centimetre in total length ; stems more or less prostrate or spreading. → **Hairy Greenweed** [*Genista pilosa*]. (Family *Leguminosæ*.)

△ Flowers not hairy (Fig. GT), more than a centimetre in length ; stems erect. → **Dyers' Greenweed** (Woad-waxen) [*Genista tinctoria*]—industrial.—Represented in colour : 3, Plate 13. (Family *Leguminosæ*.)

Leaves opposite (except sometimes on the upper part of the stems or branches) ; that is to say, leaves arranged in pairs, attached to the stem at the same level, opposite one another 479

The above figures represent examples of opposite leaves.

N.B.—Little leafy twigs are often formed in the axils of opposite leaves which may lead to the belief that the leaves are grouped in a large number at the same level on the stem, and are not merely an opposite pair ; but on looking carefully at the base of these groups of leaves the two opposite leaves will be readily distinguished.

478
(following on 470).

Leaves whorled, at least towards the middle region of the stems ; that is to say, leaves attached in 3's or 4's at the same level on the stem, and arranged regularly round its whole circumference (example : Fig. LS) 488

Leaves alternate ; that is to say, leaves attached singly to the stem at different levels 488

The above figures represent examples of alternate leaves.

Leaves grouped ; that is to say, leaves attached to the stem, 2 or more at the same level, but arranged, at that level, on the same side of the stem 488

Leaves all at the base of the plant 488

N.B.—If the plant has both alternate and opposite leaves, or both opposite and whorled leaves, either question may be followed up, and in either case the name of the plant will be reached.

479
(following on 478).

○ Plant either climbing (Fig. LC), twining its stems round other plants, or with stems prostrate on the ground or hanging; except in its young parts, the stem has the appearance and hardness of wood. → **Common Honeysuckle** [*Lonicera Periclymenum*]. 🌸—Represented in colour (with pink flowers): 4, Plate 26. (Family *Caprifoliaceæ*.)

○ Plant **not having these characteristics together** 480

480
(following on 479).

— Corolla surrounded by 5 fine spines terminating the 5 teeth of the green structure enclosing the corolla tube 481

— Corolla **not surrounded by 5 fine spines** (it may have 4) 483

481
(following on 480).

☉ Flowers **yellow**; the groups of flowers are situated **in the axils of the ordinary leaves**; leaves with a long stalk (Fig. GA : Fig. G represents a flower cut lengthwise). → **Yellow Deadnettle** (Yellow Archangel, Weasel-snout) [*Lamium Galeobdolon*]—medicinal. (Family *Labiatæ*.)

☉ Flowers **yellow, large, gaping, on stalks, solitary in the axils of sessile opposite leaves**. → **Common Monkey-flower** [*Mimulus Langsdorfii*]. (Family *Scrophulariaceæ*.)

☉ Flowers **yellowish or white spotted with yellow**; the groups of flowers are at the upper part of the plant in the axils of leaves smaller than the ordinary leaves 482

482
(following on 481).

✳ Leaves **with numerous hairs**; there are **no hairs on the 5 fine spines** of the calyx (examine with the lens) (Fig. R); lower leaves almost destitute of stalk (Fig. SR). → **Upright Woundwort** [*Stachys recta*]. 🌸 (Family *Labiatæ*.)

✳ Leaves **almost without hairs**; there are **hairs on the 5 fine spines of the calyx** (examine with the lens) (Fig. A); lower leaves borne on stalks of more or less length (Fig. AN). → **Annual Woundwort** [*Stachys annua*]. 🌸 (Family *Labiatæ*.)

483
(following on 480).

= Leaves **without stalks or with stalks less than 2 millimetres long** 484

= Leaves **with stalks more than 2 millimetres long**; flowers arranged in long clusters at the tops of the stems (Fig. S); corolla with one lip (Fig. T); leaves wrinkled between their veins.—Go on to No. 652

= Leaves **with a long stalk and corolla with two lips**.—Refer back to No. 481

484
(following on 483).

○ Leaves thick, fleshy; flowers **almost regular**; leaves alternate or grouped on the shoots (Fig. O). → Cooking Purslane [*Portulaca oleracea*]—food plant; medicinal. (Family *Portulacaceæ*.)

○ Plant **not having** the above-mentioned characteristics 485

485
(following on 484).

× Flowers of a yellowish white, slightly pinkish; leaves slightly embracing the stem by their bases; flowers singly in the axils of the leaves (Fig. GO). → **Common Gratia-Dei** (Hedge Hyssop) [*Gratiola officinalis*]—poisonous; medicinal. (Family *Scrophulariaceæ*.)

× Flowers with a long horn at their base 491

× Plant not having these characteristics 486

486
(following on 485).

□ Flowers marked with violet lines, with a tube opening widely at the top (Fig. E); plant less than 18 centimetres (5 inches) high; upper leaves alternate (Fig. O). → **Common Eye-bright** [*Euphrasia officinalis*]—medicinal. (Family *Scrophulariaceæ*.)

□ Plant **not having** the above-mentioned characteristics together 487

487
(following on 486).

✳ ✳ Corolla **with two bosses** of a bright yellow on its lower lip, one beside the other, towards the interior of the flower (Fig. MP); flowers not intermixed with numerous red leaves each divided into acute lobes (Fig. PR); the part of the flower (calyx) which encloses the base of the corolla tube is neither inflated nor flattened. → **Meadow Cow-wheat** [*Melampyrum pratense*].—Represented in colour: 5, Plate 42.[1] (Family *Scrophulariaceæ*.)

✳ ✳ Corolla **with two bosses** of a bright yellow on its lower lip; flowers intermixed with red leaves each divided into acute lobes.—Refer back to No. 174

✳ ✳ Corolla without two bosses on its lower lip; the part of the flower (calyx) which encloses the tube of the corolla is inflated and slightly flattened at its sides (Fig. MA). → **Cock's-comb Rhinanthus** (Yellow-Rattle) [*Rhinanthus Crista-galli*].—Represented in colour: 4, Plate 42. (Family *Scrophulariaceæ*.)

---

[1] For the various species of *Melampyrum* reference should be made to more comprehensive Floras.

488
(following on 478).

○ Corolla in the form of a mouth, with the lower lip in contact with the upper one 489

The above figures represent flowers with the corolla in the shape of a mouth.

○ Corolla not in the form of a mouth, and not with two lips in contact with one another 492

489
(following on 488).

⌀ Corolla with a short swelling at the base (Fig. M). → Greater Snapdragon [*Antirrhinum majus*] — ornamental; medicinal. ❀ —Represented in colour (with red flowers): 1, Plate 41. (Family *Scrophulariaceæ*.)

⌀ Corolla prolonged at its base into a narrow and more or less long tube or horn (Figs. SU, ST); leaves attached to the stem, some singly, others in 2's, 3's, or 4's at the same level, especially towards the bases of the stems. → Toad-flaxes [*Linaria*].[1]—For the chief kinds of Toad-flax [*Linaria*] with yellow flowers go on to No. 490

490
(following on 489).

✳ The upper lip of the corolla is purple on the inside; leaves not more than twice as long as they are broad, oval, pointed, attached to the stem by a very short but quite distinct stalk (Fig. S). → False Toad-flax (Male Fluellen) [*Linaria spuria*]. (Family *Scrophulariaceæ*.)

✳ The upper lip of the corolla purple on the inside; leaves halberd-shaped, that is, nearly triangular, with 3 points and slightly 3 lobed. → Elatine Toad-flax (Sharp-pointed Fluellen) [*Linaria Elatine*]. (Family *Scrophulariaceæ*.)

✳ The upper lip of the corolla is not purple on the inside; leaves more than twice as long as they are broad, oval, and elongated or very narrow 491

491
(following on 490).

⊕ Stems erect; flowers in long clusters; the green calyx, which surrounds the base of the yellow corolla, is without hairs (Fig. V). →Common Toad-flax [*Linaria vulgaris*]. ❀ —Represented in colour: 3, Plate 41. (Family *Scrophulariaceæ*.)

⊕ Stems prostrate; flowers in short clusters (Fig. SP); the green calyx, which surrounds the base of the corolla, is hairy (Fig. SU). → Prostrate Toad-flax [*Linaria supina*]. (Family *Scrophulariaceæ*.)

---

[1] For further details as to the various species of Toad-flax [*Linaria*] reference should be made to more comprehensive Floras.

⊁ Each flower has its petals separated from one another down to their bases; that is to say, that one of the petals (or parts of the flower coloured yellow or yellowish) may be detached down to its base without tearing the others. This refers to those parts of the flower which, collectively, make up the corolla or coloured structure which surrounds the little threads and other organs that occupy the centre of the flower ; when the flower fades each petal (or coloured piece) falls off or withers separately [1] 493

492 (following on 488).

Fig. RLU represents a flower with separate petals ; Fig. LU one of its petals detached. Figs. NN and TRI represent other examples of flowers with separate petals.

⊁ Each flower has its petals united together, at least at the base; that is to say, that in trying to detach one of the parts of the flower coloured yellow or yellowish, one is obliged to tear the corolla, at least at its base ; when the flower fades the corolla falls off or withers all in one piece 493

The above figures represent some examples of flowers with united petals.

493 (following on 492).

§ Upper petal prolonged at its base into a horn or narrow tube; 4 petals directed upwards and one downward (Figs. T and TRI). → Tricolor Viola (Pansy, Heart's-ease) [*Viola tricolor*]— ornamental.—Represented in colour: 2, Plate 7. (Family *Violaceæ*.)
§ Plant not having these characteristics 494

494 (following on 493).

+ Leaves not developed, reduced to yellowish or brownish scales (Fig. N); flower with 6 very unequal divisions (Fig. NN). → Bird's-nest Neottia (Bird's-nest Orchid) [*Neottia Nidus-avis*].—Represented in colour: 6, Plate 56. (Family *Orchidaceæ*.)
+ Leaves developed and green 495

---

[1] In most flowers there is, outside the corolla, another covering to the flower, generally green, which is termed the *calyx* and which surrounds the base of the corolla. In other flowers it is difficult to distinguish the calyx and corolla apart, since they are more or less blended into a single floral envelope, coloured yellow or yellowish, like a corolla. Under the names petals and corolla we here understand those pieces coloured yellow or yellowish, which immediately surround the little threads or other organs occupying the centre of the flower.

495
(follow-
ing on
494).
{ --• Flower in reality composite; that is to say, that on examining carefully what is ordinarily called the flower, it will be seen to be made up by the union of very small flowers, without stalks, either strap-shaped or tubular, the whole surrounded by a collarette of numerous little leaves or little scales.—Go on to No. 828

--• Flower not composite 496

496
(follow-
ing on
495).
{ △ Flowers in long clusters (see below, Figs. RL and LL under No. 497); each flower less than 7 millimetres across. On examining the flower carefully, it is seen that the petals, or at least the upper ones, are much divided; examine them with the lens. → Reseda (Mignon-ette) [*Reseda*].—For the chief kinds of *Reseda* go on to No. 497

△ Flowers not in long clusters (Fig. AU); each flower more than 7 millimetres across; the petals are not divided. → Goldilocks Crowfoot [*Ranunculus auricomus*]. (Family *Ranunculaceæ*.)

497
(follow-
ing on
496).
{ ✠ Leaves more or less divided (Fig. RL); the upper petals are very deeply divided (examine with the lens: Figs. RE, RS). → Yellow Reseda (Wild Mignonette) [*Reseda lutea*]. ❀ —Represented in colour: 5, Plate 7. (Family *Resedaceæ*.)

✠ Leaves not divided (Fig. LL); the upper petals are divided for about half their length (examine with the lens: Figs. RLU, LU). → Yellow-weed Reseda (Weld, Dyer's Rocket) [*Reseda Luteola*]. ❀ — Represented in colour: 6, Plate 7. (Family *Resedaceæ*.)

498
(follow-
ing on
492).
{ ○ Leaves not developed, reduced to brownish, yellowish, or whitish scales (Fig. OG); flowers yellowish, with 2 lips, one upper, the other lower (Figs. O and OG). → Greater Broom-rape [*Orobanche major*].[1] — Represented in colour: 7, Plate 42. (Family *Orobanchaceæ*.)

○ Leaves developed and green 499

499
(follow-
ing on
498).
{ — Flowers almost regular 500
— Flowers very irregular, in the form of a wide bell-mouthed tube or of a horn 501

---

[1] For the various species of *Orobanche* reference should be made to more comprehensive Floras.

500
(follow-ing on 499).

✱ Flowers yellowish, veined in dark violet or brown; flowers in a recurved cluster (Fig. HN). → Black Henbane [*Hyoscyamus niger*]—poison-ous; medicinal.—Represented in colour: 1, Plate 40. (Family *Solanaceæ*.)

✱ Flowers yellow; flowers in an erect cluster, with one petal larger than the other (Fig. ML). → Great Mullein (Hag-taper) [*Verbascum Thapsus*] —medicinal.—Represented in colour: 5, Plate 40. (Family *Scrophulariaceæ*.)

501
(follow-ing on 499).

= Flowers with the shape of a bell-mouthed tube (Fig. L), in a long cluster, all turning the same way; leaves oval elongated. → Yellow Fox-glove [*Digitalis lutea*]—dangerous. (Family *Scrophu-lariaceæ*.)

= Flowers with the shape of a horn (Fig. CL); flowers intermixed with ordinary leaves; leaves reversedly heart-shaped. → Climbing Birthwort [*Aristolochia Clemati-tis*]—medicinal.—Represented in colour: 6, Plate 46. (Family *Aristolochiaceæ*.)

502
(follow-ing on 355).

⊖ Leaves made up of a great number of little secondary leaves (leaflets); flowers in a branching cluster (Fig. F representing part of a cluster). → Meadow-rues [*Thalic-trum*].—For the chief kinds of Meadow-rue [*Thalictrum*] refer back to No. 421

⊖ Leaves, divided into 3 to 5 lobes, or with well-marked teeth, arranged in pairs (Fig. H); plant climbing. → Rough Hop [*Humulus Lupulus*]—in-dustrial; medicinal. ✿—Represented in colour: 1 and 1 bis, Plate 48. (Family *Urticaceæ*.)

⊖ Leaves neither compound, divided, toothed, or not developed 503

503
(follow-ing on 502).

✕ Leaves cylindrical like the stems (Fig. J) or not developed.

→ Rushes [*Juncus*].[1]—Refer back to No. 36

✕ Leaves reduced to a collar-ette of little scales, arranged regularly round the entire circumference of the stem, where the green twigs start from (Fig. AV) (in reality, it is a plant without flowers). → Horse-tails [*Equisetum*]—Go on to No. 1104

✕ Leaves neither cylindrical, nor reduced to scales 504

---

[1] For details as to the species of Rush [*Juncus*] reference should be made to more comprehensive Floras.

☐ Flowers **arranged in balls** which are placed one above the other (Fig. S). → **Branched Bur-reed** [*Sparganium ramosum*]. (Family *Typhaceæ*.)

☐ Flowers **enclosed in a large sheath** (Fig. AR) green or greenish. → **Spotted Arum** (Lords and Ladies, Cuckoo-pint, Wake Robin) [*Arum maculatum*] — medicinal.—Represented in colour: 2 and 2 *bis*, Plate 57. (Family *Araceæ*.)

☐ Flowers **arrang**-ed in two solid cylinders placed one above the other (Fig. L); the lower cylinder is brown. → **Reedmace** [*Typha*].—Go back to No. .. **162**

☐ Flowers **neither in balls nor cylinders; nor in a big sheath**; leaves opposite and in pairs (Figs. PE, AN).—Refer to No........... **722**

☐ Plants **not having the preceding characteristics** .. **505**

504 (*following on* 503).

* * Leaves attached to the stem by a **sheath split open length**-wise (*f, fl, g,* Fig. G) on the opposite side to the leaf; stem **more or less rounded** (*t, t,* Fig. G); the leaf has **a little tongue or a line of special hairs** at the spot where it is joined to the stem . **1069**

* * Leaves attached to the stem by a **sheath which is not split open lengthwise** (*f, g,* Fig. C); stem has **3 angles** (*l,* Fig. C), at least for part of its length; the leaf has **neither tongue nor lines of special hairs** at the spot where it is joined to the stem, above the sheath **1062**

505 (*following on* 504).

⊙ Flowers **in a compound umbel; that is to say**, all the stalks that bear flowers start from exactly the same point, like the spokes which uphold an umbrella; and themselves have stalks which start from exactly the same point, each one ending in a single flower.... **670**

Fig. C represents the arrangement of flowers in a compound umbel: IO, the principal umbel and its main spokes; *i, o, f,* the secondary umbels and their corresponding secondary spokes or rays, from which the flowers spring directly.

506 (*following on* 4).

⊙ Flowers **not in an umbel; that is to say, not having all these preceding characteristics** **507**

⌔ Each flower **regular**, that is to say, that the similar parts of the flower which are coloured white or whitish are arranged regularly round the centre of the flower, and are obviously equal to one another **508**

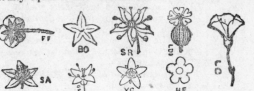

The above figures represent some examples of regular flowers.

⌔ Each flower **irregular**, that is to say, that the flower has not got the above-described character **618**

N.B.—Flowers which have their right half similar to the left are not to be considered as regular.

507
(following on 506).

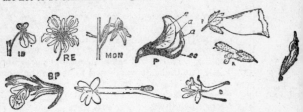

The above figures represent some examples of irregular flowers.

⌔ Each flower **reduced to little white or whitish scales** 702

The above figures represent some examples of flowers or of groups of flowers reduced to scales.

N.B.—If there is any doubt as between regular and irregular flowers, as, for example, in the case of the flowers represented by Figs. VT, L, and CA, either of the numbers to which one is referred may be taken, and in either case the name of the plant will be reached.

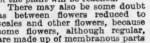

There may also be some doubt as between flowers reduced to scales and other flowers, because some flowers, although regular, are made up of membranous parts

and thus seem to be reduced to scales, as, for example, the flower represented by Fig. ML, or the group of flowers in Fig. LC. Either one or other of the numbers to which reference is made may be chosen and in either case the name of the plant will be reached.

✳ **Leaves compound;** that is to say, that the leaf, as a whole, is made up by the union of secondary leaves, called *leaflets*, each of which is often mistaken for a leaf; the whole compound leaf is attached to the stem by its base or by a stalk which bears all the leaflets. The base of the compound leaf is not situated exactly in the axil of another leaf **593**

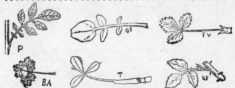

The above figures represent some examples of compound leaves.

✳ **Leaves deeply divided** (except sometimes the leaves that are quite at the upper part of the stems), that is to say, that each leaf is, as it were, cut to the extent of more than half its breadth **593**

The above figures represent examples of divided leaves.

✳ **Leaves simple;** that is to say, either not cut to the extent of more than half their breadth, or merely edged with teeth, or even without teeth on their edges **509**

The above figures represent examples of simple leaves.

✳ **Leaves not developed** or reduced to scales **511**

Figs. CS and M represent plants the leaves of which are not developed or are reduced to scales.

N.B.—It is of no consequence if there is some hesitation as between compound and deeply divided leaves, since in both cases the reference is to the same number (593). If there is doubt as between deeply divided leaves and simple leaves, either question may be followed up, and in either case the name of the plant will be reached. The same result will follow if the plant has both simple and compound or divided leaves (besides the few simple leaves which often occur at the top of flowering stems).

⊕ **Leaves opposite** (except sometimes on the upper part of the stems or branches); that is to say, leaves arranged in two's, attached to the stem at the same level, opposite to one another 560

The above figures represent examples of opposite leaves.
N.B.—Little leafy shoots not infrequently occur in the axils of opposite leaves which might lead to the belief that the leaves were grouped at the same level on the stem and were not merely an opposite pair; but, on carefully examining the base of such a group of leaves, the two opposite leaves will be readily distinguished.

⊕ **Leaves whorled**, at least about the middle region of the stems; that is to say, leaves attached 3, 4, 5, or even more together at the same level on the stem and arranged regularly round its whole circumference 584

509 (following on 508).

The above figures represent examples of whorled leaves.

⊕ **Leaves alternate;** that is to say, leaves attached singly on the stem at different levels (examples: the figures below) 510

⊕ **Leaves grouped;** that is to say, leaves attached 2 or more together at the same level on the stem, but arranged only on one side of it 510

⊕ **Leaves all at the base of the plant** (examples: Figs. V and PR) 510

N.B.—If the plant have both alternate and opposite leaves, or both alternate and whorled leaves, either question may be followed up, and in either case the name of the plant will be reached.

✠ Each flower has its petals separated from one another down to their base; that is to say, that one of the petals (or parts coloured white or whitish) can be detached down to its base without tearing the others. This refers to those parts of the flower which, collectively, form the corolla or coloured part that surrounds the little threads and other organs which occupy the centre of the flower; when the flower fades each petal (or coloured piece) falls off or withers separately [1]   512

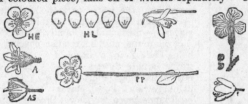

510 (following on 509).

Fig. HE represents a flower with separate petals, Fig. HL showing its petals detached. The other figures represent other examples of flowers with separate petals, as seen from above, from the side, or from below.

✠ Each flower has its petals united to one another, at least at their base; that is to say, that in trying to detach one of the parts of the flower which is coloured white or whitish, one is obliged to tear the corolla, at least at its base; when the flower fades the corolla falls off or withers all in one piece   541

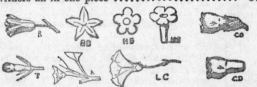

The petals are united to one another at very different heights in different flowers. Figs. BO, HE represent the corolla of a flower the petals of which are very slightly united to one another at their bases. In the flowers represented by the other figures the corolla is made up of petals united to one another for a greater or less length. To the right is shown a flower CO and its corolla (CD) detached.

511 (following on 508).

§ Plant climbing, attaching itself to other plants (Fig. CS). → Sweet-scented Dodder [*Cuscuta suaveolens*], a parasite on cultivated Lucerne — harmful to crops. (Family *Convolvulaceæ*.)

§ Plant not climbing; whitish plant which turns black as it dries (Fig. M). → Pine Bird's-nest (Fir-rape) [*Monotropa Hypopitys*]. (Family *Ericaceæ*.)

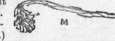

[1] In most plants there is, outside the corolla, another covering to the flower, usually green, called the *calyx*, which surrounds the base of the corolla. In other flowers it is difficult to distinguish between the calyx and the corolla,

512
(following on 510).

+ Leaves divided into lobes, with veins arranged like a fan (Fig. G); plant growing in water or in places that are flooded. → **Water Crowfoot** [*Ranunculus aquatilis*].—Represented in colour: 3, Plate 1. (Family *Ranunculaceæ*.)

+ Leaves round, with their stalks attached to the lower surface of the leaf (Fig. H); plant growing in the water or in flooded places. → **Common Marsh-pennywort** [*Hydrocotyle vulgaris*]—medicinal. (Family *Umbelliferæ*.)

+ Leaves round, stalked, reddish, covered with long hairs ending in a drop of sticky liquid; flowers small, not expanding (Fig. DR); plant growing in boggy places. → **Round-leaved Sundew** [*Drosera rotundifolia*]. (Family *Droseraceæ*.)

+ Plant not having the characteristics of the three preceding **513**

513
(following on 512).

— Flowers with 5 petals (or white or whitish parts).. **514**

— Flowers with 4 or 8 petals (or white parts) **523**

— Flowers with 3 or 6 petals (or parts coloured white, greenish white, or white with pink or red spots).. **535**

— Flowers with more than 6 petals (or white parts).. **540**

514
(following on 513).

△ Each flower more than 4 millimetres across when fully open **515**

△ Each flower 4 millimetres across or less than 4 millimetres **522**

515
(following on 514).

Flowers expanded like a star, with 5 petals slightly united at their base; each petal has two green spots at its base; leaves simple or sometimes deeply divided (Fig. DU). → **Bittersweet Nightshade** (Woody Nightshade) [*Solanum Dulcamara*]—poisonous; medicinal.—Represented in colour (with violet flowers): 2 and 2 *bis*, Plate 40. (Family *Solanaceæ*.)

Plant not having these characteristics together... **516**

516
(following on 515).

○ Plant with sticky hairs on the upper part; leaves with 3 to 8 divisions, besides those at the base (Fig. SGR). → **Tuberous Saxifrage** (Pretty Maids) [*Saxifraga granulata*].—Represented in colour: 1, Plate 23. (Family *Saxifragaceæ*.)

○ Plant without sticky hairs; leaves not divided .. **517**

they being more or less blended into a single floral envelope (Figs. AS and R, for example). Lastly, in other flowers there is really only a single floral envelope, which is coloured white or whitish, like a corolla. Under the names petals or corolla we shall here understand those pieces, coloured white or whitish, which immediately surround the little threads or other organs that occupy the centre of the flower.

517
(following on 516).

{ — Leaves all, or all except one, at the base of the plant 518
— Leaves arranged along the stem 519

518
(following on 517).

{ ✳ A solitary flower at the top of the stem (Fig. PP); within the flower, on the inner side of the petals, are 5 fan-shaped scales bordered with hairs each having a little round head. → Marsh Grass-of-Parnassus [*Parnassia palustris*]. (Family *Saxifragaceæ*.)

✳ Flowers in a cluster (Fig. PR); no special scales within the flower.→ Round-leaved Winter-green [*Pyrola rotundifolia*]—medicinal.[1] (Family *Ericaceæ*.)

519
(following on 517).

{ = Flowers with petals really united at their bases (Fig. N), spreading like a star; flowers in groups of 3 to 6 (Fig. SN); leaves irregularly toothed and with the teeth rounded. → Black Nightshade [*Solanum nigrum*]—poisonous; medicinal. (Family *Solanaceæ*.)

= Plant not having these characteristics 520

520
(following on 519).

{ ⊖ Plant fleshy, with thick, fleshy juicy leaves; leaves without stalks or nearly without stalks; flowers in the shape of a star when fully open (Fig. SR) 521

⊖ Plant not fleshy, with leaves not fleshy, each borne on a stalk of greater or less length, more or less shaped like an arrow-head or a reversed heart (Fig. FG); flowers not star-like. → Buck-wheat Knot-grass [*Polygonum Fagopyrum*]—food-plant; fodder. 🌸 —Represented in colour: 4, Plate 46. (Family *Polygonaceæ*.)

521
(following on 520).

{ × Each leaf shaped like an elongated grain (Fig. AL). → White Stonecrop (Great-Stone-crop) [*Sedum album*]—medicinal. 🌸 —Represented in colour: 4, Plate 22.

× Each leaf flat and thick, more or less toothed along its edges (Fig. TE). → Orpine Stonecrop (Livelong) [*Sedum Telephium*]—medicinal. —Represented in colour (with pink flowers): 1, Plate 22. (Family *Crassulaceæ*.)

---

[1] For details as to the species of Winter-green [*Pyrola*] reference should be made to more comprehensive Floras.

522
(following on 514).

☐ Leaves **arrow-shaped** (Fig. CO), with a more or less elongated stalk; plant climbing or trailing its stems to a great length along the ground; flowers whitish. → **Convolvulus Knot-grass** (Black Bindweed) [*Polygonum Convolvulus*]. (Family *Polygonaceæ*.)

☐ Leaves **not** arrow-shaped; flowers white, not mixed with the ordinary leaves (Fig. TR); leaves rather fleshy. → **Three-fingered Saxifrage** [*Saxifraga tridactylites*].—Represented in colour: 2, Plate 23. (Family *Saxifragaceæ*.)

☐ Leaves **not** arrow-shaped; flowers whitish or pinkish white, mixed with the ordinary leaves along the stem (Fig. AV); leaves not fleshy. → **Birds' Knot-grass** [*Polygonum aviculare*]. ✿—Represented in colour: 5, Plate 46. (Family *Polygonaceæ*.)

523
(following on 513).

⊙ Leaves **without** hairs (examine with the lens)...... 524

⊙ Leaves **with** hairs, at least along their veins, on the under surface of the leaf, or on the stalk of the leaf....... 526

524
(following on 523).

◇ Each flower **more** than 3 centimetres (1½ inches) across; upper leaves embracing the stem very much by their bases (Fig. PV). —Refer back to No. 20

◇ Each flower **less** than 3 centimetres (1½ inches) and **more** than a half centimetre (½ inch) across; upper leaves slightly embracing the stem by their bases (Fig. CP). → **Cooking Cabbage** [*Brassica oleracea*]—food plant. ✿ —Represented in colour (with yellow flowers): 6, Plate 5. (Family *Cruciferæ*.)

◇ Each flower **less** than half a centimetre across... 525

525
(following on 524).

✱ Leaves embracing the stem by their bases which are prolonged right and left in two pointed little ear-like lobes (Fig. AR); the lower leaves are not deeply divided. → **Field Penny-cress** (Mithridate Mustard) [*Thlaspi arvense*]. (Family *Cruciferæ*.)

✱ Leaves embracing the stem at their bases by two broad rounded ear-like lobes; the lower leaves are not divided. → **Perfoliate Penny-cress** [*Thlaspi perfoliatum*]. (Family *Cruciferæ*.)

✱ Leaves **not** embracing the stem by their bases which taper (Fig. G); the lower leaves are deeply divided. → **Grass-leaved Pepperwort** [*Lepidium graminifolium*]. (Family *Cruciferæ*.)

526
(follow-
ing on
523).

⊕ Flowers apparently with 8 petals (ex- amine the flowers with the lens) (Fig. VER, enlarged); in reality each of the 4 petals is divided into 2 almost to its base; leaves all at the base of the plant (Fig. V). → Spring Whitlow-grass [*Draba verna*].—Represented in colour: 4, Plate 6. (Family *Cruciferæ*.)

⊕ Flowers with 4 white petals 527

527
(follow-
ing on
526).

✠ Leaves embracing the stem by their bases, at least partly 528

✠ Leaves not embracing the stem by their bases 530

528
(follow-
ing on
527).

§ Flowering branches at the upper part of the plant often almost all coming nearly to one level (Fig. CM); leaves embracing the stem by their bases (Fig. C) and bearing hairs which are neither 2-branched nor star-shaped. → Field Pepperwort [*Lepi- dium campestre*]. (Family *Cruciferæ*.)

§ Plant not having these characteristics together.. 529

529
(follow-
ing on
528).

+ Stem stiff, unbranch- ed (Fig. AS), or, if the stem has some branches, they are close against the stem; leaves with 2-branched hairs (examine with the lens). → Hairy Rock-cress [*Arabis hir- suta*]. (Family *Cruciferæ*.)

+ Stem with branches diverging more or less from the main stem (Fig. CBP); leaves with scattered star-shaped hairs. → Common Shepherd's - purse [*Capsella Bursa - pastoris*]— medicinal. — Represented in colour: 5, Plate 6. (Family *Cruciferæ*.)

530
(follow-
ing on
527).

—• Leaves reversedly heart-shaped, with long stalks (Fig. A), with a smell of garlic when bruised. → Common Garlic- mustard (Sauce-alone, Jack-by-the-Hedge) [*Alliaria officinalis*]—medicinal. (Family *Cruciferæ*.)

—• Leaves without the smell of garlic 531

531
(following
on
530).

△ Flowers veined with violet or with brown (Fig.
RR); stems with stiff hairs. → Wild Radish
(White Charlock) [*Raphanus Raphanistrum*].
(Family *Cruciferæ*.)

△ Flowers **not** veined with violet or brown 532

532
(following
on
531).

⫟ Stems without hairs
on their upper parts;
leaves with hairs
that are 2- or 3-
branched (examine
with the lens); leaves mostly in a rosette at the base
of the plant (Fig. AT). → Thale Hedge-mustard (Thale
Cress, Wall Cress) [*Sisymbrium Thalianum*]. (Family
Cruciferæ.)

⫟ Stems with hairs on their upper parts 533

533
(following
on
532).

○ Flowers more than a
centimetre (⅖ inch)
across, with a sweet
smell; leaves pointed
at their bases and at
their tips (Fig. HM).
→ **Dame's Hesperis** (Dame's Violet) [*Hesperis matronalis*]
—ornamental. (Family *Cruciferæ*.)

○ Flowers **less** than a centimetre across, without a sweet
smell 534

534
(following
on
533).

— Flowers **yellowish**, becoming
white when they fade; leaves
small and oval (Fig. AC). → Yellow Alysson (Heal-bite) [*Alyssum
calycinum*]. (Family *Cruciferæ*.)

— Flowers **white**.—Refer back to No. 529

535
(following
on
513).

✳ A solitary **flower** at the top of the stem (Fig.
G); the three inner pieces of the flower are heart-
shaped with a green crescent-shaped mark. →
Common Snowdrop [*Galanthus nivalis*]—ornamental. (Family *Amaryllidaceæ*.)

✳ Plant not having these characteristics 536

536
(following
on
535).

= Plant growing **in** water, with leaves shaped like an
arrow-head (see Fig. S, at the top of the next page,
under No. 537) or rounded and heart-shaped ... 537

= Plant not growing in water, with leaves oval or very
elongated, neither arrow-shaped, nor rounded and heart-
shaped 538

537 *(following on 536).*

⊖ The leaves formed above water are arrow-shaped (Fig. S); flowers in an erect cluster; the plant may also have more or less rounded leaves floating on the water, or leaves very elongated, like ribbons, under water. → **Arrow-head-leaved Sagittaria** (Arrow-head) [*Sagittaria sagittifolia*].—Represented in colour: 1 and 1 *bis*, Plate 52. (Family *Alismaceæ*.)

⊖ The leaves are all rounded and reversedly heart-shaped at the base (Fig. H); flowers not in an erect cluster. → **Frog-bit Hydrocharis** (*Hydrocharis Morsus-ranæ*). (Family *Hydrocharidaceæ*.)

538 *(following on 536).*

× **The plant has only two leaves** which are oval and are each borne on an elongated stalk (Fig. AU). → **Bear's Allium** (Ramson, Broad-leaved Garlic) [*Allium ursinum*]—medicinal. (Family *Liliaceæ*.)

× **The plant has more than two leaves** which are very elongated and are not borne on a stalk **539**

539 *(following on 538).*

☐ Flowers with a green band on the under surface of each white division of the flower; stem with no branches except the flower-stalks (Fig. U). → **Umbellate Star-of-Bethlehem** [*Ornithogalum umbellatum*].—Represented in colour: 6, Plate 53. (Family *Liliaceæ*.)

☐ Flowers without any green band on the under surface of each white division; stem branched (Fig. PH). → **Branched Phalangium** [*Phalangium ramosum*]. (Family *Liliaceæ*.)

540 *(following on 513).*

✱ ✱ Plant entirely in the water; leaves rounded, and reversedly heart-shaped; each flower more than 8 centimetres (3 inches) across, with numerous petals rather pointed at their tips (Fig. NA represents a flower cut in half). → **White Nymphæa** (White Water-lily) [*Nymphæa alba*]—ornamental; medicinal.—Represented in colour: 2, Plate 4. (Family *Nymphæaceæ*.)

✱ ✱ Plant not in water; each flower less than 5 centimetres (2 inches) across. In reality what is taken for a flower is a composite flower of a great number of little strap-shaped or tubular flowers without stalks, the whole surrounded by a collarette of numerous little leaves or scales.—Go on to No. **891**

541
(following on 510).
{
⊙ Flowers with 4 divisions or with 4 white lobes, slightly irregular (Fig. VT). → Speed-wells [*Veronica*].—For the chief kinds of Speedwell [*Veronica*] refer back to No. ... **VT** .. 315

⊙ Flowers with 4 membranous brown or greenish divisions (in reality the scales of the flower are neither white nor whitish).—Refer back to No. 150

⊙ Flowers with 4 divisions, of which 2 are notched at the top and 2 are acute.—Refer back to No. 62

⊙ Flowers with 5 petals or with 5 white lobes 542

⊙ Flowers with 3 or 6 divisions or lobes 556

⊙ Flowers without divisions, with petals united to the top in the shape of a funnel 546
}

542
(following on 541).
{
↶ Plant fleshy, with thick fleshy leaves, each in the shape of an elongated grain (Fig. AL). → White Stonecrop [*Sedum album*]—medicinal. ✿ —Represented in colour: 4, Plate 22. (Family *Crassulaceæ*.)

↶ Plant not fleshy 543
}

543
(following on 542).
{
• Flower with petals united at their base only; each petal having two green spots at its base; plant with some leaves simple, others divided (Fig. DU); stems with the appear-ance and hardness of wood in their lower parts. → Bitter-sweet Nightshade (Woody Nightshade) [*Solanum Dulca-mara*]—poisonous; medicinal.—Represented in colour: (with violet flowers): 2 and 2 *bis*, Plate 40. (Family *Solanaceæ*.)

• Plant not having these characteristics together 544
}

544
(following on 543).
{
⊕ Plant with its stems climbing or trailing at length on the ground 545

⊕ Plant with stems neither climbing nor trailing... 547
}

545
(following on 544).
{
✠ Stems attaching themselves to other plants by means of threads rolled up on themselves (Fig. BR); leaves more or less divided, and with their veins arranged like a fan. → Diœcious Bryony (White Bryony) [*Bryonia dioica*]— poisonous; medicinal. ✿ —Represented in colour: 1 and 1 *bis*, Plate 21. (Family *Cucurbitaceæ*.)

✠ Stems twining themselves round other plants or trailing at length on the ground 546
}

546
(following on 545).

§ Each flower less than 3 centimetres (1½ inch) long; two very small leaves are attached to the stalk of the flower, at some distance below the flower (Fig. A). → **Field Bindweed** (Small Convolvulus) [*Convolvulus arvensis*].—Represented in colour: 3, Plate 38. (Family *Convolvulaceæ*.)

§ Each flower more than 3 centimetres long; there are two small leaves immediately below the flower (Fig. S).
→ **Hedge Bindweed** [*Convolvulus sepium*].—Represented in colour (with white flowers): 4, Plate 38. (Family *Convolvulaceæ*)

547
(following on 544).

+ Each flower with a corolla of 5 pointed petals united at their bases only by a very short tube (example: Fig. B) 548

+ Each flower with 5 petals rounded at their tips and scarcely united at their bases 520

+ Each flower with a corolla which only forms 5 lobes at the top of a long or bell-mouthed tube (examples: the figures below) 549

548
(following on 547).

—• Stems and leaves with pricking hairs; the flower expands to more than a centimetre across; the 5 green parts of the calyx show between the petals (Fig. B). → **Officinal Borage** [*Borago officinalis*]—medicinal.—Represented in colour (with blue flowers): 4, Plate 39. (Family *Boraginaceæ*.)

—• Stems and leaves with hairs that are not prickly; the flower expands to less than a centimetre across; the 5 green parts of the calyx do not show between the petals (Fig. N); leaves with rounded teeth (Fig. SN). → **Black Nightshade** [*Solanum nigrum*]—poisonous; medicinal. (Family *Solanaceæ*.)

549
(following on 547).

△ Leaves narrow and elongated, less than 4 millimetres across; flowers with lobes whitish inside and greenish outside, elongated (Fig. T); flowers in a cluster (Fig. TH). → **Prostrate Bastard-toad-flax** [*Thesium humifusum*]. (Family *Santalaceæ*.)

△ Plant not having the above characteristics together.. 550

550
(following on 549).

✠ Flowers more than 5½ centimetres (2 inches) long, with a long tube (Fig. D) with 5 pleats and 5 short acute teeth. → **Thorn - apple** Datura [*Datura Stramonium*]—medicinal; poisonous. (Family *Solanaceæ*.)

✠ Flowers less than 5½ centimetres long 551

551
(following on 550).

○ The stalks of the flowers are each attached **immediately above a little leaf** 552

○ The stalks of the flowers are attached to the stem without any little leaf at their immediate point of attachment (see the figures below) 554

552
(following on 551).

— Each flower **more than a centimetre across**, shaped like a very open funnel (Fig. CO) ; the part that surrounds the base of the corolla (calyx) grows very much when the flower has withered and forms a sort of balloon (Fig. P), at first green, then red, or orange. → **Common Winter-cherry** (Cape Gooseberry) [*Physalis Alkekengi*]—medicinal. (Family *Solanaceæ*.)

— Each flower **less than a centimetre across**, forming a tube with 5 lobes at the top (Fig. LA represents the flower cut lengthwise). → Gromwell [*Lithospermum*].[1] —For the chief kinds of Gromwell [*Lithospermum*] go on to No. 553

553
(following on 552).

✳ Each leaf with only one vein prominent on the under surface of the leaf (Fig. AV) ; the other veins are hardly prominent or hardly visible. → **Corn Gromwell** [*Lithospermum arvense*]. (Family *Boraginaceæ*.)

✳ Each leaf with **many veins** prominent on the under surface of the leaf (Fig. LO). → **Common Gromwell** (Grey Millet) [*Lithospermum officinale*]. (Family *Boraginaceæ*.)

---

[1] For further details as to the various species of Gromwell [*Lithospermum*] reference should be made to more comprehensive Floras.

554
(following on 551).

== Leaves prolonged far down the stem by their bases (Figs. SO and S); flowers more than a centimetre in length, ending in 5 very short lobes bending outwards (Fig. CD). → **Officinal Comfrey** [*Symphytum officinale*]—medicinal. 🌸 —Represented in colour (with purple flowers): 3, Plate 39. (Family *Boraginaceæ*.)

== Leaves **not** prolonged down the stem by their bases   555

555
(following on 554).

⊖ In looking at the flower from the front, 5 little scales are seen within the tube of the corolla almost completely closing it (Fig. P); the withered flowers diverge from one another (Fig. I). → **Myosote** (Scorpion-grass) [*Myosotis*].— For the chief kinds of *Myosotis* refer back to No. ...   261

⊖ In looking at the flower from the front, it will be seen that there are **not** 5 little scales within the tube; the withered flowers remain in crowded clusters below the newly opened flowers (Fig. H). → **European Heliotrope** [*Heliotropium europæum*]. (Family *Boraginaceæ*.)

556
(following on 541).

× Stem **with** branches (see below, Figs. AS and PH, under No. 557)   557

× Stem **without** branches (see below, Figs. C and P, under No. 558)   558

557
(following on 556).

☐ The stems bear short fine green branches resembling leaves and arranged in crowded tufts (Fig. P; Fig. AS represents a flowering branch).→**Seaside Asparagus** [*Asparagus maritimus*]—food plant; medicinal. 🌸 —Represented in colour (in fruit): 1, Plate 53. (Family *Liliaceæ*.)

☐ The stems do **not** bear short fine branches in crowded tufts; leaves attached singly (Fig. PH). → **Branched Phalangium** [*Phalangium ramosum*]. (Family *Liliaceæ*.)

558
(following on 556).

✳ ✳ Flowers rounded in the form of a little bell (Fig. C); leaves attached to the base of the stem. → **May Convallaria** (Lily-of-the-Valley) [*Convallaria majalis*]—medicinal; ornamental.—Represented in colour: 3, Plate 54. (Family *Liliaceæ*.)

✳ ✳ Flowers tubular (Fig. P); leaves arranged along the stem and intermixed with the flowers. → **Solomon's Seal** [*Polygonatum*].—For the chief kinds of *Polygonatum* go on to No.   559

559
(*follow-ing on 558*).

⊙ **Stem angular in section** (Fig. A represents a piece of the stem); flowers solitary or in groups of 2 (Fig. P). → Officinal Solomon's Seal [*Polygonatum officinale*].—Represented in colour: 2, Plate 54. (Family *Liliaceæ*.)

⊙ **Stem round in section** (Fig. PM); flowers grouped often 3 to 5 together (Fig. M). → **Many - flowered Solomon's Seal** [*Polygonatum multiflorum*]. (Family *Liliaceæ*.)

560
(*follow-ing on 509*).

↶ Each flower has its petals separate from one another down to their bases; that is to say, that one of the petals, or parts of the flower coloured white or whitish, can be detached without tearing the others. This refers to those parts of the flower which, collectively, make up the corolla or coloured structure surrounding the little threads and other organs that occupy the middle of the flower; when the flower fades each petal (or coloured piece) falls off or withers separately [1] .. 570

N.B.—It sometimes happens that the tube of the calyx, which encloses the petals, does not permit of its being seen at a glance that the petals are separate down to their bases (Fig. DI, below, for example); the tube of the calyx must then be torn to see the petals distinct from one another down to their bases.

The above figures represent examples of flowers with petals distinct from one another.

↶ Each flower has its petals **united together, at least at the base**; that is to say, that in trying to detach one of the parts of the flower coloured white or whitish, one is obliged to tear the corolla, at least at its base; when the flower fades the corolla falls off or withers all in one piece 561

The above figures represent examples of flowers with their petals united, at least at their base. In Figs. M and P the petals are seen to be united into a tubular corolla with lobes at the top. Figs. MC, VC, and VT represent examples of flowers with their petals only united at the base.

---

[1] In most flowers there is, outside the corolla, another covering to the flower, generally green, known as the *calyx*, which surrounds the base of the corolla. In other flowers it is difficult to distinguish the calyx and corolla apart, they being more or less blended into a single floral envelope. Lastly, in some other flowers there is actually only one floral envelope, which is coloured white or whitish, like a corolla. Under the names petals and corolla we here understand those parts, coloured white or whitish, that immediately surround the little threads or other organs occupying the centre of the flower.

561
(following on 560)

- The 4 or 5 lobes of the flower are exactly equal one with the other 562
- The 4 or 5 lobes of the flower are not exactly equal one with the other 566

The above figures represent examples of flowers whose lobes are not exactly equal one with the other.

562
(following on 561).

⊕ Each flower has 5 lobes spread out in the form of a star or of a wide cup, and united at their base by a very short tube (Figs. MC and VC) 563

⊕ Each flower has 5 lobes placed at the end of a long bell- or funnel-shaped cylindrical tube (examples: Fig. CA and E) 564

563
(following on 562).

✠ Stem upright; flowers grouped, whitish; leaves pointed at the tip (Figs. VC, D). → Officinal **Swallow-wort** [*Vincetoxicum officinale*]— poisonous; medicinal.—Represented in colour: 5, Plate 37. (Family *Asclepiadaceæ*.)

✠ Stem more or less prostrate; flowers white, attached singly at the axils of the leaves (Figs. MC and A); leaves oval. → **Field Pimpernel** (Scarlet Pimpernel, Poor Man's Weather-glass) [*Anagallis arvensis*].—Represented in colour (with blue or red flowers): 6 and 6 *bis*, Plate 36.[1] (Family *Primulaceæ*.)

564
(following on 562).

§ Each flower, bell- or funnel-shaped, with the tube widened at the top (Figs. P and G). → **Gentian** [*Gentiana*].[2] Cross-leaved Gentian [*Gentiana Cruciata*] is represented in colour (with blue flowers): 2, Plate 38. (Family *Gentianaceæ*.)—For the principal kinds of Gentians [*Gentiana*] refer to No. 278

§ Each flower having the tube either little or not at all wider at the top (see head of following page, Figs. E and CA of No. 565

---

[1] The Scarlet Pimpernel must not be confounded with the **Chickweed Star-wort** [*Stellaria media*]. The latter is represented in colour: 4, Plate 9. (Family *Caryophyllaceæ*.)

[2] For further details as to the various species of Gentian [*Gentiana*] reference should be made to more comprehensive Floras.

565
(following on 564).

+ Flowers more than half a centimetre (⅕ inch) in length; the tube of the corolla surrounded by the green tube of the calyx (Figs. E, EC). → Common Centaury [*Erythræa Centaurium*]—medicinal.—Represented in colour (with pink flowers): 1, Plate 38. (Family *Gentianaceæ*.)

+ Flowers less than 3 millimetres in width; the tube of the corolla not surrounded by the green tube (Fig. CA; Fig. OL, No. 568, represents a flowering branch). → Cooking Valerianella (Corn Salad, Lamb's Lettuce) [*Valerianella olitoria*]—food plant.[1]—Represented in colour (with blue flowers): 4, Plate 27. (Family *Valerianaceæ*.)

566
(following on 561).

—o Leaves with a strong aromatic odour when rubbed 567

—o Leaves without any strong aromatic odour 568

567
following on 566).

△ Leaves either not toothed at the edge or not very plainly so (Figs. OR and O); flowers surrounded by numerous little oval scales. → Common Marjoram [*Origanum vulgare*]—medicinal. —Represented in colour (with pink flowers): 3, Plate 43. (Family *Labiatæ*.)

△ Leaves plainly toothed at the edges; flowers not surrounded by a number of little oval scales; flowers almost regular (Fig. M). → Mint [*Mentha*]—For the principal kinds of Mints [*Mentha*] refer to No. 169

568
(following on 566).

✠ Each flower has 5 lobes (Fig. CA); flowers in closely packed groups at the top of the stalks (Fig. OL). → Cooking Valerianella (Corn Salad, Lamb's Lettuce) [*Valerianella olitoria*] —food plant.—Represented in colour (with bluish flowers): 4, Plate 27. (Family *Valerianaceæ*.)

✠ Each flower has 4 lobes 569

569
(following on 568).

O Corolla has spreading lobes (Fig. VT) united to each other by a short tube. → Speedwell [*Veronica*].[2]—For the principal kinds of Speedwell [*Veronica*] refer to No. 315

O Corolla, funnel-shaped, with upright lobes (Fig. L); leaves deeply toothed, pointed (Fig. LY), or even divided. → Common Gipsywort [*Lycopus europæus*]. (Family *Labiatæ*.)

---

[1] For the various species of *Valerianella* reference should be made to more comprehensive Floras.

[2] For further details as to the various species of Speedwell [*Veronica*] reference should be made to more comprehensive Floras.

570
(following on 560).

— Plant fleshy, with thick fleshy leaves shaped like elongated grains (Fig. AL); petals pointed at the tip (the petals are almost completely separated). → White Stonecrop [*Sedum album*]—medicinal. ❀ —Represented in colour: 4, Plate 22. (Family *Crassulaceæ*.)

— Plant not fleshy **571**

571
(following on 570).

✳ Each flower having 2 petals divided in two and 2 other parts green or reddish.—Refer to No. **62**

✳ Each flower having 5 petals, not divided, or each divided in two, but not as far as the base **573**

✳ Each flower having the appearance of 10 petals owing to the 5 petals of the flower being divided in two down to the base **572**

✳ Each flower having the appearance of 4 or 8 petals; stems with the look and hardness of wood except in the young branches; leaves very small and close together (Fig. C). → Common Ling (Heather) [*Calluna vulgaris*]. ❀ —Represented in colour (with pink flowers): 2, Plate 36. (Family *Ericaceæ*.)

572
(following on 571).

= Plant without any hairs; leaves very pointed (Fig. SG). → Grassy Starwort (Lesser Stitchwort) [*Stellaria graminea*]. (Family *Caryophyllaceæ*.)

= Plant hairy; a line of hairs may be seen on the stem extending from one pair of leaves to the following pair (Fig. MR). → Intermediate Starwort (Common Chickweed) [*Stellaria media*].—Represented in colour: 4, Plate 9. Cultivated as food for small birds. (Family *Caryophyllaceæ*.)

573
(following on 571).

⊖ Stems not hairy except sometimes towards the base **574**

⊖ Stems hairy up to the top **577**

574
(following on 573).

× Each of the 5 petals is divided in two at the top (example: Fig. CV) **576**

× None of the 5 petals divided at the top (example: Fig. AS) **575**

575
(following on 574).

☐ Petals shorter than the 5 green parts of the calyx which surrounds them; leaves very narrow and pointed (Fig. AT). → **Fine-leaved Alsine** [*Alsine tenuifolia*]. (Family *Caryophyllaceæ.*)

☐ Petals longer than the 5 green parts of the calyx which surrounds them; leaves oval (Fig. C); petals falling very easily. → **Cathartic Flax** [*Linum catharticum*]—medicinal. (Family *Linaceæ.*)

576
(following on 574).

✱ ✱ Calyx inflated round the petals (Fig. SI); leaves less than 4 times longer than they are broad. → **Broad-leaved Silene** (Bladder Campion) [*Silene latifolia*].—Represented in colour: 3, Plate 8. (Family *Caryophyllaceæ.*)

✱ ✱ Calyx not inflated round the petals; leaves more than 4 times longer than they are broad (Fig. SH). → **Bone-set Starwort** (Greater Stitchwort, Cuckoo's meat, Adder's meat) [*Stellaria Holostea*].—Represented in colour: 5, Plate 9. (Family *Caryophyllaceæ.*)

577
(following on 573).

⊙ Petals **extending beyond the** 5 little green parts of the calyx which surrounds them 578

⊙ Petals not extending beyond the 5 little green parts of the calyx which surrounds them 583

578
(following on 577).

♧ Each petal having little irregular teeth at the tip (Fig. H); flowers whose stalks all spring from the same point (Fig. HU). → **Umbelliferous Jagged-chickweed** [*Holosteum umbellatum*]. (Family *Caryophyllaceæ.*)

♧ Plant not having these characteristics together ... 579

579
(following on 578).

• Plant very viscid, sticking to the fingers if the stem is plucked by the upper part; flowers more or less drooping (Fig. N). → **Drooping Silene** (Nottingham Catchfly) [*Silene nutans*]. (Family *Caryophyllaceæ.*)

• Plant not very viscid, nor sticking to the fingers.... 580

580
(following on 579).

⊕ Flowers more or less inflated (Figs. LDI, LY); the calyx (the inflated structure surrounding the petals) is slightly contracted at its upper end and green and purplish along its sides. → **Evening Lychnis** (White Campion) [*Lychnis vespertina*]. —Represented in colour: 2 and 2 *bis*, Plate 9. (Family *Caryophyllaceæ*.)

⊕ Flowers with very spreading petals (Fig. CC); the calyx which surrounds the petals is very open; plant with lax, almost climbing, stems; leaves all stalked. → **Berry-bearing Campion** [*Cucubalus bacciferus*]. (Family *Caryophyllaceæ*.)

⊕ Plant not having the characteristics described above 581

581
(following on 580).

✠ Each petal divided into two at the tip (Fig. CV). → **Cerastium** [*Cerastium*].[1]—For the chief kinds of Mouse-ear-chickweed [*Cerastium*] go on to No. 582

✠ Each petal **not** divided into two at its tip (Fig. AS); leaves grouped, apparently whorled, that is to say, appearing to start from the same point on the stem (Fig. SC) (in reality the leaves are opposite). → **Corn Spurrey** [*Spergula arvensis*]. (Family *Caryophyllaceæ*.)

582
(following on 581).

§ Each flower more than 12 millimetres across when fully out; petals far longer than the five little green parts of the calyx which surround them (Fig. CC). → **Field Cerastium** (Mouse-ear-Chickweed) [*Cerastium arvense*].—Represented in colour: 3, Plate 9. (Family *Caryophyllaceæ*.)

§ Each flower less than a centimetre across; petals scarcely longer than the five little green parts of the calyx which surround them. → **Wayside Cerastium** [*Cerastium vulgatum*]. (Family *Caryophyllaceæ*.)

583
(following on 577).

+ Each petal distinctly divided into two at its tip (Fig. CV); leaves velvety. → **Wayside Cerastium** [*Cerastium vulgatum*]. (Family *Caryophyllaceæ*.)

+ Each petal **not** divided into two at its tip, or scarcely notched; leaves without hairs or slightly hairy (Fig. S). → **Thyme-leaved Sandwort** [*Arenaria serpyllifolia*]. (Family *Caryophyllaceæ*.)

---

[1] For further details as to the various species of *Cerastium* reference should be made to more comprehensive Floras.

584
(following on 509).

—• Leaves in opposite pairs and only apparently whorled (Fig. SC); petals separate from one another down to their bases, that is to say, that one white petal can be detached down to its base without tearing the other petals even at their bases. → **Corn Spurrey** [*Spergula arvensis*]. (Family *Caryophyllaceæ*.)

—• Leaves really whorled (Fig. GA); petals united to one another, at least at the base; that is to say, that one of the petals cannot be completely detached without tearing the corolla at least at the base 585

585
(following on 584).

△ Flowers with 5 petals or 5 lobes white or whitish ... 586

△ Flowers with 4 petals or 4 lobes white or whitish... 587

586
(following on 585).

⊬ Stems with hairs; leaves with hairs along their veins and edges; flowers with petals united at the base only (Fig. VC). → **Officinal Swallow-wort** (Tame-poison) [*Vincetoxicum officinale*]—dangerous.—Represented in colour: 5, Plate 37. (Family *Asclepiadaceæ*.)

⊬ Stems without hairs but with little hooked bristles (Fig. GA), clinging to one's clothes; the leaves have no hairs, but their edges are armed with bristles (Fig. RP); flowers with petals united at the base into a tolerably long tube. → **Wild Madder** [*Rubia peregrina*]. (Family *Rubiaceæ*.)

587
(following on 585).

○ Flowers shaped like an elongated rattle (Fig. EC); stems with the appearance and hardness of wood, except in the young twigs. → **Hoary Heath** (Fine-leaved Heath) [*Erica cinerea*]. ❀ —Represented in colour (with crimson flowers): 1, Plate 36. (Family *Ericaceæ*.)

○ Plant not having these characteristics 588

588
(following on 587).

— Each flower funnel-shaped (Fig. AC); leaves 4 in a whorl, very narrow; plant prostrate, not fragrant. → **Quinsy-wort Asperula** [*Asperula cynanchica*]—medicinal. (Family *Rubiaceæ*.)

— Each flower funnel-shaped; leaves 6 to 9 in a whorl (Fig. AO); plant erect, fragrant when dried. → **Sweet Asperula** (Sweet Woodruff) [*Asperula odorata*]. (Family *Rubiaceæ*.)

— Each flower with 4 spreading lobes only united at the base (Fig. GM). → **Bedstraw** [*Galium*].[1]— For the chief kinds of Bedstraw [*Galium*] go on to No. 589

---

[1] For further details as to the various species of Bedstraw [*Galium*] reference should be made to more comprehensive Floras.

589
(following on 588).

✳ Plant clinging to one's clothes by little hooked bristles on the angles of its stems or on its leaves **590**

✳ Plant not clinging to one's clothes **591**

590
(following on 589).

= Plant more than 45 centimetres (18 inches) long, with clambering stems supporting themselves by clinging to other plants (Fig. GG represents a flowering stem). → Cleavers Bedstraw (Clivers, Goose-grass) [*Galium Aparine*]—food plant; medicinal. (Family *Rubiaceæ*.)

= Plant less than 45 centimetres (18 inches) long, with erect, self-supporting stems (Fig. GCR represents a flowering stem). → Rough-fruited Bedstraw [*Galium tricorne*]. (Family *Rubiaceæ*.)

591
(following on 589).

⊖ Leaves rounded or slightly pointed at their tips (Fig. P). → Water Bedstraw [*Galium palustre*]. (Family *Rubiaceæ*.)

⊖ Leaves pointed or acute at their tips (example: Fig. M) **592**

592
(following on 591).

× Petals ending in a little point (Fig. GM). → Hedge Bedstraw [*Galium Mollugo*]—medicinal.—Represented in colour: 3, Plate 27. (Family *Rubiaceæ*.)

× Petals acute at the tips but without a little point (Fig. GS). → Rough Bedstraw [*Galium asperum*]. (Family *Rubiaceæ*.)

—
593
(following on 508).

□ Below the solitary flower terminating the stem there are three leaves attached to the stem at the same point (Fig. AN). → Wood Anemone (Wind - flower) [*Anemone nemorosa*]—Represented in colour: 4, Plate 1. (Family *Ranunculaceæ*.)

□ Plant not having this characteristic **594**

594
(following on 593).

✳ ✳ Flowers all very nearly at the same level; leaves with numerous toothed leaflets in two rows (Fig. AM). In reality, what is taken for each flower is a composite flower made up of a great number of very little strap-shaped or tubular flowers, the whole surrounded by a collarette of very small scales. → Milfoil Achillea (Milfoil, Yarrow) [*Achillea Millefolium*]—medicinal.—Represented in colour: 6, Plate 31. (Family *Compositæ*.)

✳ ✳ Leaves much divided into segments which are again divided into numerous leaflets; flowers small and very numerous in branching clusters.—Refer back to No. 421

✳ ✳ Plant not having these characteristics **595**

595
(following on 594).

⊙ Each flower with 4 petals or 4 lobes **596**

⊙ Each flower with more than 4 petals or 4 lobes **601**

596
(following on 595).

♥ Each flower with 4 lobes at the top, with a somewhat funnel-shaped corolla (Fig. L); leaves deeply toothed, with acute teeth (Fig. LY) or even deeply divided; flowers white spotted with red. → **Common Gipsy-wort** [*Lycopus europæus*]. ✠ (Family *Labiatæ*.)

♥ Each flower with 4 petals, separated from one another down to their bases **597**

597
(following on 596).

• Flowers less than 7 millimetres across **598**

• Flowers more than 7 millimetres across **599**

598
(following on 597).

⊕ Plant without hairs; leaves with a pungent taste, with the upper lobe more or less rounded (Fig. OF). → **Officinal Water-cress** [*Nasturtium officinale*]—medicinal; food plant.—Represented in colour: 3, Plate 6. (Family *Cruciferæ*.)

⊕ Plant with hairs (examine with the lens); leaves without any pungent taste, not divided or divided; but, in the latter case, the upper lobe of the leaf is not rounded (Fig. CBP represents a whole plant). → **Common Shepherd's-purse** [*Capsella Bursa-pastoris*]—medicinal. — Represented in colour: 5, Plate 6. (Family *Cruciferæ*.)

599
(following on 597).

✠ Each flower more than 3 centimetres (1⅕ inch) across; leaves embracing the stem by their bases (Fig. PV); petals crumpled in the flower-bud (Fig. PR). → **Opium Poppy** (Garden Poppy) [*Papaver somniferum*]—poisonous; medicinal. (Family *Papaveraceæ*.)—A variety of this plant is cultivated for industrial purposes.—Represented in colour (with lilac flowers): 2, Plate 5.

✠ Plant not having these characteristics together.... **600**

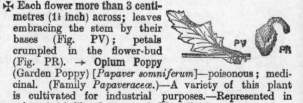

600
(following on 599).

§ Petals veined with brown or violet lines (Fig. RR); upper leaves toothed. → Wild Radish (White Charlock) [*Raphanus Raphanistrum*]. 🌼 (Family *Cruciferæ*.)

§ Petals not veined with brown or violet lines, but only more or less striped (Fig. C); upper leaves deeply divided

(Fig. CAR); lower leaves with rounded leaflets (Fig. P). → Meadow Cardamine (Lady's Smock, Cuckoo-flower) [*Cardamine pratensis*]. 🌼 —Represented in colour (with lilac flowers): 2, Plate 6. (Family *Cruciferæ*.)

601
(following on 595).

+ Plant growing in the water, with leaves divided into very narrow elongated thongs (see Figs. FL, RAQ, below, under No. 602) 602

+ Plant not having these characteristics together 603

602
(following on 601).

─• Leaves with very long divisions all directed lengthwise in the same direction (Fig. FL). → Submerged Crowfoot [*Ranunculus fluitans*]. (Family *Ranunculaceæ*.)

─• Leaves with divisions not all directed lengthwise or in the same direction (Figs. RAQ and G). → Water Crowfoot [*Ranunculus aquatilis*].—Represented in colour: 3, Plate 1.[1] (Family *Ranunculaceæ*.)

603
(following on 601).

△ Flowers with 5 to 7 petals 604

△ Flowers with more than 7 petals. In reality what is taken for a flower is a composite flower made up of numerous little strap-shaped or tubular flowers, the whole surrounded by a collarette of little leaves or little scales.— Go on to No. 891

604
(following on 603).

✠ Each flower star-shaped (Fig. N), with 5 petals scarcely united; each petal bears two green spots at its base; leaves sometimes divided (Fig. DU); plant clambering and supporting itself more or less by means of other plants. → Bittersweet Nightshade (Woody Nightshade) [*Solanum Dulcamara*]— poisonous; medicinal.—Represented in colour (with violet flowers): 2 and 2 *bis*, Plate 40. (Family *Solanaceæ*.)

✠ Plant not having these characteristics together.. 605

─────────────

[1] For further details as to the white-flowered species of Crowfoot [*Ranunculus*] reference should be made to more comprehensive Floras.

605
(follow-ing on 604).

○ Leaves with leaflets or divisions very definitely **separated** from one another, the leaflets at the end of the leaf sometimes excepted **606**

The above figures represent examples of leaves either with leaflets or divisions plainly separated from one another.

○ Leaves with divisions **not** definitely separated from one

another down to their base **616**

606
(follow-ing on 605).

— Leaves slightly fragrant, with numerous rather unequal divisions in two rows and toothed (Fig. EC); flowers with rather unequal petals and fringed at the base (examine with magnifying glass). → Hemlock Stork's-bill [*Erodium cicutarium*].— Represented in colour (with pink flowers): 2, Plate 11. (Family *Geraniaceæ*.)

— Plant not having these characteristics together... **607**

607
(follow-ing on 606).

✳ Leaves opposite; that is to say, attached in pairs opposite to one another, at the same level, on the stem (see below Figs. Y and VAL at No. 608) **608**

✳ Leaves alternate; that is to say, attached singly to the stem at different levels **609**

✳ Leaves all at the base of the plant **609**

608
(follow-ing on 607).

= Stem with 2 little unequal leaflets attached to it at right and left of the base of each leaf (Fig. E; Fig. Y represents a flowering branch). → Dwarf Elder (Danewort) [*Sambucus Ebulus*]—medicinal. ✿ —Represented in colour: 5, Plate 26. (Family *Caprifoliaceæ*.)

= Stem without 2 little leaflets attached to it at right and left of the base of each leaf (Fig. VAL). → Valerian [*Valeriana*].—For the principal kinds of Valerian refer to No. **103**

609
(following on 607).

⊖ Stems and stalks of leaves having here and there sharp prickles (Fig. RC). → **Shrubby Bramble** (Blackberry) [*Rubus fruticosus*]—medicinal; eatable. 🌸 —Represented in colour: 5, Plate 19. (Family *Rosaceæ*.)

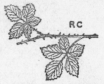

⊖ Stems and stalks of leaves **without prickles** **610**

610
(following on 609).

• Each leaf having **3 leaflets or 3 divisions** (without counting, when such are present, the 2 little leaflets attached to the stem which are at the base of the leaf) **611**

• Each leaf having **more than 3 leaflets** or more than 3 divisions **613**

611
(following on 610).

× Plant **growing in the water,** or in flooded areas, edges of leaves **not** regularly toothed (Fig. T). → **Common Buck-Bean** (Bog Bean, Marsh Trefoil) [*Menyanthes trifoliata*]—medicinal. (Family *Gentianaceæ*.)

× Plant **not growing in the water;** edges of leaves regularly toothed **612**

612
(following on 611).

☐ Each flower with **an orange ring inside it** at the base of the petals; flower-stalks have hairs lying flat (examine with magnifying glass) (Fig. FF). → **Strawberry-like** Potentil [*Potentilla Fragariastrum*].[1] (Family *Rosaceæ*.)

☐ Each flower **without any orange ring inside** at the base of the petals; flower-stalks have hairs not lying flat (Fig. FC). → **Edible Strawberry** [*Fragaria vesca*]—eatable; medicinal.—Represented in colour: 3, Plate 18. (Family *Rosaceæ*.)

613
(following on 610).

✱✱ Each flower **more than a centimetre and a half** (⅗ inch) across, the petals joined together and forming a star-shaped corolla; leaves with leaflets neither divided nor sharply toothed (Fig. P). → **Tuberous Nightshade** (Potato) [*Solanum tuberosum*] —eatable; medicinal.—Represented in colour (with pinkish flowers): 4, Plate 40. (Family *Solanaceæ*.)

✱✱ Each flower **less than a centimetre and a half** across **614**

---

[1] For the various species of white-flowered Potentils [*Potentilla*] reference may be made to more comprehensive Floras.

614
(following on 613).

⊙ Flowers in little groups; the stalks of the flowers are all attached at exactly the same point (Fig. PV) ; leaves hav-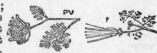ing divisions which are again much divided (Fig. P represents a branch when the flowers are over). → **Venus' Comb Scandix** (Shepherd's - Needle) [*Scandix Pecten-Veneris*]. (Family *Umbelliferæ*.)

⊙ Flowers in branching clusters; flower-stalks not attached at exactly the same point ; leaves with toothed leaflets (Figs. UL and S at No. 615). → **Spiræa** [*Spiræa*].—For the principal kinds of Spiræas see on to No. **615**

615
(following on 614).

↶ **Leaves not having more than 11 leaflets** (the leaves at the top of the stems must not be taken as examples) very unequal (Fig. UL). 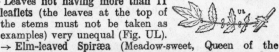→ **Elm-leaved Spiræa** (Meadow-sweet, Queen of the Meadows) [*Spiræa Ulmaria*]—medicinal.—Represented in colour : 4, Plate 18. (Family *Rosaceæ*.)

↶ Leaves having 31 to 41 leaf-lets (the leaves at the top of the stem must not be taken as examples), slightly unequal (Fig. F). → **Dropwort Spiræa** [*Spiræa Filipendula*] —medicinal. (Family *Rosaceæ*.)

616
(following on 605).

⊕ Plant climbing; stems having slender coil-ing threads (Fig. BR), by which they attach themselves to other plants. → **Diœcious Bryony** (White Bryony) [*Bryonia dioica*]—poisonous ; medicinal. 🌸 —Represented in colour : 1 and 1 *bis*, Plate 21. (Family *Cucurbitaceæ*.)

⊕ Plant not climbing. → **Saxifrage** [*Saxifraga*].[1]—For the principal kinds of Saxifrages [*Saxifraga*] see on to No. **617**

617
(following on 616).

✠ **Each flower more than a centi-metre across;** plant rather viscid in its upper part ; lower leaves rounded and toothed on the upper side (Fig. SGR). → **Tuberous Saxifrage** (Pretty Maids) [*Saxifraga granulata*]. (Family *Saxifragaceæ*.)

✠ Each flower less than a centimetre across ; the greater part of the leaves have 3 divisions (Fig. TR) ; leaves rather thick and fleshy. → **Three-fingered Saxifrage** [*Saxifraga tri-dactylites*].—Represented in colour : 2, Plate 23. (Family *Saxifragaceæ*.)

---

[1] For further details as to the various species of Saxifrage reference should be made to more comprehensive Floras.

§ **Leaves compound;** that is to say, that the leaf as a whole is made up by the union of secondary leaves, known as *leaflets,* each of which is often mistaken for a leaf; the whole compound leaf is attached to the stem either by its base or by a stalk which bears all the leaflets; the base of a compound leaf is not attached exactly in the axil of another leaf 655

The above figures represent examples of compound leaves.

§ **Leaves deeply divided** (except sometimes the leaves that are quite at the upper part of the stems); that is to say, that each leaf is, as it were, cut to the extent of more than half its breadth 655

The above figures represent examples of deeply divided leaves.

§ **Leaves simple;** that is to say, either not cut to the extent of more than half the breadth of the leaf, or merely edged with teeth, or even without teeth on their edges 619

The above figures represent examples of simple leaves.

N.B.—It is of little moment if there is any doubt as between compound and deeply divided leaves, since in either case the reference is to the same number (655).

If the doubt is as between deeply divided and simple leaves (as in Fig. A, for example) either question may be followed up, and in either case the name of the plant will be reached. The same will be the case if the plant has both simple and compound or divided leaves (not counting the few simple leaves that may occur quite at the top of the flowering stems).

618
(following on 507).

+ Leaves **opposite** (except sometimes at the upper part
of the stems or branches); that is to say, that the leaves
are arranged in pairs attached to the stem, at the same
level, opposite to one another 632

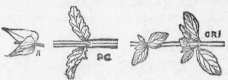

The above figures represent examples of opposite leaves.

N.B.—In the axils of opposite leaves small leafy shoots are
somewhat frequently found (as in the above Fig. ORI, on the
right) which may lead to the belief that the leaves are grouped in
a large number at the same level on the stem, instead of being only
an opposite pair; but on examining the base of such a group of
leaves carefully, the two opposite leaves will be readily distinguished.

+ Leaves **whorled**, at least towards the middle region of
the stems; that is to say,
leaves attached by 3's or 4's
at the same level on the

stem and arranged regularly round its whole circumference (example: Fig. LS) 621

619
*(follow-
ing on
618).*

+ Leaves **alternate**; that is to say, leaves attached singly
to the stem at different levels 620

The above figures represent examples of plants with alternate
leaves.

+ Leaves **grouped**; that is to say, leaves attached 2 or more
together at the same level on the stem, but arranged, at
that level, only on one side of the stem 620

+ Leaves all at the base of the
plant ....  .. 625

Fig. VP represents an example
of a plant with all its leaves at
the base.

N.B.—If a plant has both alternate and
opposite leaves (as, for example, in Fig.
PD) or both alternate and whorled leaves,
either question may be followed up, and
in either case the name of the plant will
be reached.

620
(following on 619).

—• Flower shaped like a mouth, with the lower lip inflated and in contact with the upper lip (see Figs. M and ST below, under No. 621) 621

—• Flower **not** shaped like a mouth 622

621
(following on 620).

△ Each flower more than 2 centimetres across and with a swelling at the base (Fig. M). → **Greater Snapdragon** [*Antirrhinum majus*]—ornamental; medicinal. 🌺 —Represented in colour (with red flowers): 1, Plate 41. (Family *Scrophulariaceæ.*)

△ Each flower less than 2 centimetres across, with a horn or tube at the base (Fig. ST); leaves alternate or whorled. → **Creeping Toadflax** [*Linaria repens*]. 🌺 (Family *Scrophulariaceæ.*)

622
(following on 620).

✠ Flowers white, marked with violet lines; corolla tubular at the base and opening in two lips, one upper and the other lower (Fig. E). → **Common Eye-bright** [*Euphrasia officinalis*]—medicinal. (Family *Scrophulariaceæ.*)

✠ Plant **not** having these characteristics together.. 623

623
(following on 622).

○ Flowers tubular, widely bell-mouthed (Fig. P), with a slight curve below; flowers in a long cluster and all turning towards the same side. → **Purple Foxglove** (white-flowered variety) [*Digitalis purpurea*]—poisonous; medicinal; ornamental. 🌺 —Represented in colour (with purple flowers): 5, Plate 41. (Family *Scrophulariaceæ.*)

○ Flowers **not** in the form of a bell-mouthed tube ... 624

624
(following on 623).

— Each flower with 2 free pieces placed right and left of the rest of the flower (Fig. POL). → **Common Milkwort** (Gangweed) (Fig. PV) [*Polygala vulgaris*].—Represented in colour (with pink or lilac flowers): 4, Plate 7. (Family *Polygalaceæ.*)

— Plant with flowers **not** of this shape 625

625
(following on 624).

✳ Each flower with 4 petals or 4 lobes 626

✳ Each flower with 5 petals, one of which is prolonged into a horn at the base 628

✳ Each flower with 5 lobes, with no horn at the base 500

✳ Each flower with 6 or 7 petals, or 6 white or whitish parts 629

626
(following on 625).

= **2 petals larger** than the others (Figs. IB and I). → **Bitter Candytuft** [*Iberis amara*]. ✿ (Family *Cruciferæ*.)

= **One petal larger** than the others or of a different shape **627**

627
(following on 626).

⊖ **Flower with a long horn or tube** at its base (Fig. MT). In reality the flower is made up of 6 pieces, but there are 2 petals brought towards the centre of the flower which it is not easy to make out at the first glance. → **Mountain Orchis** (*Orchis montana*].—Represented in colour: 2, Plate 55. (Family *Orchidaceæ*.)

⊖ **Flower without** either horn or tube at its base; petals only united at the base (Fig. VT). → **Speedwell** [*Veronica*].—Refer back to No. **315**

628
(following on 625).

× **2 petals directed upward** and 3 petals directed downwards (Fig. H). → **Violet** [*Viola*].—Refer back to No. **303**

× **4 petals directed upward** and one petal directed downward (Fig. TRI). → **Tricolor Viola** (Pansy, Heart's-ease) [*Viola tricolor*] —ornamental; medicinal.—Represented in colour (with yellow and violet flowers): 2, Plate 7. (Family *Violaceæ*.) —A form of this species is cultivated for ornament in gardens.

629
(following on 625).

☐ Flowers **less than a centimetre** (⅖ inch) across, with several of the petals deeply divided (examine with the lens) (Fig. RE, enlarged); flowers in a long cluster (Fig. RL); leaves not divided (Fig. U). → **Rampion Reseda** [*Reseda Phyteuma*]. ✿ (Family *Resedaceæ*.)—A related species *Reseda odorata* is the Sweet Mignonette grown for its perfume in gardens.

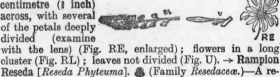

☐ Flowers **more than a centimetre** across, with **one petal very different** from the others **630**

630
(following on 629).

✱ ✱ **Flowers spotted with red or violet with a horn** or tube at the base directed downward; leaves often spotted (Fig. OT). → **Spotted Orchis** [*Orchis maculata*] —medicinal. (Family *Orchidaceæ*.)

✱ ✱ Flowers **not spotted with red or violet** **631**

631
(following on 630).

⊙ Flowers white and partly yellowish white, with a long tube at the base  (Figs. BI and B). → **Lesser Butterfly-orchid** [*Habenaria bifolia*]. (Family *Orchidaceæ*.)

⊙ Flowers of a greenish white, without a tube at the base (Fig. E). → **Broad-leaved Epipactis** [*Epipactis latifolia*]—medicinal. 🌸—Represented in colour (with rose-coloured flowers): 7, Plate 56. (Family *Orchidaceæ*.)

632
(following on 619).

↻ Plant climbing (Fig. LC) with stems twining round other plants; stems with the appearance and hardness of wood, except in the young branches. → **Common Honeysuckle** (Woodbine) [*Lonicera Periclymenum*]—medicinal. 🌸—Represented in colour: 4, Plate 26. (Family *Caprifoliaceæ*.)

↻ Plant not climbing 633

633
(following on 632).

• Flowers having, as it were, two well-marked lips; that is to say, that two divisions of the flower can be recognised, one higher, the other lower (examples: the figures below) 634

• Flowers not having two well-marked lips (examples: the figures below; but there is sometimes a single lip, as in Fig. A) 650

634
(following on 633).

⊕ Each flower with red, lilac, or brown spots on the lower lip 635

⊕ Flowers not spotted with red, lilac, or brown.... 639

635
(following on 634).

✠ Each flower more than 2½ centimetres (1 inch) long; leaves borne on very distinct  stalks; flowers solitary, or 2 or 3 together, in the axils of the leaves (Figs. MM and ME). → **Balm-leaved Melittis** (Bastard Balm) [*Melittis Melissophyllum*]—medicinal.—Represented in colour: 3, Plate 44. (Family *Labiatæ*.)

✠ Each flower less than 2½ centimetres (1 inch) long ... 636

636
(*following on 635*).

§ Flowers yellowish or yellowish white; the leaves on the upper parts of the stems ending in a small point   **637**

§ Flowers white; the leaves on the upper parts of the stems not ending in a small point **638**

637
(*following on 636*).

+ Leaves very hairy; the 5 teeth of the calyx round the tube of the corolla are like little spines, without hairs (Fig. S); leaves without stalks (Fig. R). → **Upright Woundwort** [*Stachys recta*]. 🌸 (Family *Labiatæ*.)

+ Leaves almost without hairs; the 5 teeth of the calyx round the corolla are like little long-pointed spines (Fig. A); leaves with a stalk (Fig. AR). → **Annual Woundwort** [*Stachys annua*]. 🌸 (Family *Labiatæ*.)

638
(*following on 636*).

—• Plant with a strong aromatic smell; leaves without teeth or not distinctly toothed (Fig. OR and O); there are numerous little oval scales round the flowers. → **Common Marjoram** [*Origanum vulgare*]—medicinal. 🌸 —Represented in colour: 3, Plate 43. (Family *Labiatæ*.)

—• Plant with a strong disagreeable smell; leaves rather deeply toothed (some of them, at least), reversedly heart-shaped (Fig. CT); corolla with its upper lip straight (Fig. N). → **Cat-mint Nepeta** [*Nepeta Cataria*]—medicinal. (Family *Labiatæ*.)

—• Plant without smell, either aromatic or disagreeable; leaves oval or elongated, deeply toothed (Fig. LY), or even deeply divided; corolla with indistinct lips (Fig. L). → **Common Gipsy-wort** [*Lycopus europæus*]. 🌸 (Family *Labiatæ*.)

639
(*following on 634*).

△ Flowers with the lower lip yellowish, but not inflated (Fig. E); the 5 teeth of the calyx can be seen round the tube of the corolla ending in little spines (Fig. A); leaves with a stalk (Fig. AN). → **Annual Woundwort** [*Stachys annua*]. 🌸 (Family *Labiatæ*.)

△ Plant not having these characteristics together.... **640**

640
(*following on 639*).

⚔ Each flower more than 1½ centimetres in total length **641**

⚔ Each flower less than 1½ centimetres in total length **644**

641
(*following on 640*).

○ Each flower more or less in the form of a mouth, with the lower lip slightly inflated (Fig. M) and with two little bosses within (Fig. MP) **642**

○ Stems with stiff prickly hairs, much swollen near the attachment of the leaves.—Refer back to No. **179**

○ Plant not having these characteristics **643**

642
(*following on 641*).

— Leaves alternate on the upper part of the stems; each flower with a swelling at the base (Fig. M). → **Greater Snapdragon** [*Antirrhinum majus*]—ornamental; medicinal. ✿ —Represented in colour (with red flowers): 1, Plate 41. (Family *Scrophulariaceæ*.)

— Leaves all opposite (Fig. PR); flowers without a swelling at the base, but with two little bosses on the inner part of the lower lip (Fig. MP). → Meadow Cow-wheat [*Melampyrum pratense*].—Represented in colour (with yellow flowers): 5, Plate 42. (Family *Scrophulariaceæ*.)

643
(*following on 641*).

✱ Flowers of which the upper lip has rather the shape of a sickle which has been, as it were, cut off at the top (look at the flower from the side: Figs. S and P); plant rather sticky in the upper part. → Meadow Sage (Meadow Clary) [*Salvia pratensis*]—medicinal.—Represented in colour (with blue flowers): 7, Plate 43. (Family *Labiatæ*.)

✱ Flowers of which the upper lip is not sickle-shaped (Fig. A); plant not sticky in the upper part. → White Dead-nettle [*Lamium album*]—medicinal.—Represented in colour: 6, Plate 44. (Family *Labiatæ*.)

644
(*following on 640*).

= Flowers marked with violet lines; upper leaves not opposite (Fig. O; Fig. E represents a flower). → Common Eyebright [*Euphrasia officinalis*]—medicinal. (Family *Scrophulariaceæ*.)

= Flowers not marked with violet lines; leaves all opposite **645**

645 *(following on 644).*
⊖ Flowers with two bosses on the upper part of the lower lip of the corolla and with the teeth of the calyx round the corolla ending in little straight pointed spines (Figs. T and LA represent the calyxes). → Hemp-nettles [*Galeopsis*].—Refer back to No. 179

⊖ Plant not having these characteristics together..... 646

646 *(following on 645).*
× Flowers of which the corolla is surrounded by the teeth of the calyx which are hooked at their tips (Fig. MAR). → Common White-horehound [*Marrubium vulgare*]—medicinal. (Family *Labiatæ*.)

× Plant not having this characteristic 647

647 *(following on 646).*
□ Leaves with the smell of lemon when they are bruised; leaves coarsely toothed (Fig. M); corolla with a curved tube. → Officinal Balm [*Melissa officinalis*]—medicinal. (Family *Labiatæ*.)

□ Leaves not having the smell of lemon and not having the above-mentioned characteristics together 648

648 *(following on 647).*
✱✱ Flowers the corolla of which is enclosed at the base by the tube of the calyx which is regularly pleated (Fig. BF); leaves wrinkled, generally with a strong disagreeable smell when they are bruised. → Black Horehound [*Ballota nigra*].—Represented in colour (with pink flowers): 7, Plate 44. (Family *Labiatæ*.)

✱✱ Plant not having the above characteristics together 649

649 *(following on 648).*
⊙ Stems ending in leaves; flowers intermixed with ordinary leaves (Fig. GH). → Ivy-leaved Nepeta (Ground-Ivy, Alehoof) [*Nepeta hederacea*]—medicinal. —Represented in colour (with blue flowers): 4, Plate 44. (Family *Labiatæ*.)

⊙ Stems ending in flowers crowded towards the upper part of the stem (Fig. P). → Red Dead-nettle (with white flowers) [*Lamium purpureum*]. (Family *Labiatæ*.)

650 *(following on 633).*
↳ Each flower with a long slender tube at the base closed at its apex (Fig. C): plant without hairs. → Red Spur-Valerian (with white flowers) [*Centranthus ruber*]—ornamental. (Family *Valerianaceæ*.)

↳ Each flower without a long tube at its base.... 651

651
(following on 650).

- Each flower with its corolla in the form of a tube ending above by one lower lip divided into 3 or 5 lobes (see Figs. A and T, at No. 652 below) **652**
- Each flower having a corolla not of this shape.... **653**

652
(following on 651).

⊕ Flowers white, the lower lip having 3 lobes (Fig. A). → **Bugle** (with white flowers) [*Ajuga*].—For the principal kinds of Bugle refer back to No. **336**

⊕ Flowers yellowish white or greenish white; the lower lip having the appearance of being divided into 5 lobes: the 4 side lobes are much smaller than the centre one (Fig. T); flowers in elongated clusters (Fig. S). → **Wood Germander** (Wood Sage) [*Teucrium Scorodonia*]—medicinal. ✿ —Represented in colour: 3, Plate 45. (Family *Labiatæ*.)

653
(following on 651).

✠ Each flower has 2 petals, each divided in two, and two other greenish or reddish parts.—Refer back to No. **62**

✠ Each flower has a corolla with very short tube and 4 lobes more or less spread out (Fig. VT). → **Speedwell** (with white flowers) [*Veronica*] **315**

✠ Each flower has a corolla with tube not very short and divided at the top into 4 lobes of which none are spread out, or of which one only is not spread out **654**

654
(following on 653).

§ Leaves with edges not toothed at all, or not sharply toothed (Figs. OR and O); flowers surrounded by numerous little oval scales; leaves having an aromatic odour. → **Common Marjoram** [*Origanum vulgare*]—medicinal. ✿ —Represented in colour (with pink flowers): 3, Plate 43. (Family *Labiatæ*.)

§ Leaves with sharply toothed edges; flowers not surrounded by a number of little scales, flowers almost regular; leaves having the well-known fragrance of mint. → **Mint** [*Mentha*]. — For the principal kinds of Mint [*Mentha*] refer back to No. **169**

§ Leaves very deeply toothed (Fig. LY) or even divided; flower with a rather short corolla (Fig. L), white spotted with red; leaves without any aromatic odour. → **Common Gipsywort** [*Lycopus europæus*]. ✿ (Family *Labiatæ*.)

655
(follow
ing on
618).

{ + Each flower having at its
base a long horn (Fig.
D); leaves with narrow
elongated divisions, each
one less than 3 milli-
metres in width. → Con-
sound Larkspur [*Delphinium Consolida*]—medicinal. —
Represented in colour (with purple flowers): 3, Plate 3.
(Family *Ranunculaceæ*.)

+ Flowers not having a long horn at their base 656

656
(follow-
ing on
655).

—• Corolla butterfly-shaped; that is to say, with
5 unequal petals, the petal uppermost being
the largest (Fig. *e* below), 2 petals matching
one another to right and left (Figs. *a, a* below),
and 2 under petals joined together (Figs. *cc* below) in
the form of a boat, and occasionally curled round upon
one another (Fig. P, to the right) 657

—• Flowers not butterfly-shaped; that is to say, not
arranged in the manner above described 666

657
(follow-
ing on
656).

△ Leaves terminating in a slender thread, often curling,
single, or branching; leaves with more than 3 leaflets
(example: Fig. V and Figs. P, TE at No. 660, or Fig. LE
at No. 661) 658

△ Leaves not ending in a slender thread, and having 3 leaflets
(example: Figs. ST and H below) 662

658
(follow-
ing on
657).

✠ Leaves ending in a
branched and curling
thread (example: Fig. V) .. 660

✠ Leaves ending in an unbranched
thread either straight or curled
(example: Fig. LE) 659

659
(following on 658).

○ Each flower more than 2 centimetres (⅞ inch) long and with a black mark on either side (Fig. F). → **Common Bean** (Broad Bean, Windsor Bean) [*Faba vulgaris*]—food plant. ✻—Represented in colour: 2, Plate 16. (Family *Leguminosæ*.)

○ Each flower about half a centimetre, or even less, in length and without a black mark on either side ... **661**

660
(following on 658).

— Each flower more than 1 centimetre long; the two leaflets which are at the base of each leaf, and attached to the stem, are larger than those of the leaf itself (Fig. P). → **Cultivated Pea** (Green Pea) [*Pisum sativum*]—food plant fit for fodder. ✻—Represented in colour: 1, Plate 17. (Family *Leguminosæ*.)

— Each flower half a centimetre in length or even less; the two leaflets which are at the base of each leaf, and attached to the stem, are smaller than those of the leaf itself (Fig. TE). → **Four-seeded Vetch** (Smooth Tare) [*Vicia tetrasperma*]. ✻ (Family *Leguminosæ*.)

661
(following on 659).

✳ The green calyx which surrounds the corolla is only divided into 5 lobes for about half its length (Fig. PU shows the calyx only, enlarged); at the base of the leaves near the middle of the stem, the two very small leaflets, or scales, attached to the stem, are divided into 2 lobes pointed at the top. → **Four-seeded Vetch** (Smooth Tare) [*Vicia tetrasperma*]. ✻ (Family *Leguminosæ*.)

✳ The green calyx which surrounds the corolla is divided into 5 lobes very deeply, almost to the base (Fig. L shows a flower by itself, enlarged); at the base of the leaves near the middle of the stem, the two very small leaflets, or scales, attached to the stem are oval and not divided (Fig. LE). → **Lentil Vetch** [*Ervum lens*]—food plant. (Family *Leguminosæ*.)

662
(following on 657).

= Each flower having the middle part **curled round upon itself** (Fig. P); leaves with 3 leaflets (Fig. H); plant often climbing by its twining stems. → **Common Haricot** (French Bean, Haricot Bean) [*Phaseolus vulgaris*]—food plant. ✻ —Represented in colour: 2, Plate 14. (Family *Leguminosæ*.)

= Flowers **not curled** round upon themselves **663**

663
(following on 662).

⊖ Flowers **in long clusters** (Fig. M), but rather separated from one another towards the lower end of the cluster. → **White Melilot** [*Melilotus alba*]. ✽ (Family *Leguminosæ*.)

⊖ Flowers **in crowded clusters or in rounded and crowded heads** (see Figs. TI, A, and R below, under Nos. 664 and 665) 664

664
(following on 663).

× Flowers **in clusters 4 to 6 centimetres** (1½ to 2½ inches) long, in an elongated oval (Fig. TI). → **Crimson Trefoil** (Trifolium, Crimson Clover) [*Trifolium incarnatum*]—fodder plant. ✽ —Represented in colour (with crimson flowers): 5, Plate 14. (Family *Leguminosæ*.)

× Flowers **in rounded heads or in crowded clusters** that are less than 4 centimetres long 665

665
(following on 664).

□ Flowers **in velvety heads** like tufts of wool (Fig. A); stems and leaves with hairs; leaves with rather narrow and elongated leaflets. → **Field Trefoil** (Hare's-foot Trefoil) [*Trifolium arvense*]. (Family *Leguminosæ*.)

□ Flowers **in rounded heads that are not woolly**; stems and leaves without hairs; leaves with oval leaflets; stems trailing, putting out roots here and there (Fig. R). → **Creeping Trefoil** (Dutch Clover, White Clover) [*Trifolium repens*]—fodder plant. ✽ —Represented in colour: 3, Plate 14. (Family *Leguminosæ*.)

666
(following on 656).

✳✳ Flowers **spotted with red**, with the corolla tubular at the base (Fig. L); leaves much toothed, with acute teeth (Fig. LY) or even much divided. → **Common Gipsywort** [*Lycopus europæus*]. ✽ (Family *Labiatæ*.)

✳✳ Flowers **not spotted with red**, with a corolla not tubular at its base 667

667
(following on 666).

⊙ Flowers **very small**, with all their stalks attached exactly at the same point (Fig. PV). → **Venus's Comb Scandix** (Shepherd's Needle) [*Scandix Pecten-Veneris*]. (Family *Umbelliferæ*.)

⊙ Flowers with their stalks **not all attached** at the same point 668

668
(following on 667).

♡ Leaves with a great number of little narrow divisions arranged in two rows (Fig. AM). In reality, what is taken for each flower is a composite flower made up of a considerable number of very small tubular flowers and round them a few very small strap-shaped flowers, the whole surrounded by a collarette of little crowded scales; the flowers open almost all at the same level. → **Milfoil Achillea** (Milfoil, Yarrow) [*Achillea Millefolium*] — medicinal. — Represented in colour: 6, Plate 31. (Family *Compositæ*.)

♡ Leaves divided but not into a very large number of narrow little divisions arranged in 2 rows........ **669**

669
(following on 668).

✳ Flowers in long clusters (Fig. RL); each flower less than half a centimetre across, with petals more or less divided (examine with the lens). → **Sweet Reseda** (Mignonette) [*Reseda odorata*]—ornamental. 🌼 (Family *Resedaceæ*.)

✳ Flowers not in clusters; each flower more than half a centimetre across, with 4 petals turned upward and one petal directed downward (Figs. T, TRI). → **Tricolor Viola** (Pansy, Heartsease) [*Viola tricolor*] —ornamental; medicinal.—Represented in colour (with yellow flowers): 2, Plate 7. (Family *Violaceæ*.)

670
(following on 506).

⊕ There are no little leaves or scales exactly at the base of the secondary rays (Fig. A), that is to say, at *o*, at the base of the stalks *s* which themselves bear the flowers (examine with the lens) (*p*, one of the primary rays, the rest have been cut away in the figure) **671**

⊕ There may be one or several little leaves or scales (*f*, Fig. B) exactly at the base of the secondary rays *s* (examine with the lens) (*p*, one of the primary rays, the rest have been cut away in the figure) **674**

671
(following on 670).

✠ Flowers of a greenish white; groups of flowers produced all along the plant, even towards its base (Fig. C); leaves without hairs, glossy. → **Wild Celery** (Smallage) [*Apium graveolens*]—food plant. (Family *Umbelliferæ*.)

✠ Flowers white and plant not having the above characteristics together **672**

672
(following on 671).

+ 2 to 5 primary rays each bearing a rounded group of crowded flowers (Fig. F); plant without hairs, with the stem hollow; leaves with elongated divisions (Fig. FS).—Go on to No. 681

+ 6 to 25 primary rays 673

673
(following on 672).

§ The leaves at the middle of the stems or the base of the plant have 3 divisions themselves each divided into 3 (Fig. Æ). → Common Gout-weed (Bishop-weed) [*Ægopodium Podagraria*]—medicinal. (Family *Umbelliferæ*.)

§ The leaves at the middle of the stems or the base of the plant have more than 3 divisions arranged in two rows and not themselves divided completely (Figs. PM and PS). → Common Burnet-saxifrage [*Pimpinella Saxifraga*]. (Family *Umbelliferæ*.)

674
(following on 670).

—• The little leaves just at the base of the principal rays are each cut into narrow segments (Figs. CT and CA) 675

—• The little leaves, scales, or thongs just at the base of the principal rays are not cut into narrow segments (Fig. O) 676

—• There are no little leaves, scales, or thongs at the base of the principal rays 676

675
(following on 674).

△ The largest umbels have from 23 to 40 principal rays; plant not growing in water, nor in flooded places; the flowers of the outer part of the umbels have their petals larger on the outside (Fig. CHS); Fig. DC represents an umbel seen from below. → Wild Carrot [*Daucus Carota*].—Represented in colour: 5, Plate 23. (Family *Umbelliferæ*.)

△ The largest umbels have from 9 to 22 principal rays; plant growing in water or in flooded places; flowers all nearly regular; leaflets in 2 rows (Fig. A); the little leaves at the base of the principal rays are more or less divided (Figs. B and BE). → Narrow-leaved Water-parsnip [*Sium angustifolium*]—medicinal. (Family *Umbelliferæ*.)

676
(following on 674).

✠ Stems bearing throughout their length simple, toothed leaves, attached, 4 or more at the same level, regularly all round the stem 588

✠ Plants with divided leaves, without hairs (examine with the lens) 677

✠ Plants with divided leaves, and with hairs 692

677
(following on 676).

○ At the base of the secondary rays there are 3 little elongated thongs, directed downward, which are longer than the little secondary umbel at the base of which they are (Fig. CY; the principal rays, with one exception, have been cut off); compound umbel with 5 to 10 principal rays; leaves very divided. → Dog's-parsley Æthusa (Fool's-parsley) [*Æthusa Cynapium*]—poisonous; medicinal.—Represented in colour: 2, Plate 25. (Family *Umbelliferæ*.)

○ Plant not having the above characteristics together.. 678

678
(following on 677).

— Stems prostrate on the ground; leaves with their principal divisions toothed (Fig. N); umbels with 4 to 8 principal rays. → Procumbent Marshwort [*Helosciadium nodiflorum*]. (Family *Umbelliferæ*.)

— Plant not having the above characteristics together 679

679
(following on 678).

• 2 to 5 principal rays to each compound umbel 680

• 6 to 30 principal rays to each compound umbel.... 682

680
(following on 679).

= Leaves simple, with their veins arranged like a fan (Fig. SE); groups of flowers very crowded (Fig. S), and each flower without a stalk. → **Wood Sanicle** [*Sanicula europæa*]—medicinal. (Family *Umbelliferæ*.)

= Leaves deeply divided, with very narrow divisions (see Figs. FS and PE below, under No. 681); stem hollow 681

681
(following on 680).

⊖ 2 or 3 principal rays to each compound umbel (Fig. F); leaves on the middle of the stems with divisions which are not deeply divided (Fig. FS). → **Common Water-dropwort** [*Œnanthe fistulosa*]—poisonous; medicinal. (Family *Umbelliferæ*.)

⊖ 4 or 5 principal rays to each compound umbel; leaves on the middle of the stems with divisions which are themselves deeply divided (Fig. PE).→Parsnip-leaved Water-dropwort (Sulphur-wort, Water-dropwort) [*Œnanthe peucedanifolia*]. (Family *Umbelliferæ*.)

682
*(follow-
ing on
679).*

× The widest divisions of the leaves are less **than 3 milli-**
metres across, and 4 times as long as they are wide, or
even still longer 683

× The widest divisions of the leaves are less than 4 times
as long as they are wide 686

683
*(follow-
ing on
682).*

☐ Plant growing **in water or in flooded areas.** On carefully
examining (with the lens) each of the little flowers of the
secondary umbels, there will be seen, round the white
petals, the 5 green teeth of the calyx which grow much
larger when the flowers are over................. 684

☐ Plant not growing either in water or in flooded areas. Even
if the little flowers of the secondary umbels are carefully
examined (with the lens) it will be difficult to detect, round
the white petals, the 5 green teeth of the calyx which
scarcely grow larger when the flower is over 685

684
*(follow-
ing on
683).*

✳ ✳ Each flower of the secondary umbels
has a quite distinct stalk; the petals
of the outer flowers of the umbels
are rather unequal; leaves with
main divisions which are again subdivided once or
twice (Fig. P). → Fine-leaved Water-dropwort
[*Œnanthe Phellandrium*]—poisonous; medicinal.
(Family *Umbelliferæ.*)

✳ ✳ Each flower of the secondary umbels has a very short
stalk or none at all (examine
with lens); petals of the
outer flowers on the umbels
CHS
very unequal (Fig. CHS); leaves with main divisions
subdivided more than once (Fig. PE). → Parsnip-leaved
Water-dropwort (Sulphur-wort, Water-Dropwort)
[*Œnanthe peucedanifolia*]. (Family *Umbelliferæ.*)

685
*(follow-
ing on
683).*

⊙ Leaves with longest divisions less
than 3 centimetres in length; divisions of leaves erect (Fig. SES); most
of the compound umbels have 4 to
10 principal rays. → **Mountain Seseli** (Mountain Meadow
Saxifrage) [*Seseli montanum*]. (Family *Umbelliferæ.*)

⊙ Leaves with longest divisions more than
3 centimetres in length; leaf divisions
spread out (Fig. PR); most of the compound umbels have 10 to 20 principal
rays. → **Parisian Peucedanum** [*Peucedanum parisiense*]. (Family *Umbelliferæ.*)

686
(following on 682).

⚲ Each leaf has 2 rows of leaflets not themselves deeply subdivided (Fig. A); the compound umbels have only

short stalks; the little leaves at the base of the **principal** rays may be divided or not (Figs. B and BE). → **Narrow-leaved Water-parsnip** [*Sium angustifolium*]. (Family *Umbelliferæ*.)

⚲ Each leaf (except those at top of the stem) has **divisions** entirely subdivided **687**

687
(following on 686).

• On breaking the stem the well-known scent of angelica will be perceived; leaflets of the leaves more than 2 centimetres wide and toothed all round (Figs. AS and ANG). → **Wild Angelica** [*Angelica sylvestris*]—medicinal. 🌸—Represented in colour: 1, Plate 25. (Family *Umbelliferæ*.)

• Plant without the preceding characteristics **688**

688
(following on 687).

⊕ The stalk of the compound leaf is prolonged and divided into slightly curved **parts** which follow on from one another (Fig. PO); principal leaf divisions stiff and separated from one another. → **Mountain-parsley Peucedanum** [*Peucedanum Oreoselinum*]. (Family *Umbelliferæ*.)

⊕ Plant whose leaves have **not** these characteristics **689**

689
(following on 688).

✠ Compound umbels with short stalks (Fig. PH), generally less in length than the principal rays of the umbel; there is a calyx with 5 well-marked teeth round the white petals of each flower (examine with lens) (Fig. P represents a leaf). → **Fine-leaved Water-dropwort** [*Œnanthe Phellandrium*]—poisonous; medicinal. (Family *Umbelliferæ*.)

✠ Compound umbels with long stalks, longer than the principal rays of the umbel; the calyx at the base of the 5 white petals is scarcely visible **690**

§ Flowers on the outer edge of the umbels nearly regular (Figs. CMA and SEL; this circle of flowers may be even

690
(following on 689).

less irregular than in the illustration); **leaves with very narrow** divisions (Fig. SE) all less than 4 millimetres wide. → **False Milk-parsley** [*Selinum carvifolia*]. (Family *Umbelliferæ*.)

§ Flowers on outer edge of the umbels irregular; the petals turned towards the outer border of the umbels are larger than those in the interior (Figs. BL and CHS); leaves having some divisions more than 4 millimetres across 691

691
(following on 690).

+ There are 3 to 7 small reversed scales at the base of the principal rays (Fig GC); the largest compound umbels have 11 to **20 principal rays;** stems blotched with purple particularly towards the base. → **Spotted Hemlock** [*Conium maculatum*]— poisonous; medicinal.—Represented in colour: 3, Plate 25. (Family *Umbelliferæ*.)

+ No little leaves or scales at the base of the principal rays (Fig. ASI); the largest compound umbels have 5 to 10 principal rays. → **Wild Chervil** (Wild-beaked Parsley) [*Chærophyllum sylvestre*]—poisonous; medicinal. (Family *Umbelliferæ*.)

692
(following on 676).

—• Each exterior flower of the umbel has outer petals less than 3 times larger than the interior petals of the same flower (Fig. BL shows a secondary umbel); the largest umbels have more than 12 rays; stem with rough hairs. → **Common Cow - parsley** (Hog - weed) [*Heracleum Sphondylium*]—medicinal. 🐝 —Represented in colour: 3, Plate 24. (Family *Umbelliferæ*.)

—• Plant not having these characteristics together.. 693

693
(following on 692).

△ Stems covered at the upper part with stiff hairs all turning downwards (Fig. TOR); leaves more or less rough to touch. → **Hedge-parsley** [*Torilis*].—For the principal kinds of Hedge-parsley [*Torilis*] see on to No. ... 694

△ Plants not having the preceding characteristics together 696

694
(following on 693).

✠ Each compound umbel has a very short, barely visible, stalk (Fig. TN); the little leaves at the base of the secondary rays are longer than the stalks of the flowers. → **Knotted Hedge-parsley** [*Torilis nodosa*]. (Family *Umbelliferæ*.)

✠ Plant not having these characteristics together.. **695**

695
(following on 694).

○ The outer flowers of the umbel nearly regular (Fig. TA represents one of the secondary umbels); there are, generally speaking, 5 little leaves or scales at the base of the secondary rays. → **Upright Hedge-parsley** [*Torilis Anthriscus*]. (Family *Umbelliferæ*.)

○ The outer flowers of the umbel very irregular (Fig. TI represents one of the secondary umbels); there are at most 4 little leaves or scales at the base of the secondary rays: there may not be any. → **Spreading Hedge-parsley** [*Torilis infesta*]. (Family *Umbelliferæ*.)

696
(following on 693).

— Each compound umbel has in general 2 to 5 principal rays (count the rays on several umbels) **697**

— Each compound umbel has in general 6 to 15 principal rays (count the rays on several umbels) **700**

697
(following on 696).

✱ Stem very hairy; 2 to 3 principal rays, very short (Fig. SP; the white petals open out at the top of a long beak which forms part of the flower). → **Venus' Comb Scandix** (Shepherd's Needle) [*Scandix Pecten-Veneris*]. (Family *Umbelliferæ*.)

✱ Stem not hairy or only slightly so **698**

698
(following on 697).

= Leaves with the well-known odour of chervil; having at their base a little crowded mass of whitish hairs exactly above the point to which the leaves are attached: umbels often have very short stalks (Fig. CER). → **Cultivated Chervil** [*Cerefolium sativum*]—food plant; medicinal.—Represented in colour: 4, Plate 25. (Family *Umbelliferæ*.)

= Leaves without the well-known odour of chervil; when there are hairs above the point to which the leaves are attached, they are not crowded in little whitish masses **699**

699
(following on 698).

⊖ Each compound umbel attached to the stem by a rather short stalk opposite the leaf (Fig. AN); by carefully examining a flower (with the lens) a calyx surrounding the base of the 5 white petals can just be distinguishable. → **Common Beaked-parsley** [*Anthriscus vulgaris*]. (Family *Umbelliferæ*.)

⊖ Each compound umbel at the head of the stem or branch (Fig. CA); by carefully examining a flower (with the lens) the 5 little green parts surrounding the base of the 5 white petals can be plainly distinguished. → **Small Bur-parsley** [*Caucalis daucoides*]. (Family *Umbelliferæ*.)

700
(following on 696).

× Leaves with very narrow divisions (each less than 2 millimetres in width) and **upright** (Fig. SES); stems more or less prostrate at their base. → **Mountain Seseli** (Mountain Meadow Saxifrage) [*Seseli montanum*]. (Family *Umbelliferæ*.)

× Leaves with **spreading** divisions, **not very narrow**; stems usually upright from their base 701

701
(following on 700).

☐ Stems **with reddish brown or purple spots** (or becoming reddish brown altogether) on their lower side; stems solid, or only slightly hollow within (Figs. CH and CP); leaves covered with small hairs (examine with the lens). → **Rough Chervil** [*Chærophyllum temulum*]—poisonous. (Family *Umbelliferæ*.)

☐ Stems **not spotted** with reddish brown or purple on their lower side; stems very hollow (Fig. AN); leaves without hairs, or with a few only, chiefly on the veins. → **Wild Chervil** (Wild-beaked Parsley) [*Chærophyllum sylvestre*]—poisonous. (Family *Umbelliferæ*.)

702
(following on 507).

✳✳ Leaves attached to the stem by a sheath **split open down its length** (see *F, ft, g*, Fig. G) on the side opposite to that on which the leaf springs from the stem; stem **more or less cylindrical** (see *t, t*, Fig. G); the leaf has a little scale or a line of fine hairs at the spot where it is joined to the stem above the sheath 1069

✳✳ Plant **not having these characteristics together** 703

703
(following on 702).

⊙ Each flower has a tuft of white silky hairs (Fig. A); leaves attached to the stem by a long sheath (Fig. L). → **Many-ranked Cotton-grass** [*Eriophorum polystachion*].[1]—Represented in colour: 1, Plate 58. (Family *Cyperaceæ*.)

⊙ Plant not having the above characteristics **704**

704
(following on 703).

⌢ Each flower with 6 divisions (examine with the lens); the leaves are more than 15 times as long as they are broad (Fig. NI). → **Snowy Wood-rush** [*Luzula nivea*]. (Family *Juncaceæ*.)

⌢ Each flower with 4 divisions (examine with the lens: Fig. LC); leaves less than 15 times as long as they are broad (examples: Figs. LA, MA, and ME, below); all the small flowers are collected into a single crowded head at the top of the stem. → **Plantains** [*Plantago*].—Refer back to No. **150**

The above figures represent different examples of the leaves of Plantains [*Plantago*]. Fig. ME represents a whole plant.

705
(following on 4).

✱ Plant which yields a white milk when the stem is cut or broken **706**

✱ Plant without white milk **711**

706
(following on 705).

⊕ Leaves with fine teeth on their edges, at least on the upper half of the leaf (see Figs. SR and HE, below) **707**

⊕ Leaves without teeth on their edges **708**

---

[1] For the various species of Cotton-sedge [*Eriophorum*] reference should be made to more comprehensive Floras.

707
(following on 706).

✠ **Leaves pointed at the base and rounded at the tip** (Figs. HE and HLC); the leaves are often all fallen except those at the base of the umbel.—(A detached flower (enlarged) is shown at H). → **Sun Spurge** [*Euphorbia Helioscopia*]—medicinal; dangerous.—Represented in colour: 3, Plate 47. (Family *Euphorbiaceæ.*)

✠ **Leaves** (towards the middle of the stem) **more or less pointed at the tip** (Fig. SR). → **Upright Spurge** [*Euphorbia stricta*]—poisonous. (Family *Euphorbiaceæ.*)

708
(following on 706).

§ **Below the groups of flowers there are rounded leaves which appear to be pierced by the branches**; leaves generally **collected in a rosette** near the middle of the flowering stems; below this rosette the stem bears no more leaves (Fig. S). → **Almond-scented Spurge** (Wood Spurge) [*Euphorbia amygdaloides*]—poisonous. ❀ —Represented in colour: 5, Plate 47. (Family *Euphorbiaceæ.*)

§ **There are no rounded leaves appearing as if pierced** by the branches below the groups of flowers; leaves not collected into a rosette at the middle of the stems **709**

709
(following on 708).

+ **The chief branches which spring from one point at the top of a stem or of a flowering branch are 6 or more in number;** the leaves of the branches without flowers are long and narrow; branches without flowers, bearing leaves smaller than those on the stem, are grouped below the flowering branches (Fig. C). → **Cypress Spurge** [*Euphorbia Cyparissias*]—poisonous.—Represented in colour: 4, Plate 47. (Family *Euphorbiaceæ.*)

+ **The chief branches which spring from one point are 3 to 5 in number** **710**

710
(following on 709).

—• **Leaves all opposite** (Fig. LT), that is to say, attached in pairs, one opposite the other; plant usually more than 50 centimetres (1½ feet) in height; the smaller leaves at the base of the chief flower-bearing branches are arranged in a cross (Fig. L). → **Caper Spurge** [*Euphorbia Lathyris*]—medicinal. (Family *Euphorbiaceæ.*)

—• **Leaves almost all alternate,** that is to say, attached singly to the stem at different heights; leaves oval (Fig. PE). → **Petty Spurge** [*Euphorbia Peplus*]. (Family *Euphorbiaceæ.*)

△ Leaves **opposite** (except sometimes at the top of the stems or branches); that is to say, leaves arranged in pairs, attached to the stem, at the same level, one opposite the other **712**

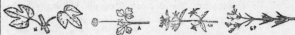

The above figures represent examples of opposite leaves.

N.B.—In the axils of opposite leaves there are not uncommonly little leafy shoots which might lead to the belief that the leaves are grouped in a large number at the same level on the stem (Fig. SP, on the right, for example), and not merely in opposite pairs; but a careful examination of the base of such a group of leaves will readily distinguish the two opposite leaves.

△ Leaves **whorled**, at least towards the middle of the stems; that is to say, leaves attached 3, 4, 5, or even more, together at the same level on the stem, and arranged regularly round its whole circumference **712**

The above figures represent examples of whorled leaves.

△ Leaves **alternate**; that is to say, leaves attached singly to the stem at different levels **727**

711 (following on 705).

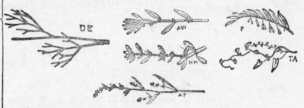

The above figures represent examples of alternate leaves.

△ Leaves **grouped**; that is to say, leaves attached at the same level on the stem but arranged, at that level, on one side of the stem (Fig. AC, for example) **727**

△ Leaves all at the base of the plant **727**

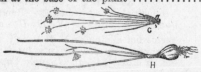

Figs. C and H represent examples of plants with all their leaves at the base.

N.B.—If the plant has both alternate and opposite leaves, or both alternate and whorled leaves, either question may be followed up, and in either case the name of the plant will be reached.

✠ Compound leaves of 5 to 7 leaflets arranged like a fan (Fig. C). → Cultivated Hemp (Common Hemp) [*Cannabis sativa*] —industrial; medicinal.—Represented in colour: 2 and 2 *bis*, Plate 48. (Family *Urticaceæ*.)

✠ Leaves deeply divided (except sometimes those at the upper part of the stem); that is to say, each leaf is, as it were, cut to the extent of more than half its width ... 713

712
(*following on* 711).

The above figures represent examples of plants with deeply divided leaves.

✠ Leaves simple; that is to say, either without teeth on their edges, or toothed, or divided, but not cut to the extent of more than half the breadth of the leaf ... 716

The above figures represent examples of plants with simple leaves.

713
(*following on* 712).

○ Leaves in whorls of 4 to 10; plant growing in water ... 714
○ Leaves opposite; plant not growing in water 715

714
(*following on* 713).

— Leaves in whorls of 4 or 5; flowers arranged in an erect spike (Fig. S). → Spiked Water-milfoil [*Myriophyllum spicatum*]. (Family *Haloragaceæ*.)

— Leaves in whorls of 6 to 10 (Fig. CD); flowers not in an erect spike. → Common Hornwort [*Ceratophyllum demersum*]. (Family *Ceratophyllaceæ*.)

715
(*following on* 713).

• Stems climbing (Fig. H) twining themselves round stems or round supports; there are numerous leaves in pairs. → Rough Hop [*Humulus Lupulus*] —industrial; medicinal. ❀ —Represented in colour: 1 and 1 *bis*, Plate 48. (Family *Urticaceæ*.)

• Stems not climbing; there is only one pair of leaves (Fig. A). → Tuberous Moschatel [*Adoxa Moschatellina*]. (Family *Caprifoliaceæ*.)

716
(*following on* 712).

= Leaves without hairs 717
= Leaves with hairs (examine with the lens) 723

717
(following on 716).

⊖ There are only two oval leaves on the stem (Fig. O); each flower with 6 irregular divisions. → **Egg - shaped Listera** (Twayblade) [*Listera ovata*].—Represented in colour: 5, Plate 56. (Family *Orchidaceæ*.)

⊖ There are **more than 2 leaves** on the stem; **flowers regular**, that is to say, that the similar parts of the flower are regularly arranged round the centre of the flower and equal to one another 718

718
(following on 717).

× Plant attached to the branches of a tree, with leaves without teeth, some opposite (Fig. VI), others whorled. → **White Mistletoe** [*Viscum album*]—medicinal. ✿ — Represented in colour: 3 and 3 *bis*, Plate 26. (Family *Loranthaceæ*.)

× Plant growing in the soil, or in water 719

719
(following on 718).

☐ Each flower more **than 1½ centimetres (⅔ inch)** in total length 720

☐ Each flower less than 1½ centimetres in total length 721

720
(following on 719).

✳ ✳ Leaves oval, in regular whorls of 4 or 5 (Fig. PA); there are no other leaves on the stem; flower with 8 or 10 narrow divisions. → **Four-leaved Paris** (Herb Paris) [*Paris quadrifolia*]—medicinal; dangerous. (Family *Liliaceæ*.)

✳ ✳ Leaves more or less divided, attached to the stem at various heights; flower of 5 oval parts, of a more or less yellowish green (Fig. AUR). → **Goldilocks Crowfoot** [*Ranunculus auricomus*]. (Family *Ranunculaceæ*.)

721
(following on 719).

☉ Plant floating in water or at the surface of the water; flowers in erect spikes (Figs. PE, R, G). → **Floating Pondweed** [*Potamogeton natans*].[1]—Represented in colour: 1, Plate 57. (Family *Naiadaceæ*.)

☉ Plant **not growing in water** 722

---

[1] For the numerous species of Pond-weeds [*Potamogeton*] reference must be made to more comprehensive Floras.

722
(following on 721).

♀ Stems erect; leaves oval (Figs. AN and PE) more than a centimetre across. → **Annual Mercury** [*Mercurialis annua*]—medicinal; harmful to crops.—Represented in colour: 2 and 2 *bis*, Plate 47. An allied species, **Dog's Mercury** [*Mercurialis perennis*], with a perennial underground stem, is more abundant in woods. (Family *Euphorbiaceæ*.)

♀ Stems flat on the ground (Fig. G); leaves less than a centimetre across. → **Smooth Rupture - wort** [*Herniaria glabra*]—medicinal. (Family *Illerebraceæ*.)

723
(following on 716).

✱ Leaves with hairs that pierce and sting the fingers on being touched; leaves toothed all round their edges (Fig. D). → **Diœcious Stinging - Nettle** (Great Stinging Nettle) [*Urtica dioica*]—food plant; industrial; medicinal.[1]— Represented in colour: 4, Plate 48. (Family *Urticaceæ*.)

✱ Leaves with hairs that do not pierce or sting...... **724**

724
(following on 723).

⊕ Stems flat on the ground (Fig. HH); leaves oval and without teeth; there are little membranous scales at the base of the leaves (examine with the lens). → **Hairy Rupture-wort** [*Herniaria hirsuta*]. (Family *Illerebraceæ*.)

⊕ Stems erect **725**

725
(following on 724).

⊬ Each flower with a corolla in the form of a tube having at its top a 5-lobed hanging portion (Figs. T and S).—Refer back to No. **483**

⊬ Each flower with a corolla in the form of a tube having at its top an erect portion and a hanging portion, not 5-lobed **482**

⊬ Flowers without a tubular corolla **726**

726
(following on 725).

= Leaves oval and toothed at their edges (Figs. AN and PE).→**Annual Mercury** [*Mercurialis annua*]—medicinal; harmful to crops.—Represented in colour: 2 and 2 *bis*, Plate 47. (Family *Euphorbiaceæ*.)

= Leaves long, narrow, without teeth (Fig. A). → **Annual Knawel** [*Scleranthus annua*].[2] (Family *Caryophyllaceæ*.)

---

[1] For the various species of Nettle [*Urtica*] reference should be made to more comprehensive Floras.

[2] For the various species of Knawel [*Scleranthus*] reference should be made to more comprehensive Floras.

+ Leaves **compound**; that is to say, that the leaf, as a whole, is made up of a collection of secondary leaves, known as *leaflets*, each of which is often mistaken for a leaf; the compound leaf is attached to the stem by its base or by a stalk which bears all the leaflets. The base or stalk of a compound leaf does not stand exactly in the axil of another leaf 728

The above figures represent examples of compound leaves.

+ Leaves **deeply divided** (except sometimes those leaves that are quite at the upper part of the stems); that is to say, that each leaf is, as it were, cut to the extent of more than half its width 728

The above figures represent examples of divided leaves.

727
(*follow-
ing on
711*).

+ Leaves **simple**; that is to say, either not cut to the extent of more than half the width of the leaf, or merely edged with teeth, or even without teeth on their edges ... 738

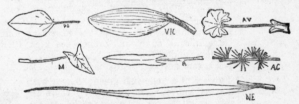

The above figures represent examples of simple leaves.

+ Leaves **not developed** 738

N.B.—If there is any hesitation as between compound and deeply divided leaves it is of no consequence, since in both cases the reference is to the same number (728).

If there is any doubt as between deeply divided and simple leaves either question may be followed up, and in either case the name of the plant will be reached. It will be the same thing if the plant happens to have both simple and compound or divided leaves (in addition to the few simple leaves which may occur quite at the top of the flowering shoots).

728
(following on 727).

—• Corolla butterfly-shaped, that is to say, with 5 unequal petals, one upper larger petal (*e* in Figs. P and PS), two equal to one another, placed right and left (*a, a*), and two lower ones united together and curved in the shape of a boat 729

—• Corolla not butterfly-shaped 730

729
(following on 728).

△ Flowers of a more or less blackish or purplish green; leaves with three leaflets (Fig. SAT); each flower is over a little very acute scale (Fig. SA). → Cultivated Medick (Lucerne) [*Medicago sativa*]—fodder plant.
—Represented in colour (with violet flowers): 2, Plate 15. (Family *Leguminosæ*.)

△ Flowers of a greenish yellow in a somewhat crowded cluster (Fig. AG); leaves with 7 to 13 leaflets (Fig. GLY). → Sweet Milk-vetch [*Astragalus glycyphyllos*]. (Family *Leguminosæ*.)

730
(following on 728).

⊁ Flowers in a compound umbel; that is to say, with the stalks all starting from one point, like the spokes which hold up an umbrella; each of these principal rays itself bears, at its extremity, other rays forming a smaller or secondary umbel and each ending in a flower. (Fig. C shows the arrangement of a compound umbel: I, O is the principal umbel; *i, o, f,* are the secondary umbels. For examples of compound umbels see Figs. PER and AP below, under No. 731) 731

⊁ Flowers not in a compound umbel 732

731
(following on 730).

○ Flowers of a yellowish green; leaves with the well-known smell of parsley; there are very small scales or green scales at the base of the secondary rays (Fig. PER). → Cultivated Parsley [*Petroselinum sativum*]—condiment; medicinal. (Family *Umbelliferæ*.)

○ Flowers of a greenish white; leaves without the smell of parsley; there are no very small leaves or green scales at the base of the secondary rays (Fig. AP). → Wild Celery (Smallage) [*Apium graveolens*]—food plant; medicinal. (Family *Umbelliferæ*.)

732
(following on 730).

— Flowers in clusters (example : Fig. AV) and, in reality, composite ; that is to say, that on careful examination (with the lens, if necessary) it will be seen that what is taken for a single flower is in reality made up of a great number of excessively small tubular flowers, the whole surrounded by a collarette of very small scales (Figs. GLA, AR, CAM).—Fig. ABS shows the collarette of scales with all the little tubular flowers of the composite flower removed **733**

— Flowers not composite **734**

733
(following on 732).

✳ Leaves without hairs on the upper and with whitish hairs on the under surface, divided into rather broad lobes (Fig. VU). → **Common Artemisia** (Mugwort) [*Artemisia vulgaris*]— medicinal.—Represented in colour : 1, Plate 32. (Family *Compositæ*.)

✳ Leaves green, with silvery silky hairs on both surfaces, divided into rather narrow lobes (Fig. AB). → **Bitter Artemisia** (Wormwood) [*Artemisia Absinthium*]—industrial ; medicinal. (Family *Compositæ*.)

734
(following on 732).

⹀ Flowers collected in balls (Fig. PS), solitary at the top of the stem or of the branches ; leaves with 11 to 17 leaflets, toothed, arranged in two rows in opposite pairs and with smaller leaflets intercalated between them. → **Bloody Burnet** (Salad Burnet) [*Poterium Sanguisorba*]—fodder plant ; salad plant.—Represented in colour : 6, Plate 19. (Family *Rosaceæ*.)

⹀ Plant not having these characteristics together.. **735**

735
(following on 734).

⊖ Plant climbing, having long filaments coiled on themselves (Fig. BR) ; flowers of a greenish white, or rather yellowish ; leaves more or less cut, with veins arranged like a fan. → **Diœcious Bryony** (White Bryony) [*Bryonia dioica*] — poisonous ; medicinal.—Represented in colour : 1 and 1 *bis*, Plate 21. (Family *Cucurbitaceæ*.)

⊖ Plant not climbing **736**

736
(following on 735).

✕ Each flower less than half a centimetre long ; flowers green, grouped and crowded in the axils of the leaves (Fig. AA) ; plant less than 35 centimetres high. → **Field Lady's-mantle** (Parsley-piert) [*Alchemilla arvensis*]. (Family *Rosaceæ*.)

✕ Each flower less than half a centimetre long ; flowers yellowish, in an elongated cluster.—Refer back to No. **497**

✕ Each flower more than a centimetre long **737**

737
(following on 736).

☐ Flowers green, **often edged with purple;** leaves with leaflets arranged like a fan (Fig. HF). → Stinking Hellebore (Setterwort) [*Helleborus fœtidus*] ✿ —poisonous; medicinal.—Represented in colour: 2, Plate 3. (Family *Ranunculaceæ*.)

☐ Flowers **of a more or less yellowish green;** leaves at the base of the plant not deeply divided; upper leaves much divided into long narrow lobes (Fig. AUR represents a flower). → Goldilocks Crowfoot [*Ranunculus auricomus*]. (Family *Ranunculaceæ*.)

—
738
(following on 727).

✱ ✱ Each flower **more than half a centimetre long**   739

✱ ✱ Each flower **less than half a centimetre long** (without taking count of the length of the hairs that sometimes occur in some flowers) 751

739
(following on 738).

⊙ Flowers **reduced** to scales and overlapping one another (examples: Figs. PU, S, and T, below) 1069

⊙ Flowers **not** reduced to scales 740

740
(following on 739).

♀ Flowers **regular;** that is to say, that the similar parts of the flower are arranged regularly round the centre of the flower and are equal to one another (examples: the figures below) 741

♀ Flowers **irregular;** that is to say, that each flower does not show the arrangement described above (examples: the figures below) 747

N.B.—Those flowers which, when looked at from the front, have similar right and left halves, are not to be looked upon as regular.

741
(following on 740).

- **Plant climbing,** having long filaments coiled on themselves (Fig. BR). → **Diœcious Bryony** (White Bryony) [*Bryonia dioica*]—poisonous; medicinal. ❀ —Represented in colour: 1 and 1 *bis*, Plate 21. (Family *Cucurbitaceæ*.)

- **Plant not climbing** **742**

742
(following on 741).

⊕ **Leaves not divided** **743**

⊕ **Leaves more or less deeply divided,** with veins arranged like a fan, except sometimes the upper and some other leaves; leaves at the lower part of the plant on long stalks (Fig. AUR represents a flower). → **Goldilocks Crowfoot** [*Ranunculus auricomus*]. (Family *Ranunculaceæ*.)

743
(following on 742).

✠ **Leaves more than 6 times as long as they are broad 744**

✠ **Leaves less than 6 times as long as they are broad 746**

744
(following on 743).

§ **Leaves apparently arranged in little groups along the**

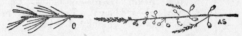

stem and branches (Fig. O). In reality, these green elongated structures are not leaves but slender green branches in tufts, united at their bases, above a little membranous scale which represents a very much reduced leaf (Fig. AS represents a flowering top). → **Seaside Asparagus** [*Asparagus maritimus*]—food plant; medicinal. ❀ —Represented in colour (in fruit): 1, Plate 53. (Family *Liliaceæ*.)

§ **Leaves all at the base of the plant** **745**

745
(following on 744).

+ **A solitary flower at the top of the stem;** the 3 inner divisions of the flower are heart shaped (Fig. G) and each have a green crescent-shaped mark. → **Common Snowdrop** [*Galanthus nivalis*]—ornamental. (Family *Amaryllidaceæ*.)

+ **Flowers clustered at the top of the stem** (Fig. U); the 3 inner divisions of the flower are oval and pointed at their tips, like the 3 outer divisions. → **Umbellate Star-of-Bethlehem** [*Ornithogalum umbellatum*].—Represented in colour: 6, Plate 53. (Family *Liliaceæ*.)

746
(following on 743).

—• Each flower tubular with 6 small lobes at the top; flowers all hanging on the same side of the stem (Fig. P). → Solomon's-seal [*Polygonatum*].—For the chief kinds of *Polygonatum* refer back to No. 559

—• Each flower cup-shaped, with 5 well-marked lobes (Figs. CO and A); the calyx (the part which surrounds the base of the corolla) enlarges when the flower is over (Fig. P) and forms a globe first green, then orange red. → **Common Winter-cherry** (Cape Gooseberry) [*Physalis Alkekengi*]—medicinal; poisonous. (Family *Solanaceæ*.)

747
(following on 740).

△ Flower having the appearance of a large rolled up cone (Fig. IT). In reality, this sheath is formed by a special leaf which encloses the top of the stem, which is swollen into a purple or violet club, and bears lower down a very great number of small yellow or reddish flowers. → **Spotted Arum** (Lords-and-ladies, Cuckoo-pint) [*Arum maculatum*]—medicinal.—Represented in colour: 2 and 2 bis, Plate 57. (Family *Araceæ*.)

△ Flower not in a conical sheath 748

748
(following on 747).

✠ Flowers white, or slightly greenish; the flower is made up of 6 divisions, but appears to have only 4 because 2 petals are folded forwards towards the interior of the flower (Fig. MT). → **Mountain Orchis** [*Orchis montana*].—Represented in colour: 2, Plate 55. (Family *Orchidaceæ*.)

✠ Flowers greenish, more or less mingled with purple or rose colour 749

749
(following on 748).

○ Leaves developed all along the stem, even among the flowers; the petal that has a special shape is neither longer nor much larger than the five other petals of the flower (Fig. E). → **Broad-leaved Epipactis** [*Epipactis latifolia*]—medicinal. ❀ —Represented in colour (with rose-coloured flowers): 7, Plate 56. (Family *Orchidaceæ*.)

○ Leaves chiefly developed at the base of the plant; the petal with a special shape is much longer or much larger than the other petals 750

750
(following on 749).

— The petal with a special shape is much longer than the other, and more or less coiled on its
(Fig. LO represents the whole spike of flowers); plant with a very disagreeable smell, especially after it is picked. → **Goat Orchis** (Lizard Orchis) [*Orchis hircina*]—Represented in colour: 6, Plate 55. (Family *Orchidaceœ*.)

— The petal with a special shape is **much broader than the others** (Fig. OA) and velvety, marked with patches that are not velvety. → [*Ophrys*].—Refer back to No. **135**

751
(following on 738).

✳ Stems **climbing**, twining themselves round the stems of other plants or round supports; leaves reversedly heart-shaped (Fig. TA). → **Common Tamus** (Black Bryony) [*Tamus communis*]. (Family *Dioscoreaceœ*.)

✳ Stems **not** climbing **752**

752
(following on 751).

= Stems bearing **tufts of slender green branches** which resemble leaves; each flower with 6 divisions **744**

= Stems **striped** lengthwise with **white and green;** leaves having on their under surface the appearance of very minute whitish scales (examine with the lens); leaves halberd-shaped (Fig. HS) or elongated (Fig. AP). → **Spreading Orache** [*Atriplex patula*]. (Family *Chenopodiaceœ*.)

= Plant not having these characteristics **753**

753
(following on 752).

⊖ Leaves **with hairs** (examine with the lens) **754**
⊖ Leaves **without hairs, or nearly without** hairs.... **758**

754
(following on 753).

× Leaves with veins arranged like a fan (Fig. AV), regularly toothed at the edges. → **Common Lady's-mantle** [*Alchemilla vulgaris*]—medicinal. (Family *Rosaceœ*.)

× Leaves with veins **not** arranged like a fan **755**

755
(following on 754).

☐ Withered flowers mixed with little prickly scales and leaves with strong branched veins (Fig. R represents a flowering branch of the plant). → **Reflexed Amaranth** [*Amarantus retroflexus*]. (Family *Amarantaceœ*.)

☐ Plant **not** having these characteristics together... **756**

756
(following on 755).

✳ ✳ At the base of each leaf there is a sheath enclosing the stem (Figs. H and C, for example) **761**

✳ ✳ At the base of each leaf there is no sheath... **757**

757
(following on 756).

☉ Stems flat and prostrate on the ground (Fig. HH) ; there are little membranous scales at the bases of the leaves (examine with the lens). → **Hairy Rupture-wort** [*Herniaria hirsuta*]. (Family *Illecebraceæ*.)

☉ Stems not prostrate or flat on the ground ; there are no little membranous scales at the bases of the leaves (Fig. P). → **Official Pellitory** (Pellitory-of-the-wall) [*Parietaria officinalis*]—medicinal.—Represented in colour : 3, Plate 48. (Family *Urticaceæ*.)

758
(following on 753).

◇ At the base of each leaf, there is a sheath enclosing the stem **759**

◇ At the base of each leaf, there is no sheath **766**

759
(following on 758).

• Groups of flowers in closely-packed balls (Fig. S) ; leaves very long and floating in water. → **Branched Bur-reed** [*Sparganium ramosum*]—medicinal. (Family *Typhaceæ*.)

• Plant not having these characteristics together ... **760**

760
(following on 759).

⊕ Leaves cylindrical like the stems (Fig. J) or reduced to scales which are on the lower part of the stems ; each flower either consists of 6 divisions arranged regularly (Fig. SL) and of a dry texture, or is replaced by a little oval body.—Refer back to No........ **158**

⊕ Leaves more or less flat and not reduced to scales **761**

761
(following on 760).

✠ Leaves more than 12 times longer than they are broad (except sometimes the upper ones), or leaves not developed ; flowers of a dry texture **762**

✠ Leaves less than 12 times longer than they are broad ; flowers not of a dry texture **765**

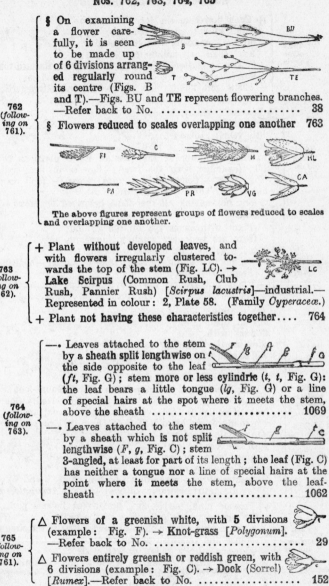

762
(*following on 761*).

§ On examining a flower carefully, it is seen to be made up of 6 divisions arranged regularly round its centre (Figs. B and T).—Figs. BU and TE represent flowering branches.—Refer back to No. 38

§ Flowers **reduced to scales overlapping one another** 763

The above figures represent groups of flowers reduced to scales and overlapping one another.

763
(*following on 762*).

+ Plant **without developed leaves**, and with flowers irregularly clustered towards the top of the stem (Fig. LC). → Lake Scirpus (Common Rush, Club Rush, Pannier Rush) [*Scirpus lacustris*]—industrial.—Represented in colour: 2, Plate 58. (Family *Cyperaceæ*.)

+ Plant **not having these characteristics together**.... 764

764
(*following on 763*).

—• Leaves attached to the stem by a **sheath split lengthwise on** the side opposite to the leaf (*ft*, Fig. G); stem more or less cylindric (*t, t*, Fig. G): the leaf bears a little tongue (*lg*, Fig. G) or a line of special hairs at the spot where it meets the stem, above the sheath 1069

—• Leaves attached to the stem by a sheath which **is not split lengthwise** (*F, g*, Fig. C); stem 3-angled, at least for part of its length; the leaf (Fig. C) has neither a tongue nor a line of special hairs at the point where it meets the stem, above the leaf-sheath 1062

765
(*following on 761*).

△ Flowers **of a greenish white**, with **5** divisions (example: Fig. F). → Knot-grass [*Polygonum*].—Refer back to No. 29

△ Flowers **entirely greenish or reddish green**, with **6** divisions (example: Fig. C). → Dock (Sorrel) [*Rumex*].—Refer back to No. 152

766
(following on 758).

✠ Each flower in the form of a tube (Fig. T) with 5 teeth at the top; flowers whitish; leaves narrow, less than 4 millimetres across; flowers in clusters (Fig. TH). → Prostrate **Bastard-toad-flax** [*Thesium humifusum*]. (Family *Santalaceæ.*)

✠ Plant **not** having the above-described characteristics together 767

767
(following on 766).

○ Leaves glossy, with whitish or reddish veins; there is a thick ring within the flower at the base of its 5 divisions (Fig. BT) (examine with the lens); flowers in long spikes (Fig. BV). → Common **Beet** [*Beta vulgaris*]—food plant; industrial. (Family *Chenopodiaceæ.*)

○ Plant **not** having all the above-described characteristics together 768

768
(following on 767).

— Plant with stems flat on the ground; there are two very small membranous scales at the base of each leaf (Fig. G). → Smooth **Rupture-wort** [*Herniaria glabra*]—medicinal. (Family *Illecebraceæ.*)

— Plant **not** having the above-described characteristics together 769

769
(following on 768).

• On examining an open flower with care (use the lens), 5 **green divisions** will be seen **arranged regularly** round the centre of the flower. → Goose-foot [*Chenopodium*]. (Figs. BH, OP, AL represent kinds of Goose-foot.) **White Goose-foot** (Fat Hen) [*Chenopodium album*] and **Good-King-Henry Goose-foot** (Mercury) [*Chenopodium Bonus-Henricus*] are represented in colour: 1 and 2, Plate 46. (Family *Chenopodiaceæ.*)

• On examining a flower with care (use the lens), 5 green divisions arranged regularly round the centre of the flower will **not** be seen (Figs. B and V). → Blite **Amaranth** [*Amarantus Blitum*]. (Family *Amarantaceæ.*)

770
(following on 3).

= Flowers pink, purple, red, brown—or flowers pink at the circumference and yellow at the centre...... 771

= Flowers blue, lilac, violet—or flowers lilac at the circumference and yellowish at the centre 810

= Flowers entirely yellow or yellowish 828

= Flowers white, whitish, or white at the circumference and yellow or yellowish at the centre 891

= Flowers green or greenish 928

① Leaves **opposite** (except sometimes at the upper part of the stems or of the branches); that is to say, leaves arranged in pairs and attached to the stem, at the same level, opposite to one another...................... 772

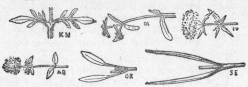

The above figures represent examples of opposite leaves.

N.B.—Not uncommonly in the axils of opposite leaves little leafy shoots occur that may give rise to the belief that the leaves, instead of being merely an opposite pair, are grouped in a large number at one level on the stem; but if the base of such a group of leaves be carefully examined the pair of opposite leaves can be readily distinguished.

① Leaves **whorled**; that is to say, leaves attached, 3, 4, 5, or even more, together at the same level on the stem and arranged regularly round its whole circumference; groups of very small flowers surrounded by a collarette of scales (Fig. SA). → **Field Sherardia** (Field Madder) [*Sherardia arvensis*]. (Family *Rubiaceæ*.)

771
(following on 770).

① Leaves **alternate**; that is to say, leaves attached to the stem singly at different levels 781

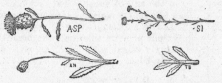

The above figures represent plants with alternate leaves.

① Leaves **grouped**; that is to say, leaves attached to the stem, 2 or more at the same level, but arranged, at that level, only on one side of the stem 781

① Leaves **all at the base** of the plant 781

The above figures represent examples of plants with all their leaves at the base.

N.B.—If the plant has both alternate leaves (in addition to those at the upper part of the stem) and opposite ones, either question may be followed up, and in either case the name of the plant will be reached.

772
(*following on 771*).

× The little flowers which make up the composite flower are larger at the circumference and spread out like rays all round the expanded composite flower (Fig. COL) **773**

× The little flowers which make up the composite flower do not spread out like rays all round the composite flower **774**

773
(*following on 772*).

○ At the base of the lavender corolla of each little flower of the composite flower, there are 6, 7, or 8 stiff white hairs (Fig. K). → **Field Knautia** (Field Scabious) [*Knautia arvensis*]—medicinal.—Represented in colour : 4, Plate 28. (Family *Dipsaceæ*.)

○ At the base of the lavender corolla of each little flower of the composite flower there are 5 stiff blackish hairs (Fig. S). → **Dove's** Scabious [*Scabiosa Columbaria*]—Represented in colour : **2**, Plate 28. (Family *Dipsaceæ*.)

774
(*following on 772*).

✳ ✳ Leaves compound; that is to say, that the leaf as a whole is made up by the union of secondary leaves, known as *leaflets*, each of which is often mistaken for a leaf ; the whole compound leaf is attached to the stem by its base or by a stalk that bears all the leaflets ; the base of the compound leaf is not attached in the axil of another leaf **775**

Figs. SR and CA represent examples of compound leaves.

✳ ✳ Leaves simple; that is to say, either not cut to the extent of more than half the breadth of the leaf, or merely edged with teeth, or even without teeth on their edges **776**

The above figures represent examples of simple leaves.

775
(*following on 774*).

☉ Each leaf with 3 leaflets not pointed at their tips (example : Fig. SR) with very small teeth at the edges. → **Trefoil** (Clover) [*Trifolium*].—Refer back to No. **222**

☉ Each leaf with 3 or 5 leaflets or divisions pointed at their tips (Fig. CA), with large teeth at their edges. → **Hemp Eupatorium** (Hemp Agrimony) [*Eupatorium cannabinum*]—medicinal. —Represented in colour : 1, Plate 31. (Family *Compositæ*.)

776
(following on 774).

✳ Leaves **with a strong aromatic** smell when they are bruised **777**

✳ Leaves without any strong aromatic smell when bruised **779**

777
(following on 776).

♡ Each flower of the group of flowers that appears to be a composite flower is very irregular, with two well-marked lips (Fig. ACI) (that is to say, with two divisions, one upper, the other lower); leaves more or less greyish on their under surface (Fig. CC shows the flowering top of the plant). → **Foot-stool Calamint** (Wild Basil) [*Calamintha Clinopodium*]. 🌸 —Represented in colour: 2, Plate 43. (Family *Labiatæ*.)

♡ Plant not having the above-described characteristics together **778**

778
(following on 777).

✳ Leaves **not toothed or not dis**tinctly toothed (Figs. OR, O); the flowers are surrounded by numerous little reddish-purple scales; flowers rather irregular, nearly 2-lipped, the upper lip with 2 slightly marked lobes, the lower lip 3-lobed. → **Common Marjoram** [*Origanum vulgare*]—medicinal. 🌸 —Represented in colour: 3, Plate 43. (Family *Labiatæ*.)

✳ Leaves **distinctly tooth**ed; no numerous little red-purple scales surrounding the flowers; flowers almost regular (Figs. AQ and A). → Mint [*Mentha*] —Refer back to No. **169**

779
(following on 776).

⊕ Each flower of the group of flowers (examples: Figs. P, CM) that may appear to be a composite flower has 5 petals distinct from one another down to their bases (on tearing the tube of the calyx which encloses the base of the 5 petals of a flower, these 5 petals, very narrow towards their bases, can be seen to be completely separated from one another down to their bases); leaves narrow, each pair of leaves having a sheath at its base. → Pinks [*Dianthus.*] Refer back to No. **70**

⊕ Each flower of the composite flower (or of what may appear to be a composite flower) forms a tube ending in 4 or 5 lobes at the top **780**

780
(following on 779).

✠ Each composite flower surrounded by a collarette of very numerous little leaves or green scales overlapping one another SCS (Figs. SSU, SCS); each little flower of the composite flower ending in 4 lobes. → Devil's-bit Scabious [*Scabiosa Succisa*]—medicinal.—Represented in colour: 3, Plate 28. (Family *Dipsaceæ*.)

✠ Each group of flowers (appearing to be a composite flower) without a collarette of very numerous little green leaves overlapping one another (Fig. OL); each of the little flowers of the group ends in 5 lobes. → Cooking Valerianella (Corn Salad, Lamb's Lettuce) [*Valerianella olitoria*]—food plant.—Represented in colour: 4, Plate 27. (Family *Valerianaceæ*.)

—
781
(following on 771).

§ Plant prickly either by its leaves, by its stems, or by the scales which surround each composite flower 782

§ Plant with the green scales that surround each composite flower ending in hooks (Fig. LA); the composite flower can cling to one's clothes. → Great Burdock [*Arctium Lappa*]—medicinal. ❀ —Represented in colour: 3, Plate 30. (Family *Compositæ*.)

§ Plant not prickly and without hooks on the scales of the composite flower 792

—
782
(following on 781).

+ Plant with leaves not prickly; the scales that surround the composite flower each ending in a long spine (Fig. CA). → Star-Thistle Knapweed [*Centaurea Calcitrapa*]—medicinal. (Family *Compositæ*.)

+ Plant with prickly leaves 783

783
(following on 782).

—• Stem with spinous flanges which, even below the composite flowers, are at least 3 times as wide as the stem and are continued right up to the base of the composite flowers (Fig. O); leaves woolly on their under surface. → Acanthus-leaved Cotton-thistle (Scottish Thistle) [*Onopordum Acanthium*]. ❀ —Represented in colour: 1, Plate 29. (Family *Compositæ*.)

—• Plant not having these characteristics together. → Thistles and Plume-thistles [*Carduus and Cirsium*].[1] For the chief kinds of Thistles go on to No. 784

---

[1] For further details as to the various species of Thistle [*Carduus and Cirsium*] reference must be made to more comprehensive Floras.

△ Stems and branches with spinous flanges down their sides, except sometimes towards the upper part (see the figures below) 785

784
(following on 783).

△ Stems and branches without spinous flanges (see the figures below) 789

△ No stem visible; the compound flower appears to be in the middle of the rosette of leaves 790

785
(following on 784).

✠ Each composite flower more than 2 centimetres (⅘ inch) across 786

✠ Each composite flower less than 2 centimetres across 787

786
(following on 785).

○ Each composite flower is surrounded by a collarette of **more than 200 scales**; a scale taken towards the base of the composite flower is rather abruptly terminated by a very slender spine (Fig. CLA); composite flower longer than it is broad (Fig. LA). → Spear Plume-thistle [*Cirsium lanceolatum*]. ❀ —Represented in colour: 4, Plate 29. (Family *Compositæ*.)

○ Each composite flower is surrounded by a collarette of **less than 100 scales**; a scale taken towards the base of the composite flower tapers **gradually** into a spine (Fig. CNU); composite flower hardly longer than it is broad, or even broader than it is long (Fig. N). → Nodding Thistle (Musk Thistle) [*Carduus nutans*]. ❀ —Represented in colour: 3, Plate 29. (Family *Compositæ*.)

787
(following on 785).

— The scales of the collarette of the composite flower are terminated by a rather short spine and are more than 2 millimetres broad at their bases (Fig. CTE, natural size); these scales are recurved outwards; each composite flower is longer than it is broad (Fig. TE). → Slender-flowered Thistle [*Carduus pycnocephalus*]. ❀ (Family *Compositæ*.)

— Plant not having these characteristics together.... 788

788
(following on 787).

✳ Plant growing in damp places or marshes; scales of the collarette of the composite flower oval (Fig. CPA); composite flowers often on very short stalks (Fig. PA). → Marsh Plume-thistle [*Cirsium palustre*]. 🌺 (Family *Compositæ*.)

✳ Plant growing in waste, not marshy, places; scales of the collarette of the composite flower narrow and elongated (Fig. CRI); composite flowers generally with a fairly long stalk (Fig. CR) → Welted Thistle [*Carduus crispus*]. (Family *Compositæ*.)

789
(following on 784).

═ Each compound flower more than 5 centimetres (2 inches)

across; leaves covered with very small spines on their upper surfaces (Fig. E represents a lobe of a leaf [enlarged]); the scales of the collarette which surrounds the composite flower end in a recurved point (Fig. ERI), or (towards the lower part of the collarette) end in a slightly widened structure (Fig. ER). → Woolly-headed Plume-thistle [*Cirsium eriophorum*]. (Family *Compositæ*.)

═ Each composite flower less than 5 centimetres (2 inches) across **790**

790
(following on 789).

⊖ Plant with a stem extremely short or not developed (Fig. AC); leaves (Fig. A) all, or nearly all, at the base of the plant. → Stalkless Plume-thistle (Ground Thistle) [*Cirsium acaule*]. (Family *Compositæ*.)

⊖ Plant with a stem generally more than 25 centimetres (10 inches) high; several leaves up the stem **791**

791
(following on 790).

✕ A solitary composite flower (rarely 2 or 3) at the top of the plant (Fig. AN); flowers crimson; leaves not much divided (Figs. AN, AG); scales of the collarette slightly spinous (Fig. ANG represents one of these scales). → Meadow Thistle (Gentle Thistle) [*Carduus pratensis*]. (Family *Compositæ*.)

✕ Numerous composite flowers at the top of the plant (Fig. AR); flowers of a slightish greyish purple. → Corn Plume-thistle (Corn Thistle) [*Cirsium arvense*]—harmful in crops. 🌺 —Represented in colour: 2, Plate 29. (Family *Compositæ*.)

☐ Leaves **compound**; that is to say, that the leaf as a whole is made up of the combination of secondary leaves, known as *leaflets*, each of which is often mistaken for a leaf; the compound leaf as a whole is attached to the stem by its base or by a stalk which bears all the leaflets. The base of the compound leaf is not situated in the axil of another leaf 793

The Figs. AN, AG, SV, OC represent examples of compound leaves.

☐ Leaves **deeply divided** (except sometimes those quite on the upper part of the stems); that is to say, that each leaf is, as it were, cut to the extent of more than half its breadth 793

The above figures represent examples of deeply divided leaves.

☐ Leaves **simple**; that is to say, either not cut to the extent of more than half the breadth of the leaf, or merely edged with teeth, or even without teeth on their edges ... 797

The above figures represent examples of simple leaves.

☐ Leaves **not developed** 797

792
(*following on* 781).

N.B.—It is of no consequence if there is any hesitation as between compound and deeply divided leaves, since in either case the reference is to the same number (793).

If there is hesitation as between deeply divided and simple leaves either question may be followed up, and in either case the name of the plant will be reached. So, too, will it be if the plant happens to have both simple and compound or divided leaves (without considering the few simple leaves that may often be found at the top of flowering stems).

793
(following on 792).

✳✳ Leaves with 3 leaflets (Figs. AG, OC, for example); compound flower (or group of flowers) surrounded only by some leaves at its base. → Trefoil (Clover) [*Trifolium*]. —Refer back to No. 222

✳✳ Leaves with numerous leaflets or deep lobings, with teeth round the whole edge 794

✳✳ Leaves with divisions not toothed all round and not distinctly separated from one another at their bases (see figures under Nos. 795 and 796) 795

794
(following on 793).

☉ Flowers of a greenish red; each composite flower (or group of little flowers) is in the form of a ball (Fig. PS). → Bloody Burnet (Salad Burnet) [*Poterium Sanguisorba*]—fodder plant; salad plant.—Represented in colour: 6, Plate 19. (Family *Rosaceæ*.)

☉ Flowers pink, expanding almost all at the same level; each compound flower is not in the form of a ball (Fig. AM). → Milfoil Achillea (Milfoil, Yarrow)[*Achillea Millefolium*]—medicinal.—Represented in colour: 6, Plate 31. (Family *Compositæ*.)

795
(following on 793).

ᗡ Each composite flower less than 1½ centimetres (⅝ inch) across; leaves without hairs, or almost without hairs (examine with the lens); composite flowers spreading slightly outward in rays (Fig. SER). → Dyers' Saw-wort [*Serratula tinctoria*].— Represented in colour: 4, Plate 30. (Family *Compositæ*.)

ᗡ Each composite flower more than 1½ centimetres (⅝ inch) across; leaves with hairs 796

796
(following on 795).

• The scales of the collarette of the composite flower are green in the centre, edged with brown (Fig. CSG; the green parts are at *v*); leaves often deeply divided (Fig. SC). → Great Knapweed (Matfellon) [*Centaurea Scabiosa*]. (Family *Compositæ*.)

• The scales of the collarette of the composite flower are not green in the centre, but are edged with brown

(Figs. CJA and CNI); the scales may have rather different shapes (examples: Figs. JA, AM, NG). → Black Knapweed [*Centaurea nigra*]—medicinal. (Family *Compositæ*.)

⊕ Flowers reduced to scales, or to little oval bodies, or **entirely of a dry texture** 805

The above figures represent examples of composite flowers (or groups of small flowers) reduced to scales or to little oval bodies.

⊕ Flowers **not** reduced to scales, nor to little oval bodies, nor entirely of a dry texture **798**

797
(following on 792).

798
(following on 797).

⊬ Each composite flower **yellow at the centre** (a mass of very small tubular yellow flowers) and pink or pinkish white at the circumference (little flowers each strap-shaped) 799

⊬ Each composite flower **not yellow at the centre**, that is to say, without a number of little tubular yellow flowers in the middle of the composite flower 800

799
(following on 798).

§ Leaves all at the base of the plant (Fig. B); a solitary composite flower at the top of the plant. → **Perennial Daisy** (Common Daisy) [*Bellis perennis*]—ornamental.—Represented in colour: 5, Plate 30. (Family *Compositæ*.)

§ Leaves arranged along the stem (Fig. EA); several composite flowers at the top of the plant (Fig. A shows one composite flower of natural size). → **Blue Erigeron** [*Erigeron acris*]. (Family *Compositæ*.)

800
(following on 798).

+ Leaves without hairs or nearly without hairs ... 801

+ Leaves with numerous hairs (examine with the lens) 804

801
(following on 800).

—• Flowers brown, brownish, or of a brownish green.—Go on to No. 806

—• Flowers pink or purplish 802

205

802
(following on 801).

△ Several composite flowers grouped at the top of the plant (Fig. SER). → Dyers' Saw-wort [*Serratula tinctoria*].—Represented in colour : 4, Plate 30. (Family *Compositæ*.)

△ A solitary composite flower at the top of the plant   803

803
(following on 802).

⊬ Each little flower of the composite flower (or group of flowers) (Fig. SM) with **6** divisions (Fig. CE). → **Garlic, Onion** [*Allium*].—Refer back to No. 42

⊬ Each little flower of the composite flower with 5 divisions (Fig. AP); leaves all at the base of the plant ; on the upper part of the flowering stem a sort of long membranous sheath will be seen (Fig. PL). → **Sea-side Thrift** [*Armeria maritima*]. (Family *Plumbaginaceæ*.)

804
(following on 800).

○ Plant **succulent,** with thick, juicy leaves, with shoots at the base like little artichokes (Fig. ST). (In reality, what has been taken for a composite flower is a simple flower with numerous petals.) → **Roof Sempervivum** (House-leek) [*Sempervivum tectorum*] —medicinal. 🌼 —Represented in colour : 5 and 5 *bis*, Plate 22. (Family *Crassulaceæ*.)

○ Plant **not succulent** ; collarette of the composite flower made up of numerous scales (Figs. CJA, CNI) ; **these**

scales may vary in shape (Figs. JA, NG, AM). → **Black Knapweed** [*Centaurea nigra*]—medicinal. 🌼 —(Family *Compositæ*.)

805
(following on 797).

— Flowers enveloped in a large green or greenish leaf rolled up in a cone (Fig. IT) ; leaves triangular on long stalks (Fig. M) springing from the base of the plant. → **Spotted Arum** (Lord-and-Ladies, Cuckoo-pint) [*Arum maculatum*]—medicinal.—Represented in colour : 2 and 2 *bis*, Plate 57. (Family *Araceæ*.)

— Flowers not having the above-described characteristics together 806

✳ Each little flower of the composite flower with 4 divi-

806
(follow-ing on 805).

sions (examine with the lens) (Figs. CA, LC); leaves more or less oval and all at the base. → Plantains [*Plantago*].—Refer back to No. **150**

✳ Each little flower of the composite flower with 6 divisions (examine with the lens) (Fig. LZ); leaves very narrow and much elongated **807**

✳ Each little flower of the composite flower reduced to **1, 2, or 3 scales** or to little oval bodies **808**

= Leaves without hairs (Fig. J) or reduced to scales. →

807
(follow-ing on 806).

Rushes [*Juncus*].—Refer back to No. 36

= Leaves with **long hairs** here and there along their edges

(Fig. V); groups of little flowers crowded (Fig. C) (so that they may be believed to be united into a composite flower). → **Field Wood-rush** (Chimney-sweeps, Good Friday Grass) [*Luzula campestris*].—Represented in colour: 5, Plate 57. (Family *Juncaceæ*.)

⊖ The little flowers of the composite flower (or group of crowded flowers) are each replaced by a little oval body (Fig. V). → Garlic, Onion [*Allium*]. (Each flower is replaced by a little oval body (*bulbil*) which can be detached and grown.)

808
(follow-ing on 806).

⊖ The little flowers of the composite flower (or group of crowded flowers) are arranged in balls one above the other, the lower ones being larger than the upper ones (Fig. S). → Branched Bur-reed [*Sparganium ramosum*]—medicinal. (Family *Typhaceæ*)

⊖ The little flowers of the composite flower are arranged in two cylinders one above the other, the lower one brown (Fig. L). → **Reed-mace** (Bulrush) [*Typha*].—Refer back to No.................... 162

⊖ The little flowers of the composite flower are neither replaced by oval bodies, nor in superposed balls, nor in two superposed cylinders of which the lower one is brown **809**

× **No leaves developed**; plant growing in the water... **158**

× **Leaves attached to the stem by
a sheath which is split lengthwise**
(F, ft, g, Fig. G) on the side opposite to the leaf; stem **more or less**
cylindrical (t, t, Fig. G); the leaf has a little tongue (lg,
Fig. G) or a line of special hairs at the point where it reaches
the stem, above the sheath **1069**

809
*(follow-
ing on
808).*

× **Leaves attached to the stem by
a sheath which is not split lengthwise** (F, g, Fig. C); stem **3-angled**
(t, t, Fig. C), at least at one part of
its length; the leaf has neither a tongue nor a line of
special hairs at the top of the sheath **1062**

810
*(follow-
ing on
770).*

☐ **Plant prickly** either by its leaves, its stems or the
collarette which surrounds the composite flower.. **811**

☐ **Plant not prickly** **812**

811
*(follow-
ing on
810).*

✳ ✳ **Leaves all opposite** (that is to say, arranged in pairs
facing each other); those towards the middle or lower
part of the stem are so united to one another as to

make a sort of basin (Fig. DSI); the composite flower
is more than 3 centimetres long and of an elongated
oval form (Fig. DS); not only the leaves but the stem
and branches also bear prickly points. → Wild Teasel
[*Dipsacus sylvestris*].—Represented in colour: 1,
Plate 28. (Family *Dipsaceæ*.)

✳ ✳ **Leaves almost all alternate** (that is to say,
attached singly to the stem at different levels);
the composite flower **less than 2 centimetres**
long and not of an elongated oval form (Fig.
E). The leaves have prickly points along their edges;
but the stem has no prickly points; **flowers of a bluish
white.** → Field Eryngo (Watling-street Thistle, Hundred-
headed Thistle) [*Eryngium campestre*]—medicinal. ❀ —
Represented in colour: 4, Plate 23. (Family *Umbelliferæ*.)

✳ ✳ **Plant not having the above-described characteristics 783**

⊙ **Leaves opposite** (except sometimes at the upper part of the stems or branches), that is to say, leaves arranged in pairs, attached at the same level on the stem and opposite to one another 813

The above figures represent examples of opposite leaves.

N.B.—In the axils of opposite leaves little leafy shoots may not uncommonly be found which may lead to the belief that the leaves are not merely in opposite pairs, but grouped in large numbers at the same level on the stem ; if, however, the base of such a group of leaves be carefully examined, the two opposite leaves may very readily be distinguished.

⊙ **Leaves whorled**, at least towards the middle of the stems, that is to say, leaves attached 4, 5, 6 or even more together at the same level on the stem and arranged regularly round its whole circumference 818

The above figures represent examples of whorled leaves.

⊙ **Leaves alternate**, that is to say, leaves attached singly to the stem at different levels 819

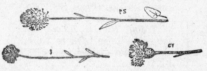

The above figures represent examples of plants with alternate leaves.

⊙ **Leaves grouped**, that is to say, leaves attached, 2 or more together, at the same level on the stem, but arranged at that level on one side of the stem only 819

⊙ Leaves **all at the base** of the plant 819

N.B.—If the plant have both alternate and opposite or both alternate and whorled leaves, either question may be followed up, and in either case the name of the plant will be reached.

812 (following on 810).

813 (following on 812).

↶ The little flowers which collectively make up the composite flower are larger at the circumference, spreading out as rays all around it (example : Fig. COL) cou .. 814

↶ The flowers which collectively form the composite flower do not spread out as rays all round it ....,,,, 815

814
(following on 813).

- There are 6 to 8 stiff white hairs at the base of each corolla of the little flowers which collectively make up the composite flower (Fig. K shows the base of one of the little flowers, without the corolla). → **Field Knautia** (Field Scabious) [*Knautia arvensis*]—medicinal.—Represented in colour: 4, Plate 28. (Family *Dipsaceæ*.)

- There are 5 stiff black hairs at the base of each corolla of the little flowers which collectively make up the composite flower (Fig. S shows the base of one of the little flowers, without the corolla). → **Dove's Scabious** [*Scabiosa Columbaria*].—Represented in colour: 2, Plate 28. (Family *Dipsaceæ*.)

815
(following on 813).

⊕ Each flower of the composite flower (or group of flowers) is 2-lipped (Fig. BV) (that is to say, with an upper division different from the lower); among the flowers are broad green or greenish plates embracing the stem and ending in a pointed tip (Fig. B; Fig. V shows the top of the flowering stem.) → **Common Self-heal** [*Prunella vulgaris*]—medicinal. ✿ —Represented in colour: 6, Plate 43. (Family *Labiatæ*.)

⊕ Plant not having the above-described characteristics **816**

816
(following on 815).

✠ Leaves each divided into three leaflets (Figs. SU, AG) or secondary leaves. → **Trefoil** (Clover) [*Trifolium*].—Refer back to No. **348**

✠ Leaves not divided (see Figs. SS and OL, under No. 817) **817**

817
(following on 816).

§ There is a collarette of numerous little green scales right round each composite flower (Figs. SSU and SCS; Fig. SS shows a leaf taken from near the base of the plant). → **Devil's-bit Scabious** [*Scabiosa Succisa*]—medicinal.—Represented in colour: 3, Plate 28. (Family *Dipsaceæ*.)

§ There is not a collarette of numerous little scales right round each composite flower (or group of flowers) (Fig. OL; Fig. CA represents one of the little flowers enlarged). → **Cooking Valerianella** (Corn Salad, Lamb's Lettuce) [*Valerianella olitoria*]—food plant.—Represented in colour: 4, Plate 27. (Family *Valerianaceæ*.)

818
(following on 812).

① Flowers of a lilac pink; each little flower in the group has a very long tube (Fig. S); each group of little flowers is surrounded by little leaves fringed with scarcely visible hairs (Fig. SA). → **Field Sherardia** (Field Madder) [*Sherardia arvensis*]. (Family *Rubiaceæ*.)

① Flowers **blue**; each little flower is funnel-shaped; each group of little flowers is surrounded by little leaves fringed with long hairs (Fig. AA). → **Field Asperula** [*Asperula arvensis*]. (Family *Rubiaceæ*.)

819
(following on 812).

+ Composite flowers **reduced to scales** which overlap one another.. 827

+ Composite flowers **not reduced to scales** 820

820
(following on 819).

—• The little flowers which collectively make up the composite flower are larger at the circumference and **spread out like rays** all round the expanded composite flower (examples: Figs. CY and CI) 821

—• The little flowers which collectively make up the composite flower are not larger at the circumference and do **not spread out like rays** all round the composite flower 824

821
(following on 820).

△ **All** the little flowers of the composite flower are **lilac**; leaves without hairs, more or less deeply cut (Fig. LP); it yields a white milk when the stem is broken. → **Perennial Lettuce** [*Lactuca perennis*].—Represented in colour: 5, Plate 33. (Family *Compositæ*.)

△ Plant **not having all these characteristics** together.. 822

822
(following on 821).

✠ The little flowers of the composite flower are **lilac at the circumference and yellowish at the centre**; the lilac flowers of the circumference are strap-shaped; the yellowish flowers of the central part are very small and tubular; leaves not cut but covered with very small hairs (Fig. EA shows the top of the plant in flower). → **Blue Erigeron** [*Erigeron acris*]. (Family *Compositæ*.)

✠ There are no little yellowish flowers at the centre of the composite flower; all the little flowers of the composite flower are **blue** (rarely violet) 823

823
(following on 822).

○ Composite flowers **solitary or in groups at the side of the branches;** all the little flowers of the composite flower are strap-shaped (those of the centre being often still rolled up on themselves, not being as yet expanded) (Fig. CI); the upper leaves are simple; those at the base more or less deeply divided. → **Succory Chicory** (Succory) [*Cichorium Intybus*]—food plant. 🌸 —Represented in colour: 2, Plate 33. (Family *Compositæ*.)

○ Composite flower **solitary at the top of the stems or branches;** the little flowers of the composite flower are tubular, regular at the centre and larger, and shaped like a horn with unequal lobes, at the circumference; the leaves are simple or more or less divided. → **Blue Knapweed** (Corn-flower, Blue Bottle) [*Centaurea Cyanus*] —medicinal. 🌸 —Represented in colour: 1, Plate 30. (Family *Compositæ*.)

○ Plant not having the above-described characteristics 795

824
(following on 820).

— Leaves each divided into 3 leaflets or secondary leaves (Figs. P and SC). → **Trefoil** (Clover) [*Trifolium*].—Refer back to No.................. 348

— Leaves not with 3 distinct leaflets 825

825
(following on 824).

✳ Each flower of the composite flower is bell-shaped (Fig. CA) and more than 1½ centimetres long. → **Clustered Bellflower** [*Campanula glomerata*].—Represented in colour: 2, Plate 35. (Family *Campanulaceæ*.)

✳ Plant not having the above-described characteristics 826

826
(following on 825)

= Each little flower of the composite flower is **on a small stalk** (examine with the lens); composite flowers round (Fig. I); violet, with a collarette; leaves narrow. → **Mountain Sheep's-bit** (Sheep's Scabious) [*Jasione montana*].—Represented in colour: 1, Plate 35. (Family *Campanulaceæ*.)

= Each little flower of the composite flower is **without a stalk** (examine with the lens); composite flowers round, becoming oval, dark blue, without a collarette at the base (Fig. PO). → **Round-headed Rampion** (*Phyteuma orbiculare*]. 🌸 (Family *Campanulaceæ*.)

= Plant not having the above-described characteristics 798

827
(following on 819).

** Leaves attached to the stem by a sheath which is split lengthwise on the side opposite to the leaf (*ft*, Fig. G); stem more or less cylindrical (*t, t*, Fig. G); the leaf *F* bears a little tongue (*lg*, Fig. G), or a line of special hairs at the spot where it meets the stem, at the top of the sheath **1069**

** Leaves attached to the stem by a sheath which is not split lengthwise (*g*, Fig. C); stem 3-angled, at least for part of its length; the leaf does not bear either a little tongue or a line of special hairs at the spot where it meets the stem at the top of the sheath of the leaf...... **1062**

828
(following on 770).

☉ Plant with **prickly points**, which may sometimes be very small, either on the leaves or on the collarette of the composite flower **829**

☉ Plant without **prickly points** on the leaves or on the collarette of the composite flower **837**

——
829
(following on 828).

⌔ A white milk flows from the stem when cut or broken; it is better to break the stalk of a composite flower when expanded or in bud **830**

⌔ No white milk from the stem when cut or broken below a composite flower when expanded or in bud **834**

830
(following on 829).

* The green collarette of the composite flower is more than 6 millimetres in its greatest breadth; the stem is not hard about half way up **831**

* The green collarette of the composite flower is less than 6 millimetres in its greatest breadth; the stem is hard, from about half way up, down to its base; the leaves have little prickles, especially on the main vein on the under side (Fig. SC); stem without hairs, usually much branched in its upper portion. → **Prickly Lettuce** [*Lactuca Serriola*]—medicinal; food plant. (Family *Compositæ*.) [1]—Various varieties of this plant are grown under the names Cos Lettuce, Cabbage Lettuce, Curly Lettuce, etc.

---

[1] For the various species of Lettuce [*Lactuca*] reference may be made to more comprehensive Floras.

831
(following on 830).

⊕ Leaves covered with some-what prickly hairs; leaves not embracing the stem at their bases (Fig. PH); the collarette of the composite flower has its lowest scales slightly recurved outwards (Fig. PC). → Hawkweed Picris [*Picris hieracioides*]. (Family *Compositæ*.)

⊕ Leaves without hairs or hairy and with very small prickles; leaves embracing the stem by their bases. → Sow-thistles [*Sonchus*].[1]—For the chief kinds of Sow-thistle [*Sonchus*] go on to No. 832

832
(following on 831).

⊁ Each leaf embraces the stem by two little ear-like lobes which are short, rounded and not recurved (Fig. AR). → Corn Sow-thistle [*Sonchus arvensis*]. (Family *Compositæ*.)

⊁ Each leaf embraces the stem by two little ears which are acute or more or less recurved or very large (see Figs. ASP and OL, under No. 833) 833

833
(following on 832).

§ The little ears which embrace the stem are twisted in a spiral (Fig. ASP). → Rough Sow-thistle [*Sonchus asper*]. (Family *Compositæ*.)

§ The little ears which embrace the stem are only slightly curved, not twisted in a spiral (Fig. OL). → Cooking Sow-thistle (Milk-Thistle) [*Sonchus oleraceus*].—Represented in colour: 1, Plate 34. (Family *Compositæ*.)

834
(following on 829).

+ Leaves without little prickles; collarette of the compound flower with each scale ending in a long sharp point (Fig. SOL). → Yellow Knapweed (Yellow Star-Thistle) [*Centaurea solstitialis*]. (Family *Compositæ*.)

+ Leaves with little prickles 835

835
(following on 834).

—• Flowers yellow; the little flowers of the cir-cumference of the composite flower are larger than the flowers of the centre, but not spreading out like rays (Fig. K); the collar-ette of the composite flower has its little spinous leaves erect (Fig. K). → Woolly Kentrophyllum (Parisian Blessed Thistle) [*Kentrophyllum lanatum*]—medicinal. (Family *Compositæ*.)

—• Flowers yellowish or yellowish white 836

[1] For further details as to the various species of Sow-thistle [*Sonchus*] reference must be made to more comprehensive Floras.

836
(following on 835).

△ Collarette of the composite flower with prickly scales radiating all round the flower when it is expanded (Fig. C). → **Common Carline-thistle** [*Carlina vulgaris*]—medicinal. ❀ —Represented in colour: 5, Plate 28. (Family *Compositæ*.)

△ Collarette of the composite flower with prickly scales not radiating; leaves rather weakly spinous (Fig. OL). → **Edible Plume-thistle** [*Cirsium oleraceum*]. (Family *Compositæ*.)

837
(following on 828).

✠ Flowers of the circumference of the composite flower spreading out like rays all round the flower when expanded 838

The above figures represent examples of composite flowers with rays.

✠ Flowers of the circumference of the composite flower not radiating 872

838
(following on 837).

○ **A white milk** exudes when the stem is cut or broken a little below a young composite flower or bud ... 839

○ **No white milk** exudes when the stem is cut 860

839
(following on 838).

— The collarette of the composite flower is made up of 5 to 12 scales or little green leaves arranged very nearly at the same level and all apparently equal (not counting a few very small scales sometimes occurring at the base) **840**

The above figures represent examples of composite flowers with the collarette made up of 5 to 12 principal scales attached nearly at one level.

— The collarette of the composite flower is made up of more than 12 scales or little green leaves which are unequal and arranged at different levels (examine with the lens, if needful) .... 84?

The above figures represent examples of composite flowers with a collarette of more than 12 scales attached at different levels.

840
(follow-ing on 839).

✳ The composite flower has only 5 little strap-shaped flowers (Fig. P; Fig. PH represents one of the little strap-shaped flowers) so that it might at first sight be taken for a simple (not composite) flower with 5 petals. → **Wall Lettuce** (Ivy-leaved Lettuce) [*Lactuca muralis*]. (Family *Compositæ*.)

✳ The composite flower has more than 5 little flowers **841**

841
'follow-ing on 840).

= Each of the composite flowers more than 2 centimetres (⅘ inch) long; leaves long and narrow (Fig. TP). → **Meadow Goat's-beard** (Jack Go-to-bed-at-noon) [*Tragopogon pratensis*]. ❀—Represented in colour: 4, Plate 33. (Family *Compositæ*.)

= Each of the composite flowers less than 2 centimetres long; leaves oval, acute, toothed or divided; the divided leaves attached about the middle of the stem have the terminal lobe much broader than the others (Fig. LC; Fig. LA represents a composite flower seen from the side). → **Common Nipplewort** [*Lapsana communis*]—medicinal.—Represented in colour: 1, Plate 33. (Family *Compositæ*.)

= Each of the composite flowers less than 2 centimetres long; leaves tooth-ed or divided; the divided leaves attached about the middle of the stem have not got the terminal lobe much broader than the others (Fig. CVR; Fig. CV represents a composite flower seen from the side). → **Smooth Hawk's-beard** [*Crepis capillaris*]. (Family *Compositæ*.)

842
(follow-ing on 839).

⊖ Leaves all or nearly all at the base of the flowering stem **843**

⊖ Leaves attached singly along the flowering stem.. **852**

843
(follow-ing on 842).

× The collarette of the composite flower less than 7 millimetres across; leaves almost without hairs; the green scales of the collarette are pressed against the collection of small flowers of the composite flower (Figs. CV and CVR). → **Smooth Hawk's-beard** [*Crepis capillaris*]. (Family *Compositæ*.)

× The collarette of the composite flower more than 7 millimetres across (measure several composite flowers) .. **844**

844
(following on 843).

☐ The scales which make up the collarette of the composite flower are more or less hairy (sometimes the hairs are very minute : examine with the lens) **845**

☐ The scales which make up the collarette of the composite flower are without hairs **850**

845
(following on 844).

✱✱ The scales which make up the collarette of the composite flower are hairy over their whole outer surface (Figs. LH and AT, for example ; sometimes the hairs are very minute : examine with the lens) ; hairs not stiff and not hard like little prickles **846**

✱✱ The scales which make up the collarette of the composite flower have stiff hairs often even hard like little prickles (the hairs may be over the whole surface of the scale [Fig. HI], or over part of the surface only [Figs. RD and R, for examples]) **849**

846
(following on 845).

⊙ Stems pressed flat on the ground, except those bearing the flowers (Fig. PI) ; leaves hairy and whitish underneath ; the composite flower is of a rather light yellow, often slightly reddish on the outside at the circumference. → Mouse-ear Hawkweed [*Hieracium Pilosella*]. —Represented in colour : 3, Plate 34. (Family *Compositæ*.)

⊙ Stems not pressed flat on the ground **847**

847
(following on 846).

⌃ Leaves generally less than 4 times longer than their

breadth (Figs. M and MU) ; the scales which make up the collarette of the composite flower have, amidst other hairs, hairs each ending in a little ball (examine with the lens : Fig. HM) ; there is usually a single leaf on the stem, above the rosette of leaves at the base of the plant. → Wall Hawkweed [*Hieracium murorum*].[1] (Family *Compositæ*.)

⌃ Leaves generally more than 4 times longer than their breadth; the scales which make up the collarette of the composite flower are hairy, but have no hairs ending in a little ball (examine with the lens : Figs. SHU, AT) ; all the leaves are at the base of the plant **848**

---

[1] For further details as to the various species of Hawkweed [*Hieracium*] reference must be made to more comprehensive Floras.

848
(following on 847).

• Each composite flower more than 2½ centimetres (1 inch) long; leaves without divisions or teeth on their edges (Fig. SH; Fig. HUM represents a composite flower seen from the side). → Dwarf Scorzonera [*Scorzonera humilis*]. (Family *Compositæ*.)

• Each composite flower less than 2½ centimetres long ; leaves divided and more or less toothed (Fig. LA ; Fig. AT represents one of the scales of the collarette of the composite flower). → Autumnal Hawk-bit [*Leontodon autumnalis*]. 🐝 —Represented in colour: 2, Plate 34.[1] (Family *Compositæ*.)

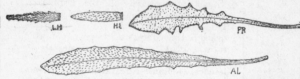

849
(following on 845).

⊕ Below the composite flower, the stem is covered with numerous stiff hairs or sometimes by little hairs (Figs. LH and HI ; Figs. PR and AL represent the more or less divided leaves). → Rough Hawk-bit [*Leontodon hispidus*]. 🐝 (Family *Compositæ*.)

⊕ Below the composite flower, the stem is without hairs (Fig. HRD ; Figs. R and RD represent scales of the collarette of the composite flower). → Long-rooted Cat's-ear [*Hypochœris radicata*]. (Family *Compositæ*.)

850
(following on 844).

⊁ Leaves without divisions or teeth on their edges, narrow and long (Fig. SH); each composite flower (Fig. HUM) more than 2½ centimetres long (Fig. HUM represents a composite flower seen from the side). → Dwarf Scorzonera [*Scorzonera humilis*]. (Family *Compositæ*.)

⊁ Leaves divided or toothed along their edges 851

---

[1] For the various species of *Leontodon* reference should be made to more comprehensive Floras.

851
(following on 850).

§ The outer scales of the collarette of the composite flower are **recurved outwardly or reflexed** (Figs. DE and DT; these figures represent the composite flower seen from the under side or divided down the middle: *ff*, little flowerets of the composite flower; *co*, collarette; Fig. T represents the entire plant). → **Officinal Dandelion** (Common Dandelion) [*Taraxacum officinale*]—food plant; medicinal. ❀—Represented in colour: 3, Plate 33. (Family *Compositæ*.)

§ The outer scales of the collarette of the composite flower are **neither recurved outwardly** nor reflexed **849**

852
(following on 842).

+ Leaves **without hairs** or almost hairless (with the exception of the little bristles sometimes found along the veins) **853**

+ Leaves **with hairs** (examine with the lens) **855**

853
(following on 852).

—• The scales forming the collarette of the composite flower are covered **with little white hairs often interspersed with black ones**; leaves without little prickly hairs or bristles on the principal vein and more or less cut up (Fig. CVR; Fig. CV represents a composite flower); **stems not hollow.** → **Smooth Hawk's-beard** [*Crepis capillaris*]. (Family *Compositæ*.)

—• The scales forming the collarette of the composite flower are **not** covered with little white hairs interspersed with black ones; leaves often have little prickles or bristles on the principal vein (see Figs. SA and SC at No. 854); **stems not hollow.** → **Lettuce** [*Lactuca*].—Go on to No. 854

—• The scales of the collarette are without hairs, or have hairs each one of which ends in a tiny ball (examine with lens); **stems hollow** **832**

854
(following on 853).

△ Leaves attached about midway up the stem, and embracing the stem at their base by **two lobes** pointed at the tips; **edges not toothed** (Fig. SA). → **Willow-leaved Lettuce** [*Lactuca saligna*]. (Family *Compositæ*.)

△ Leaves attached about midway up the stem fringed with small sharp bristles on their edges, and embracing the stem at their base by two slightly pointed or rounded lobes with **toothed edges** (Fig. SC). → **Prickly Lettuce** [*Lactuca Scariola*]—medicinal. (Family *Compositæ*.)—Several varieties of this kind of Lettuce are cultivated for food under the names of Cabbage Lettuce, Cos Lettuce, and Curly Lettuce.

855
(following on 852).

✠ The outer row of green scales of the collarette belonging to the composite flower are more or less recurved outwards, or, at any rate, are much separated from the other green scales, and several are placed below the collarette and at some distance from one another (Fig. PC); these scales are covered with stiff hairs; leaves slightly toothed and not embracing the stem at their base (Fig. PH). → Hawkweed Picris [*Picris hieracioides*]. (Family *Compositæ*.)

✠ Plant not having these characteristics together 856

856
(following on 855).

○ Leaves deeply cut up or divided, except sometimes when quite at the top of the stem 857

○ Leaves toothed, or without toothed edges, or with edges slightly cut 859

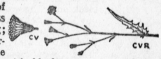

857
(following on 856).

— The green collarette of the composite flower less than 7 millimetres long; green scales of the collarette covered with little white hairs interspersed with black ones; upper leaves very little divided (Fig. CVR represents the upper part of the plant; Fig. CV represents a composite flower seen in profile). → Smooth Hawk's-beard [*Crepis capillaris*].[1] (Family *Compositæ*.)

— The green collarette of the composite flower more than 7 millimetres long 858

858
(following on 857).

✱ Plant having a disagreeable odour mingled with that of bitter almonds when the leaves are rubbed; the young buds of the composite flower are often drooping. → Fetid Hawk's-beard [*Crepis fœtida*]. (Family *Compositæ*.)

✱ Plant having no particular odour when the leaves are rubbed; the young buds of the composite flowers are often erect. → Dandelion-leaved Hawk's-beard [*Crepis taraxacifolia*]. (Family *Compositæ*.)

---

[1] For the various species of *Crepis* reference should be made to more comprehensive Floras.

859
(following on 856).

— The outer scales of the collarette are slightly recurved at the tips (Fig. HU); the leaves which are quite at the base of the plant disappear or wither off when the plant is in flower (Fig. UM). → Umbellate Hawkweed [*Hieracium umbellatum*].—Represented in colour: 4, Plate 34.[1] (Family *Compositæ*.)

= The outer scales of the collarette, like the other scales, are pressed against the composite flower (Fig. HMR); the

leaves quite at the base of the plant are still green and fully expanded (Fig. M) when the plant is in flower; sometimes there is only one leaf along the stem (Figs. M, MU), sometimes many (example: Fig. SI). → Wall Hawkweed [*Hieracium murorum*]. (Family *Compositæ*.)

860
(following on 838).

⊖ Leaves all at the base of the plant (Fig. L; in LA and PR may be seen examples of the leaves). → Hawk-bit [*Leontodon*].—Autumnal Hawk-bit [*Leontodon autumnalis*] is represented in colour: 2, Plate 34. (Family *Compositæ*.)

⊖ Leaves attached along the stem 861

861
(following on 860).

× Each composite flower expands to more than 5 centimetres in width; plant generally 1 to 2 metres (3 to 6 feet) in height 862

× Plant not having the preceding characteristics together 864

862
(following on 861).

☐ Each fully opened composite flower droops, and generally measures more than 10 centimetres (4 inches) in width. → Annual Sunflower [*Helianthus annuus*]. (Family *Compositæ*.)

☐ Each fully opened composite flower erect, and generally measuring less than 10 centimetres in width 863

---

[1] For further details as to the various species of Hawkweed [*Hieracium*] reference must be made to more comprehensive Floras.

863
(following on 862).

＊＊ Leaves green on both sides; leaves opposite, that is to say, attached in pairs, at the same level, to the stem, excepting the upper leaves which are attached singly to the stem. → Tuberous Sunflower (Jerusalem Artichoke) [*Helianthus tuberosus*]—food plant. (Family *Compositæ*.)

＊＊ Leaves hairy, whitish on underside; leaves all attached singly to the stem (Fig. HE represents a composite flower seen in profile (very reduced size)). → Helen's Elecampane (Wild Sunflower) [*Inula Helenium*]—medicinal. (Family *Compositæ*.)

864
(following on 861).

⊙ Leaves deeply divided (except sometimes those quite at the top of the stem); that is to say, each leaf is cut to the extent of more than half its width 865

The above figures represent examples of deeply divided leaves.

⊙ Leaves simple; that is to say, either not cut to the extent of more than half their width, or only toothed on the edges, or even not toothed 867

The above figures represent examples of simple leaves.

⊙ Leaves not developed 867

Note.—If you are in any doubt between leaves deeply divided and simple leaves (as, for example, in the case of a leaf such as that represented in Fig. A) either question may be taken; in both cases the name of the plant will be reached. It will be the same if the plant has simple, composite, and divided leaves all at once (with the exception of the few simple leaves which may be found quite at the top of the flowering stems).

865
(following on 864).

⚘ Composite flowers singly at the top of the stem or of elongated branches (Fig. CS); each fully open composite flower is generally 3 to 4 centimetres across; leaves glaucous, not hairy. → Yellow Chrysanthemum (Yellow Ox Eye, Corn Marigold) [*Chrysanthemum segetum*]. ⚘ (Family *Compositæ*.)

⚘ Plant not having these characteristics together.... 866

866
(following on 865).

- Each composite flower expands to more than a centimetre in width; the little strap-shaped yellow flowers, which are at the circumference of the composite flower, are not rolled outwards (Fig. JC). → Ragwort Senecio [*Senecio Jacobæa*]—medicinal.—Represented in colour: 5, Plate 31. (Family *Compositæ*.)

- Each composite flower expands to less than a centimetre in width; the little strap-shaped yellow flowers, which are at the circumference of the composite flower, are rolled outwards (Fig. VS). → Viscid Senecio [*Senecio viscosus*]. (Family *Compositæ*.)

867
(following on 864).

⊕ Leaves reduced to scales (Fig. F). → Colt's-foot Tussilago (Colt's-foot) [*Tussilago Farfara*]—medicinal. 🌼 —Represented in colour: 2, Plate 31. (Family *Compositæ*.)

⊕ Leaves developed 868

868
(following on 867).

⊬ Leaves with numerous hairs, at least on their edges and chief veins (examine with the lens) 869

⊬ Leaves without hairs or nearly so 870

869
(following on 868).

§ Leaves more or less whitish beneath, embracing the stem widely by their bases (Fig. DY); the collarettes of the composite flowers are covered with slightly woolly hairs. → Common Flea-bane [*Pulicaria dysenterica*]—medicinal. 🌼 (Family *Compositæ*.)

§ Plant not having all these characteristics together .. 870

870
(following on 869).

+ Composite flowers arranged in a cluster (Fig. SO); each composite flower when expanded not more than a centimetre across. → Goldenrod Solidago [*Solidago Virgaurea*]—medicinal. 🌼 —Represented in colour: 5, Plate 32. (Family *Compositæ*.)

+ Plant not having all these characteristics together 871

871
(following on 870).

-• Leaves with hairs (examine with the lens); the upper leaves more or less embracing the stem by their bases (Fig. C). → Field Calendula (Common Marigold) [*Calendula arvensis*]—medicinal.— Represented in colour: 3, Plate 31. (Family *Compositæ*.)

-• Leaves without hairs; the upper leaves not embracing the stem by their bases (Fig. CS). → Yellow Chrysanthemum (Corn Marigold, Yellow Ox-eye) [*Chrysanthemum segetum*]. 🌼 (Family *Compositæ*.)

The above figures represent examples of compound leaves.

The above figures represent examples of deeply divided leaves.

872
(follow-
ing on
837).

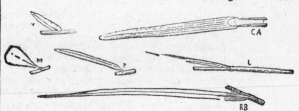

The above figures represent examples of simple leaves.

N.B.—It is of no consequence if there is some doubt as between compound and deeply divided leaves, since in either case the reference is to the same number (873)

If there is any hesitation as between deeply divided and simple leaves (as, for example, in the case of such a leaf as that shown in Fig. A) either question may be followed up, and in either case the name of the plant will be reached. It will be the same thing if the plant happens to have both simple and compound or divided leaves (apart from the few simple leaves that may occur at the top of the flowering stems).

873
(follow-
ing on
872).

✠ Leaves with 3 leaflets, not toothed, or with very small teeth on their edges, not count-ing the two little leaflets attached to the stem at the base of each leaf (Fig. PR) **465**

✠ Leaves with more than 3 leaflets; each flower of the com-posite flower is irregular; the collarette is made up of little fan-shaped leaves **463**

✠ Plant not having these characteristics **874**

874
(follow-
ing on
873).

○ Leaves opposite, attached in pairs, at the same level on the stem, opposite to one another (Figs. A and TRI under No. 875) **875**

○ Leaves alternate, attached singly at different levels **876**

875
(follow-
ing on
874).

— A solitary composite flower (or group of little flowers crowded together), of a greenish yellow, more or less in the form of a ball; there is no collarette of scales below the flowers (Fig. A); on the stem there are only two opposite leaves; the other leaves are all at the base of the plant. → Tuberous Moschatel [*Adoxa Moschatellina*]. (Family *Capri-foliaceæ*.)

— Flowers yellow; each composite flower is surrounded by a collarette of green scales and by the leaves (Fig. B); leaves often divided into 3 segments toothed and acute at the tip (Figs. T and TRI). → Tri-fid Bur-Marigold [*Bidens tri-partita*]. (Family *Compositæ*.)

876
(follow-
ing on
874).

✱ The scales of the collarette of each little composite flower are whitish and very hairy, numerous and arranged in several rows overlapping one another; the composite flowers are collected into more or less elongated clusters (Fig. AV) **877**

✱ Plant not having the above-described characteristics together **878**

877
(follow-
ing on
876).

= Leaves white beneath, with rather broad lobes (example: Fig. VU). → Common Arte-misia (Mugwort) [*Artemisia vulgaris*]—medi-cinal.—Represented in colour: 1, Plate 32. (Family *Compositæ*.)

= Leaves green and with silky hairs on both surfaces, with rather narrow lobes (Fig. AB). → Bitter Artemisia (Wormwood) [*Artemisia Absinthium*] —medicinal; industrial. (Family *Compositæ*.)

⊖ There are little yellow strap-shaped flowers recurved outwards round the circumference of the composite flowers 866

⊖ There are no recurved strap-shaped little flowers; collarette of the composite flower with very long scales arranged in a single row; but below there are some very small scales (Fig. VU) 884

878
(following on 876).

⊖ There are no recurved strap-shaped little flowers; collarette of the composite flower with scales arranged in several rows (Fig. TVU); the composite flowers are each about twice as broad as they are long, generally expanding nearly at one level (Fig. TV). → Common Tansy [*Tanacetum vulgare*]—medicinal.—Represented in colour : 2, Plate 32. (Family *Compositæ*.)

879
(following on 872).

× A white milk exudes when the stem is cut or broken. → Spurges [*Euphorbia*].—Refer back to No. 706

× No white milk when the stem is cut ..:......... 880

880
(following on 879).

□ Flowers reduced to scales (examples: Figs. LT and

VG, A or S) or with little crowded bodies wrapped round by a large sheath (Fig. IT) 888

□ Flowers not reduced to scales and regular, that is to say, that the similar parts of the flower are arranged regularly round the centre of the flower and are obviously equal to one another 881

881
(following on 880).

✱ ✱ Leaves with hairs (examine with the lens) 882

✱ ✱ Leaves without hairs 886

882
(following on 881).

⊙ The scales of the collarette of the composite flower are whitish and hairy 885

⊙ The scales of the collarette of the composite flower are without hairs or nearly so 833

883
(following on 882).

⌒ The scales of the collarette of the composite flower (with the exception of the upper scales) are recurved outwards at their tips (Fig. CO). → Scurfy Elecampane (Ploughman's Spikenard) [*Inula squarrosa*]. —Represented in colour : 4, Plate 32. (Family *Compositæ*.)

⌒ The scales of the collarette of the composite flower are not recurved outwards at their tips 884

884
(follow-ing on 883).

- The little flowers of the circumference of the composite flower are larger than those of the centre; leaves edged with hairs (Fig. C shows a composite flower; Fig. EC shows a flowering stem). → **Canadian Erigeron** (Canadian Flea-bane) [*Erigeron canadensis*]—medicinal. Represented in colour: 3, Plate 32. (Family *Compositæ*.)
- The little flowers of the circumference of the composite flower are of the same length as those of the centre (Fig. VU); leaves not edged with hairs. → **Common Senecio** (Groundsel, Birdseed) [*Senecio vulgaris*]—medicinal.— Represented in colour: 4, Plate 31. (Family *Compositæ*.)

885
(follow-ing on 882).

⊕ Each composite flower more than 7 millimetres across; little strap-shaped flowers at the circumference of the composite flower erect and scarcely longer than the little flowers of the centre (Fig. IP); upper leaves embracing the stem by their bases (Fig. V). → Small Flea-bane [*Pulicaria vulgaris*]. (Family *Compositæ*.)

⊕ Each composite flower less than 7 millimetres across. →

Cudweeds [*Gnaphalium*].[1]—Figs. U, GS, LA represent some examples of Cudweeds [*Gnaphalium*]. (Family *Compositæ*.)

886
(follow-ing on 881).

⋈ Flowers membranous, of a dry texture (Fig. LA represents a detached flower). → **Rushes** [*Juncus*].—Refer back to No..................... 36

⋈ Flowers not membranous...................... 887

887
(follow-ing on 886).

§ Leaves more than 10 times as long as they are broad (Fig. FL); each little flower of the group which is taken for a composite flower has six divisions separate or nearly separate from one another down to their bases. → **Yellow Allium** (Yellow Garlic) [*Allium flavum*]. (Family *Liliaceæ*.)

§ Leaves less than 10 times as long as they are broad; each little flower of the composite flower is tubular (Fig. VU represents a composite flower). → **Common Senecio** (Groundsel, Birdseed) [*Senecio vulgaris*]—medicinal.—Represented in colour: 4, Plate 31. (Family *Compositæ*.)

---

[1] For the various species of Cudweed [*Gnaphalium*] reference must be made to more comprehensive Floras.

+ **Leaves cylindrical like the stems (Fig. J) : or reduced to**

scales, but not arranged regularly round the stem. →
Rushes [*Juncus*].—Spreading Rush (Soft Rush) [*Juncus
effusus*] is represented in colour : 4, Plate 57. (Family
Juncaceæ.)

+ **Leaves (or branches resembling leaves) whorled or**

888
*(follow-
ing on
880).*

**reduced to toothed
sheaths;** that is to
say, attached 5 or
more at the same
level on the stem (Figs. A, AV, AR). (In reality this is
a flowerless plant.) → Horsetail [*Equisetum*].—Go on to
No. **1104**

+ **Leaves developed, flat and elongated** **889**

889
*(follow-
ing on
888).*

─• **Flowers arranged in long
cylinders** (Fig. A). → Reed-
mace (Bulrush) [*Typha*].—Refer back to No. **162**

─• **Flowers arranged
in balls placed one
above the other** (Fig.
R).→Branched Bur-
reed [*Sparganium
ramosum*]. (Family
Typhaceæ.)

─• **Flowers enclosed in a large
sheath** (Fig. IT). → Spotted
Arum (Lords - and - ladies,
Cuckoo-pint) [*Arum maculatum*]—medicinal.—Represented in colour : 2 and 2 *bis*, Plate 57. (Family *Araceæ*.)

─• **Flowers not arranged as in Figs. A, R, or IT** **890**

890
*(follow-
ing on
889).*

△ **Leaves attached to the stem
by a sheath split lengthwise** (*F,
fi, g*, Fig. G) on the side opposite to the leaf ; stem more or
less cylindrical (*t, t*, Fig. G); the leaf bears a little
tongue (*lg*, Fig. G) or a line of special hairs at the spot
where it meets the stem, above the sheath..... **1069**

△ **Leaves attached to the stem by
a sheath which is not split lengthwise** (*F, g*, Fig. C); stem 3-angled
(*t*, Fig. C), at least for a part of
its length ; the leaf has neither a little tongue nor a line
of special hairs at the point where it meets the stem,
above the sheath **1062**

891
(following on 770).

✠ Plant **prickly either on the leaves, stems, or scales of the** composite flower 892

✠ Plant having the collarette scales of the composite flower ending in a hook (Fig LA); the composite flower when detached hooks itself easily thus on to clothes. → **Great Burdock** [*Arctium Lappa*]—medicinal. 🏵 —Represented in colour (with pink flowers): 3, Plate 30. (Family *Compositæ*.)

✠ Plant **not prickly and without hooked scales** 896

892
(following on 891).

○ Leaves **spinous** 893

○ Leaves **not spinous**; each collarette scale of the composite flower ending in a sharp spine (Fig. CA). → **Star-thistle Knapweed** (Common Star-Thistle) [*Centaurea Calcitrapa*]—medicinal. (Family *Compositæ*.)

893
(following on 892).

— Leaves **opposite**; that is to say, attached regularly in pairs, at the same level, on the stem; the lower leaves are united at their base in the shape of a cup (Fig. DSI; Fig. DS represents a composite flower). → **Wild Teasel** [*Dipsacus sylvestris*]. 🏵 —Represented in colour: 1, Plate 28. (Family *Dipsaceæ*.)

— Leaves **alternate**; that is to say, attached one by one to the stem at different levels 894

894
(following on 893).

✳ Leaves **hairy**, at least on their under side 895

✳ Leaves **not hairy**; of a rather bluish green (Fig. E represents a composite flower). → **Field Eryngo** (Watling Street Thistle, Hundred-headed Thistle) [*Eryngium campestre*]—medicinal. 🏵 —Represented in colour: 4, Plate 23. (Family *Umbelliferæ*.)

895
(following on 894).

= The outer scales of the composite flower arranged in regular rays around the composite flower (Fig. C); the little flowers of the composite flower are **yellowish**. → **Common Carline-thistle** [*Carlina vulgaris*]—medicinal. 🏵 —Represented in colour: 5, Plate 28. (Family *Compositæ*.)

= The outer scales of the composite flower do **not radiate** regularly round the flower; the little flowers of the composite flower are white, or white with a tinge of pink. → **Thistles and Plume-thistles** [*Carduus* and *Cirsium*].—Refer back to No. 784

896
(following on 891).

⊖ The little flowerets forming the circumference of the composite flower are larger than those in the centre and radiate all round the composite flower (Figs. MA and M represent a rayed composite flower seen on the upper and under side: *co*, collarette; *flt*, little tubular flowerets; *fll*, little strap-shaped flowerets) **897**

⊖ The flowers forming the circumference of the composite flower do not radiate around the flower... **910**

—
897
(following on 896).

× The little flowers of the composite flower are strap-shaped, and white or pinkish white on the outer circle of the flower, and tube-shaped, very small and yellow, in the centre **898**

× The little flowers of the composite flower are all white except, occasionally, those in the centre which, in some cases, are yellowish **901**

898
(following on 897).

☐ Leaves all at the base of the plant; there is only one composite flower at the top of each stem (Fig. B). → Perennial Daisy (Common Daisy) [*Bellis perennis*].— Represented in colour: 5, Plate 30. (Family *Compositæ*.)

☐ Leaves arranged along the stem **899**

899
(following on 898).

✳ ✳ Leaves deeply divided into narrow and elongated lobes; these lobes are less than 3 millimetres in width (see figures at No. 900) **900**

✳ ✳ Leaves toothed or divided, but not very deeply, into narrow and elongated lobes. → White Chrysanthemum (Ox-eye Daisy, Moon Daisy, Marguerite) [*Chrysanthemum Leucanthemum*]—medicinal.—Represented in colour: 6, Plate 30. (Family *Compositæ*.)

900
(following on 899).

⊙ Leaves not hairy. → Feverfew [*Matricaria*]. (Figs. MC and I represent Feverfew leaves.)[1]—Chamomile Matricaria (Wild Chamomile) [*Matricaria Chamomilla*] is medicinal.—Represented in colour: 7, Plate 30. (Family *Compositæ*.)

⊙ Leaves hairy. → Chamomile [*Anthemis*]. (Fig. M represents a Chamomile leaf.)[2]—The Common Chamomile [*Anthemis nobilis*] is medicinal. (Family *Compositæ*.)

---

[1] For the various species of *Matricaria* reference must be made to more comprehensive Floras.

[2] For the various species of *Anthemis* reference must be made to more comprehensive Floras.

901
(following on 897).

♀ Leaves **opposite**; that is to say, arranged in pairs, at the same level, on the stem, and facing one another (Fig. CO represents a single leaf); composite flower much enlarged (Fig. COL). → **Dove's Scabious** (with white flowers) [*Scabiosa Columbaria*].—Represented in colour (with purple flowers): 2, Plate 28. (Family *Dipsaceæ*.)

♀ Leaves **not** opposite **902**

902
(following on 901).

• Leaves toothed pretty regularly like a saw along their edges (Fig. AP); each composite flower comprises in its outer circle 8 to 12 strap-shaped flowers. → **Sneeze-wort Achillea** [*Achillea Ptarmica*]—medicinal. (Family *Compositæ*.)

• Leaves not having these characteristics together .. **903**

903
(following on 902).

⊕ Leaves **not hairy** (examine with lens if necessary).. **904**
⊕ Leaves **hairy**, at any rate on their under-sides or edges **905**

904
(following on 903)

⊠ Leaves **partially divided into 3 or 5 rather wide lobes** (Fig. SE), with veins arranged like a fan; flowers grouped more or less irregularly; there are 2, 3, or 4 small leaves at the spot where the main stalks supporting the groups of flowers are united (Fig. S). → **Wood Sanicle** [*Sanicula europæa*]—medicinal. (Family *Umbelliferæ*.)

⊠ Leaves **deeply divided into very narrow sections** (Fig. FS); flowers in rather small groups; no little leaves at the spot where the principal stalks supporting the composite flower (or groups of flowers) are united (Fig. F). → **Water-Dropwort** [*Œnanthe*]. (Family *Umbelliferæ*.)—Refer back to No. **681**

905
(following on 903).

§ Each of the little flowers at the circumference of the composite flower **opens out into the shape of a wide funnel divided into lobes at the mouth**; these flowers are much larger than those in the centre of the flower (Fig. CY represents a composite flower); leaves silky on the under-side and more or less whitish. → **Blue Knapweed** (Cornflower) (with white flowers) [*Centaurea Cyanus*]—medicinal. —Represented in colour (with blue flowers): 1, Plate 30. (Family *Compositæ*.)

§ Plant not having these characteristics **906**

906
(following on 905).

+ On careful examination it will be seen that **each of the** little flowers of the composite flower (or group of flowers) is supported by a short stalk, and that the little stalks of the neighbouring flowers are attached at exactly the same point (see figures below) **909**

+ On careful examination it will be seen that the little flowers of the composite flower have **no stalk,** and that they are surrounded by a collarette of little scales arranged in several rows **907**

907
(following on 906).

—• Each composite flower **more than a centimetre** across when fully open ; the composite flowers arranged here and there along the flowering stem (Fig. C represents a composite flower fully open). → **Succory Chicory** (Succory) [*Cichorium Intybus*]—food plant ; medicinal. ✿ —Represented in colour (with blue flowers): **2, Plate 33.** (Family *Compositæ.*)

—• Each composite flower **less than a centimetre across** **908**

908
(following on 907).

△ Leaves with very numerous divisions in two opposite rows (Fig. AM); flowers nearly at the same level when just opened. → **Milfoil Achillea** (Yarrow) [*Achillea Millefolium*]—medicinal. — Represented in colour : **6, Plate 31.** (Family *Compositæ.*)

△ Leaves **not divided;** flowers in elongated clusters (Fig. EC). → **Canadian Erigeron** [*Erigeron canadensis*]—medicinal. — Represented in colour : **3, Plate 32.** (Family *Compositæ.*)

909
(following on 906).

✠ Stems **rough,** with the hairs turned downwards (Fig. TOR) (examine with lens). → **Hedge-parsley** [*Torilis*].—Refer back to No. **694**

✠ Stems **not rough** ; hairs directed in various ways (Fig. PV represents a flowering branch ; Fig. P represents the flowers gone over). → **Venus' Comb Scandix** (Shepherd's Needle) [*Scandix Pecten-Veneris*]. (Family *Umbelliferæ.*)

○ Leaves compound; that is to say, that the leaf as a whole is formed by the union of secondary leaves, called *leaflets*, each of which is often mistaken for a leaf; the entire compound leaf is attached to the stem by its base or by a stalk which supports all the leaflets. The base of the compound leaf is not placed just at the axil of another leaf 911

The above figures represent some examples of compound leaves.

○ Leaves deeply divided (those sometimes excepted that are quite at the top of the stems); that is to say, each leaf is as though cut to the extent of more than half its width 911

The above figures represent examples of deeply divided leaves.

○ Leaves simple; that is to say, either not cut to the extent of more than half their width, or only toothed on their edges, or even not toothed 916

The above figures represent examples of simple leaves.

Note.—If there seems any doubt between leaves compound and leaves deeply divided, it is of no importance, as in both cases you are referred to the same number (911).

If there seems any doubt between leaves deeply divided and simple leaves, either question may be taken; in both cases the name of the plant will be found. It will be the same if the plant possesses at the same time simple leaves and compound or divided leaves (without speaking, of course, of the few simple leaves which may be found at the top of the flowering stems).

910
(following on 896).

911
(following on 910).

— Leaves having 3 leaflets (Figs SR and P) with no teeth or very little ones on their edges (the two small leaflets at the base of the leaf stalk and attached to the stem are not counted).
→ Trefoil (Clover) [*Trifolium*].—Refer to No. 664

— Leaves not having these characteristics 912

912
(following on 911).

❋ Leaves divided in 3 to 5 lobes (Fig. SE); veins disposed like a fan; flowers grouped more or less irregularly (Fig. S). → **Wood Sanicle** [*Sanicula europœa*]—medicinal. (Family *Umbelliferæ*.)

❋ Leaves not having these characteristics together **913**

913
(following on 912).

= Leaves covered with plentiful hairs (examine with lens) **914**

= Leaves hairless or almost so **915**

914
(following on 913).

⊖ Stems rough; hairs turned downwards (Fig. TOR) (examine with lens). → **Hedge-parsley** [*Torilis*].—Refer back to No. **694**

⊖ Stems not rough, hairs turned in various directions (Fig. PV represents a flowering branch; Fig. P represents the flowers gone over). → **Venus' Comb Scandix** (Shepherd's Needle) [*Scandix Pecten-Veneris*]. (Family (*Umbelliferæ*.)

915
(following on 913).

✕ All the stalks of the composite flowers (or united groups of flowers) start from the same point exactly. → **Water-dropwort** [*Œnanthe*].—Refer back to No. **681**

✕ The stalks of the composite flower are attached at various heights along the upper part of the stem (Fig. SER). → **Dyers' Saw-wort** [*Serratula tinctoria*].—Represented in colour (with pink flowers): 4, Plate 30. (Family *Compositæ*.)

916
(following on 910).

☐ Leaves opposite; that is to say, arranged in pairs on the stem, and attached at the same level and facing one another (examples: Figs. AQ and SSU below).. **917**

☐ Leaves alternate; that is to say, attached one by one on the stem at different heights (examples: Figs. I and SER below) **920**

☐ Leaves all at the base of the plant **920**

917
(following on 916).

✱ ✱ Plant with leaves having a strong aromatic odour when rubbed **918**

✱ ✱ Plant whose leaves have no special odour when rubbed **919**

918
(following on 917).

☉ Leaves slightly toothed or not at all (Figs. OR and O) ; each composite flower (or group of little flowers) surrounded by numerous small scales. → Common Marjoram (with white flowers) [*Origanum vulgare*]—medicinal. ❀ —Represented in colour (with pink flowers) ; 3, **Plate 43.** (Family *Labiatæ*.)

☉ Leaves toothed all round; the composite flower (or group of little flowers) is not surrounded by numerous small scales. → Mints [*Mentha*]. (Figs. AQ and A represent examples of Mints.)—Refer back to No. **169**

919
(following on 917).

♋ Each composite flower (or crowded group of small flowers) is only surrounded at its base by 2 or 4 little green leaves, not forming a collarette (Fig. OL) ; the whole of the little group of crowded flowers is less than a centimetre and a half in width. → Cooking Valerianella (Corn-Salad, Lamb's Lettuce) [*Valerianella olitoria*]—food plant.—Represented in colour (with lilac flowers) : 4, **Plate 27.** (Family *Valerianaceæ*.)

♋ Each composite flower is surrounded at its base by numerous green scales forming a collarette (Figs. SCS, SSU), and is more than a centimetre and a half across when fully open. → Devil's-bit Scabious [*Scabiosa Succisa*]—medicinal.—Represented in colour (with lilac flowers) : 3, **Plate 28.** (Family *Dipsaceæ*.)

920
(following on 916).

• Leaves attached to the stem by a sheath which is split lengthwise along the side opposite to the leaf (*ft*, Fig. G) ; stem more or less cylindrical (*t, t*, Fig. G) ; the leaf *F* has a little tongue (*lg*, Fig. G) or a line of special hairs at the place where it meets the stem above the sheath **1069**

• Plant not having these characteristics together... **921**

921
(following on 920).

⊖ Leaves not hairy or scarcely so (examine with lens) **922**

⊖ Leaves hairy or leaves fringed at edge **926**

922
(following on 921).

⊕ Leaves with veins arranged like a fan, and with 3 or 5 lobes (Fig. SE); the groups of flowers (which have each been taken for a composite flower) are borne on stalks starting from the same point (Fig. S). → Wood Sanicle [*Sanicula europœa*]—medicinal. (Family *Umbelliferœ*.)

⊕ Plant not having all these characteristics together   **923**

923
(following on 922).

§ Leaves toothed, or more or less cut at their edges (Fig. SER). → Dyers' Saw-wort [*Serratula tinctoria*].—Represented in colour (with red flowers): 4, Plate 30. (Family *Compositœ*.)

§ Leaves neither toothed nor cut **924**

924
(following on 923).

+ Each flower of the composite flower (or group of flowers at the top of the stem) has 6 divisions (Fig. MOS); leaves very elongated. → Onions [*Allium*].—Refer back to No. **538**

+ Plant not having these characteristics **925**

925
(following on 924).

— Leaves all at the base of the plant (example: Fig. ME); each little flower of the composite flower (or group of flowers) has 4 brownish or greenish divisions. → Plantains [*Plantago*].—Refer back to No.   **150**

— Leaves arranged along the stem (Fig. PS); each little flower of the composite flower (or group of flowers) has 5 white divisions which remain united by their tips when the flowers are still young. → Spiked Rampion [*Phyteuma spicatum*] —medicinal. ❀ (Family *Campanulaceœ*.)

926
(following on 921).

△ On carefully examining the little flowers which, collectively, make up the composite flower, each is seen to be borne on a small stalk and to have 5 narrow divisions united by their tips when the flowers are young. → Mountain Sheep's-bit (Sheep's Scabious) [*Jasione montana*] (Fig. J).—Represented in colour (with blue flowers): 1, Plate 35. (Family *Campanulaceœ*.)

△ The little flowers making up a composite flower (or a collection of very crowded flowers) are without stalks and have not 5 narrow divisions **927**

✠ **A solitary composite flower (or crowded** group of flowers) at the top of the stem; leaves all at the base of the plant (example: Fig. ME). → Plantain [*Plantago*].—Refer back to No. .... 15(

927
(following on 926).

✠ **Numerous composite flowers** (each less than a centimetre across) arranged at the upper part of the plant; leaves arranged along the stem (Fig. EC). → Canadian Erigeron [*Erigeron canadense*]—medicinal.—Represented in colour : 3, Plate 32. (Family *Compositæ*.)

928
(following on 770).

○ Leaves **compound**; that is to say, that the leaf as a whole is made up of a collection of secondary leaves, known as *leaflets*, each of which is often mistaken for a leaf; the compound leaf is attached to the stem by its base or by a stalk that bears all the leaflets (Fig. A represents a flower with two compound leaves) 929

○ Leaves **deeply divided** (except sometimes those leaves which are quite at the upper part of the stems); that is to say, that each leaf is, as it were, cut to the extent of more than half its width (Figs. VU, AB) 929

○ Leaves **simple**; that is to say, either not cut to the extent of more than half the width of the leaf, or merely edged with teeth, or even without teeth on their edges 931

The above figures represent examples of simple leaves.

○ Leaves not developed 931

929
(following on 928).

— Leaves not opposite, with **11 or more leaflets**; flowers of a more or less reddish green (Fig. PS represents the top of a flowering branch). → Bloody Burnet (Salad Burnet) [*Poterium Sanguisorba*]—fodder plant; salad plant.—Represented in colour: 6, Plate 19. (Family *Rosaceæ*.)

— Leaves each with **3 leaflets**; there are two opposite leaves on the stem at the same level (Fig. A). → Tuberous Moschatel [*Adoxa Moschatellina*]. (Family *Caprifoliaceæ*.)

— Leaves more or less divided, edged with slender spines 836

— Plant not having the above-described characteristics 930

930
(following on 929).

— Leaves (Fig. VU) white beneath. → Common Artemisia (Mugwort) [*Artemisia vulgaris*]— medicinal. — Represented in colour: 1, Plate 32. (Family *Compositœ*.)

= Leaves (Fig. AB) hairy, silky, and green on both surfaces. → Bitter Artemisia (Wormwood) [*Artemisia Absinthium*]—industrial; medicinal. (Family *Compositœ*.)

931
(following on 928).

⊖ A white milk exudes from the stem when it is cut or broken. → Spurges [*Euphorbia*].—Refer back to No. 706

⊖ No white milk when the stem is cut 932

932
(following on 931).

× Flowers reduced to scales overlapping one another (examples: Figs. LT and A, below) or to little oval bodies enclosed in a large sheath (Fig. IT) 938

× Flowers not reduced to scales overlapping one another (examples: Figs. C, LP, ALB) nor to little oval bodies enclosed in a large sheath. If the flowers are reduced to scales it is seen that each little flower of the composite flower (or group of flowers) has 4 or 6 divisions 933

933
(following on 932).

☐ Leaves with hairs or leaves fringed along their edges (examine with the lens) 934

☐ Leaves without hairs 937

934
(following on 933).

✳ ✳ Leaves all at the base of the plant (example: Fig. ME). → Plantains [*Plantago*].—Refer back to No. 150

✳ ✳ Leaves arranged along the stem 935

935
(following on 934).

① Leaves opposite; that is to say, attached to the stem in pairs at the same level, or apparently whorled, that is to say, attached more than two together at the same level on the stem (Fig. A). → Sand Plantain [*Plantago arenaria*]. (Family *Plantaginaceœ*.)

① Leaves alternate; that is to say, attached singly to the stem, at different levels 936

⊙ Leaves hairy and whitish. → Cudweeds [*Gnaphalium*].[1]—

936
(following on 935).

Figs. GS, GA, SM represent examples of different kinds of Cudweed [*Gnaphalium*]. (Family *Compositæ*.)

⊙ Leaves only fringed at their edges **927**

⊙ Leaves edged with slender spines, and more or less divided **836**

937
(following on 933).

⌒ Leaves more than 6 times as long as they are wide or reduced to small scales which are at the bases of the stems; each little flower of the composite flower (or group of flowers) has 6 divisions (Fig. SL).— Refer back to No. **36**

⌒ Leaves developed but not more than 6 times as long as they are wide (Figs. LA and I); each little flower of the composite flower (or group of flowers) has 4 divisions. → Plantains [*Plantago*].—Refer back to No. **150**

938
(following on 932).

• Leaves (scales) or branches whorled, that is to say, attached 5 or more together, at the same level, and arranged regularly round the whole circumference of the stem (Fig. AR) or leaves forming toothed sheaths (Fig. AV) placed one above the other. → Horse-tails [*Equisetum*].[2]— Go on to No. **1104**

• Leaves not whorled **939**

939
(following on 938).

⊕ Flowers enclosed in a large greenish, whitish green, or sometimes more or less purplish sheath (Fig. IT); leaves triangular, on long stalks, all attached towards the base of the plant. → Spotted Arum (Lords-and-ladies, Cuckoo-pint) [*Arum maculatum*]—medicinal.—Represented in colour: 2 and 2 *bis*, Plate 57. (Family *Araceæ*.)

⊕ Plant not having all these characteristics together ... **940**

---

[1] For the various species of Cudweed [*Gnaphalium*] reference must be made to more comprehensive Floras.

[2] In reality this is a flowerless plant; what has been taken for the flowers is the collection of sporanges (containing the spores or germs of the plant) collected into an oval head at the top of the stem.

940
(following on 939).

⚜ Flowers forming a series of balls, some larger than the others (Fig. R); plant growing in water and with very much elongated submerged leaves. → Branched Bur-reed [*Sparganium ramosum*]—medicinal. (Family *Typhaceæ*.)

⚜ Plant not having these characteristics together.. **941**

941
(following on 940).

§ Leaves attached to the stem by a sheath which is split lengthwise (*F*, *ft*, *g*, Fig. G) on the side opposite to the leaf; stem more or less cylindrical (*t*, *t*, Fig. G); the leaf bears a little tongue (*lg*, Fig. G) or a line of special hairs at the point where it meets the stem, above the sheath **1069**

§ Leaves attached to the stem by a sheath which is not split lengthwise (*F*, *g*, Fig. C); stem 3-angled (*t*, *t*, Fig. C), at least for part of its length **1062**

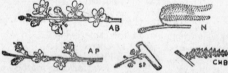

942
(following on 2).

+ Flowers appearing before the leaves............ **943**

The above figures represent examples of branches of trees or shrubs, the flowers of which appear before their leaves.

+ Flowers appearing after the leaves **or at the same time as the leaves** **961**

The above figures represent examples of the branches of trees or undershrubs, the flowers of which appear after, or at the same time as, their leaves.

Note.—If there is any doubt as between these two questions either may be followed up, and in either case the name of the plant will be reached.

—. Flowers with a fully-formed corolla, either white, pink, yellow or yellowish **944**

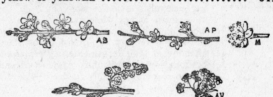

The above figures represent some examples of branches of trees, shrubs, or undershrubs, with flowers having a fully formed corolla.

—. Flowers with no corolla, or with the corolla **reduced to scales** **950**

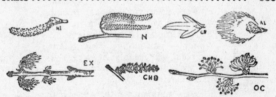

The above figures represent some examples of flowers with no corolla or with the corolla reduced to scales, or of branches of trees bearing groups of flowers without corolla and reduced to scales.

943 (*following on 942*).

---

944 (*following on 943*).

△ Flowers **yellow or yellowish** **945**

△ Flowers **bright pink or pinkish** **946**

△ Flowers **white** **948**

---

945 (*following on 944*).

✠ In each group of flowers the stalks of the flowers all start very nearly from the same point (Fig. CM); the buds are usually in opposite pairs. → Male Cornel (Cornelian Cherry) [*Cornus mas*]—food plant; industrial. 🌸 (Family *Cornaceæ*.)

✠ In each group of flowers the stalks of the flowers are all attached at different points (Fig. GR); the buds are not opposite to one another. → Red Currant [*Ribes rubrum*]—food plant. 🌸 —Represented in colour: 3, Plate 23. (Family *Ribesiaceæ*.)

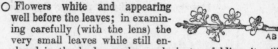

946
(following on 944).

○ Flowers white and appearing well before the leaves; in examining carefully (with the lens) the very small leaves while still enclosed in the bud, or when only just unfolding, it will be seen that they are rolled up on themselves in the direction of their length (Fig. AB represents a flowering branch). → **Apricot Prunus** (Apricot) [*Prunus Armeniaca*] —food plant. (Family *Rosaceæ*.)—Several varieties of this tree are cultivated.

○ Flowers pink or white; when white, they appear almost at the same time as the leaves; on examining carefully the very small leaves still enclosed in the bud, or scarcely unfolded, they will be seen to be folded in two in the direction of their length **947**

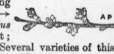

947
(following on 946).

— Flowers deep rose-colour, opening well before the leaves (Fig. AP). → **Peach Almond** (Peach) [*Amygdalus Persica*]—poisonous; food plant; medicinal. (Family *Rosaceæ*.)—Several varieties of this tree are cultivated: one of them (the Nectarine) has fruit without hairs.

— Flowers pinkish white, appearing almost at the same time as the leaves (Fig. AC). → **Common Almond** [*Amygdalus communis*]— food plant; medicinal. (Family *Rosaceæ*.) — Various forms of this tree are cultivated, some yielding sweet almonds and others bitter almonds.

948
(following on 944).

• Plant with spinous branches (Fig. SP). → **Spinous Prunus** (Blackthorn, Sloe) [*Prunus spinosa*]—food plant.—Represented in colour: 2 and 2 *bis*, Plate 18. (Family *Rosaceæ*.)

• Plant without spines and with flowers almost without stalks (Fig. AB); the little leaves when still in the bud, or which have hardly unfolded (examine with the lens) are rolled up on themselves lengthwise; tree with spreading branches. → **Apricot Prunus** (Apricot) [*Prunus Armeniaca*] — food plant. (Family *Rosaceæ*.)

• Plant without spines and with flowers on tolerably long stalks (Fig. AV); the stalks of the flowers all start from nearly the same point: the little leaves when still in the bud. or scarcely unfolded, are folded in two lengthwise **949**

949
(following on 948).

⊕ Buds **almost rounded** (Fig. PC); the small branches are spreading and drooping. → **Cherry Prunus** (Dwarf Cherry) [*Prunus Cerasus*] — food plant. (Family *Rosaceæ*.)

⊕ Buds **pointed** (Fig. PA); the small branches are usually erect. → **Birds' Prunus** (Black Cherry, Gean) [*Prunus Avium*]. (Family *Rosaceæ*.)—Varieties of this tree are cultivated for their edible fruits (Black-heart, Sweet and Bigaroon Cherries) — food plant; industrial. 🌺 —Represented in colour: 1, Plate 18.

950
(following on 943).

× Buds **black** and mostly **opposite** (Fig. EX); groups of flowers of a purple or dark violet colour. → **Lofty Ash** (Common Ash) [*Fraxinus excelsior*]—industrial; medicinal. 🌺 —Represented in colour: 1, Plate 37. (Family *Oleaceæ*.)

× Buds **not** opposite 951

951
(following on 950).

☐ Flowers in clusters which are **not elongated** (Fig. OC); each flower is regular, divided into **4 or 5 lobes** (Fig. O), fringed with hairs. → Common Elm [*Ulmus campestris*]—industrial; medicinal. 🌺 (Family *Ulmaceæ*.)

☐ Flowers in more or less **elongated** groups, erect or pendant; each flower is **reduced to a scale or to a few scales** ... 952

(See the above figures and the figures under Nos. 952 and 953.)

952
(following on 951).

✳✳ Buds and flowers **with a strong smell**; buds with two opposite scales (Fig. N); the groups of flowers resemble those shown in Fig. JR, and the two forms of groups of flowers may occur on the same plant. → Common Walnut [*Juglans regia*] — food plant; industrial; medicinal. (Family *Juglandaceæ*.)

✳✳ Buds and flowers **without a strong smell**; the buds **have not got two opposite scales** 953

— • Buds with a single scale (Figs. CP, SV), woolly or cottony within ; *the groups of flowers are erect and resemble those represented below* 954

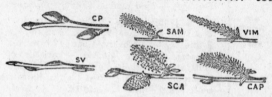

953
(follow-ing on 952).

— • Buds with 2, 3, or more scales (Figs. BL, CH, CO, PN, AL) ; groups of flowers resembling the figures below 955

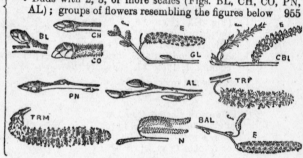

⊙ Branches **tapering and flexible even when tolerably old**; buds narrow and very acute (Fig. SV) ; the groups of flowers resemble either that represented in Fig. SAM or

that in Fig. VIM. → **Osier Willow** [*Salix viminalis*]—industrial. 🌸—Represented in colour (in leaf): 6, Plate 50. (Family *Salicaceæ*.)

954
(follow-ing on 953).

⊙ Branches **not tapering and not flexible** when tolerably old; buds more or less oval (Fig. CP) ; the groups of flowers resemble either that represented by Fig. CAP,

or that represented by Fig. SCA. → **Goat Willow** [*Salix caprea*]—industrial. 🌸—Represented in colour: 4 and 4 *bis*, Plate 50. (Family *Salicaceæ*.)

955
(following on 953).

- **Young** branches slender, reddish, flexible, and mostly pendulous; the groups of flowers resemble *m* or *f* (Fig. BAL) and may both  occur on the same tree; buds with more than 3 scales visible from outside (Fig. BL); when the tree is of some age, its bark is whitish and satiny. → **Silver Birch (Common Birch)** [*Betula alba*]—industrial. 🌼 —Represented in colour: 2, Plate 51. (Family *Betulaceæ*.)
- **Tree or shrub not having all these characteristics together** 956

956
(following on 955).

- ⊕ **Young shoots hairy** 957
- ⊕ **Young shoots without hairs, glossy** 958

957
(following on 956).

✠ **Buds and young shoots often** slightly sticky, with hairs each having a little ball at the tip (Fig. CO) (examine with the lens); buds slightly pointed, with numerous scales (Fig. N represents groups of flowers). → **Hazel Nut (Nut-tree)** [*Corylus Avellana*]—food plant; medicinal. 🌼 —Represented in colour: 3 and 3 *bis*, Plate 49. (Family *Cupuliferæ*.)

✠ **Buds sticky, but young shoots not sticky; young shoots covered with short hairs, not woolly or cottony; the groups**

of flowers resemble those shown in Figs. TRF and TRM (any one tree bearing only one or the other sort of group of flowers); the buds at the side of the shoots are very pointed (Fig. TR) and sticky. → **Tremulous Poplar (Aspen)** [*Populus tremula*]—industrial.—Represented in colour: 2, Plate 50. (Family *Salicaceæ*.)

✠ **Buds and young shoots not sticky; young shoots covered with white and slightly woolly or cottony hairs; the groups of flowers resemble those shown in Figs. ALB and PAL**

(any one tree bearing only one or the other sort of these groups of flowers): the buds at the sides of the shoots are slightly pointed (Fig. PB). → **White Poplar (Abele)** [*Populus alba*]—industrial. 🌼 (Family *Salicaceæ*.)

I

958
(follow-ing on 956).

§ Buds at the sides of the shoots are borne on short stalks (Fig. AL); the groups of flowers resemble *m* or *f* (Fig. GL) and may both occur on the same tree. → **Sticky Alder (Common Alder)** [*Alnus glutinosa*]—industrial; medicinal.—Represented in colour: **3 and 3** *bis*, Plate 51. (Family *Betulaceæ*.)

§ Plant not having these characteristics **959**

959
(follow-ing on 958).

+ Buds not sticky, more or less rounded at the tip (Fig. CH); the groups of flowers resemble *m* or *f* (Fig. CBL) and may both occur on the same tree. → **Birch-like Hornbeam (Common Hornbeam)** [*Carpinus Betulus*]—industrial.—Represented in colour: **1 and 1** *bis*, Plate 50. (Family *Cupuliferæ*.)

+ Buds sticky, pointed (see Figs. PN and TR, under No. 960) **960**

960
(follow-ing on 959).

—• The buds at the sides of the shoots are closely pressed against the branch (Fig. PN); the scales of the flowers are without hairs. → **Black Poplar** [*Populus nigra*]—medicinal; industrial. (Family *Salicaceæ*.) — A variety of this species, the pyramidal **Lombardy Poplar**, with all its branches erect, is often planted.—Represented in colour: **3 and 3** *bis*, Plate 50.

—• The buds at the sides of the shoots are not closely pressed against the branch (Fig. TR); the scales of the flowers are very hairy. → **Tremulous Poplar** (Aspen) [*Populus tremula*]—industrial.—Represented in colour: **2**, Plate 50. (Family *Salicaceæ*.)

△ Flowers reduced to scales (see, for example, the figures below) **1044**

961
(follow-ing on 942).

△ Flowers not reduced to scales **962**

962
(following on 961).

✠ Plant prickly, either with spinous branches, by prickles here and there on the stem, by leaves edged with spines, ending in a little sharp point or bearing prickles..   963

✠ Plant not prickly   980

963
(following on 962).

○ Flowers violet; with petals united in a funnel opening with 5 lobes (Fig. L). → Chinese Box-thorn (Duke of Argyll's Tea-tree [*Lycium chinense*]. 🌸 —Represented in colour: 3 and 3 *bis*, Plate 40.   (Family *Solanaceæ*.)

○ Flowers yellow, yellowish, reddish yellow, or greenish   964

○ Flowers white or pink   970

964
(following on 963).

— Flowers irregular with 5 petals, one of which partly covers the two petals below and they partly cover the other two which are united.—See the figures under No. 965   965

— Flowers regular, that is to say, that the similar parts of the flower are regularly arranged round the centre of the flower and are obviously equal to one another   966

965
(following on 964).

• All the leaves and all the branches of the plant are transformed into spines (Fig. U); the yellow petals of the flower are surrounded by two green or yellowish parts separated down to the base (calyx) (Fig. UE). → European Furze (Gorse, Whin) [*Ulex europæus*]—fodder plant. 🌸 —Represented in colour: 1, Plate 13.   (Family *Leguminosæ*.)

• The spinous branches bear flowering branches that are not spinous and oval leaves (Fig. AN); the yellow petals of the flower are surrounded by two green parts (the upper with 2 teeth, the lower with 3 teeth) united to one another in the lower part. → English Greenweed (Petty Whin, Needle Whin) [*Genista anglica*].   (Family *Leguminosæ*.)

966
(following on 964).

= Flowers greenish, apparently attached to the upper surface of the leaf, either solitary, or less commonly two together. In reality, the leaf-like branch that bears the flower is flattened and forms an oval leathery plate, persisting through the winter and ending in a spinous tip (Fig. R). → Spine-pointed Ruscus (Butcher's-Broom, Knee-holm) [*Ruscus aculeatus*]—medicinal.—Represented in colour: 1, Plate 54.   (Family *Liliaceæ*.)

= Flowers sulphur-yellow, in hanging clusters, with 12 principal divisions, 6 of which are inner; leaves grouped (Fig. B), edged with stiff bristles. → Common Barberry [*Berberis vulgaris*]—harmful to crops; medicinal. 🌸 —Represented in colour: 3 and 3 *bis*, Plate 4.   (Family *Berberidaceæ*.)

= Plant not having the characteristics of either of these two preceding plants   967

967
(follow-ing on 966).

↻ **Flowers** apparently with **very many yellow petals.** In reality, what is taken for a flower is a composite flower of many little strap-shaped flowers, the whole surrounded by a collarette of numerous little green or greenish scales. There are no spinous branches; but only very minute prickles on the leaves (Figs. SA and SC); plant **nearly herbaceous.** → **Lettuce** [*Lactuca*].—Refer back to No... **854**

↻ **Flowers yellowish, greenish, or slightly reddish, with 4 or 5 inner divisions** (corolla) and 4 or 5 little outer divisions (calyx); **shrub or under-shrub** **968**

968
(follow-ing on 967).

⊖ **Below the groups of leaves there are 3-branched spines** (Fig. RU); leaves with hairs; flowers hairy outside (Fig. U). → **Gooseberry Currant** (Common Gooseberry) [*Ribes Uva-crispa*]—food plant. (Family *Ribesiaceæ*.)

⊖ **There are no 3-branched spines** below the groups of leaves; leaves without hairs **969**

969
(follow-ing on 968).

× **Leaves without teeth on their edges or with wide little-marked teeth;** the chief veins not all curving to the tip of the leaf (Fig. FR; Fig. F represents a flower cut in half). → **Alder Buckthorn** (Berry-bearing Alder) [*Rhamnus Frangula*]—industrial; medicinal. ❀ (Family *Rhamnaceæ*.)

× **Leaves with little teeth on their edges;** the chief veins all curving more or less to the tip of the leaf (Fig. CA; Figs. R and RC represent the two sorts of flowers which may occur on the same shrub). → **Cathartic Buckthorn** (Common Buckthorn) [*Rhamnus catharticus*]—medicinal. (Family *Rhamnaceæ*.)

970
(follow-ing on 963).

☐ **Corolla butterfly-like,** that is to say, with 5 unequal petals: one upper petal the largest (*e*, Figs. P and PS), two petals equal to one another, placed right and left (*a, a*), and two lower petals united to one another (*cc*) in the shape of a boat **971**

☐ **Flowers not butterfly-like, regular,** that is to say, that the similar parts of the flower are arranged regularly round the centre of the flower and are obviously equal to one another **972**

971
(following on 970).

✽✽ Pink flowers intermingled with the leaves (Fig. O); very small undershrub with stems more or less prostrate on the ground, and branches here and there transformed into spines. → **Creeping Rest-harrow** (Wild Liquorice) [*Ononis repens*]—dangerous; medicinal.—Represented in colour: 1, Plate 15. (Family *Leguminosæ*.)

✽✽ Flowers white, very seldom pink, **in hanging clusters** (Fig. RPA); **tree** with an erect main stem; there are 2 spines at the base of most of the leaves (Fig. RO). → **False Acacia** (Locust-tree) [*Robinia Pseudacacia*]—industrial. ❀—Represented in colour: 5, Plate 15. (Family *Leguminosæ*.)

972
(following on 970).

⊙ Plant prickly only in its leaves, either by a spine at the tip of the leaf, or also by spines on the edge of the leaf (see the figures under No. 973) 973

⊙ Plant prickly by prickles here and there both on the leaves and on the stems (see the figures under No. 975) 974

⊙ Plant prickly by its branches ending in spines.... 976

973
(following on 972).

☙ Leaves broad, more or less oval, often with spines on their edges (Fig. H), or at least at the tip (Fig. IA); flowers white, with spreading lobes. → **Needle-leaved Holly** [*Ilex Aquifolium*]—industrial. ❀—Represented in colour: 3 and 3 *bis*, Plate 12. (Family *Ilicineæ*.)

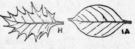

☙ Leaves **very small and very narrow,** scarcely prickly at their tips; flowers crimson, very seldom white, in the shape of a slightly elongated rattle (Fig. EC). → **Hoary Heath** (Fine-leaved Heath, Crimson Heather) [*Erica cinerea*]. ❀—Represented in colour: 1, Plate 36. (Family *Ericaceæ*.)

974
(following on 972).

• The flower has a swollen structure below its expanded petals (Fig. RO represents a flower when over blown cut lengthwise). → **Dog-Rose** [*Rosa canina*][1]—medicinal.—Represented in colour: 4 and 4 *bis*, Plate 19. (Family *Rosaceæ*.)

• The flower has no swollen structure below its expanded petals (Fig. RU represents an over-blown flower cut lengthwise) 975

---

[1] For the numerous species of Roses [*Rosa*] reference must be made to complete Floras.

975
(following on 974).

⊕ The petals of the open flower are spreading; stems more or less hanging and arching; the leaves have 3 leaflets (Fig. RF) or 5 leaflets arranged like a fan (Fig. RC). → Shrubby Bramble (Blackberry) [*Rubus fruticosus*]—medicinal. 🐝 —Represented in colour: 5, Plate 19. (Family *Rosaceæ*.)

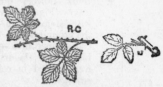

⊕ The petals of the open flower remain erect; stems erect; the leaves on the flowering branches have 3 leaflets; those on the branches without flowers have 5, not arranged like a fan (Fig. I). → Mt. Ida Bramble (Raspberry) [*Rubus Idæus*]—medicinal. 🐝 (Family *Rosaceæ*.)

976
(following on 972).

✠ Leaves more or less deeply divided (Fig. CR); flowers with a smell recalling that of bitter almonds. → Sharp-spined Hawthorn (Whitethorn, May) [*Cratægus Oxyacantha*] — ornamental; medicinal. — Represented in colour: 1 and 1 *bis*, Plate 20. (Family *Rosaceæ*.)

✠ Leaves not divided 977

977
(following on 976).

§ Petals white, surpassed by the five green divisions of the calyx which surround them (Fig. GE); leaves with hairs on both surfaces, even when old (Fig. MG represents a leaf). → Common Medlar [*Mespilus germanica*]—food plant. 🐝 (Family *Rosaceæ*.)

§ Petals white or pink, not surpassed by the five green or reddish green divisions of the calyx that surrounds them 978

978
(following on 977).

+ Flowers slightly rosy; leaves lightly downy beneath, or with some cobwebby hairs, having less than 9 secondary veins on each side of the principal vein (Fig. MC); flowers almost all starting from the same point (Fig. M). → Common Apple (Crab Apple) [*Malus communis*]—industrial. 🐝 —Represented in colour: 4, Plate 20. (Family *Rosaceæ*.)

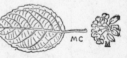

+ Flowers white; leaves without hairs beneath, when they are developed 979

979
(following on 978).

⌐⌐• Flowers in clusters; each flower attached separately (Fig. MA). → **Mahaleb Prunus** (St. Lucie Cherry) [*Prunus Mahaleb*]. (Family *Rosaceæ*.)

—• Flowers all attached almost at the same point (Fig. P); leaves with generally more than 9 secondary veins on each side of the principal vein (Fig. PC). → **Common Pyrus** (Pear-tree) [*Pyrus communis*] — industrial. ✿ —Represented in colour: 3, Plate 20. (Family *Rosaceæ*.)

980
(following on 962).

△ Plant climbing or trailing along the ground or with branches resting on other plants 981

△ Plant with its main stem erect and not climbing.. 990

⊁ Leaves **opposite** (except sometimes on the upper part of the stems or branches); that is to say, leaves arranged in pairs attached to the stem at the same level, opposite one another (examples: Figs. P and LC below) 982

N.B.—Little leafy shoots often occur in the axils of opposite leaves which might lead to the belief that the leaves, instead of being merely in opposite pairs, are grouped in large numbers at the same level, but on a careful examination of the base of such a group of leaves, the two opposite leaves will be readily distinguished.

981
(following on 980).

⊁ Leaves **alternate**; that is to say, leaves attached singly to the stem at different levels (example: Fig. DU) 985

⊁ Leaves **grouped**; that is to say, leaves attached two or more together at the same level on the stem, but arranged at that level on one side of the stem only (example: Fig. L) 985

N.B.—If the plant have both opposite leaves and alternate leaves (in addition to those on the upper part of the stem) either question may be followed up, and in either case the name of the plant will be reached.

982
(following on 981).

○ Flowers **regular** (Figs. C and PY); that is to say, that the similar parts of the flower are arranged regularly round its centre and are obviously equal to one another 983

○ Flowers **irregular**; that is to say, not having the arrangement described above (examples: Figs. P and NU) 984

983
(following on 982).

— Flowers **blue**, with 5 lobes (Fig. PY); leaves not divided; plant prostrate on the ground, not climbing. → **Lesser Periwinkle** [*Vinca minor*]—medicinal.—Represented in colour: 4, Plate 37. (Family *Apocynaceæ*.)

— Flowers **white**, with 4 lobes (Fig. C); leaves completely divided into secondary leaves or leaflets; plant climbing. → **Wild Clematis** (Traveller's Joy, Old Man's Beard) [*Clematis Vitalba*]—dangerous.
—Represented in colour: 6, Plate 1. (Family *Ranunculaceæ*.)

984
(following on 982).

✳ Very small undershrub with **pink flowers**; leaves without teeth and with an aromatic smell (Fig. S). → **Wild Thyme** [*Thymus Serpyllum*]—medicinal; condiment. ✿ (Family *Labiatæ*.)

✳ Very small undershrub with pink flowers; leaves strongly toothed and with no aromatic smell **165**

✳ Undershrub with much elongated stems, with flowers white, yellow, or mingled with pink, with a long tube ending in lobes at the top (Fig. LC). → **Common Honeysuckle** (Woodbine) [*Lonicera Periclymenum*]. ✿ —Represented in colour: 4, Plate 26. (Family *Caprifoliaceæ*.)

985
(following on 981).

= Flowers **violet, purple, or white** **986**

= Flowers **greenish, yellowish, yellow, or pink** **987**

986
(following on 985).

⊖ Flowers **star-shaped** (Fig. DC), not funnel-shaped at the base; each petal bears two green spots edged with white at its base. → **Bittersweet Nightshade** (Woody Nightshade) [*Solanum Dulcamara*]—poisonous; medicinal.—Represented in colour: 2 and 2 *bis*, Plate 40. (Family *Solanaceæ*.)

⊖ Flowers **funnel-shaped** at the base (Fig. L); there are not two green spots edged with white at the base of each petal. → **Chinese Box-thorn** (Duke of Argyll's Tea-tree [*Lycium chinense*]. ✿ —Represented in colour: 3 and 3 *bis*, Plate 40. (Family *Solanaceæ*.)

987
(following on 985).

× Flowers **regular**; that is to say, that the similar parts of the flower are arranged regularly round its centre and are equal to one another **988**

× Flowers **irregular**; butterfly-shaped (see, for example, Fig. GP under No. 989) **989**

▢ **Flowers in umbels** (Fig. H); that is to say, that in each little group of flowers, the stalks of the flowers start from the same point, like the spokes that support an umbrella (Fig. H); leaves without hairs. → **Climbing Ivy** (Common Ivy) [*Hedera Helix*]—medicinal. — Represented in colour: 1 and 1 *bis*, Plate 26. (Family *Araliaceæ*.)

988 (*following on 987*).

▢ **Flowers in clusters** (Fig. VV); that is to say, that the stalks of the flowers do not all start from the same point; leaves more or less hairy (examine with the lens, if necessary); on examining the flowers it will be seen that the green petals of each remain united at the top and come off whole like a little hood (Fig. V). → **Grape Vine** [*Vitis vinifera*]—food plant; medicinal. (Family *Vitaceæ*.)

989 (*following on 987*).

✶✶ **Flowers pink**, without hairs on their petals (Fig. O represents a flowering branch). → **Creeping Rest-harrow** (Wild Liquorice) [*Ononis repens*]—dangerous; medicinal.—Represented in colour: 1, Plate 15. (Family *Leguminosæ*.)

✶✶ **Flowers yellow**, with little hairs on the petals (Fig. GP). → **Hairy Greenweed** [*Genista pilosa*]. (Family *Leguminosæ*.)

990 (*following on 980*).

⊙ Each flower **regular**; that is to say, that the similar parts of the flower are arranged regularly round its centre and are obviously equal to one another (examples: the figures below) **991**

⊙ Each flower **irregular**; that is to say, that the flowers have not got the arrangement described above (examples: the figures below) **1037**

N.B.—Flowers that have their right and left halves similar are not to be considered regular.

*I

↶ Leaves compound; that is to say, that the leaf as a whole is made up of a collection of secondary leaves, known as *leaflets*, each of which is often mistaken for a leaf; the whole compound leaf is attached to the stem by its base or by a stalk that bears all the leaflets; the base of the compound leaf is not in the axil of another leaf **992**

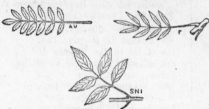

The above figures represent examples of compound leaves.

↶ Leaves deeply divided (except sometimes the leaves quite at the upper part of the stems); that is to say, that each leaf is, as it were, cut to the extent of more than half its width **992**

The above figures represent examples of deeply divided leaves or of branches bearing deeply divided leaves.

↶ Leaves simple; that is to say, either not cut to the extent of more than half their width, or merely edged with teeth, or even without teeth on their edges **1000**

The above figures represent examples of simple leaves or of branches bearing simple leaves.

N.B.—It is of no consequence if there is some doubt as between compound and deeply divided leaves, since in both cases the reference is to the same number (992).

If there is any hesitation as between deeply divided and simple leaves, either question may be followed up, and in either case the name of the plant will be reached. So, too, if the plant happens to have both simple and compound or deeply divided leaves (not counting the few simple leaves that may occur quite at the top of flowering stems).

991
(following on 990).

254

992
(following on 991).

- • Flowers in the shape of a 5-rayed star (Fig. N); flowers violet, rarely white; plant almost herbaceous, with leaves sometimes deeply divided (Fig. DU); other leaves are simple. → Bittersweet Nightshade (Woody Nightshade) [*Solanum Dulcamara*]—poisonous; medicinal.—Represented in colour: 2 and 2 *bis*, Plate 40. (Family *Solanaceæ*.)

- • Plant not with these characteristics together **993**

993
(following on 992).

- ⊕ Flowers green, greenish, or yellowish **994**
- ⊕ Flowers white **997**

994
(following on 993).

✠ Plant almost herbaceous, less than a metre in height; the 5 green parts of the flower are often edged with purple-brown; the leaves are almost completely divided into long toothed leaflets arranged like a fan (Fig. HF). → Stinking Hellebore (Setterwort) [*Helleborus fœtidus*]—poisonous; medicinal. 🌸 —Represented in colour: 2, Plate 3. (Family *Ranunculaceæ*.)

✠ Shrub less than 2 metres in height; leaves often slightly reversedly heart-shaped at their base (Fig. RB), not in opposite pairs; flowers in more or less pendulous clusters (Fig. RB). (Figs. R and N represent separate flowers of Currants). → Currants [*Ribes*].—Go on to No. **1009**

✠ Tree more than 2 metres high; leaves opposite (that is to say, attached to the stem in pairs, opposite to one another, at the same level) with veins arranged like a fan (see the figures under Nos. 995 and 996). → Maples [*Acer*].—For the chief kinds of Maple [*Acer*] go on to No. **995**

995
(following on 994).

§ Leaves with their principal divisions toothed all round (see Figs. AP and PP, under No. 996) **996**

§ Leaves with not many teeth on their main divisions (Fig. AC), pale green on the under surface; flowers greenish and erect. → Field Maple (Common Maple) [*Acer campestre*] — industrial. 🌸 —The fruit is represented in colour: 6, Plate 11. (Family *Aceraceæ*.)

996
(following on 995).

+ Leaves with deep and very acute teeth (Fig. AP), green on both surfaces; flowers yellowish and erect. → Norway Maple [*Acer platanoides*].[1] 🌸 —The fruit is represented in colour: 5, Plate 11. (Family *Aceraceæ*.)

+ Leaves with teeth not deeply cut (Fig. PP), whitish green beneath; flowers greenish in hanging clusters. → Sycamore Maple (Sycamore, Greater Maple) [*Acer Pseudo-platanus*].[1] 🌸 —Represented in colour: 4 and 4 bis, Plate 11. (Family *Aceraceæ*.)

997
(following on 993).

— Leaves opposite, that is to say, arranged in pairs, attached two together to the stem at the same level, and opposite to one another (Fig. SNI, which represents a leaf and the base of the leaf which is opposite to it); each flower has its petals united by their bases. → Black Elder [*Sambucus nigra*]—medicinal.—Represented in colour: 6, Plate 26. (Family *Caprifoliaceæ*.)

— Leaves alternate, that is to say, attached one by one to the stem at different levels. → Sorbs (Service-trees) [*Sorbus*].—For the chief kinds of Service-trees [*Sorbus*] go on to No. 998

998
(following on 997).

△ Leaves compound with distinct leaflets (example: Fig. AU) 999

△ Leaves rather deeply divided (Fig. ST). → Wild Sorb (Wild Service-tree) [*Sorbus torminalis*]—industrial; medicinal. 🌸 (Family *Rosaceæ*.)

999
(following on 998).

✠ The leaflets of the compound leaf are toothed almost down to their base (Fig. SA); buds hairy. → Fowler's Sorb (Rowan-tree, Fowler's Service, Mountain Ash) [*Sorbus Aucuparia*] — industrial; medicinal. 🌸 (Family *Rosaceæ*.)

✠ The leaflets of the compound leaf only toothed along the upper two-thirds (Fig. SD); buds not hairy. → Cultivated Sorb (Service-tree) [*Sorbus domestica*]—food plant; industrial. 🌸 —Represented in colour: 2, Plate 20. (Family *Rosaceæ*.)

---

[1] The Maples must not be confounded with the Plane, which differs from them in having its leaves not opposite and its very small flowers collected in balls. The Plane is represented in colour: 1, Plate 51.

○ Leaves **opposite** (except sometimes at the upper part of the stems or the branches) ; that is to say, leaves arranged in twos, attached to the stem at the same level, opposite to one another 1026

The above figures represent examples of opposite leaves (Figs. V and S show one whole leaf and the base of the leaf opposite to it).

N.B.—Little leafy shoots rather frequently occur in the axils of opposite leaves which may give rise to the belief that the leaves, instead of being merely in opposite pairs, are grouped in a large number at the same level on the stem ; but if the base of such a group of leaves be examined carefully, the two opposite leaves will readily be distinguished.

○ Leaves **whorled;** that is to say, leaves attached, 3, 4, 5, or even more, together, at the same level on the stem, and arranged regularly round its whole circumference.. 1026

The above figure represents an example of a plant the leaves of which (except the highest ones) are whorled. (Note the leaves near the letters LS.)

○ Leaves **alternate;** that is to say, leaves attached one by one to the stem at different levels 1001

The above figures represent plants with alternate leaves.

○ Leaves **grouped;** that is to say, leaves attached, 2 or more together, to the stem at the same level, but arranged, at that level, on one side only of the stem 1001

The above figures represent examples of grouped leaves.

N.B.—If the plant have both alternate leaves (in addition to those at the upper part of the stem) and opposite ones, or both alternate and whorled leaves, either question (1001 or 1026) may be followed up, and in either case the name of the plant will be reached.

1000
(follow-
ing on
991).

1001 *(following on 1000).*

—• Each flower has its petals separate from one another down to their bases; that is to say, that one of the petals (or part of a flower of some colour other than green) can be detached without tearing the others. This refers to those parts of the flower which, collectively, form the corolla or coloured structure surrounding the little threads and other organs that occupy the centre of the flower; when the flower fades, each petal (or coloured piece) falls off or withers separately [1] 1002

Fig. HE represents a flower with separate petals; Fig. HL its petals detached. The other figures represent examples of flowers with separate petals as seen from above, from the side, or from below.

—• Each flower has its petals united to one another, at least at their bases; that is to say, that in trying to detach one of the parts of the flower which is coloured otherwise than green, one is obliged to tear the corolla, at least at its base; when the flower fades the corolla falls off or withers all in one piece 1023

The above figures represent examples of flowers with united petals.

1002 *(following on 1001).*

✳ Flowers yellow, yellowish, greenish, brown, or greenish mingled with reddish 1003

✳ Flowers white, whitish, pink or pinkish 1011

1003 *(following on 1002).*

= Large tree with leaves pointed at the tip and reversedly heart-shaped; each flower appears to be attached to the upper surface of an elongated little leaf of a special shape (Fig. TI). → Small-leaved Linden (Lime-tree) [*Tilia cordata*] [2]—medicinal. ❀ —Represented in colour: 3, Plate 10. (Family *Tiliaceæ*.)

= Undershrub or plant almost herbaceous not having all these characteristics together 1004

---

[1] In most flowers there is, outside the corolla, another covering to the flower, generally green, known as the *calyx*, which surrounds the base of the corolla. In other flowers it is difficult to distinguish the calyx and the corolla, which are more or less combined into a single floral envelope (Figs. PA and ST, for example). In other flowers, again, there is really only a single floral envelope, coloured otherwise than green, like a corolla. Under the names petals and corolla we here understand those parts coloured otherwise than green which immediately surround the little threads or other organs occupying the centre of the flower.

[2] For the various species of Linden [*Tilia*] reference should be made to more comprehensive Floras.

1004
(following on 1003).

⊖ Flowers yellow 1005

⊖ Flowers greenish or yellowish, sometimes mingled with reddish 1007

1005
(following on 1004).

× Each flower with 5 petals (Fig. HE) which are surrounded by 5 green, or slightly reddish, parts of which 2 are much the smaller (Fig. VG). → Common Rock-rose [*Helianthemum vulgare*]—medicinal.—Represented in colour: 1, Plate 7. (Family *Cistaceæ*.)

× Each flower with 4 petals (Fig. ES) which are surrounded by 4 green, or slightly reddish, parts 1006

1006
(following on 1005).

☐ Leaves all without either teeth or divisions (Fig. GV); flowers with a sweet smell. → Common Wallflower (Gilliflower) [*Cheiranthus Cheiri*]—ornamental. ✿ — Represented in colour: 1, Plate 6. (Family *Cruciferæ*.)

☐ Leaves more or less deeply divided and toothed (Fig. DTE); flowers without a particularly sweet smell. → Slender-leaved Wall-rocket [*Diplotaxis tenuifolia*]. ✿ (Family *Cruciferæ*.)

1007
(following on 1004).

✳ ✳ Apparently the leaves are very slender, very elongated and grouped at the side of the stems (Fig. O) (in reality, these are slender little green branches); each flower is made up of 6 parts; plant almost herbaceous. → Seaside Asparagus (Common Asparagus) [*Asparagus maritimus*]—food plant; medicinal. ✿ — Represented in colour (in fruit): 1, Plate 53. (Family *Liliaceæ*.)

✳ ✳ Shrub or undershrub not having these characteristics 1008

1008
(following on 1007).

⊙ Small shrubs with leaves more or less divided; flowers in clusters (Fig. RB) 1009

⊙ Shrubs with undivided leaves; flowers not in clusters 1010

1009
(following on 1008).

♀ Flowers without hairs (Fig. R); flowers and leaves with no strong smell. → Red Currant [*Ribes rubrum*] —food plant. ✿ —Represented in colour: 3, Plate 23. (Family *Ribesiaceæ*.)

♀ Flowers hairy on their lower part (Fig. N); flowers and leaves with a strong smell. → Black Currant [*Ribes nigrum*]—food plant. ✿ (Family *Ribesiaceæ*.)

1010
(follow-ing on 1008).

- Leaves without teeth on their edges or from scarcely any to wide slightly-marked indentations, with veins not all curving to the tip of the leaf (Fig. FR); leaves glossy beneath. → Alder Buckthorn (Berry-bearing Alder) [*Rhamnus Frangula*]—industrial; medicinal. 🌺 (Family *Rhamnaceæ.*)

- Leaves regularly toothed at the edges, with veins all curving more or less to the tip of the leaf (Fig. CA). → Cathartic Buckthorn [*Rhamnus catharticus*]—medicinal. (Family *Rhamnaceæ.*)

1011
(follow-ing on 1002).

⊕ Plant almost herbaceous, with a long cluster of rose-red flowers (Fig. LS). → Willow-leaved Lythrum (Purple Loosestrife) [*Lythrum Salicaria*]—medicinal. 🌺 —Represented in colour: 4, Plate 21. (Family *Lythraceæ.*)

⊕ Tree or shrub 1012

1012
(follow-ing on 1011).

Each flower appears to be attached to the upper surface of a small special leaf of elongated shape (Fig. TI); leaves reversedly heart-shaped, and pointed at the tip. → Small-leaved Linden (Lime-tree) [*Tilia cordata*]—medicinal. 🌺 —Represented in colour: 3, Plate 10. (Family *Tiliaceæ.*)

Tree or shrub not having these characteristics ... 1013

1013
(follow-ing on 1012).

§ Flowers almost without stalks, or with a stalk shorter than the flower 1014
§ Flowers with a stalk longer than the flower, at least among the lower flowers 1017

1014
(follow-ing on 1013).

+ Leaves without hairs beneath 1015
+ Leaves more or less whitish with hairs on their under surface 1016

1015
(follow-ing on 1014).

- Flowers of a bright pink (Fig. AP represents a flowering branch). → Peach Almond (Peach) [*Amygdalus Persica*]—poisonous; food plant; medicinal. 🌺 (Family *Rosaceæ.*)

- Flowers of a pinkish white (Fig. AC represents a flowering branch). → Common Almond [*Amygdalus communis*]—food plant; medicinal. 🌺 (Family *Rosaceæ.*)

Nos. 1016, 1017, 1018, 1019, 1020

1016
(following on 1014).

△ Each flower has its petals overtopped by the ends of the 5 green parts that surround them (Fig. GE). → **Common Medlar** [*Mespilus germanica*]—food plant. 🌼 (Family *Rosaceæ.*)

△ Each flower has not got its petals overtopped by the ends of the 5 green parts that surround them (Fig. CY). → **Common Quince** [*Cydonia vulgaris*]—food plant; medicinal. 🌼 (Family *Rosaceæ.*)

1017
(following on 1013).

✠ Leaves more or less deeply divided (Fig. CR). → **Sharp-spined Hawthorn** (Whitethorn, May) [*Cratægus Oxyacantha*]—medicinal. — Represented in colour: 1 and 1 *bis*, Plate 20. (Family *Rosaceæ.*)

✠ Leaves not divided 1018

1018
(following on 1017).

○ Leaves hairy beneath when young or of a dull green and more or less whitish beneath 1019

○ Leaves without hairs beneath or only hairy on the veins, even when young, not of a dull green and whitish beneath 1022

1019
(following on 1018).

— Flowers slightly rosy; leaves rather downy beneath, with less than 9 secondary veins on each side of the principal vein (Fig. MC); buds pressed against the branches (Fig. MA). → **Common Apple** (Crab Apple) [*Malus communis*]—industrial; food plant. 🌼 —Represented in colour: 4, Plate 20. (Family *Rosaceæ.*)

— Tree not having these characteristics together 1020

1020
(following on 1019).

✱ Old leaves of a dull green, shining and more or less whitish beneath, with more than 9 secondary veins on each side of the principal vein (Fig. PC); buds more or less divergent (Fig. PI). → **Common Pyrus** (Pear-tree) [*Pyrus communis*]—industrial; food plant. 🌼 —Represented in colour: 3, Plate 20. (Family *Rosaceæ.*)

✱ Tree not having these characteristics together... 1021

1021
(following on 1020).

— Flowers usually in groups of more than 2 (Fig. AV); leaves folded in two in the direction of their length, when very young; there are some very minute rounded and reddish bodies on the edges and towards the base of the leaves (*g*, Fig. A). → **Birds' Prunus** (Black Cherry, Gean) [*Prunus avium*]. (Family *Rosaceæ*.)—Varieties of this tree are cultivated, such as the Sweet and Bigaroon Cherries—food plant; industrial. ✿—Represented in colour: 1, Plate 18.

— Flowers usually 2 together or solitary (Fig. DOM); leaves rolled on themselves in the direction of their length when very young; there are **no** distinct minute rounded and reddish bodies towards the base of the leaves. → **Cultivated Prunus** (Plum) [*Prunus domestica*]—food plant. ✿ (Family *Rosaceæ*.)

1022
(following on 1018).

⊖ Flowers with their stalks attached almost exactly at the same point (Fig. PC); young branches without hairs (examine with the lens). → **Cherry Prunus** (Dwarf Cherry) [*Prunus Cerasus*]—food plant. ✿ (Family *Rosaceæ*.)

⊖ Flowers with their stalks attached **at different levels** (Fig. MA); young branches hairy (examine with the lens). → **Mahaleb Prunus** (St. Lucie Cherry) [*Prunus Mahaleb*]—condiment. (Family *Rosaceæ*.)

1023
(following on 1001).

✕ Each flower shaped like a rattle widened out (Fig. MY); flowers of a greenish, reddish, or pinkish white. → **Common Whortleberry** (Bilberry, Whin-berry, Huckleberry) [*Vaccinium Myrtillus*]—food plant; medicinal. (Family *Ericaceæ*.)

✕ Each flower bell-shaped; stems almost entirely herbaceous.—Refer back to No. 53

✕ Each flower not in the shape of a rattle or a bell... 1024

1024
(following on 1023).

▢ Flowers of a greenish yellow, tubular; very small erect undershrub (Fig. L represents the top of a flowering branch). → **Spurge-laurel Daphne** [*Daphne Laureola*]—poisonous; medicinal. ✿ (Family *Thymelæaceæ*.)

▢ Flowers violet, purple, or white, in the shape of a star or of a funnel 1025

1025 *(following on 1024).*

✱✱ Flowers star-shaped with 5 petals united to one another at their bases only; there are two green spots edged with white at the base of each petal; leaves sometimes deeply divided (Fig. DU); an undershrub more or less climbing or supporting itself on other plants; the flowering branches have neither the appearance nor hardness of wood. → **Bittersweet Nightshade** (Woody Nightshade) [*Solanum Dulcamara*]—poisonous; medicinal.—Represented in colour: 2 and 2 *bis*, Plate 40. (Family *Solanaceæ*.)

✱✱ Flowers more or less **funnel-shaped** spreading in 5 lobes; there are not two green spots edged with white; leaves oval-elongated, narrow, often grouped two together at one level, never divided (Fig. L). → **Chinese Boxthorn** (Duke of Argyll's Tea-tree) [*Lycium chinense*]. ❀ —Represented in colour: 3 and 3 *bis*, Plate 40. (Family *Solanaceæ*.)

1026 *(following on 1000).*

⊙ Each flower has its petals separate from one another down to their bases; that is to say, that one of the petals (or parts coloured otherwise than green) can be detached without tearing the others. This refers to those parts of the flower which, collectively, make up the corolla (or coloured structure surrounding the little threads and other organs that occupy the centre of the flower); when the flower fades each petal (or coloured piece) falls off or withers separately [1] 1027

Fig. HE represents a flower with separate petals; Fig. HL shows the petals detached.—The other figures represent examples of flowers with separate petals or of branches bearing flowers with separate petals.

⊙ Each flower has its petals united to one another, at least at their bases; that is to say, that, in trying to detach one of the pieces of the flower coloured otherwise than green, one is obliged to tear the corolla; when the flower fades the corolla falls off or withers all in one piece (examples: Figs. TE and MS) 1033

---

[1] In most flowers there is, outside the corolla, another covering to the flower, generally green, known as the *calyx*, which surrounds the base of the corolla. In other flowers it is difficult to distinguish the calyx and the corolla

—
1027
(follow-ing on 1026).

⌒ Flowers yellow; plant almost herbaceous; below the flower there are 5 little green or brownish parts, 3 of which are much larger than the others (Fig. VG); flowers in a cluster (Fig. VUL). → **Common Rock-rose** [*Helianthemum vulgare*]—medicinal.— Represented in colour: 1, Plate 7. (Family *Cistaceæ*.)

⌒ Flowers pink **1028**

⌒ Flowers whitish, yellowish, or greenish **1029**

1028
(follow-ing on 1027).

• Leaves very small, narrow, crowded and arranged in 4 rows. → **Common Ling (Heather)** [*Calluna vulgaris*]. —Represented in colour: 2, Plate 36. (Family *Eri-caceæ*.)

• Leaves flat, oval, elongated, attached singly, in pairs, or by 3's (Fig. LS). → Willow-leaved **Lythrum (Purple Loosestrife)** [*Lythrum Salicaria*].—Represented in colour: 4, Plate 21. (Family *Lythraceæ*.)

1029
(follow-ing on 1027).

⊕ Flowers white; groups of numerous flowers opening very nearly all at the same level; leaves with their chief veins curving towards the tip of the leaf (Fig. SA). → **Bloody Cornel** (Dogwood, Bloody Twig) [*Cornus sanguinea*]—industrial. —Represented in colour: 2 and 2 *bis*, Plate 26. (Family *Cornaceæ*.)

⊕ Flowers whitish, yellowish, or greenish **1030**

1030
(follow-ing on 1029).

✠ Plant fixed on the branches of a tree; leaves opposite or whorled (Figs. VI and V). → **White Mistletoe** [*Viscum album*]—medicinal. —Represented in colour: 3 and 3 *bis*, Plate 26. (Family *Loranthaceæ*.)

✠ Tree or shrub growing in the ground **1031**

1031
(follow-ing on 1030).

§ The principal veins of the leaf curve and tend to reunite towards the tip of the leaf (Fig. CA). → **Cathartic Buckthorn** [*Rhamnus catharticus*]—medicinal. (Family *Rhamnaceæ*.)

§ The principal veins of the leaf do not curve towards the tip of the leaf **1032**

which are more or less combined into a single floral envelope. In other flowers, again, there is really only a single floral envelope coloured like a corolla. Under the names of petals and corolla we here include those pieces of the flower coloured otherwise than green which immediately surround the little threads or other organs that occupy the centre of the flower.

1032
(following on 1031).

+ Leaves more or less cut, with veins arranged like a fan (Figs. AC, AP, and PP). → Maples [*Acer*].—Refer back to No. 995

+ Leaves not cut, with veins not arranged like a fan (Fig. EV). → European Spindle-tree (Gatteridge, Prickwood) [*Evonymus europæus*]—industrial.—Represented in colour: 2 and 2 *bis*, Plate 12. (Family *Celastraceæ*.)

—
1033
(following on 1026).

—• Flowers shaped like a rattle elongated (Fig. EC); leaves very narrow and pointed, almost prickly at the tip. → Hoary Heath (Fine-leaved Heath, Crimson Heather) [*Erica cinerea*]. 🌺 —Represented in colour: 1, Plate 36. (Family *Ericaceæ*.)

—• Flowers not shaped like a rattle; leaves flat, not prickly at the tip 1034

1034
(following on 1033).

△ Flowers solitary, more than 1½ centimetres across, with 5 lobes spreading and, as it were, cut across a little at their tips (Fig. PY); stems prostrate; leaves opposite (Fig. P). → Lesser Periwinkle [*Vinca minor*]—medicinal.—Represented in colour: 4, Plate 37. (Family *Apocynaceæ*.)

△ Flowers in more or less elongated clusters 1035

△ Flowers in widely spreading clusters 1036

1035
(following on 1034).

⚕ Leaves more or less heart-shaped or rounded at the base, borne on rather long stalks (Fig. S). → Common Lilac [*Syringa vulgaris*]—ornamental.—Represented in colour: 3, Plate 37. (Family *Oleaceæ*.)

⚕ Leaves pointed at the base, borne on very short stalks (Figs. V and LI). → Common Privet [*Ligustrum vulgare*]—industrial. 🌺—Represented in colour: 2 and 2 *bis*, Plate 37. (Family *Oleaceæ*.)

1036
(following on 1034).

○ Flowers all alike; leaves not divided (Fig. L). → Mealy Guelder-rose (Wayfaring-tree) [*Viburnum Lantana*].—Represented in colour: 7, Plate 26. (Family *Caprifoliaceæ*.)

○ Outer flowers in the clusters of flowers considerably larger than the others; leaves more or less divided into 3 lobes (Fig. O). → Common Guelder-rose (Water Elder) [*Viburnum Opulus*]—ornamental. (Family *Caprifoliaceæ*.)—A variety of this tree is grown in gardens under the name of Snowball-tree.

265

— Leaves **compound**, that is to say, that the leaf as a whole is made up of a collection of secondary leaves, known as *leaflets*, each of which is often mistaken for a leaf; the whole compound leaf is attached to the stem by its base or by a stalk bearing all the leaflets; the base of the compound leaf is not attached in the axil of another leaf **1041**

1037
(following on 990).

The above figures represent examples of compound leaves.

— Leaves **simple**, that is to say, not made up of leaflets **1038**

The above figures represent examples of simple leaves.

—
1038
(following on 1037).

✳ Flowers yellow.—Refer back to No. **474**

✳ Flowers pink, blue, violet, or yellowish more or less mixed with pink **1039**

1039
(following on 1038).

= Flowers pink; stems more or less prostrate **1040**

= Flowers blue or violet; plant nearly herbaceous with erect stems (Fig. HY represents the plant in flower). → **Officinal Hyssop** [*Hyssopus officinalis*]—medicinal. 🌼 (Family *Labiatæ*.)

= Flowers yellowish mingled with pink, grouped in two's; shrub. → **Woody Honeysuckle** (Upright Fly Honeysuckle) [*Lonicera Xylosteum*]. (Family *Caprifoliaceæ*.)

1040
(following on 1039).

⊖ Each flower **tubular ending in 2 lips**; leaves opposite, attached in pairs at the same level on the stem (Fig. S). → **Wild Thyme** [*Thymus Serpyllum*]—medicinal. 🌼 (Family *Labiatæ*.)

⊖ Each flower **with 5 unequal petals**, free from one another down to their bases; leaves not opposite. → **Creeping Restharrow** (Wild Liquorice) [*Ononis repens*]—dangerous; medicinal.—Represented in colour: 1, Plate 15. (Family *Leguminosæ*.)

✕ Flowers yellow **1042**

1041
(follow-ing on 1037).

✕ Flowers white, not flecked with pink or red (occasionally with pink flowers); leaves with numerous leaflets; tree with flowers in drooping clusters (Fig. RPA). → **False Acacia (Locust-tree)** [*Robinia Pseudacacia*]—industrial. 🐝 —Represented in colour: 5, Plate 15. (Family *Leguminosæ*.)

✕ Flowers white, flecked with pink or red (occasionally with red flowers); leaves of trees have 5 or 7 leaflets arranged in fan shape (Fig. A); flowers in upright clusters. → **Common Horse - Chestnut** [*Æsculus Hippocastanum*]—ornamental; industrial; medicinal.—Represented in colour: 1 and 1 *bis*, Plate 12. (Family *Sapindaceæ*.)

✕ Flowers bright pink; leaves with 3 leaflets; a very small undershrub with stems more or less prostrate, and flowers more or less mingled with the ordinary leaves (Fig. O). → **Creeping Rest-harrow (Wild Liquorice)** [*Ononis repens*] —dangerous; medicinal.—Represented in colour: 1, Plate 15. (Family *Leguminosæ*.)

1042
(follow-ing on 1041).

☐ Flowers with more than 3 leaflets arranged in 2 rows (Fig. CO); the flowers are succeeded by swollen out fruits (Fig. U). → **Shrubby Bladder-senna** [*Colutea arborescens*] —ornamental; medicinal.—Represented in colour: 6, Plate 15. (Family *Leguminosæ*.)

☐ Leaves with 3 leaflets **1043**

1043
(follow-ing on 1042).

✱ ✱ Tree with flowers in hanging clusters (Fig. LA). → **Laburnum Cytisus (Labur-num, Golden Chain)** [*Cytisus Laburnum*] —ornamental; industrial. 🐝 — Represented in colour: 4, Plate 13. (Family *Leguminosæ*.)

✱ ✱ Shrub with flowers not in hanging clusters (Fig. GB); the flowering branches do not possess in general either the look or hard-ness of wood. → **Common Broom** [*Sarothamnus scoparius*] — industrial; poison-ous; medicinal. 🐝 —Represented in colour: 2, Plate 13. (Family *Leguminosæ*.)

⊕ **Leaves opposite;** that is to say, leaves arranged in pairs, attached to the stem at the same level, and facing one another (Fig. VI) **1045**

⊕ **Leaves whorled** (at least towards the middle of the stem); that is to say, 3, 4, or more leaves attached to the stem at the same level and arranged regularly around it **1045**

1044 *(following on 961).*

The above figures represent examples of whorled leaves.

⊕ **Leaves alternate;** that is to say, leaves attached singly to the stem at different levels (Figs. CN, P, T, PSP) **1047**

⊕ **Leaves grouped;** that is to say, 2 or more leaves attached to the stem at the same level, but arranged, at that level, on the same side of the stem .. **1047**

—
1045 *(following on 1044).*

⟊ **Leaves prickly,** attached by threes to the stem at the same level (Fig. CO). → **Common Juniper** [*Juniperus communis*] —industrial; medicinal.—Represented in colour: 4, Plate 62. (Family *Coniferæ*.)

⟊ **Leaves not prickly** **1046**

1046 *(following on 1045).*

§ Plant attached to the branches of a tree; leaves flat and oval; some opposite, others whorled. → **White Mistletoe** [*Viscum album*]—medicinal. ✿ —Represented in colour: 3 and 3 *bis*, Plate 26. (Family *Loranthaceæ*.)

§ Plant growing on the ground with very slender green branches, whorled, or with leaves reduced to scales and whorled (Figs. AR and AV). → **Horse-tail** [*Equisetum*]. In reality this is a plant without flowers.—Refer on to No. **1104**

1047
(following on 1044).

+ Leaves **hard, leathery, and thick** (enduring through the winter) 1048

The above figures represent the leafy branches of trees, shrubs, or bushes with hard, thick, and leathery leaves.

+ Leaves **not hard, leathery, and thick at the same time** (falling in autumn) 1054

The above figures represent leaves or leafy branches of trees, shrubs, or undershrubs having leaves not hard, thick, and leathery at the same time.

1048
(following on 1047).

—• Flowers **regular**, with 6 divisions apparently attached to the upper surface of the leaves (Fig. R). → Spine-pointed Ruscus (Butcher's-Broom, Knee-holm) [*Ruscus aculeatus*]—medicinal.—Represented in colour (in fruit): 1, Plate 54. (Family *Liliaceæ*.)

—• Flowers **reduced to scales**, and not apparently attached to the upper surface of the leaves 1049

1049
(following on 1048).

△ Leaves **oval**, length less than 4 times their width (Fig. BU); shrub sometimes very small. → Evergreen Box [*Buxus sempervirens*] —industrial; medicinal. 🌑 —Represented in colour: 1, Plate 47. (Family *Euphorbiaceæ*.)

△ Leaves **narrow and elongated**, length more than 4 times their width 1050

1050
(following on 1049).

✠ Leaves **grouped in pairs** (Figs. S and SIL). → Pine [*Pinus*].—Follow on to No. 1051

✠ Leaves **attached singly to the stem** 1052

1051
(*following on 1050*).

○ Leaves usually from 11 to 16 centimetres (4-6 inches) in length (measure a number of leaves). → Maritime Pine (Cluster-Pine) [*Pinus maritima*]—industrial; medicinal. 🌸 (Family *Coniferæ*.)

○ Leaves usually from 5 to 10 centimetres (2-4 inches) in length (measure a number of leaves) → Forest Pine (Scots Fir) [*Pinus sylvestris*]—industrial; medicinal. 🌸 —Represented in colour: 1, Plate 62. (Family *Coniferæ*.)

1052
(*following on 1050*).

— Each leaf having 2 white lines on the under side (Fig. A). → Comb-like Fir (Silver Fir) [*Abies pectinata*]—industrial; medicinal. 🌸 —Represented in colour (in leaf): 3, Plate 62. (Family *Coniferæ*.)

— Leaves without white lines on the under side 1053

1053
(*following on 1052*).

✳ Leaves arranged all round the branches (Fig. P). → Lofty Spruce (Common Spruce) [*Picea excelsa*]—industrial. 🌸 —Represented in colour (in fruit): 2, Plate 62. (Family *Coniferæ*.)

✳ Leaves of branches arranged distinctly in two opposite rows (Fig. T). → Common Yew [*Taxus baccata*]—poisonous; medicinal. (Family *Coniferæ*.)

1054
(*following on 1047*).

═ Each group of flowers forms a mass, more or less ball-shaped, as wide, or almost as wide, as it is long 1055

═ Each group of flowers forms a cluster or a spike more or less elongated, and either upright or drooping.. 1057

1055
(*following on 1054*).

⊖ Leaves more or less cut; principal veins arranged like a fan; flowers in hanging balls. → Oriental Plane [*Platanus orientalis*].—Represented in colour: 1, Plate 51. (Family *Platanaceæ*.)

⊖ Leaves not cut, and principal veins not arranged like a fan 1056

1056
(*following on 1055*).

✕ Leaves oval (Fig. FSI); flowers in rounded groups. → Woodland Beech (Beech) [*Fagus sylvatica*]—industrial; medicinal. — Represented in colour: 1 and 1 *bis*, Plate 49. (Family *Cupuliferæ*.)

✕ Leaves narrow and very elongated (Fig. M). → European Larch [*Larix europæa*] — medicinal. 🌸 (Family *Coniferæ*.)

1057 *(following on 1054).*

☐ Leaves cut; with lobes more or less rounded (Fig. O ; the groups of flowers are represented by Fig. R). → **Strong Oak** (Common Oak) [*Quercus Robur*]—industrial ; medicinal. 🌼 —Represented in colour: 2 and 2 *bis*, Plate 49. (Family *Cupuliferœ*.)

☐ Leaves not cut but finely toothed on their edges ... **1058**

1058 *(following on 1057).*

✱✱ Leaves (when not very old) **more or less pleated** (Fig. CAR ; the groups of flowers are represented by Fig. CBL) ; groups of flowers drooping. → **Birch-like Hornbeam** (Common Hornbeam) [*Carpinus Betulus*]—industrial.—Represented in colour: 1 and 1 *bis*, Plate 50. (Family *Cupuliferœ*.)

✱ ✱ Tree not having these characteristics together **1059**

1059 *(following on 1058).*

⊙ Young branches **drooping and reddish ;** leaves glossy on the upper side and pale green on the lower (Fig. BA represents a leaf ; Fig. BAL represents the group of flowers *f* and *m*). → **Silver Birch** (Common Birch) [*Betula alba*]—industrial ; medicinal. 🌼 —Represented in colour: 2, Plate 51. (Family *Betulaceœ*.)

⊙ Young branches **spreading or upright** **1060**

1060 *(following on 1059).*

♥ Leaves **sharply toothed; teeth pointed** and sometimes rather recurved ; clusters of flowers slender, very elongated and upright (Fig. CVU). → **Cultivated Chestnut** (Spanish Chestnut) [*Castanea sativa*] — industrial ; medicinal. 🌼 —Represented in colour : 4 and 4 *bis*, Plate 49. (Family *Cupuliferœ*.)

♥ Leaves **toothed** and usually **rounded at the tip** (Fig. AG) ; clusters of flowers, some small and erect; (*f*, Fig. GL) ; others **drooping** (*m*, Fig. GL) ; buds sticky. → **Sticky Alder** (Common Alder) [*Alnus glutinosa*] —industrial ; medicinal.—Represented in colour : 3 and 3 *bis*, Plate 51. (Family *Betulaceœ*.)

♥ Tree **not having these characteristics together** .. **1061**

1061
(following on 1060).

- **Leaves** with silvery hairs on both sides and finely toothed (Fig. A). →
  White Willow (Huntingdon Willow) [*Salix alba*]—industrial; medicinal. 🌱 (Family *Salicaceæ*.)
- **Leaves** green on the upper side, silky or without hairs on the lower, and finely toothed (as in Fig. A); branches snapping easily at the point where they are attached. → **Crack Willow** (Withy) [*Salix fragilis*]. 🌱 —Represented in colour: 5, Plate 50. (Family *Salicaceæ*.)
- **Leaves** green on the upper side and with silky hairs on the lower; not toothed (Fig. VI); branches flexible (Figs. SAM and VIM represent groups of flowers).
  → **Osier Willow** [*Salix viminalis*].—Represented in colour (in leaf): 6, Plate 50.[1] (Family *Salicaceæ*.)

1062[2]
(following on 764).

- ⊖ Each of the little clusters of flowers is flat, and has scales regularly arranged in two rows (Fig. FUS). (Flowering stem Fig. FU.) → **Brown Cyperus** [*Cyperus fuscus*]. (Family *Cyperaceæ*.)
- ⊕ Plant not having these characteristics together.. **1063**

1063
(following on 1062).

- ✠ The little groups of flowers are slightly elongated, and are separate from one another. These little groups are on numerous, very slender, and widely spreading branches (Fig. SI). → **Wood Scirpus** [*Scirpus sylvaticus*]. (Family *Cyperaceæ*.)
- ✠ The little groups of flowers are oval, few in number, and crowded together and are overtopped by one or two narrow elongated leaves (Fig. MA). → **Sea-side Scirpus** (Sea Club-rush) [*Scirpus maritimus*]. (Family *Cyperaceæ*.)
- ✠ Plant not having the preceding characteristics. → **Sedge** [*Carex*].—Go on to No. **1064**

---

[1] For the numerous species of Willows [*Salix*] reference must be made to more comprehensive Floras.

[2] The plants to which you are directed by Nos. 1062 to 1068 are only examples taken from the most common of the group of the Cyperaceæ. For the other members of the Family reference must be made to more comprehensive Floras.

1064
(following on 1063).

§ All the groups of flowers are **alike** (Figs. CM and CV) **1065**

§ The groups of flowers that terminate the stem (or the one group that does so) **different** from those below (examples: the figures below) **1066**

1065
(following on 1064).

+ **More than 12** groups of flowers (Fig. CV); stem with **3 very sharp angles** and 3 slightly hollowed-out sides (Fig. VU). → Fox Sedge (Great Sedge) [*Carex vulpina*]. (Family *Cyperaceæ*.)

+ **6 to 12** groups of flowers (Fig. CM); stem with 3 slightly acute angles (Fig. CMU). → Prickly Sedge [*Carex muricata*]. (Family *Cyperaceæ*.)

1066
(following on 1064).

—• Envelope of the withered flowers (in the lower groups of flowers) **covered with hairs** (examine with the lens) (Figs. H and F) **1067**

—• Envelope of the withered flowers (in the lower groups of flowers) **without** hairs or slightly hairy at their angles (examine with the lens) (Figs. R, S, and G) **1068**

1067
(following on 1066).

△ The **2 or 3 upper** groups of flowers are different from the others (Fig. AT); the sheaths of the leaves are velvety (Fig. HI). → Hairy Sedge (Hammer Sedge) [*Carex hirta*]. (Family *Cyperaceæ*.)

△ **One solitary** group of flowers, at the top, is different from the others (Fig. PX); the sheaths of the leaves are not velvety. → Spring Sedge [*Carex præcox*]. (Family *Cyperaceæ*.)

✠ Stems with 3 slightly marked angles AM (Fig. AM); the lower groups of flowers become drooping, but only after the flowers have gone over (Fig. GL); at the top, there are usually 2 or 3 groups of flowers different from the rest and brown or yellowish. → **Glaucous Sedge** [*Carex glauca*]. (Family *Cyperaceæ*.)

✠ Stems with 3 well marked angles CA (Fig. CA); the lower groups of flowers are drooping (Fig. SI); at the top, there is **one solitary group** of flowers different from the others and of a greenish white. → **Wood Sedge** [*Carex sylvatica*].—Represented in colour: 3, Plate 58. (Family *Cyperaceæ*.)

✠ Stems with 3 cutting angles (Fig. PL); the lower groups of flowers remain erect, even when the flowers have gone over (Fig. RI); at the top, there are **three or four groups** of flowers different from the others and brown or yellowish. → **Pond Sedge** [*Carex paludosa*].—Represented in colour: 4, Plate 58. (Family *Cyperaceæ*.)

1068
(following on 1066).

○ Leaves at least 6 centimetres (2 inches) across; the groups of flowers at the top of the plant are very different from those lower down (Fig. Z). → **Maize Zea** (Indian Corn) [*Zea Mays*]—food plant; medicinal.—Represented in colour: 5, Plate 58. (Family *Gramineæ*.)

○ Groups of flower elongated, all attached at the same point (Fig. D) or nearly at the same point; leaves hairy beneath; flowers ordinarily purple. → **Creeping Dog's-tooth-grass** [*Cynodon Dactylon*]—medicinal. (Family *Gramineæ*.)

○ Plant both with leaves less than 3 centimetres (1 inch) across and with groups of flowers not all starting from the same point 1070

1069[1]
(following on 764).

---

[1] The plants referred to by the Nos. 1069 to 1091 are only examples of some of the most common plants belonging to the group of the Grasses [*Gramineæ*]. For other members of the group reference must be made to more comprehensive Floras.

— Each little group of flowers is without a stalk or nearly so, attached more or less directly to the stem that bears all the groups of flowers. The whole of the flowers forms a spike 1071

1070
(follow-ing on 1069).

The above figures represent examples of plants with the groups of flowers without, or nearly without, stalks.

— Each little group of flowers is borne on a stalk more or less long, attached to a little branch, which is more or less directly attached to the stem that bears all the groups of flowers. The whole of the groups of flowers forms a cluster 1078

The above figures represent examples of plants with the groups of flowers each borne on a stalk (see also the figures under Nos. 1079 to 1091).

✳ The little groups of flowers are all attached directly to the stem 1072

1071
(follow-ing on 1070).

The above figures represent examples of plants with the groups of flowers attached directly to the stem. Fig. SE shows 3 groups of flowers attached together directly to the stem.

✳ The little groups of flowers appear to be attached one to another and the whole of these groups to be attached to the main stem 1076

The above figures represent examples of plants with the groups of flowers attached one to another.

1072
(following on 1071).

⚊ **The little groups of flowers overlap one another very closely;** the whole collection of flowers forms a very crowded spike (examples: Figs. V, VL, S, V, and M, under Nos. 1073 and 1074) **1073**

⚊ **The little groups of flowers do not overlap one another closely;** the whole collection of flowers forms a rather loose spike (examples: Figs. PE and RE, under No. 1075) **1075**

1073
(following on 1072).

⊖ **Each little group of flowers is as broad or nearly as broad as it is long** (Figs. VG and TV; Figs. V and VL re-present the flower-ing top of the stem, in two different

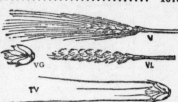

varieties of the plant); **V,** with the groups of flowers bearing long awns (Bearded Wheat); **VL,** with the groups of flowers without the long awns (Unbearded Wheat) → **Cultivated Wheat** [*Triticum sativum*]—food plant.—Repre-sented in colour: 1, Plate 59. (Family *Gramineæ*.)

⊖ **Each little group of flowers is very much longer than it is broad** (see the figures under No. 1074) **1074**

1074
(following on 1073).

× **A single little group of flowers** is attached direct-ly on each inden-tation of the stem (Figs. C and S). →

Cereal Rye [*Secale cereale*]—food plant.—Represented in colour: 2, Plate 59. (Family *Gramineæ*.)

× **Three little groups of flowers** are attached directly and together (Fig. SE) on each indentation of the stem, **which is erect from its base;** the plant is usually more than 50 centimetres (20 inches) in height (Fig. V represents the flowering top of the stem). → **Common Barley** [*Hordeum vulgare*]—food plant; in-dustrial; medicinal.—Represented in colour: 3, Plate 59. (Family *Gramineæ*.)

× **Three little groups of flowers** attached directly and to-gether on the stem which is **prostrate at its base and then erect;** the plant is usually less than 50 centimetres (20 inches) in height. (Fig. M represents the top of a flowering stem.) → **Wall Barley** [*Hordeum murinum*]. (Family *Gramineæ*.)

□ A single scale (*g*, Fig. LP) occurs at the base of each little group of flowers, and is attached directly to the indentation of the stem which bears the little group of flowers (Fig. PE); the little groups of flowers are flattened and have each of them one of their sides towards the stem. → Perennial Rye-grass (Way-Bent) [*Lolium perenne*]—ornamental.—Represented in colour: 5, Plate 59. (Family *Gramineæ*.)

1075 (follow-ing on 1072).

□ Two scales (Fig. R), one opposite the other, occur at the base of each little group of flowers and are attached directly to the indentation of the stem which bears the little group of flowers (Fig. RE); the little groups of flowers are flattened and each turns its flattened surface towards the stem. → Creeping Couch-grass [*Agropyrum repens*]—medicinal; harmful to crops.—Represented in colour: 4, Plate 59. (Family *Gramineæ*.)

1076 (follow-ing on 1071).

✱✱ Each very small group of flowers (nearly reduced to one flower) is accompanied by 2 long stiff hairs covered by minute bristles directed downwards (examine with the lens) (Fig. SV; Fig. VI represents the top of a flowering stem); leaves slightly rough along their edges. → Green Bristle-grass [*Setaria viridis*].—Represented in colour: 7, Plate 59. (Family *Gramineæ*.)

✱✱ Plant not having the above-described characters together **1077**

1077 (follow-ing on 1076).

⊙ Outside each flower is a slender, stiff hair which is longer than each of the scales that occur at the base of each little group of flowers (Figs. AA and APP); flowers often purple. → Mousetail-like Foxtail (Black Grass) [*Alopecurus myosuroides*]—fodder plant.—Represented in colour: 8, Plate 59. (Family *Gramineæ*.)

⊙ At the tip of each scale that occurs at the base of each little group of flowers is a stiff hair which is shorter than the rest of the scale (Fig. PPR; Figs. B and PP represent the tops of flowering stems); leaves usually of a light green. → Meadow Cat's-tail (Timothy Grass) [*Phleum pratense*]—fodder plant.—Represented in colour: 6, Plate 59. (Family *Gramineæ*.)

1078
(following on 1070).

⚘ Each little group of flowers **much overtops** the two scales at its base 1079

The above figures represent groups of flowers in which the collection of flowers much overtops the two scales at its base.

⚘ Each little group of flowers **does not overtop** the two scales that enclose it 1090

The above figures represent groups of flowers in which the collection of flowers does not overtop the two scales that enclose it.

1079
(following on 1078).

• There is a long, slender, stiff hair attached **right on the back** of the scale of each flower (Fig. E). The little groups of flowers are shining whitish or sometimes purplish-green, arranged on slender very spreading branches (Fig. EL). → Taller **False-Oat** (Oat-grass) [*Arrhenatherum elatius*]—fodder plant. (Family *Gramineæ*.)

• There is a long, slender, stiff hair attached **at the tip,** or nearly at the tip, of the scale of each flower (examples: Figs. E, M, and S) 1080

• There is **no** long, slender, stiff hair attached to the scale of each flower (examples: Figs. PR, A, and N) 1080

1080
(following on 1079).

⊕ Flowers **intermingled** with long hairs; plant 1 to 2 metres (3 to 6 feet) high; the collection of flowers forms a large plume (Fig. C). → **Common Reed** [*Phragmites communis*]—fodder plant.—Represented in colour: 1, Plate 60. (Family *Gramineæ*.)

⊕ Flowers **not** intermingled with long hairs 1081

1081
(following on 1080).

✠ The outer scale of each flower bears a long, slender, stiff hair attached a little below the tip of the scale of the flower (examples: Fig. C; see also the figures under Nos. 1083 and 1084) (examine with the lens). → Brome-grasses [*Bromus*].[1]—Go on to No. **1082**

✠ The outer scale of each flower bears a long, slender, stiff hair attached exactly at the tip of the scale of the flower (example: Fig. R) (examine with the lens) **1085**

✠ The outer scale of each flower bears **no** long, slender, stiff hair (example: Fig. A) .. **1085**

1082
(following on 1081).

§ The slender, stiff hair on the scale of each flower is much longer than that scale (see Figs. S and T, under No. 1083, below) **1083**

§ The slender, stiff hair on the scale of each flower is shorter than that scale (see Figs. E and M, under No. 1084) **1084**

1083
(following on 1082).

+ The scales of the flowers are **without** hairs (Fig. S); stem without, or nearly without, hairs on its upper portion; groups of flowers more or less drooping. → Barren Brome [*Bromus sterilis*]. (Family *Gramineæ*.)

+ The scales of the flowers are **covered with fine hairs** (Fig. T); stem hairy on its upper portion; groups of flowers becoming quite drooping (Fig. TE). → **Roof Brome** [*Bromus tectorum*]. (Family *Gramineæ*.)

1084
(following on 1082).

—• Scales of the flowers **without** hairs and **more than 5** times as long as they are broad (Fig. E). → **Upright Brome** [*Bromus erectus*]—fodder plant.— Represented in colour: 5, Plate 60. (Family *Gramineæ*.)

—• Scales of the flowers **covered with fine hairs** (Fig. M). → **Soft Brome** (Lop Grass) [*Bromus mollis*]—fodder plant. —Represented in colour: 4, Plate 60. (Family *Gramineæ*.)

[1] For further details as to the **various** species of Bromes [*Bromus*] reference must be made to more comprehensive Floras.

1085
(following on 1081).

△ Groups of flowers arranged in compact masses (Fig. D); each little group of flowers is borne on a stalk shorter than the little group of flowers. → **Clustered Dactylis** (Cock's-foot Grass) [*Dactylis glomerata*]—fodder plant.—Represented in colour: 4. Plate 61. (Family *Gramineæ*.)

△ Groups of flowers **not** arranged in compact masses   **1086**

1086
(following on 1085).

✠ Each little group of flowers is **broader than it is long**, almost in the shape of a reversed heart (Fig. B; Fig. ME represents the flowering top of a stem). → **Intermediate Briza** (Quaking-grass, Totter-grass) [*Briza media*]—fodder plant. —Represented in colour: 1, Plate 61. (Family *Gramineæ*.)

✠ Each little group of flowers is **longer than it is broad** (examples: Figs. under Nos. 1088 and 1089)...   **1087**

1087
(following on 1086).

○ The scales of the flowers are **prolonged into points** (see the figures under No. 1088) and are rounded at the back   **1088**

○ The scales of the flowers are **acute at the tips** (see the figures under No. 1089) and have an angle at the back   **1089**

1088
(following on 1087).

— **All the leaves are rolled up**, or nearly rolled up, on themselves lengthwise; each little group of flowers is, usually, but slightly elongated (Figs. TE, OVI, and O). → **Sheep's Fescue** [*Festuca ovina*] — fodder plant. — Represented in colour: 5, Plate 61. (Family *Gramineæ*.)

— **All the leaves are flat**, or nearly flat; each little group of flowers is, usually, rather long (Fig. PR). → **Meadow Fescue** [*Festuca pratensis*]. (Family *Gramineæ*.)

1089
(following on 1087).

✳ Plant generally **less than 30 centimetres** (1 foot) high; the slender branches which attach the groups of flowers to the stem are solitary or start 2 (or rarely 3) together from the same point on the stem (Fig. A). → **Annual Poa** [*Poa annua*].—Represented in colour: 2, Plate 61. (Family *Gramineæ*.)

✳ Plant generally **more than 30 centimetres** (1 foot) high; the slender branches which attach the groups of flowers to the stem spring from 3 to 5 together from the same point of the stem, towards the base of the flowering portion (Fig. PP). → **Meadow Poa** [*Poa pratensis*]—fodder plant. — Represented in colour: 3, Plate 61. (Family *Gramineæ*.)

1090
(following on 1078).

= Scales of the flowers less than 2 millimetres long (Fig. CA represents one of the little groups of flowers which only contains one developed flower (enlarged); Fig. CN represents the flowering stem). → **White Agrostis** (Fiorin-grass, Marsh Bent) [*Agrostis alba*] —fodder plant. (Family *Gramineæ*.)

= Scales of the flowers **more than 2** millimetres and less than a centimetre long (Fig. HM represents one of the little groups of flowers enlarged;

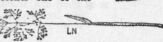

Fig. LN represents the flowering stem); **stems velvety at the places where they are** swollen at the bases of the sheaths of the leaves. → **Soft Holcus** [*Holcus mollis*]—fodder plant.—Represented in colour: 6, Plate 61. (Family *Gramineæ*.)

= Scales of the flowers **more than a centimetre long** 1091

1091
(following on 1090).

⊖ Groups of flowers hanging on slender branches spreading in all directions (Fig. SA; Fig. AS represents one of the little groups of flowers). → **Cultivated Oat** [*Avena sativa*] — food plant; medicinal.—Represented in colour: 2, Plate 60. (Family *Gramineæ*.)

⊖ Groups of flowers **not** hanging, arranged on erect slender branches (Fig. AP); there is often only a single little group of flowers on each branch. → **Meadow Oat** [*Avena pratensis*]. —Represented in colour: 3, Plate 60. (Family *Gramineæ*.)

1092
(following on 1).

× Branches or scales whorled (Figs. A, AR); or leaves

reduced to collarettes toothed at their tops (Fig. A) and placed one above the other; sporanges (that is to say, the little bags containing the spores or germs of the plant) grouped at the top of the stem in an oval mass (Fig. AV) 1104

× Plant **not** having these characteristics together 1093

1093
(following on 1092).

☐ Plants with leaves **1094**

☐ Plants without leaves. (The plants to which this question refers are not described in this book.[1])

1094
(following on 1093).

✳✳ Stems developed above ground and bearing numerous little leaves crowded upon one another and each less than half a centimetre (⅕ inch) broad; the leafy stem is not as a rule more than 10 centimetres in height. (The plants to which this question refers are not described in this book.[2])

✳✳ Plant not having all these characteristics together (see the figures under Nos. 1095 and the following ones) **1095**

1095
(following on 1094).

⊙ Leaves **undivided**; groups of sporanges in long lines

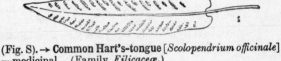

(Fig. S). → **Common Hart's-tongue** [*Scolopendrium officinale*] —medicinal. (Family *Filicaceæ*.)

⊙ Leaves **deeply divided** **1096**

---

[1] Those plants that are without flowers, without stems, and without leaves, comprise :—

1st. The *Algæ* which live in water or in damp air, and which contain the green substance that occurs in the leaves of higher plants. The green substance may be directly visible (Green Algæ), or it may be hidden by another substance (Red and Brown Algæ). Algæ can nourish themselves by means of air and water, without organic matter. In the sea hardly any plants occur except Algæ which are very abundant on the coast, where they are often made use of as manure.

2nd. The *Fungi* which live upon plants, animals, and organic matter, and which never contain the green colouring-matter of leaves. The best known are those that are called Pileate or Cap-mushrooms, such as the cultivated Mushroom, the Bolete, the Oronge, and the Chantarelle, which are edible, but which we must be on our guard against confusing with other Agarics that resemble them but are very poisonous. Others, such as the Morel and Truffle, which are also edible, are of an entirely different shape ; others, again, very much smaller, are the causes of certain diseases among plants, such as mildew, or sometimes in animals, or even in man (thrush in children, etc.) : lastly, other extremely minute Fungi are useful to us, such as the yeasts which are employed in making bread, beer, etc.

3rd. The *Lichens* formed by the close union of certain Algæ and Fungi. The Lichens contain the green colouring-matter of leaves and can grow, like the Algæ, without organic matter ; but they can bear drought, whilst Algæ are usually killed by desiccation. Lichens grow in the form of scales or plates or tree-like shapes on rocks, on the bark of trees, or on the ground.

[2] Those plants that have no flowers or roots but have usually stems and leaves comprise :—

1st. The *Mosses*, the leaves of which are usually attached all round the branches. They are commonly small plants growing abundantly in woods, on trees, on rocks, or on walls. The best known is the Gardeners' Moss, which is used to put round the base of pot plants.

2nd. The *Liverworts*, the leaves of which are attached on one side of the stem. They are small plants, often prostrate on the ground, growing in damp places, near springs, on rocks, or banks, or sometimes on trees.

1096
(following on 1095).

℧ Leaves whose principal divisions are all **joined together** at their base (see Figs. B and V at No. 1102) **1102**

℧ Leaves whose principal divisions are **separated from each other down to the base** (see figures at Nos. 1098 to 1102) **1097**

1097
(following on 1096).

• Plant usually **from 5 to 40 centimetres (2-16 inches)** (see

Figs. T, AN, and RM at Nos. 1098 and 1099); groups of sporanges oval or elongated in shape (Figs. AT and AR), sometimes united with one another (Fig. AR) **1098**

• Plant not having these characteristics together **1100**

1098
(following on 1097).

⊕ Lobes of leaves round-ed and arranged in two opposite rows (Figs. T and AT); the main stalk of the leaf is brownish black and glossy. → **Maidenhair Spleen-wort** [*Asplenium Trichomanes*]—medicinal.—Represented in colour: 2, Plate 63. (Family *Filicaceæ*.)

⊕ Plant not having these characteristics together.. **1099**

1099
(following on 1098).

✠ Leaves usually from **10 to 40 centimetres (4-16 inches)** in their **entire length** (including the main leaf-stalk); the principal lobes of the leaf are **sharply pointed at the tip**

(Fig. AN); the main leaf-stalk is blackish brown towards the base. → **Black-Maidenhair Spleenwort** (French Fern) [*Asplenium Adiantum-nigrum*]. (Family *Filicaceæ*.)

✠ Leaves usually from **5 to 15 centimetres (2-6 inches)** in total length; the principal lobes of the leaf **slightly pointed at the tip** (Figs. RM and AR); the main leaf-stalk is brownish green, or dark brown down towards the base. → **Wall-rue Spleenwort** [*Asplenium Ruta-muraria*]. — Represented in colour: 3, **Plate 63**. (Family *Filicaceæ*.)

1100
(following on 1097).

§ A single large leaf, often more than a metre in height (and which might be taken for a stem bearing leaves); the leaf has no little brown scales at the base of the main stalk (Fig. A represents the final divisions of the leaf). → **Eagle-marked Bracken (Common Bracken)** [*Pteris aquilina*] — industrial; medicinal. — Represented in colour: 4, Plate 63. (Family *Filicaceæ*.)

§ Plant not having these characteristics together; there are little brown scales at the base of the main leaf-stalk (Fig. P) **1101**

1101
(following on 1100).

+ The lobes of the leaf are toothed all round, and with very pointed teeth, almost like small, very slender spines (Fig. S);

the large divisions of the leaf are nearly 3 times as long as they are wide (Fig. SP). → **Spiny Polystichum** [*Polystichum spinulosum*]. (Family *Filicaceæ*.)

+ The lobes of the leaves are slightly toothed (Fig. E, No. 1103), or toothed all round but not with very sharp teeth (Fig. AF, No. 1103); the large divisions of the leaf are 4 to 7 times longer than their width (example: Fig. FM at No. 1103) **1103**

1102
(following on 1096).

① Leaves whose lobes diminish in size little by little towards

the base (Fig. B). → **Upright Blechnum (Hard Fern)** [*Blechnum Spicant*]. (Family *Filicaceæ*.)

① Leaves whose lobes do not diminish in size little by little towards the base (Fig. V). → **Common Polypody** [*Polypodium vulgare*]—medicinal.—Represented in colour: 1, Plate 63. (Family *Filicaceæ*.)

—• The lobes of the principal divisions are deeply toothed all round; teeth not pointed (Fig. AF; Fig. PP represents one of the principal divisions of a leaf with a large number of lobes). → **Lady-fern Athyrium** [*Athyrium Filix-femina*]. (Family *Filicaceæ*.)

1103 (*following on 1101*).

—• The lobes of the principal divisions are not very deeply toothed; they are chiefly toothed towards the tip, and sometimes more than in Fig. F (Fig. FM represents part of a leaf with its principal divisions and their lobes). → **Male-fern Polystichum** (Male-fern) [*Poly-*

stichum Filixmas]—poisonous; medicinal.—Represented in colour: 1, Plate 64. (Family *Filicaceæ*.)

△ Sheaths more than a centimetre and a half in width (Fig. T, natural size), edged with 30 to 40 teeth. → **Greatest Horsetail** [*Equisetum maximum*]. —Represented in colour (stems green): 3, Plate 64. (Family *Equisetaceæ*.)

1104 (*following on 1046*).

△ Sheaths less than a centimetre and a half in width

edged with less than 20 teeth (Fig. A, natural size; Figs. AR and AV represent two kinds of stems on the same plant). → **Field Horse-tail** [*Equisetum arvense*]—industrial; medicinal.—Represented in colour: 2 and 2 *bis*, Plate 64. (Family *Equisetaceæ*.)

ABRIDGED TABLES

For finding out the Names of Plants more quickly.

The reader already sufficiently acquainted with this work, can arrive more quickly at the names of the plants by beginning to look them out through the aid of the following tables.

These tables refer directly to one of the numbers of the preceding pages (numbers with a little line over them). On starting from the number to which you are referred in these tables the name of the plant will be found in the preceding pages by means of the successive questions.

Begin with the General Table below.

GENERAL TABLE

Plant having flowers.

Herbaceous plant. — Flowers not composite.

⊢ Tree, shrub, or undershrub. → *See A, lower down on this page.*

✳ Flowers composite .... → *See B, page* 287.

× Flowers pink, red, purple, reddish, brown, brownish, or of a blackish brown .... → *See C, page* 288.

× Flowers blue, bluish, lilac, violet or purplish .... → *See D, page* 288.

× Flowers yellow or yellowish .... → *See E, page* 289.

× Flowers white or whitish .... → *See F, page* 289.

× Flowers green or greenish .... → *See G, page* 289.

○ Plant never having flowers .... → *See on to No.* 1092

A.—Trees, Shrubs, or Undershrubs.

⊕ Flowers opening before the leaves.

= Flowers with a fully developed corolla...... **944**

= Flowers without corolla, or with one reduced to scales **950**

⊕ Flowers opening after the leaves, or at the same time.

⊙ Flowers reduced to scales.

△ Leaves opposite or whorled **1045**

△ Leaves alternate. or grouped.

—• Leaves hard, leathery, and thick (lasting through the winter) ... **1048**

—• Leaves not hard, leathery, and thick at the same time (falling in autumn) **1054**

⊙ Flowers not reduced to scales.

+ Tree, shrub, or undershrub prickly **963**

+ Tree, shrub, or undershrub climbing or creeping.. **981**

+ Tree, shrub, or undershrub not prickly or climbing.

○ Flowers regular.

□ Leaves compound or deeply divided.. **992**

• Leaves opposite or whorled.

— Petals separated ... **1027**

— Petals joined together **1033**

□ Leaves simple.

• Leaves alternate or grouped.

⊕ Petals separated ... **1002**

⊕ Petals joined together **1023**

○ Flowers irregular.

✳ ✳ Leaves compound **1041**

✳ ✳ Leaves simple **1038**

B.—Flowers composite.

⊕ Flowers pink, purple, red, and brown ; or flowers pink in their outer circle, yellow in the centre.

⊙ Leaves opposite 772
⊙ Leaves whorled 818
⊙ Leaves alternate, grouped, or all at the base, or not developed.
= Plant prickly 782
= Leaves of the collarette ending in a hook 781
= Plant not prickly and without hooks on the scales of the collarette.
• Leaves compound or deeply divided.. 793
• Leaves simple or not developed 797

⊞ Flowers blue, lilac, or violet, or lilac in the outer circles and yellow in the centre.

⌒ Plant prickly 811
⌒ Plant not prickly.
+ Leaves opposite 813
+ Leaves whorled 818
+ Leaves alternate or all at the base 819

⊞ Flowers entirely yellow or yellowish.

△ Plant having sharp spines (sometimes very small) 829
△ Plant without sharp spines.
⊖ The little flowers of the outer circles radiate all round the expanded flower.
— Plant which exudes a white milk (cut below the flower).. 839
— Plant without this white milk 860
⊖ Flowers not radiating.
• Leaves compound or deeply divided 873
• Leaves simple or not developed 879

⊞ Flowers white, whitish, or white flowers in the outer circles and yellow or yellowish in the centre.

✳ Plant prickly 892
✳ Scales of the collarette ending in a hook.. 891
✳ Plant not prickly and without hooks on the scales of the collarette.
○ Flowers in the outer circles radiating all round the expanded flower 897
○ Flowers not radiating 910

⊞ Flowers green or greenish.

▢ Leaves compound or deeply divided... 929
▢ Leaves simple or not developed 931

C—Plant herbaceous, with flowers (not composite ones) **pink, red, purple, reddish, brown, brownish, or blackish brown.**

✠ Flowers regular.	△ Leaves compound or deeply divided.	⊙ Leaves opposite	89
		⊙ Leaves whorled	104
		⊙ Leaves alternate or all at the base	107
	△ Leaves simple.	= Leaves opposite. { + Petals separated	61
		{ + Petals joined together..	77
		= Leaves whorled	85
		= Leaves alternate, grouped, or all at the base. { • Petals separated.	9
		{ • Petals joined together	45
	△ Leaves not developed {	— Petals separated	9
		— Petals joined together..	45
✠ Flowers irregular.	⊖ Leaves compound or deeply divided.	△ Corolla butterfly-shaped	212
		△ Corolla not butterfly-shaped. { —• Leaves opposite .	202
		{ —• Leaves alternate.	206
	⊖ Leaves simple.	× Leaves opposite. { ☐ Flower with 2 lips	173
		{] Flower with 1 lip	165
		{ _] Flower with neither 1 lip nor two	166
		× Leaves whorled	1104
		× Leaves alternate, or all at the base	126
	⊖ Leaves not developed		125
✠ Flowers reduced to scales			146

D.—Plants herbaceous, with flowers (not composite) blue, bluish, lilac, violet, or purplish.

○ Flowers regular.		• Leaves compound or deeply divided	284
	Leaves simple.	① Leaves opposite or whorled. { — Petals separated	268
		{ — Petals joined together..	271
		① Leaves alternate, grouped, or all at the base. { ✳ Petals separated	232
		{ ✳ Petals joined together	242
		• Leaves not developed (see *Colchicum*, at No. 423).	
○ Flowers irregular.	☐ Leaves compound or deeply divided.	♡ Corolla butterfly-shaped	341
		♡ Corolla not butterfly-shaped ...	349
	Leaves simple.	✠ Leaves opposite	324
		✠ Leaves whorled (see Toadflax [*Linaria repens*] at No. 310).	
		✠ Leaves alternate, grouped, or all at the base. { × Petals separated	300
		{ × Petals joined together	307
○ Flowers reduced to scales			352

E.—Plant herbaceous, with flowers (not composite) yellow or yellowish.

F.—Plant herbaceous, with flowers (not composite) white or whitish.

G.—Plant herbaceous, with flowers (not composite) green or greenish.

HOW PLANTS ARE CLASSIFIED

In the preceding pages our only aim has been to find out the names of plants, and we have not troubled ourselves at all about their classification. Let us now see how different plants can be grouped and classified systematically.

Those different plants which much resemble one another so that they appear almost identical, are known by the same name and are said to belong to the same kind or *species*. Thus, two stalks of Red Clover resemble one another much more than they resemble a stalk of Lucerne or Sainfoin or White Clover. If the seeds of these Red Clovers are sown, they produce plants that resemble them as much as the two stalks resemble one another ; and all these similar plants form the species Red Clover.

Since the number of species of plants is considerable, in order to classify them more easily, we unite those species which show certain likenesses to one another into one group which is termed a *genus,* and in naming plants in English we put a name for each species before that of the genus. For example, the species known as Dutch Clover, Red Clover, and Hare's-foot Trefoil have much likeness and belong to one genus, the genus Trefoil or Clover. In Latin the order of the names is reversed, that is to say, the name of the genus—in this case *Trifolium*—comes first, and is followed by that peculiar to the species, such as *Trifolium repens, Trifolium pratense*, and *Trifolium arvense*.

The number of genera is, however, also very great ; and it is, therefore, convenient, in order to classify them readily, to unite those genera that most resemble one another into one group, and this is called a *Family*. For example, the Trefoil genus, the Lucerne genus, the Sainfoin genus, etc., resemble one another in their butterfly-shaped flowers, and they are accordingly classed together in one family known as *Papilionaceæ*, from the Latin *papilio*, a butterfly. Thus the species popularly known as Red Clover belongs to the family Papilionaceæ, to the genus Trefoil, and to the species Red ; it is known by the name Red Clover, that is to say, by the name of the genus (Clover or Trefoil) preceded by that of the species (Red). Our coloured Plates 13, 14, 15, 16, and 17 are all devoted to species belonging to the family Papilionaceæ. In the same way all the species represented on Plate 22 are fleshy plants with regular flowers which belong to the family Crassulaceæ.

The families themselves are arranged in a definite order ; and it is in accordance with this order that they appear in our coloured plates.

DETAILED EXAMPLES

Of how to find the Names of Plants by the Simple Way

At the beginning of the book we gave an example of how to find the name of a plant (the Corn Poppy). We will now examine some other examples, first following out the search for the name, as we did for the Poppy, by starting from page 2 which has Nos. 1, 2, 3, 4 as a heading ; and then, for the reader who has become sufficiently used to the book, by means of the Abridged Tables beginning on page 286, which is readily found by the tab fixed to the top of page 287.

Note 1.—*It is most important to bear in mind that when there is a doubt between two alternatives, or between several included under one bracket, either of these questions may be chosen and followed up, and in any case the name of the plant will be reached. For example, if a flower is pink or rather purplish, its name will be found just the same whether we chose " flowers pink " or " flowers purplish."*

→ See also Note 2 on page 292, and Note 3 on page 294.

First Example : *Yellow Iris.*

Supposing that in early summer we have gathered some flowering stems of the beautiful plant generally known as the Yellow Iris or Flag, and that we want to know what it is called botanically, what are its various popular names, and what are its properties ; or let us suppose that we do not know any name for it.

We open the book at page 2, where we find Nos. 1, 2, 3, 4 at the heading of the page, and begin with No. 1 which gives us the choice between two questions or alternatives, each having the sign + before it. We should choose " Plant with flowers," which refers us on to No. 2, where we are faced by two questions preceded by the sign —• ; the plant not being either a tree, a shrub, or an undershrub, we should choose the first " Herbaceous plant," which refers us on to No. 3, where two fresh questions met us, each preceded by the sign △. From the explanations that are given we should choose the second question, " Flower not composite," which refers us on to No. 4. Under No. 4, at the bottom of the same page, we are met by five questions at once —under one bracket—each preceded by the sign ⊁ ; we should choose the third of these, " Flowers yellow or yellowish," which carries us on to No. 354. We accordingly turn over the pages till we find that number, an easy matter since the numbers in each page are put at the top of the page.

Under No. 354 we find two questions, each preceded by the sign ⊖ ; of these it is the second that suits, because the flowers in our plant are not arranged in a compound umbel; and that carries us on to No. 355, which is on the next page.

There three questions are propounded. We easily recognise, by the explanations given on that page and by Fig. IA, that it is the first of these that suits. We choose, therefore, the alternative, "Each flower regular," which directs us to No. 356, on the following page. Under No. 356 four questions, each preceded by the sign □, present themselves together. Thanks to the explanations and the figures, we should choose the third of these, "Leaves simple," which directs us to No. 357, on the following page. There we take the third alternative, "Leaves alternate," which carries us on to No. 358, where we should choose the first alternative, "Each flower with petals separated from one another down to their bases;" and we then go on to No. 361, on the following page. We cut the stem, but no white milk exudes; and this directs us to No. 362. The leaves are not thick, fleshy, and juicy, so we go on to "Plant not fleshy" and to No. 363. No such little scale is to be seen on the inner side of each of the yellow petals of our flower as is represented in Fig. R; and that brings us to No. 364. There are more than five parts coloured yellow or yellowish, so that we go on to No. 380.

Under No. 380, since we see that the similar parts of the flower are arranged in 3's, that its leaves are elongated and acute and have unbranched veins, and as we recognise Fig. IP as resembling our plant, we arrive at the name of the plant as Acorus-like Iris, also commonly known as Corn Flag or Yellow Iris, the Latin botanical name of which is *Iris Pseudacorus*. We are told at once that the plant is medicinal; but on looking out "Iris, Acorus-like" in the alphabetical index of English botanical names, the first of the three indexes at the end of the book, we shall see what its properties are. We are also referred, both under No. 380 and in this index, to Fig. 5 on Plate 54, where we shall at once recognise our plant represented in colour.

NOTE 2, with reference to turning back.—*Under each number is given, in parentheses, the number from which it follows on, that is to say, the number which has guided us to the one before us. Thus we read "380 (following on 364)," and so on, if we retrace our steps. If we think we have made any mistake, these references enable us to go back, number by number, to reconsider the choice of each successive question. One number may sometimes be reached by different routes; in this case it is only possible for the retracing of our steps to be indicated in one direction, that, namely, which is the more ordinary and normal.*

SECOND EXAMPLE: *Cornflower.*

Let us suppose that we have gathered a Cornflower in a field and that we may try to find out its botanical name, its other popular names, etc.

Let us open the book at page 2, which has Nos. 1, 2, 3, 4 as a heading. We should, at No. 1, choose "Plant with flowers," at No. 2, "Herbaceous plant," which brings us to No. 3. There we recognise that we are concerned with a composite flower, because what is usually spoken of as the flower of the Cornflower is made up of a great number of little flowers without stalks, the whole surrounded by a collarette of scales crowded one upon another. We should, therefore, choose the first alternative, that which carries us on to No. 770.

Let us turn over the pages of the book until we come to that number, and we then find five questions together, each preceded by the sign =. Our plant having blue flowers, we should choose the second question, that which directs us to No. 810. Our plant not being prickly, we go on to No. 812. As the leaves of our plant are attached to the stem singly, at different levels, we should choose the third question, " Leaves alternate," which refers us to No. 819. As the flower is not reduced to scales, we go on to No. 820.

The composite flower has the little flowers at its circumference larger and radiating outwards all round it when it is fully out ; and we shall also recognise that the flower resembles that represented in Fig. CY. We are thus led to No. 821. Our plant not having the characteristics of the Perennial Lettuce, we are led to No. 822 ; when, since the composite flower of our plant has not got little yellowish flowers in its centre but has all its little flowers blue, we are carried on to No. 823. There we recognise that the composite flowers are solitary at the tops of the stems or branches, and that our flower resembles Fig. CY. This brings us to the name of the plant : → Blue Knapweed, also popularly known as Cornflower or Bluebottle, its Latin botanical name being *Centaurea Cyanus.* It is here stated also that the plant is medicinal, and its properties may be found in the index of English names. The sign 🐝 tells us that the plant is honey-bearing, that is to say, that it is visited by bees which suck a sugary liquid from its blossoms. Lastly, we see that it is figured in Fig. 1 of Plate 30, among our coloured plates.

Third Example : *Acacia.*

Let us try to find out the name of the tree commonly called Acacia, which expands its clusters of white flowers in June. Let us pick a branch with a bunch of flowers on it.

We begin its analysis at page 2, where we are referred from No. 1 to No. 2, which directs us to No. 942, because our plant is a tree.

As the blossoms appear on the tree at the same time as, or after, the leaves, we are sent on to No. 961 ; and, as the flowers are not reduced to scales, we are directed to No. 962.

At this number, it is asked whether the plant is, or is not, prickly. Usually we shall have noticed that there are spines on this tree, and we shall, therefore, choose " Plant prickly " ; but it may happen that we have gathered a bunch of flowers and some leaves on a branch that is without spines. In either case we shall be led to the name of the tree.

Supposing, in the first place, that we have ascertained that spines are present, we are then directed to No. 963, whence, by the third alternative question, we go on to No. 970. As each flower of our tree has a butterfly-shaped corolla and agrees with the explanation given of it under No. 970, we are directed to No. 971. The second alternative under this number brings us to the name of the plant to which Figs. RPA and RO refer. We thus come to → False Acacia or Locust-tree, named in Latin *Robinia Pseudacacia*. We are told that the tree has industrial uses (see Acacia, in the index of English names). The sign 🐝 tells us that it is a tree the flowers of which are visited by bees ; and, lastly, we are referred to Fig. 5 on Plate 15, where we see a branch of the Acacia represented in colour.

Supposing, however, that the flowering branch of this tree that we have gathered has no spines. At Nô. 962 we shall then have chosen the alternative " Plant not prickly," which carries us on to No. 980. The plant not being a climber and not trailing on the ground, we are carried on to No. 990. We see that each flower is irregular, which directs us to No. 1037. Under this number we see clearly that each leaf of the tree is a compound leaf of the same type as Fig. CO (see Note 3, below). This brings us to No. 1041, where we shall choose the second alternative, which is the Acacia.

Note 3, with reference to compound leaves.—*With regard to compound leaves, it is necessary not to confound the secondary leaves or*

"leaflets" of a compound leaf with simple leaves on a branch. The base of a compound leaf is attached to the stem without being at the same point as, and immediately above another leaf.

On the contrary, a young branch, such as the branch r *(Fig. A), bearing leaves (a leafy branch which might be confused with a compound leaf) is attached to the stem* t *immediately above another leaf* f *and at the same point as that leaf* (Fig. A). Fig. GLY *represents, not a branch, but a leaf made up of leaflets which is attached to the stem not immediately above another leaf.*

This may be stated otherwise by saying that a compound leaf may be recognised by not being situated in the axil of another leaf, while a young branch is attached to the stem in the axil of a leaf.

Fourth Example : *Wheat.*

Let us gather an ear of Wheat in flower, that is to say, at the time when the spike is still green. Under No. 1, on page 2, we will take the first alternative, because we are there told that flowers may be green or scarcely visible, and we will not take the second alternative because Wheat in no way resembles the Ferns and Horsetails figured under Nos. 1092 to 1104. This carries us on to No. 2, where two other questions present themselves. Wheat being neither a tree, a shrub, nor an undershrub, we should choose the first alternative, " Herbaceous Plant," which brings us to No. 3. There we may hesitate, perhaps, and, as the flowers of Wheat are without stalks, very crowded and surrounded by little scales, we might choose " Flower composite "; but since these little scales are not clearly arranged in a collarette, we may choose " Flower not composite." As is always the case when there is any doubt, either alternative may be followed up, and in either case the name of the plant will be reached.

Examples of the Search for a Name

Let us then take the first alternative, looking upon each group of the flowers of the Wheat, or even the entire ear, as a composite flower. That will refer us to No. 770, where we should choose the last question, since the flowers are green, and we are then referred to No. 928. As the leaves are simple, we take the third question which directs us to No. 931. There is no exudation of white milk when the stem is broken, which takes us to No. 932, where we should choose the first question, which conducts us to No. 938. Wheat not resembling Figs. AR, AV, IT, or R in any way, and not presenting the characteristics of the first alternatives under Nos. 938, 939, or 940, we are led on to No. 941. If we look at the way in which the leaf of Wheat is attached to the stem, we shall easily see that it is by means of a sheath that is split lengthwise and that there is a little tongue at the point where the leaf appears to join the stem, above the sheath. Furthermore, the stem of the Wheat is cylindrical and not three-angled. For all these reasons, we should choose the first alternative which brings us to No. 1069.

At this number we recognise at the first glance that Wheat does not resemble Fig. Z or Fig. D. Moreover, the leaves of Wheat are less than 3 centimetres (1¼ inches) wide, and the spikes are not united to the same point at their bases. We are thus brought to No. 1070. We recognise readily that it is the first alternative that suits, from which the reference is to No. 1071. We ascertain that each little group in the spike is attached directly to the stem, or, we may say, to the axis of the spike; and this carries us on to No. 1072. As the little groups of flowers in the spike overlap one another very closely, we go on to No. 1073, where we recognise Figs. VG and VL if we have gathered an ear of beardless Wheat, or Figs. TY and V if we have gathered Bearded Wheat. We ascertain also that each little group of flowers is almost as broad as it is long. We have thus reached the name of the plant : → Cultivated Wheat, popularly known as Wheat or Corn, the Latin botanical name of which is *Triticum sativum*, and which is represented in colour by Fig. 1 on Plate 59. The word " food plant " refers us to the index of English names.

Suppose, on the other hand, that at No. 3 we have chosen " Flower not composite," that would conduct us to No. 4, where we should choose the last question, the reference from which is to No. 705. From this point, choosing in succession : at 705 the second question ; at 711, the third ; at 727, the third ; at 738, the first (or if we have any doubt and at this point choose the second, it will still lead us to the name of the plant) ; at 739, the first question which refers us to 1069, where, as before, we arrive by means of several questions at No. 1073 → Cultivated Wheat.

Supposing, however, that we have gathered an ear of Wheat almost ripe and already yellow or yellowish, we shall still reach the name of the plant, by different routes, whether we consider its flowers as composite or as simple.

If we take the Wheat as having composite yellow or yellowish flowers, we shall determine it by passing in succession through the questions numbered : 1, 2, 3, 770, 828, 837, 872, 879, 880, 888, 889, 890, 1070, 1071, 1072, 1073 → Cultivated Wheat.

If, however, we look upon the Wheat as having simple yellow or yellowish flowers, we shall again determine it very easily by passing in succession through Nos. 1, 2, 3, 4, 354, 355, 502, 503, 504, 505, 1069, 1070, 1071, 1072, 1073 → Cultivated Wheat.

It sometimes happens that the ears of Wheat are of a russet brown colour. In this case, we shall still find the name of the plant if we look upon its flowers as composite (by the Nos. 1, 2, 3, 770, 771, 781, 792, 797, 805, 806, 808, 809, 1069, 1070, 1071, 1072, 1073 → Cultivated Wheat), or considering it as having simple flowers (by the Nos. 1, 2, 3, 4, 5, 146, 157, 159, 160, 161, 163, 164, 1069, 1070, 1071, 1072, 1073 → Cultivated Wheat).

Other varieties of the same species, that is to say, of this same Wheat, may have their spikes whitish. In this case we shall reach the name of the plant quite as readily, whether we take it as having composite flowers (by the Nos. 1, 2, 3, 770, 891, 896, 910, 916, 920, 1069, 1070, 1071, 1072, 1073 → Cultivated Wheat), or whether we take it as having simple flowers (by the Nos. 1, 2, 3, 4, 506, 507, 702, 1069, 1070, 1071, 1072, 1073 → Cultivated Wheat).

OTHER EXAMPLES

We will also give here, in an abridged form, the way in which we shall find out the names of a few plants, merely indicating the order of the numbers that show the sequence of questions to be chosen.

Daisy.—Nos. 1, 2, 3, 770, 891, 896, 897, 898 ; 1st question under No. 898 → Perennial Daisy [*Bellis perennis*].

Hawthorn.—Nos. 1, 2, 942, 961, 962, 963, 970, 972, 976 ; 1st question under No. 976 → Sharp-spined Hawthorn (White-thorn, May) [*Cratægus Oxyacantha*].

Sainfoin.—Nos. 1, 2, 3, 4, 5, 123, 200, 212, 218, 219, 226, 227 ; 1st question under No. 227 → Cultivated Sainfoin [*Onobrychis sativa*].

Honesty.—Nos. 1, 2, 3, 4, 5, 6, 7, 8, 9, 10, 11, 12, 13, 14 ; 2nd question under No. 14 → Biennial Lunaria (Honesty) [*Lunaria biennis*].

Mallow.—Nos. 1, 2, 3, 4, 5, 6, 7, 8, 9, 21, 22 ; 2nd question under No. 22 → Mallow [*Malva*]. Supposing that a particular species of Mallow is being traced, we may continue, for example, by Nos. 57, 58 ; the 2nd question under No. 58 → Common Mallow [*Malva sylvestris*]. The same species may be reached by Nos. 1, 2, 3, 4, 5, 6, 7, 8, 45, 47, 48, 53, 54, 55, 56, 57, 58, and the 2nd question under No. 58. It may also be reached by Nos. 1, 2, 3, 4, 228, 229, 230, 231, 242, 257, 258, 260, 264, 265, 57, 58, and the 2nd question under No. 58.

Buttercup.—Nos. 1, 2, 3, 4, 354, 355, 356, 416, 422, 438, 439, 440, 441 ; 1st question under No. 441 → Buttercup (Crowfoot), and for one of the species, for example, 442, 443, 444, 445, 446 ; 1st question under No. 446 → Common Crowfoot [*Ranunculus acris*].

Dandelion.—Nos. 1, 2, 3, 770, 828, 837, 838, 839, 842, 843, 844, 850, 851 ; 1st question under No. 851 → Common Dandelion [*Taraxacum Dens-leonis*]

Mercury.—Nos. 1, 2, 3, 4, 705, 711, 712, 716, 717, 718, 719, 721, 722 ; 1st question under No. 722 → Annual Mercury [*Mercurialis annua*]. The name of this plant may also be reached if at No. 716 the other alternative be chosen, by Nos. 723, 724, 725, 726 ; 1st question under No. 726.

Bracken.—Nos. 1, 1092, 1093, 1094, 1095, 1096, 1097, 1100 ; 1st question under No. 1100 → Eagle-marked Bracken [*Pteris aquilina*].

HOW TO USE THE ABRIDGED TABLES

The reader who is already accustomed to this book can find the names of plants more quickly by making use of the Abridged Tables which begin on page 286, which is found by means of the tab fastened to the top of page 287. By their means he will obviate the necessity for turning over a great number of pages and of constantly going over again various detailed explanations that he already knows and which have thus become useless to him.

The alternative questions between which a choice has to be made are in these tables preceded by identical signs ; and in passing from one bracket to another, one is referred in a few words to one of the numbers on the preceding pages (6 to 281). Starting from this number, which has a line over it, the name of the plant will be attained by means of the succeeding questions.

Let us take once more one of our examples, the Yellow Iris, and search for its name by means of the Abridged Tables.

Let us begin by choosing the alternative questions in the General Table on page 286.

We pass at once, by " plant with flowers," and " herbaceous " to " flowers not composite," and " yellow," and so to Table E, on page 289. There, we are taken, by " flowers not in a compound umbel," " flowers regular," " leaves simple, alternate," " petals separate," and " no white milk " to No. 362. Following up the search in the earlier pages, starting from No. 362, we pass, by Nos. 363, 364, and 380, to the name of the plant → *Acorus-like Iris, Corn Flag*, or *Yellow Iris*.

The Daisy may be determined, in the same way, by means of the Abridged Tables, as follows :—

General Table (page 286) : plant with flowers, herbaceous, with composite flowers → See B (page 287).—Table B : flowers white at the circumference and yellow in the centre, plant not prickly, flowers at the circumference radiating. → 897, thence to 898 → *Common Daisy*.

These two examples will serve to show the method of using these Abridged Tables, which enable the names of plants to be found more rapidly.

In Case the Name of the Plant is not Found

It is possible that, after following up the alternative questions chosen in succession, we may come to descriptions and to figures which do not agree with the plant we have in our hands. For this there may be two divers reasons.

—In the first place, we may have made some mistake, either misunderstanding one of the questions propounded, or making a blunder as to a number. In this case we must retrace our steps to the successive questions, by means of the indications ("following on") which are given after the number of each bracket.

For example, we are looking for the name of the Hawthorn and, by mistake, we come to No. 975, which includes only the Bramble or Blackberry and the Wild Raspberry. Neither the figures nor the descriptions of these two plants agree with the branch we have in our hands. We notice then that 975 follows on 974, and we accordingly turn back to 974. It is not there (we may suppose) that we have made our mistake; but we see that 974 follows on 972. Let us go back to 972. It is here, we may suppose, that our error lies. Let us re-read the three questions under No. 972. We have chosen the second alternative, "Plant prickly by prickles here and there both on the leaves and on the stems," and we did not take the precaution of looking at the figures under No. 975 to which we were referred. We thus failed to choose the third alternative, our branch, in fact, having its twigs ending in spines and not prickles scattered here and there on leaves or stems. This third alternative carries us to No. 976, where we find the Hawthorn.

In the case in which we have made a mistake of a number by taking one number for another, it will be necessary to begin our search afresh from the beginning.

—In the second place, we may fail to get to the name of a plant because that particular plant, not being one *generally* distributed or very common in Britain, France, Belgium, the lowlands of Switzerland, etc., is not in this book. The plant may be found in abundance at the spot where we gathered it, but yet be extremely rare.

Under these circumstances two cases may arise.—1stly, the descriptions and figures under the number to which we find ourselves directed very nearly agree with the plant we have in our hands. In this case these descriptions and figures may serve as a suggestion as to the group of plants among which we may find the plant we have in our hands described in some more comprehensive and advanced Flora.

2ndly, the descriptions and figures under the number to which we are referred in no way resemble the plant we have in our hands. This shows that this plant, relatively uncommon, not only is not described in this book, but is not even nearly related to any of the plants here described. In this case we must give up all idea of finding its name with the help of this book, though it may, of course, be found by consulting a complete Flora.

SOME PRACTICAL SUGGESTIONS

As to the Collection and Preservation of Plants

It is essential to be careful to pick plants as low down as possible in order to make out the characteristics of their leaves. If the plant has all its leaves at the base, it is necessary either to uproot it, or, at least, to take some of the lower leaves.

When it is wished to bring plants home for examination, it is necessary to prevent their fading. For this purpose it is usually enough to make a somewhat tightly packed parcel of the plants gathered and to wrap them completely in grass enclosed in paper. It is more convenient, however, to use one of the well-known japanned metal boxes, known as *vascula*, which are made for the purpose.

To preserve plants that have been gathered, a collection of dried specimens, known as a *herbarium*, may be made.

The preparation of a herbarium is a very simple matter. When one wishes to dry plants it is only necessary to put them between the pages of a big dictionary no longer in use or an out-of-date directory. On top of the book some heavy stones are placed, so as to press heavily upon the plants. By shifting the plants from time to time from one page to another they become dry and they may then be placed between sheets of paper. By the side of each plant its name should be written on a label, together with the place where it was collected, its properties and uses.

In this way a collection may be gradually got together which will be very useful for reference.

INDEX

OF THE

ENGLISH BOTANICAL NAMES OF PLANTS

with an indication of the properties of the plants and their applications to agriculture, industrial uses and herbal medicine

— Such entries as 2, pl. 7,—8, pl. 59, etc., in this Index, refer to the Coloured Plates and signify Figure 2 on Plate 7, Figure 8 on Plate 59, etc.

Explanation of some terms employed in describing the medical properties of plants.

Note.—The doses—such as 10 grams to the litre of water—refer, in the absence of any statement to the contrary, to the quantity which can be taken by an adult, the weights referring to the plant when dried. The doses are given in grams (*gr.*), a gram being equal to 15.432 grains.

Anti-ophthalmic, employed against diseases of the eyes.
Anti-spasmodic, employed to check paroxysms of nervous disorders.
Anti-scorbutic, employed to purify the blood.
Appetising, used to provoke appetite.
Carminative, soothing.
Corrosive, attacking the skin.
Depuratory, employed to purify the blood.
Diuretic, increasing the action of the kidneys.
Emollient, that which relaxes and softens the tissues.
Febrifuge, employed to counteract fever.
Pectoral, employed to afford relief in maladies of the respiratory organs.
Resolvent, employed to improve the condition of sores.
Solvent, serving to break down tissues, in cases of tumour, for example.
Sternutatory, producing sneezing.
Stomachic, favouring digestion.
Sudorific, employed to induce perspiration.
Vermifuge, employed to prevent or cure maladies due to the development of parasitic worms in the intestines.
Vulnerary, employed in treating wounds.

A

	No.
Acacia, False (5, pl. 15).—Wood very hard, resisting the action of water	971
Achillea, Milfoil (6, pl. 31).—Tonic, excitant; used against slight intermittent fevers: dried flowering tops (20 gr. to the litre of water)..	207
Achillea, Sneezewort.—The roots and leaves, dried and powdered, are sternutatory	902
Aconite, Monk's-hood (1, pl. 3).—Roots and leaves employed against neuralgia and congestion; but the plant is *dangerous* and should only be used under a doctor's orders; very poisonous	351
Æthusa, Dog's-parsley (2, pl. 25).—A *very poisonous* plant, often mistaken for Chervil or Parsley. Its use medicinally is *very dangerous*	677
Agrimony, Eupator's (3, pl. 19).—Astringent, employed in gargles (20 gr. to a litre of water), resolvent	439
Agrostis, White.—Good forage	1090

Index of the English Botanical Names of Plants

Index of the English Botanical Names of Plants

303

Index of the English Botanical Names of Plants

C

Index of the English Botanical Names of Plants

Index of the English Botanical Names of Plants

Index of the English Botanical Names of Plants

No.

Hawthorn, Sharp-spined (1 and 1 *bis*, pl. 20).—Grown as an ornamental tree. The flowers are employed as a cardiac tonic and against simple ailments of the throat: infusion (10 gr. to the litre of water)...... 976

Heath, Hoary (1, pl. 36) 85

Hedge-mustard, Common.—The whole plant when in flower (dried) is stimulant and is used for coughs, laryngitis and hoarseness: infusion (30 gr. to the litre) 428

Hedge-mustard, Flixweed.—The whole plant, triturated, is applied as a vulnerary to sores 427

Hedge-mustard, Rocket.. 428

Hedge-mustard, Thale 532

Hedge-parsley, Knotted 694

Hedge-parsley, Spreading 695

Hedge-parsley, Upright 695

Heliotrope, European... 256

Hellebore, Stinking (2, pl. 3).—The root was used formerly in veterinary medicine as a vermifuge; a dangerous plant.................... 118

Hemlock, Spotted (3, pl. 25).—A very poisonous plant; employed medicinally to soothe local pain: a very *dangerous* plant, only to be used under a doctor's orders 691

Hemp, Cultivated (2 and 2 *bis*, pl. 48).—Textile plant; the seed serves as food for poultry and small birds.—A variety of this plant is used for making hashish 712

Hemp-nettle, Common... 179

Hemp-nettle, Scented (2, pl. 44) 179

Henbane, Black (1, pl. 40).—A *very poisonous* plant: its leaves and seeds are narcotic: a *dangerous* plant, only to be used under a doctor's orders 314

Hesperis, Dame's 14

Holcus, Soft (6, pl. 61).—Good forage 1090

Holly, Needle-leaved (3 and 3 *bis*, pl. 12).—Wood hard, used for whip-handles, inlaying and turnery 973

Honeysuckle, Common (4, pl. 26) 173

Honeysuckle, Woody 1039

Hop, Rough (1 and 1 *bis*, pl. 48).—Scales of fruit used to preserve and flavour beer.—The flowers before fruiting are soothing and diuretic: infusion or decoction (10 gr. to the litre of water)............... 398

Horehound, Black (7, pl. 44) 196

Hornbeam, Birch-like (1 and 1 *bis*, pl. 50).—Wood hard, used for cogs and printers' rollers; good for fuel 959

Hornwort, Common 714

Horse-chestnut, Common (1 and 1 *bis*, pl. 12).—Seeds may be used as food for cattle; wood used for making battens and in poker-work. The seeds are used as an extract or tincture against rheumatism, neuralgia and skin affections: the powdered bark is tonic (1-4 gr. a day) and febrifuge (15-20 gr. a day) 1041

Horseshoe-vetch, Tufted 469

Horsetail, Field (2 and 2 *bis*, pl. 64).—Can be used for polishing wood and metals; harmful in meadows.—The whole plant, dried, is diuretic and can be used to stop hæmorrhage: decoction (8 to 15 gr. to the litre of water) 1104

Horsetail, Greatest (3, pl. 64) 1104

Hottonia, Marsh 105

Hound's-tongue, Official.—Soothing and narcotic: a *dangerous* plant, only to be used under a doctor's orders 52

Hyacinth, Uninscribed (5, pl. 53) 241

Hyssop, Official.—Sometimes used as a condiment.—The tops of the flowering stems are used for cough and act as a stomachic stimulant: infusion (10 gr. to the litre of water) 330

Index of the English Botanical Names of Plants

I

Index of the English Botanical Names of Plants

Index of the English Botanical Names of Plants

Index of the English Botanical Names of Plants

R

S

Index of the English Botanical Names of Plants

Index of the English Botanical Names of Plants

T

V

INDEX OF POPULAR NAMES

(Where these are not used as English Botanical Names and do not, therefore, occur in the preceding Index.)

The numbers refer to the questions, *i.e.* are those on the left-hand side of the pages.

INDEX

OF THE LATIN NAMES OF THE PLANTS

Note.—Such entries as 3, pl. 62; 6, pl. 11, etc., refer to the coloured plates, signifying Figure 3 on Plate 62; Figure 6 on Plate 11, etc.

Index of the Latin Names of the Plants

Index of the Latin Names of the Plants

Index of the Latin Names of the Plants

Index of the Latin Names of the Plants

Index of the Latin Names of the Plants

EVERYMAN'S LIBRARY

A LIST OF THE 983 VOLUMES
ARRANGED UNDER AUTHORS

Anonymous works are given under titles.

Anthologies, Dictionaries, etc., are arranged at the end of the list.

LONDON: J. M. DENT & SONS LTD.

NEW YORK: E. P. DUTTON & CO. INC.

*The Publishers regret that, owing to wartime
difficulties and shortages, some of the volumes
may be found to be temporarily out of print.*